For Teresa

Resonare Christum

with respect,
admiration + love.

JH.

28/ june
1988

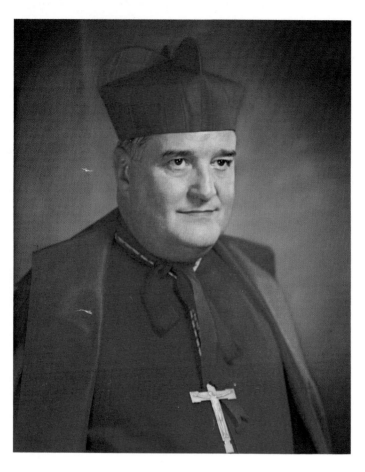

Portrait by Jonas

Resonare Christum

Volume II
1959–1969

A Selection from the Sermons,
Addresses, Interviews, and Papers
of

Cardinal John J. Wright

Prepared and Edited by
R. Stephen Almagno, O.F.M.

RESONARE CHRISTUM

Ignatius Press   San Francisco

Imprimi Potest: Alban V. Montella, O.F.M.
                 Minister Provincial
                 Provincial Curia
                 New York City

Imprimatur: + John R. Quinn
                 Archbishop of San Francisco

Cover by Victoria Hoke Lane

All monies accruing to the editor from the publication of this book will be paid to the Catholic Institute of Pittsburgh, Inc., for works of religion, charity, and education.

Memoriae et Laudi

Iohannis I. Wright
Cardinalis

Sanctae Romanae Ecclesiae

Summis Honoribus Functi

De Humanis Pariter et Christianis Litteris

Optime Meriti

Contents

Tribute

Cardinal John Wright served as the initial inspiration for my stewardship at the University of Pittsburgh. In giving the blessing at my inauguration, he articulated the core of the philosophy that has guided me through two decades into the Bicentennial Year of this University. There can be no more fitting tribute to his memory and to the reverence he held for education than to quote his own words from the prayer, which now graces a wall in my office in an illumination provided by the Vatican:

> May all the loves blended here—love of learning, love of life, love of liberty, love of one another, divine charity itself—help bring it to pass that all those privileged to enjoy under the auspices of this University the banquet of the good, the true, and the beautiful will be inspired to play their part in building a world where every man, no matter what his race, religion, nationality or family background, can live a fully human life, freed from servitude imposed upon him by ignorance, by other men, or by natural forces over which he has not sufficient control; a world where freedom is not an empty word, and where the poor man Lazarus can sit at the same table with the privileged!

Wesley Wentz Posvar
President

The University of Pittsburgh
Bicentennial
1787–1987

Preface

The task of preparing for publication this selection from the sermons, addresses, interviews, and papers of Cardinal John Wright (1909–1979) has been an entirely pleasant affair. Pleasant, because of the trust placed in me by the Wright Family and by the Cardinal's executors. Pleasant, because I was able to work—during this Bicentennial Year—in the congenial atmosphere of this university, which was an object of Wright's love and concern. Pleasant, because of the encouragement and co-operation from so many of his friends and admirers. And, finally, pleasant, because "to be reminded" of Cardinal Wright "is always the greatest delight to me, whether I speak myself or hear another speak of him" (*Phaedo*).

The Cardinal's words are presented with as little intrusion as possible. This is his book. Each text speaks for itself. The notes endeavor, simply, to put a background to the text.

I know that this text will be welcomed by Cardinal Wright's friends, and I hope that this book may possibly be of interest and give insight to someone who had not the privilege of knowing him.

It remains only for me to thank, especially, President Wesley W. Posvar, Ph.D., for gracing this volume with his *Tribute*; and the Most Reverend Anthony G. Bosco, for his *Introduction*. I also want to thank Dean Toni Carbo Bearman, Ph.D., the Most Reverend Anthony J. Bevilacqua, the Most Reverend Norbert G. Gaughan, the Reverend Alban V. Montella, O.F.M. (my Minister Provincial), the Very Reverend Leo V. Vanyo, J.C.D., Professor Roy B. Stokes, Dr. Ellen G. Detlefsen, Ph.D., Jo Ann Hartz, Lisa Dallape, Sandra Collins, and the Reverend Louis L. De Ninno for their cooperation and assistance.

The work on this volume was started at the University of Pittsburgh and completed at Serra Friary, McKeesport, Pennsylvania, during a long period of convalescence. To my Franciscan brothers—in whom I saw incarnated Saint Francis' exhortation "If any one of them becomes sick, the other brothers should serve him as they would wish to be served themselves" (*Rule* VI: 9)—my deepest gratitude.

R. Stephen Almagno, O.F.M.

The University of Pittsburgh
School of Library and Information Science

Serra Friary
McKeesport, Pennsylvania
May 26, 1987

Acknowledgments

Publication of this book was made possible by the generous donation of Mr. and Mrs. John F. Donahue.

The literary executor is grateful to the following for permission to reproduce copyright material:

America for "Conciliar Rome".

Harper and Row for *Richard Wright, Black Boy: A Record of Childhood and Youth*.

The Thomas More Association and *The Critic* for "Reflections on Conscience and Authority", and "Unspoken Tribute".

The Pittsburgh Years
1959–1969

Introduction

On January 23, 1959, the news spread quickly through the Diocese of Pittsburgh. The Church of Pittsburgh had a new shepherd—and he was a *Yankee*! Surprise mixed with apprehension was the mood of the diocese. We Pittsburghers are probably more provincial than we would like to admit. In 1959, New England seemed far, far away from Pittsburgh. But in the typical spirit of the faithful and clergy of Pittsburgh, we were prepared to accept him who was being sent.

We had heard of John Wright. He was, after all, not an unknown figure. The departing Cardinal Dearden's remark to some of us was, "I know you are going to like him." Many of us, of course, took a wait-and-see attitude.

When Bishop Wright started to make preparations for his installation here, we began to get our first hint of the type of person with whom we were dealing. At the installation ceremony, on March 18, Cardinal Cushing, who in a sense had come along to give Bishop Wright away, told us that if we weren't satisfied with John Wright, New England would be very happy to have him back. At that stage of the game, we weren't too sure whether we might not want to send him back.

With characteristic sensitivity, Bishop Wright seemed to sense our concern about the "Yankee invasion". He said at the time of his installation that he knew we would accept him. He said he came *in the Name of the Lord*—and *Benedictus qui venit in Nomine Domini*. He was giving us his credentials. He had come to Pittsburgh *in the Name of the Lord*, and he knew that the faithful everywhere accepted their shepherds *in the Name of the Lord*.

We also became aware of the type of man he was by an event he scheduled and insisted upon—against the advice of some around him. That event was a public reception at Duquesne University's Rockwell Hall on one of the first Sundays after his installation. He told us that on that day he wanted to shake hands with the whole world. Those of us accustomed to less exposure of this kind saw it as a grandiose and probably impossible gesture—until we saw him do it!

The lines surrounding Rockwell Hall were happy and cheerful. They stopped traffic. Little did we realize then how many times in the next ten years this man would literally stop traffic. Inside Rockwell Hall he stood—without eating, and perhaps with just a sip of something occasionally—for about eight hours. We were amazed at his stamina. He shook hands with anyone who wanted to meet him. He had a witty remark and a kind word for each person. For many, it was the first time they had ever come so close to a bishop. It was a grand day, and in many ways that day was very typical of the life we were to see unfolded before us during the ten years that John Wright was Bishop of Pittsburgh.

Shortly after he came to the Chancery Office—and he arrived there on the day after his installation—Bishop Wright convened a staff meeting. From his talk to us, it was clear that he intended to have a very real working relationship with the staff. He made it clear to us that the administration of John Wright as Bishop of Pittsburgh was going to center around the people of the diocese. And he served notice—subtly, by example, and sometimes more explicitly—that his curia and staff must love people and that our chief purpose was to serve people.

We learned soon that the newly installed Bishop of Pittsburgh was quite at ease with the media. He was a media figure. He was in constant demand by television, radio, and the press. He was a news-maker. The diocese began to sense a feeling of pride that our Bishop was listened to, that people wanted to know what he thought on important issues. We soon became aware that at least some bishops—certainly *our* Bishop—could do more than pray the Rosary over the radio.

John Wright was at ease not only with the media but with

any group. One of the first groups he addressed in Pittsburgh was the Press Club, whose members included all the major media people. The talk was John Wright at his best. He was dazzling, charming, and intelligent. As I walked out of the Press Club, I listened very carefully and proudly to the remarks made by club members and their wives. They were impressed and even astonished. And they too were beginning to realize that some very fascinating pages in the history of the Diocese of Pittsburgh were about to be written.

Protestants and Jews began to ask him to address their groups—another first for Pittsburgh. He spoke at Christian Mothers' communion breakfasts and grade-school graduations. He once told me that if his schedule were open, he would speak at any event, as long as he was invited. In fact, he often spoke without invitation. Even his remarks given off the cuff were polished and profound. He always felt he had something to say. It was clear that there was within him a drive, an impelling force—the love of Christ. He had to preach the gospel. And so he spoke everywhere and to everyone, to anyone who would listen: to Protestants, to Jews, to labor and to management, to the man on the street, to students. He was at home with all of them.

By anticipating many of the moods and thrusts of the Second Vatican Council, John Wright proved himself a visionary in the Diocese of Pittsburgh. Long before *Christus Dominus* (no. 27) and *Presbyterorum Ordinis* (no. 7), he established here in Pittsburgh a Diocesan Pastoral Council, which brought together priests, religious, and laity, men and women from all walks of life and from every corner of the diocese. He insisted that all of the Chancery staff attend the meetings of the Pastoral Council. But he muzzled us. We weren't allowed to say a word. All we were allowed to do was listen to the *vox populi*. Of course, as Bishop of the diocese, he exempted himself from that injunction. He was allowed to talk. He did, but he also listened carefully.

Again, before the Second Vatican Council he set to work on

21

the reorganization of parish councils. As is evident from some of the items in this volume, John Wright was always concerned about the role of the laity in the Church. Lay leadership was a great concern of his life. Some petty minds thought he was pro-laity but anti-clergy. But certainly those of us who knew him and knew his understanding of the ministerial priesthood never had that feeling.

The Eighteenth Synod of the Diocese of Pittsburgh was one of the major events during the years that John Wright was our Bishop. Convoked on December 8, 1968, the Synod's aim and purpose was to implement in the Diocese of Pittsburgh the recently concluded Vatican Council. In his "Formal Call of the Synod", which you will find in this volume, Bishop Wright put it this way: "What is the purpose of this historic Synod?" The Synod was taking place during the one hundred and twenty-fifth anniversary of the diocese.

> It is . . . to apply to our diocese the teachings and the spirit of the Second Vatican Council; not the one without the other, nor either without reference to the other, but both together, literally in the case of the teaching, fully in the case of the spirit. It is to do for the diocese what the Council sought to do for the Church, the Church universal. Our purpose in calling the Synod, then, is that of Pope John in calling the Ecumenical Council and which Pope Paul has summed up in these words: "To reawaken, reform, rejuvenate the Church; to enlighten her conscience, to strengthen her forces, to purify her defects; to strengthen her structures, to widen her frontiers, to recompose her unity, to prepare her for new defenses and new contacts with the world; to place her in renewed contact with her own sources". . . .

One of the great bequests that the Cardinal left the diocese, a bequest that is still alive and vigorous, was the formation of the Christian Associates of Southwest Pennsylvania. When the Protestant community and the old Council of Churches approached him saying that no ecumenical agency in this area could exist without the support of the Catholic Church, Bishop

Wright said he would be happy to work with these groups. But, he added, he wanted to work toward creating a new organization more in the spirit of the time. He did not wish to involve himself merely in the refurbishing of tired and outmoded structures. Those of us, Protestants and Catholics alike, who today are still active in Christian Associates continue to hear John Wright's name as *the* founding father of this major ecumenical organization, which has attracted not only national but international attention.

He loved the poor. The Fund to Assist Neighbors in Need tithed diocesan receipts and gave those monies to self-help groups in need of seed money. The poor from all over the world sought his assistance. He helped them all generously but quietly. Again, his love for the poor was seen in his work for better housing in the diocese. To this end he established a committee, insisting that it be an ecumenical committee made up of Catholics, Protestants, and Jews, to seek new homes for the homeless and dispossessed.

He introduced the Pittsburgh Oratory into the diocese. As a neighbor of the University of Pittsburgh, and loving academia as he did, John Wright was always interested in the university. He had a pastoral concern for the spiritual life and growth of the Catholic professors, students, and staff who frequented or worked at the university. So he entrusted this concern to the Fathers of the Oratory, the sons of Saint Philip Neri and of Cardinal John Henry Newman, with the hope that they would bring, as indeed they have brought, a new dimension to the Diocese of Pittsburgh. By his interest in the university and through the friendships he established with the Chancellor, the Provost, and the administration of the University of Pittsburgh, he remedied what was certainly a defect. Relations between what was known as a *Presbyterian* University and the Roman Catholic Diocese of Pittsburgh were not always what they should have been, but John Wright, the Bishop of Pittsburgh, the *pontifex*, the bridge-builder, brought about through the

Oratory and his own personal contacts the now-happy relationship between the University of Pittsburgh and the Roman Catholic Diocese of Pittsburgh.

When the time came, he immersed himself in the Second Vatican Council. Before he left Pittsburgh for the first session of the council, he gathered together the priests of the diocese and spoke to us of what we might expect from the council. Since he had been involved in the preparatory sessions, he had some idea of what the council would do. He told us on that day that it would take fifty years for us to begin to realize what the council was all about. At that time, I was much younger and I believed that in fifty years one could build a universe in addition to understanding a council. The few words he addressed to us that day have stayed with me so long because I begin now to see how correct he was. Those of us who might have misunderstood what happened in the immediate wake of the Second Vatican Council are slowly discovering that today, years after the council, we are only now beginning to understand what happened at the council. John Wright knew that, I think, because he understood history better than most of us. He understood that history was not a series of isolated events. He certainly knew that events cannot be digested within thirty seconds after they have happened. The threads are woven slowly. The total tapestry takes time to emerge.

John Wright was an intellectual. No one who knew him would hesitate for a moment to attribute that term to him. He was a true intellectual in the sense that he looked to basic core truths. He was a philosopher and as such was concerned with ultimate causes and reasons. John Wright was a voracious reader. He had a huge library. He devoured books the way a hungry man devours food. He remembered what he read. He was a thinker, a craftsman of ideas. He thought synthetically, and from the storehouse of his mind he brought forth treasures, old and new. He was able to furnish others with fresh and new insights. To see something through the intellect of John Wright was an experience that carried with it new nuances, new visions.

He was very generous in sharing the experience of the council with the priests, religious, and laity of the diocese. He did this not only by the lectures that he gave upon his return after each session but also through the courier system that he had organized. We couriers carried the mail overseas. We knew John Wright well enough by then to know that when we arrived in Rome with the attaché cases filled with mail, the fact that he greeted the mail bag more enthusiastically than he greeted us was not an indication that he loved us less. It meant rather that he was eager to get to the business of his beloved Diocese of Pittsburgh. He wanted to see what his people were telling him. And since his mail came from all sorts of people, he was always well informed. He loved these letters from home, and he answered every one.

By the late 1960s, we in the Diocese of Pittsburgh had become quite accustomed to surprises. But we were not quite ready for the shock—*the joyful shock*—of March 28, 1969, when we were told that our Bishop had been named a cardinal of the Roman Catholic Church. I remember the press conference he held at *the house*. He always called his Warwick Terrace residence *the house*. There he was amidst the lights, the wires, and the reporters, at ease and jovial and personal with all of them. The announcement had us scratching our heads wondering what it might mean. We really didn't think that John Wright, now a cardinal, would remain in Pittsburgh. And in due time, on April 4, 1969, it was announced that Pope Paul VI had named him Prefect of the Sacred Congregation for the Clergy. One of the things that John Wright did was to have stationery printed with the cardinalatial coat of arms. He told us that he wanted it clear in the archives of the diocese that a cardinal once occupied the See of Pittsburgh. It was clear to me that the reason he did this was not personal pride but his great love for the Church of Pittsburgh.

My mood on the plane ride to Rome for the ceremonies, on April 28, 1969, afforded me a chance to reflect on the man who was John Wright. That plane carried the oddest conglomeration of human beings that one could have ever hoped to see. We were going to Rome for the creation of a cardinal of the Roman Catholic Church. Aboard were of course priests, religious, and laity of the Diocese of Pittsburgh. One would have expected that. But with us were rabbis, ministers, a black labor leader, and the varied assortment of human beings who always seemed drawn to John Wright. I was always astonished at the people who sat around table with him. He brought the strangest types of people together. He was the catalyst. I was always happy to be invited to dinner with him because I never knew whom I was going to meet. I might meet Billy Graham (see, for example, the Cardinal's statement published in this volume: "Billy Graham in Pittsburgh") or the Dalai Lama or the gardener. It was always fascinating. Now that I have read in this volume his talk entitled "The Use Christ Made of Public Dinners", I understand John Wright even more.

But the plane ride to Rome and the planeload of people and the entire Pittsburgh delegation were very symbolic of what had happened in the ten years he had been with us. I know what the plane ride would have looked like ten years before: we could have chanted the Liturgy of Hours together.

After the ceremonies in Rome, the Cardinal returned to the diocese for a short time. His last days in the diocese were as hectic as his previous ten years. I know that when the time came to leave his beloved Diocese of Pittsburgh, he had genuine regret. His attitude at the airport ceremonies—a high school band played, he passed out silver dollars with a kind word of remembrance to each person—made it somewhat easier for those of us who knew that we and the Diocese of Pittsburgh were losing a great man, a shepherd, a churchman, and a friend.

Still, John Wright never really left Pittsburgh. He went to Rome with a sense of adventure. He knew that he was being called to the Vatican and to the Sacred Congregation for the Clergy so that he might serve the Universal Church, which he loved so well and so deeply. But he never forgot Pittsburgh. And we who had been concerned and worried that the Yankee Bishop might not make it here in Pittsburgh finally decided that he was probably more a Pittsburgher than we.

He took up his duties in Rome with delight. He loved the Vatican, the work, the City of Rome, and the Italian people. He was one of the most *Italian Yankees* I have ever known. When I saw him in Italy or in one of the Italian churches of the Diocese of Pittsburgh, he would go native quite easily and naturally. He spoke some of the Italian dialects. He knew the songs and the customs. He was very much at home. His Italian always had a New England—better, a Bostonian—accent about it, but his heart was Italian through and through.

In the Introduction to Cardinal Wright's Rome Years, Bishop Wuerl will deal with the Cardinal's time and work there. I simply want to say from a Pittsburgh point of view that the offices of the Sacred Congregation for the Clergy in the Vatican were never the same after John Wright got there. Youths, school children, visitors of all sorts dropped in to see him. And he was delighted, especially if they were from Pittsburgh. People would come back to the diocese and tell me "We saw the Cardinal!" "He took us out for a spaghetti dinner." "He asked about my mother." John Wright seemed to remember everyone and everything about Pittsburgh. His visitors were touched and delighted. They felt very important, and for him they were.

Each year during the time he spent in Rome, the Cardinal would return to the diocese, usually late in August, for a visit. When word would come out that he was returning, electricity sparked in the air. People who had reason to see him began to prepare for his return with the hope that they would be able to visit with him. He saw as many people as he possibly could and was most generous with his time.

I am very grateful to the editor for this selection of the

sermons, addresses, and papers of John Wright. Those of us who heard many of them delivered will now in the reading hear reecho in our minds and hearts and souls the accents of the "Yankee Bishop of Pittsburgh", the universal churchman, the man who taught us what being all things to all people really means. We will hear again the echo of his voice and be reminded of the depths of his thought, the joy of his wit, the sound of his laughter, his love for Christ and the Church, his compassion for people.

I am grateful too for this selection of his sermons, addresses, and papers because it should put to rest the idea, for some unfortunately, the conviction that John Wright, the champion liberal of the 1940s and 1950s, became in the 1960s and 1970s a conservative. Even a casual reading of his sermons, addresses, and papers—*but the reading must be done in chronological order*—will show that there was in the mind and heart and therefore on the lips of John Wright a *verum aeternum*. And while various themes might be developed to a greater or lesser degree throughout his lifetime, still the root truths remained changeless. Why? Because John Wright did not change! He was ever and always traditional in theology and liberal in social questions.

Finally, I am grateful for this selection of his sermons, addresses, and papers because I hope that those who never met or knew John Wright will meet the man in his sermons, addresses, and papers. For his talks were the man, and the man was his talks. Read the talks and you meet John Wright. Read the talks and you will know the things he cared about, the things that mattered to him. Read the talks and you will know that he was always concerned about the things of God and mankind. I hope that you too will pick up the echo of his laughter and the depth of his person.

+ *Anthony G. Bosco*

I

Leadership in Serra and the Church

Here in Pittsburgh the works of Serra are long- and well-established, and Serra has become one of the strongest ties between typical priests and representative lay people in the diocese which is privileged to be your host during this Convention. As a matter of fact, this might even be called a Serra hotel, because the Penn-Sheraton is managed by one of the most loyal of our Serrans, present here at the breakfast this morning as a Serran, but keeping an eye on your comfort as manager of the hotel. He has even brought his beloved mother from Omaha to be his guest at the Serra Convention. Let me introduce Charlie Carey.[1]

I would like to explain to you before the convention gets underway what you think you see as you look out the windows of the hotel today. Californians and Floridians will not recognize it, because it is fog, and it is strictly temporary. There is only one thing that it definitely is not; that's *smoke*. We have *no smog* and *no smoke* in Pittsburgh.

It is true that sometimes during the late afternoon you will see small wisps of yellow smoke rising from the plants along the banks of the rivers, and during the night you may be under the illusion that you see smoke going up to the stars together with the flames from the forges. I want you to look at those flames with great reverence. It means that men are at work. I beg you all to pray God that we'll see it next month, too.

Serra Clubs began with an emphasis on leadership. The initial hope for Serra in the minds of those who conceived it and who first became identified with its idealism was that Serra

This address was delivered at the Penn-Sheraton Hotel, Pittsburgh, Pennsylvania, on June 22, 1959.

was to produce an elite among the laymen of the dioceses where it would flourish. Serra has justified that hope. It has done it so well that many who should know better have an excessive, or, perhaps better to say, a mistaken idea about the elite that Serra aspires to produce. Only yesterday in Canada I asked a bishop whether he had Serra in his diocese. He said that he hadn't and that he regretted it. He regretted it, he said, because he would very much welcome having Serra in the diocese. "But", he said, "in my diocese, I have no rich men!"

I didn't say, but I thought, "Good Lord, who has?" Then I said aloud, "I think you're thinking of some other organization, but Serra does not seek that kind of an elite." The elite to which Serra aspired in the beginning and which, on the record, it has achieved, is an elite of Catholics with special insight into the needs of the Church and into the nature of the Church, together with a special solicitude to play a prayerful, privileged part in meeting those needs and in translating into the order of action their understanding of the nature of the Church.

There are many other ways in which Serra has helped produce an elite among us. Serra is made up of elite men in the sense that they are usually those who, in each diocese, are closest, by desire and deed, to the interests of their bishops; in the theoretical and actual organization of the Catholic Church this fact identifies them as an elite. President Jordan has just reminded us that most of the charter members of Serra in each diocese are such by invitation of their bishops, and it is no secret that frequently the beginnings of Serra in a diocese depend on men suggested or at least approved by the bishop or by trusted priests close to the bishop in the life of the diocese. Men of Serra are a Catholic elite in that they are close to their clergy and their bishops. They are also a Catholic elite in that they are close to their wives, as the presence of so many wives at so many of their special meetings and at all of their conventions verifies!

They are a Catholic elite, finally, because they are the heads

30

or members of the kind of families which pray for their priests and which would be the most likely to produce priests. It is, of course, this concern with the problem of the need for priests which constitutes the cement which keeps Serra so close to the Church and makes Serrans an elite within the Church in America.

Typical Serrans may or may not belong to some other groups with a primacy of social standing in a given diocese. But by and large, we have no differences of social class in the church of America yet. Sometimes one fears we may be headed for them, but family and blood relationships still link us all to just about every *class*. Catholic Americans are still close to the class to which we belonged when first we arrived in this country. We have picked up a few advantages, one or two social *aspirations* or *pretensions* perhaps, but no social class yet divides us, by and large, here in America. If we are divided into different social sets as a result of some of the clubs to which we belong, country clubs or professional groups which we have achieved, we return to our unchanged social class whenever there is a death in the family and we meet our relatives at the wakes. We're still one class at these! So we have, by God's mercy, no notable social elite on our hands, although some emergent social *classes* are developing in some areas among some of our wives, or our daughters, and their boyfriends!

The Serra elite is of an entirely different kind. It is an elite based not on a primacy of social consideration, but on a primacy of spiritual solicitude. It is made up of those who have a refined and sensitive solicitude with respect to the interests of the Church.

Surely in our day such a solicitude will center around vocations to the priesthood. The number and quality of such vocations constitute assuredly the major objects of the prayerful solicitude of those sensitive to the needs of the Church in our generation and in our area. For this reason, the establishment of Serra a quarter century ago may well prove to have been providential in terms of anticipating the likelihood that the church in America might otherwise have been headed toward the embarrassment which confronts the Church in some other nations in this matter of vocations to the priesthood.

It is common knowledge that some of the older nations, even nations which are traditionally considered characteristically Catholic, have long suffered, and suffered painfully, from a critical shortage of vocations to the priesthood. For my part, I think there is no nation the history of which is so identified with the history of Christendom, certainly in the Western world, as is France. There is no nation to which we are more indebted for great saints, no nation which has exercised beyond its own frontiers, throughout the world, so powerful a role in the formation of what we usually mean by Christian culture than has France. And yet, there is also no nation so embarrassed as is France by the shortage of vocations. Once while working there as a *supply*, I discovered that one French diocese, a diocese with shrines one thousand and five hundred years old and a cathedral that is one of the wonders of the Western world, as well as monasteries and churches which were glorious in the high peak of Catholic civilization in France, now has almost one thousand churches but approximately two hundred and twenty priests.[2]

This is an embarrassing situation, but one which is typical of the condition in many of the dioceses of the Old World. True, there are also nations where vocations to the priesthood and to the religious life continue to be strong. These favored nations are countries which have been outside the influences which presumably account for the distressing shortage of vocations elsewhere in Europe; such fortunate nations are Ireland, Holland, Switzerland, one or two other nations. But what caused the appalling lack of vocations in a country like France? It is worthwhile reflecting on this question, because like forces could operate here in America unless we are vigilant in recognizing them and militant in preventing, so far as we can, the operation of such forces.

Many explanations of the French crisis in vocations have been offered. Perhaps one explanation is the social and economic, but reductively moral, problem of the decline in the size of French families. The plain fact is that small families do not produce vocations to the priesthood, at least when the smallness of the families is a calculated thing, independent of the Will of God or in defiance of that Divine Will. The motives of selfishness, materialism, and purely personal convenience which account for contrived small families—*planned parenthood* in the cynical sense the phrase usually has—are motives destructive of the spirit that inspires religious vocations. The prevailing spirit of such families is a spirit inconsistent with choosing a life of special cooperation with God's graces, the life required of people who give themselves to the service of others. Accordingly, frequently the decline in the number of vocations in a nation closely parallels the decline in the size of families; and, of course, the root cause of both declines is selfishness.

When the smallness of a family is itself a reflection of God's mysterious will for a given couple, then there is likely to be present in such a family unit a spirit of resignation to the Will of God and a spirit of prayer not only consistent with but positively conducive to the fostering of vocations. But a small family which is *planned* for reasons which reduce to strictly personal convenience, reductively selfish and immoral, is not likely to be the breeding place of anything—but assuredly not of vocations to the religious life or to the priesthood.

It is interesting to reflect on how many of our vocations to the religious life and the priesthood come from large families, having been nourished by the idealism characteristic of people who count on God's Providence and who therefore follow the laws of Nature and of Nature's God, and, be it noted, as often as not live to see their children and their children's children gather for their Golden Jubilees and sometimes the Silver Jubilees in the priesthood or religious life of their children. The history of modern France on this point is a grave warning to the rest of the world and particularly to us. There are, of course, many large and holy families in France; but those of us who love France lament that there are not more, noting, as we must, the parallel between race suicide and the decline in religious vocations.

A second explanation is indubitably the establishment in France, during and after the Napoleonic era, of permanent compulsory peace-time military service. Cardinal Gasparri, one of the shrewdest of all of the observers of modern European history, did not hesitate to pinpoint this program as among the explanations of the moral plagues which have, epidemic-wise, overrun Europe in recent generations. Others than he have not less candidly denounced permanent compulsory peace-time military service as the source of serious social immoralities, with the weakening of family instincts and the corruption of psychological and spiritual forces in the development of young men, all of which have been so wide-spread and tragic consequences of peace-time compulsory military service regimes. So, one is bound to see this system as related fatally to the decline of the specific moral standards which are presupposed for vocations to the priesthood, and to see adequate vocations as unlikely to flourish in a place where this system becomes entrenched and its corollaries become engrained.

A third probable explanation of the decline of vocations in nations of the Old World like France is one less likely to apply here in America. It is the identification of the priesthood with a social class. This can take a number of different forms; sometimes it involves identification of the priesthood with the so-called *upper classes*, the aristocratic classes; sometimes the identification of priesthood is with the so-called *lower classes*, the peasants or proletariat. There follows, when this is frozen into a class pattern, a decline of priestly influence and of the

34

appeal of the priestly life among those of the classes left out by whatever social identification may characterize a given time or place. This, one feels, is something perhaps less likely to be operative in our country for reasons we have already suggested, but nevertheless we should keep on our guard against social patterns fraught with such serious spiritual danger.

A fourth and powerful factor explaining the shortage of vocations in the Old World is one which must definitely be a preoccupation in our country, since this factor is more aggravated here than it has been certainly in France. I refer to the irrelevance of much of the educational program to the formation of the kind of mind and personality most consistent with effective and numerous vocations to the priesthood. Once the school systems, public, private, and parochial, break with the liberal arts tradition on the collegiate level and with preparation for liberal arts education on the secondary school level, then the intellectual climate in which vocations are likely is bound to be badly affected.

We might as well face the fact that for the indefinite future the study of philosophy, theology, and much of the spiritual literature of the Western world will presuppose a reasonably educated man's knowledge of Latin, some little Greek, and the kind of education that includes the study of history, including ancient history. Therefore, if I were a Communist agent in the world of education, or if I were someone seeking to create an intellectual climate in which it would be unlikely that we would have learned priests, I would do everything possible to get Latin out of the schools. I would bring upon the country a situation not too different from that which actually has been brought upon it, namely that few students are encouraged to study Latin anywhere, and all manner of subjects likely to produce superficial people are encouraged, disciplines with scant roots either in time or eternity. These I would substitute for Latin; current events—the reading of *Time*, *Newsweek*, *U.S. News and World Report*—I would put in place of the history of the race; civics, which often means only what the League of Women Voters can give you in one mailing the week before an election, I would substitute for the traditional disciplines which might make the youngsters suspect that prior to 1492 there was any civilization. Any such suspicion I'd get out of the schools, just as it has been fairly effectively exorcised from the universities, where I was a subversive agent.

If, on the other hand, I wanted to help implement my prayers for increased vocations to the priesthood and for the prosperity of Christian culture, then I would watch for every opportunity to hold the line for authentic education in the schools, for the restoration of languages, Latin, history, and whatever else will make students work. I would introduce boys and girls to the Christian tradition and the humane traditions of the ancient world which the gospel ennobled and perfected.

These are some of the probable explanations of the decline in vocations elsewhere. These things happened abroad; they could happen here. Perhaps it is providential that the Prayer Crusade of Serra for vocations began in our country when it did. But it is a commonplace of spiritual theology that we cannot pray in one way and work in another. You remember the cynical prayer of Augustine before his conversion: "Lord, make me chaste, but not too soon."[3] Some of us pray that way, you know. "Lord, make me honest, as soon as I can afford to be." "Lord, make me charitable, when I've paid off this score." We must be sure that our prayer in Serra is not "Lord, give us many and holy priests, in some way that won't inconvenience me or my family in the slightest degree, or that will not require of me anything beyond this prayer which I now offer with fingers crossed so far as my personal involvement is concerned."

So each Serran should be vigilant about these factors we have mentioned on the practical levels of life—personal life, family life, social and national life—so that forces which elsewhere have made prayers for vocations inefficacious, sometimes hypocritical, in any instance ineffectual, will not embarrass us here. Serrans must strive to develop all around us that which Serra assuredly develops within its own ranks, namely, a sense of intimate love for and friendship with our priests, plus insight into their problems. One of the most attractive things about Serra is the easy comradeship that it fosters between good laymen and good priests. Good laymen love the Church as much as any priest, and good priests realize that the Church belongs to the laymen as much as it does to the priests. Their easy friendship and common solicitude for the future of the Church, their common prayers for their common intentions and their sympathetic prayers for the problems of each, laymen praying for vocations to the priesthood, priests praying for God to bless the marriages and the lives of laymen—these are the great virtues of Serra.

It is to be hoped that out of the community of prayer and interest Serrans will derive, as a further motive to their prayers, a fresh appreciation of the extraordinary dignity and beauty of the secular priesthood, the diocesan priesthood. Sometimes diocesan priests suffer from a certain disadvantage in popular estimation. The members of the great religious orders have as their fathers saintly personalities who lived relatively close to our times and our understanding. They are remembered for the magnificent, even glamorous, priests that they were. Who can possibly be unresponsive to the appeal of Saint Ignatius? Who doesn't instinctively love Saint Francis? Who hasn't been attracted by Saint Vincent, Saint John Bosco? Well, I hesitate to tell you who was the Founder of our diocesan priesthood, the helpers of the bishops! You'd probably think I was being blasphemous or taking unfair advantage. However, the fact is that our secular priests, who don't renounce things as do the religious, but sometimes have to do without them even *without* renouncing them, which makes it twice as tough; our secular priests, who spend as many years in study as in novitiate or postulancy, are nonetheless called to do the universal work of the priesthood as established by Christ. They don't take special vows, the magnificent vows of obedience of the Jesuits, although the Lord knows it can be tough to follow the letters that we get from our bishops, and all without special merit of being *religiously* obedient. They don't have the special humility that goes with Franciscan poverty, or the religious perfection of the common table, which is ordinarily without a tablecloth but otherwise fairly well provided. (One rarely goes to a convention as a secular priest on a train and passes a monk walking! Somehow they always arrive at the same time the imperfect seculars do and usually the same way!) We say these things in jest, of course, but your laughter tells me you know what I mean. You also know that I am not poking fun at the religious orders; I am saying a word, a needed word, for diocesan priests.

I ask you to speak up for the secular priesthood more often and more militantly. Let me add: When you speak up for the beauty and dignity, the indispensability of the secular priesthood, you will be doing exactly what our professors in the Jesuit, Dominican, Holy Ghost, Franciscan, and other colleges have traditionally done and still do, or we would not have most of the vocations which we have. There has never been any difficulty on this point between the secular priests and the great priests and spiritual directors who are the Jesuits, Dominicans, Benedictines, Franciscans, Salesians, Vincentians, and others who watch for and encourage vocations to the secular priesthood. Where this curious and unfounded snobbery usually reveals itself is not among *priests*, but among their aunts. They are the ones who are responsible for the tired little jokes about the *great religious orders* and the *ordinary parish priests*; not the Jesuits, who guide to us so many of our best vocations in their colleges and preparatory schools; not the other religious who, as our confessors, spiritual directors, and loyal aides share the authentic spirit of the Catholic priesthood and the Catholic Church concerning the respective shares we and they have in the priesthood we all share with Jesus Christ.

It is appropriate that I say these things about the priesthood today, because today is the Feast of Saint Paulinus of Nola. Paulinus of Nola was a convert to the Faith. He had been a pagan, and so he appreciated, as *born Catholics* sometimes appear not to do, the great need for the priesthood and the sublime office of the priest. He lived in that period of history when the old Roman classical civilization was breaking up and the best parts of it were being integrated in the new Christian culture. He wrote magnificent Latin verse, and where his predecessors in the tradition of Latin poetry had written on secular and pagan themes, Paulinus wrote in the same language and verse forms about the gospel of Jesus Christ, and His revelations and the dogmas which are the core of Catholic Christian Faith and culture.

One of the most magnificent poems of this Paulinus of Nola, whose Mass we read together this morning, was written to a young friend of his who had been named a bishop in Dalmatia. In the poem he told the young bishop what would be his function as a shepherd for Christ. Now, our priests are the auxiliaries of the bishops, and the functions of Paulinus' friend are the functions of all bishops and of all priests.

Paulinus summed up the role of our priests and its influence on civilization in the words he addressed to his friend: "In this mute region of the world, the barbarians through your schooling learn to make Christ's name resound from Roman hearts, and to live in purity and tranquil peace."[4]

That was the social effect of the influence of priests when Christendom was first forming out of the chaos that followed the collapse of ancient civilization. It is the function still of the bishops of the Holy Catholic Church, wherever in the world they may be, and of the priests who are their auxiliaries, none more than the priests of your own dioceses. It is their vocation, in modern times as in ancient, to teach people to echo Christ in their thoughts and words, to speak in the accents of their various nationalities the unique and eternal Wisdom of God made known through Jesus Christ. Just as in the days of Paulinus of Nola, so now, thanks to the worldwide ministry of reconciliation in the hands of our bishops and priests, the scattered tribes of men are united in Roman loyalty as they profess, each in his own tongue, the universal Catholic Faith. Just as in the days of Paulinus, so today our bishops and priests are sent to refine, to inspire, to instruct the untutored, whether these untutored be in mission countries or in our own parishes, parish schools, and American communities.

Not all the untutored are among the savages of the mission fields. Some of them are the *little savages* of whom you, their parents, speak so affectionately—and for whose sanctification and bringing to maturity in the Lord you rely on your priests—the priests of the present to whom Serra makes you such good friends, the priests of the future for whom Serra bids you earnestly to pray.

The Bicentennial of the Founding of Pittsburgh

We meet for a cherished devotion, the Holy Hour of Adoration, at the principal civic shrine of our city, one of the major shrines of American patriotism in all the land. *The Point* at this end of Pittsburgh is a symbol of the saga and destiny of America herself, our mighty nation into the bloodstream of which, making it strong and productive, have flowed the streams of the blood of many nations, even as the mighty Ohio River, flowing from this very point, blends the waters of two great streams and their many tributaries, to the enriching of our region and of all America.

Even if we were heathens, our minds and hearts would be lifted by patriotic pride at the contemplation of this place and at reflection on the part it has played in the lives and fortunes, the freedom and prosperity of millions of families.

But since we are Christians, conscious of the presence of God in history and of the dominion of His Providence over the fortunes of men and nations, our patriotic sentiments in a place like this are further ennobled by religious piety, and the pride of our patriotism is at once refined and made stronger by the humility of grateful prayer.

This is as it should be. For religion and patriotism are twin virtues. Supernatural love of the devout for the Faith and their natural love for the fatherland flow from the same piety toward God, our Creator; they are two duties of the first order from which no man, in this life, can exempt himself. When authentic piety grows strong, it reveals itself in deeper religious

This sermon was preached at Point State Park, Pittsburgh, Pennsylvania, on June 28, 1959, on the occasion of a Holy Hour in prayerful observance of the city's bicentennial.

devotion and more profound civic patriotism; when either religion or patriotism deteriorates, both suffer eclipse at the same time; and with the decline of either or both, all the loyalties of the good man are weakened and disintegrate.

The men who made America powerful understood this happy relationship between religion and patriotism when both are strong, as they also understood the fatal effect on both of anything that undermines either. And so in the national documents which established us as a people apart among the nations of the earth, as in our State constitutions, notably that of Pennsylvania, they included as integral, interrelated elements of our American idealism expressions of religious acknowledgment of our debt to God and to divine religion, together with clauses protective of the freedoms cherished by our patriotic heritage.

A civic shrine so hallowed as this *Point* is an appropriate place to meditate devoutly upon the vocation for which God called America into being, bringing together, in His wonderful Providence, the peoples who make up our nation from all the ends of the earth. It is an ideal place for a collective examination of conscience on how well we are cooperating in the pursuit of that national vocation, and what part we are playing in the attainment of America's destiny within the family of nations.

Nations, even as individuals, have their particular destinies, and, even as individuals, so nations are prosperous or wretched, powerful or important, according as they are faithful or renegade to their vocations. God is the Father of Nations as well as the Father of individual souls. And so, as Saint Pius X pointed out, He gives to individual nations special missions to perform for the accomplishment of His designs for mankind. God rewards nations for their fidelity to their collective vocations and punishes them for their negligence or abuse of their national destiny. All nations are Chosen Peoples in the Christian understanding of God's Providence, and all nations stand in danger of His judgment or in the way of His blessing, each according as it fulfills its divinely appointed destiny.[1]

The vocation of America is clear to a~
superficially, the evidence of God's s~
land. One of our presidents, Woodrov
on the mystery of God's Providence for .
he gave to the students at West Point.[2] He c.
let their imagination range for a moment over
continent that God gave us to dwell in. He bade .
as they did so, on how God's Providence had stoc.
lakes, rivers and mountains, its fields, forests, and the .
of its earth, with every resource needed to make a pe~
prosperous and independent. He reminded them that God ha~
left it, unknown and unoccupied, until a moment when, under
circumstances without parallel in human history, men and
women from every nation under the sky would begin to
gather together here, coming out of their Old World countries
to seek in this new land freedom to work together and to
worship God at a time when these freedoms were in peril in
their respective countries. What a strange story this is, this
story of a new nation coming into being not as the daughter of
another great people, but as a nation made up of the children of
scores of nations, all meeting here almost within a century. It is
the story of a people free to do as they chose with a new
continent, rich beyond compare, and prepared by God at the
hour of creation to be kept waiting for centuries in order that
here a new people, called out of many peoples, might bear
witness, with fresh human enthusiasm and renewed divine faith,
to how the children of God should use strength, prosperity,
and freedom in loyal comradeship with one another and in
grateful loyalty to their Creator and their Provident God.

This is the destiny of America, and we shall be judged
grievously if we are renegade to it or prove unworthy of the
sublime vocation it involves. We shall incur the wrath of
heaven itself and the contempt of the world if we permit
inter-class, inter-credal, inter-group conflicts or tensions of
any kind to undermine or weaken that unity of brothers in the

yment of good things and in the love of God and one another ich America was clearly called into being to demonstrate to e jaded, divided Old World.

In this witness to which America is called by God, the witness to mankind that is her special destiny, she will find the Church of Christ both her loyal aid and her spiritual exemplar. The Catholic Church is made up of all nations. The Catholic Church, like America, is strong and beautiful in the diversity of the tongues and tribes and traditions she brings together. The Holy Catholic Church knows no difference of color or class, culture or human condition. All are at home within her spiritual household, the family of God, drawn out of all nations, even as is America on the temporal level. Her children are united by one Faith under one Lord. It is that Lord whom we adore in the Blessed Sacrament present here today. It is He whom we thank for the freedom and faith in which we are privileged to meet in this twice hallowed place that is the center of so many civic and spiritual traditions which make us one in love and hope.

Here, indeed, is the place to offer the prayer for that unity which is the supreme aspiration of our times: O God of unity and peace, grant, we beseech Thee in the Holy Name of Jesus, that we who are of many races and tongues may be united in heart and mind in all that pertains to the advancement of religion and the best interests of our country. Through the same Christ our Lord. Amen.

III

Khrushchev in Pittsburgh

Nikita Khrushchev is scheduled to be in Pittsburgh in connection with a visit to this country arranged by the national administration. As all know, this visit is linked to that of our Vice President to Communist-dominated Russia and Poland. It is strictly political and is presumably part of an effort of our government to reduce world tensions and avert war.

The wisdom of even well-intentioned association with the Red chieftains, especially if it might strengthen their despotic hand in the captive countries behind the Iron Curtain, has been widely debated, pro and con, by persons qualified to comment on political and diplomatic policies. The record of Khrushchev and his associates with respect to religious freedom, regard for the natural dignity of man, and respect for the right of nations does not admit of debate; it is a clear record, which all may read, of violence and cynicism.

As American citizens we each have our own opinions of the arguments, pro and con, concerning the political and diplomatic aspects of the projected visit of Nikita Khrushchev to the United States. As Catholic Christians, painfully aware of the appalling suffering of our brethren in the Faith under the tyranny of which Khrushchev is now the leader, our only proper and effective response to his visit is that of instant prayer that God's purposes, merciful and pacific, may somehow be served in the midst of the human efforts, wise or unwise, of our government in an event so fraught with consequences for our nation and all mankind.

As Bishop of a See city included on Nikita Khrushchev's

This official statement, written on September 10, 1959, was addressed to the clergy, religious, and laity of the Diocese of Pittsburgh, Pennsylvania.

itinerary, I have no political opinion to express. No political opinions will be expressed from the pulpits of our churches, especially in times of such emotion, lest some ill-considered word of ours, unbecoming to Catholic Christians, complicate further a situation which is already dangerously charged with understandably strong feeling. We, the Bishop and priests of this diocese, in the tradition of our spiritual forefathers in every period of history when tyrants have momentarily mocked Divine Law and human hopes, shall speak in our churches neither violence nor politics, but only fervent, unceasing prayer.

Accordingly, I call on our people and their prayerful neighbors to make the occasion of the Soviet dictator's intended visit a time of meditation. We should reflect on the spiritual ties which unite us to those millions behind the Iron Curtain for whom Jesus died and who belong to Him and to His Kingdom, in fact or by right, as a result of His saving death.

We should meditate on the special gratitude we owe to God for our freedom publicly to proclaim His sovereignty over us and over all the nations of mankind. We should be grateful for the traditions of civil liberty and religious faith to which we are the heirs in this blessed country.

Without any public demonstrations unworthy of the dignity and spiritual commitments we have as Christians, we shall spend the day of Nikita Khrushchev's visit in prayer that Almighty God will convert to His benign purposes the hearts of the hostile, while strengthening the minds and wills of those responsible for the protection of our heritage and the attainment of our peaceful hopes.

At all Masses in our churches on the day that Khrushchev visits the area, priests and people are asked to recite aloud and together the Apostles' Creed and the Lord's Prayer, immediately after the Last Gospel and before kneeling for the vernacular prayers traditionally offered for the conversion of Russia. During the rest of the day we shall have recourse to silent prayer—and nothing else.[1]

IV

Exceptional Children

As one who by official duty and personal inclination must be the best of the friends of Saint Anthony School, I must first thank those who have planned and those who have come to this evening's meeting to discuss and encourage the work that the school seeks to accomplish.

Permit me to thank first of all Dr. Humphreys for the paper that he prepared for this evening's meeting. I would hope that the wise, practical, and profoundly spiritual things that you had to say to us, Dr. Humphreys, might reach an audience much larger than this. And so I respectfully ask if I may have your paper for appropriate publication and distribution to friends of this school and to others who are interested in this tremendous area of special education.[1]

I wish to thank also those who have come simply to encourage us by showing their solidarity, intellectual and spiritual, with the sisters and the director of the school. I notice in the audience many doctors, many teachers, and not a few leaders from local colleges and universities, from the area's public schools, special education departments, local hospitals, and kindred institutions. We are deeply grateful to them for the encouragement and for the endorsement evidenced by their presence.

I am grateful to the priests who have come to encourage us and to the representatives of the Knights of Columbus who have pledged themselves in this part of the State to make the work of Saint Anthony School the major object of their continuing charitable benefactions.

This address was delivered at the Saint Anthony School for Exceptional Children, Oakmont, Pennsylvania, on November 13, 1959.

I bespeak the gratitude of the school, and I speak not only officially for the school but also out of intense personal feeling when I thank Mr. Kennedy and Mr. Shriver for coming personally to bring their contribution, so generous and so well timed, to the work of Saint Anthony School. By now almost everyone in America must know that it is characteristic of the Kennedys to do what they do in an intensely personal fashion. Almost anyone in their position to help could mail you a check; very busy and important people would not hesitate to mail it or to send someone along to give it to you. But Kennedys come themselves. I am deeply grateful to them for coming and encouraged by their presence as well as by their magnificent contribution to the work at the school.[2]

I have known the Kennedy family as far back as I have known my own home town. When I was a small boy, Mr. Kennedy's mother's father was engaged in the effort to give my native city what he called in his campaigns "a Bigger, Better, and Busier Boston". He went a long way toward doing it. I think we would have had a considerably bigger, better, and busier Boston if some of the Kennedy values had been confined to Boston. A wider national community has benefited from the vision and zeal inherited in no small part from the man who planned to give us "a Bigger, Better, Busier Boston". These aggressive qualities have been passed along to the present generation of Kennedys through the most attractive and welcome of channels, through Mayor Fitzgerald's daughter, the gentle, spiritual, and sensitive personality that is the mother of the Kennedy family.

As a young priest in Boston, I knew Mr. Kennedy's mother particularly well. My field was not politics then any more than it is now. It was religion and education. And so I came to know Mrs. Kennedy and her many attractive daughters. The daughter that I and many have found to be the most attractive was Eunice, and the best thing I know about Sargent Shriver, present here tonight, is that she was willing to marry him.

I mention these things to show that I know many things

about the Kennedy family, but the best thing I know about them, in each generation of the three generations that, as a boy and a man, I have known, is their attitude toward and their work for children, more particularly exceptional children.

I was secretary to the Archbishop of Boston immediately after World War II when the Kennedy Foundation was established. It was then my privilege to act for the Archbishop in working out details with the Kennedy family for the first major institutional program which the Kennedy Foundation made possible in behalf of exceptional children: the Joseph P. Kennedy, Jr., Memorial Hospital in Brighton, Massachusetts. I had occasion then to see not merely the intelligence and acumen, but the dynamic passion with which the members of this family approach the problem of the plight of the exceptional child. I saw it again in connection with like work in Hanover, Massachusetts; in journeying about the country, I have seen what they have helped make possible in Wisconsin, Chicago, New York, and the nation's capital. These are the places that I have personally visited and about which I am able to bear personal witness, but they are far from the only places that the foundation has made possible in its work for exceptional children.

It was one of my ambitions while Bishop of Worcester to establish there a school for exceptional children which would embody the new ideas and directions coming out of the research that the Kennedy Foundation has made possible, together with some of my own ideas and prejudices in the education and care of exceptional children. Mr. Joseph Kennedy had planned and earmarked a generous contribution to the work there. In order to make sure that I went ahead with the work, he gave a substantial down payment on his pledge. That, too, is in the Kennedy tradition. They do not waste money, private or public. I was transferred out of Worcester before we could break ground for the new school, but I read in the *New York Times* that ground was broken last week for the School for Exceptional Children which Kennedy money is helping make possible in Worcester. No sooner did I arrive in Pittsburgh than I found that the Kennedys were here before me, and that Saint Anthony's has been the object of their keen interest, intelligent study, and princely generosity.

I have said that of the many things I know about the Kennedy family, the best thing is their attitude toward work for exceptional children. Well, in the months that I have been in western Pennsylvania I have come to learn many things about Saint Anthony School, and one of the best things I know about it is the fact that its program commends it to the Kennedy Foundation. That is a high recommendation of the program, the soundness of its premises, and of the manner in which the sisters, the lay staff, and the others identified with the school are doing their work. The Kennedys have a passionate interest in the problems of exceptional children, but it is not a sentimental one. It is a spiritual one, but it is an objective and sound one. It does not blind them to imperfect procedures or to inadequate programs. Quite the contrary, it serves as a motive for making certain that whatever is being done in any program to which they contribute is in accord with sound educational, therapeutic, and scientific standards, as well as with lofty spiritual idealism. And so the best thing I know about Saint Anthony School is that its program and its procedures commended themselves to those who came here in the name of the Kennedy Foundation to study the school and its work.

I am happy and proud to speak for the school and for the community which the school serves in expressing gratitude to the Kennedy family through Mr. Robert Kennedy and Mr. Sargent Shriver for the encouragement and the help that they have given us.

The measure of civilization is likely to be the manner in which its less privileged members are protected. The measure of any civilization, of its basic decency, its worth, and its likelihood to survive is to be found, one thinks, in how well it provides for those who cannot provide for themselves. It is not the measure of a civilization to see how well the kings make out. They usually land standing up. The measure of a civilization is not how well the intellectuals, the bright, the strong, the able, the competent make out. They always make out fairly well. But the measure of the worth and the decency of a civilization is how well those who are shortchanged by nature make out in the institutions, public policies, and social philosophies of the civilizations in question; we identify the good society not by how well the strong are able to take care of themselves, but by how the weak count in the plans of the strong and in the provisions which the strong make for them.

I don't think that a fairly careful reader of history can condemn with particular wrath the civilization which Hitler tried to build because of the outrageous things that it did on the level of military or diplomatic action. One would have to condemn most of our English ancestors in that case. The measure of the evil of Hitler's civilization, in the eyes of those who are sensitive to what civilization means, is what he intended to do with those who were physically or mentally unprepared to take care of themselves: what he intended to do with the aged; what he intended to do with those whom he judged unfit, whether physically or culturally; what he intended to do with *lesser breeds*, what he intended to do with the stunted; not the things that he did in the prison camps to captured soldiers (that evil is as old as mankind), but what he intended to do with his own German children who did not fit his insane concept of the standard of human excellence and perfection. It was the gas chamber and the annihilation camps, the work of his doctors and his scientists, that damned in the eyes of the sensitive and the civilized what Hitler was offering as a civilization.

So it is throughout the course of history. The thing that makes Sparta remembered with such grim regret is what was done to unfit children. Any of you who saw the film that Miss Bergman did on *The Inn of the Sixth Happiness* were reminded of something you might have forgotten since the days when you were children: how the measure of the inadequacy of Chinese civilization was not the sort of political or economic things the newspapers tell us about. It was what they did to little girls, the way they bound girls' feet in making them fit into a preconceived pattern and the manner in which they exposed to death children who were born physically inadequate. The ancient tragedy of Oriental civilizations has been the plight of the underprivileged, the crippled, the sick child. If the measure of civilization is what is done for children, then the measure of the extent to which our civilization deserves to survive is not what is provided in fringe benefits for those in capital or labor, those who are more than able to take care of themselves, but what is done on the front of education, hospital care, and specialized attention for those who cannot possibly take care of themselves and who, therefore, test our civilization by the demand they make on our protection and our guidance.

This standard of the worth of a civilization, of its ultimate decency, is the one which Jesus announced when He said, "For inasmuch as you have done it to the least of these, my brethren, you did it unto Me."[3] He appointed one of His apostles to be His Vicar. But He never said that the measure of our worth would be how much we liked him or how much we liked any others of the bright and powerful. He gave them their job to do, and us our obligation to help them in the doing of that job. But the measure of our ultimate relationship to Him and therefore to the standards, temporal and eternal, which He came to teach is what we do for the least of the brethren, what is done therefore for the very type of child whom Saint Anthony's exists to serve, to make better, happier, and more useful.

What is done for Saint Anthony's constitutes a good norm for the measure of the decency of the hearts of those who do it. On this premise, I express your thanks and mine to Mr. Kennedy, Mr. Shriver, and all their associates in the Kennedy Foundation.

V

Prayer at the Dedication
Of the Pittsburgh Hilton Hotel

During this season we commemorate the coming of Him for Whom "there was no room in the inn" (Lk 2:7).

Almost two thousand years have gone by since that strange, wond'rous night, and still there are places—including inns—in which there is no room for Him. There is room for power, room for intrigue, room for misery and for hate. But all too often there is no room for faith, no room for hope, no room for charity, no room for the liberty of the sons of God.

We pray this morning that in this new inn, so modern and so proud, and in all our city, everywhere and always, there may be room for the good things, the true and beautiful things, made possible by the traditions of faith and freedom inspired by the coming of Him for Whom "there was no room in the inn".

To this end we adapt for the blessing of this beautiful hotel some prayers from the ancient liturgy for the blessing of a monastery and the guest house which was once a part of all monastic foundations. During a thousand years of Christendom the medieval monasteries, hospices, and religious guest houses, all along the roads of the great pilgrimages of Europe and high in the mountains across which strangers passed from nation to nation, served as prototypes of the later inns and modern hotels. It is good to remember them as we dedicate this new hotel and pray that the ancient virtues of hospitality will flourish here as once they flourished in the guest houses blessed with the prayers we recall today:

These remarks and this prayer were delivered at the Pittsburgh Hilton Hotel, Pittsburgh, Pennsylvania, on December 3, 1959.

O God, Whose Son has declared that He is received by whoever receives graciously the stranger as a guest, grant that we may serve Him fraternally and well in those who come here . . . that He may be a guest in our hearts as we receive His people as guests in our home. Bless, O Lord, this place of shelter for Thy servants; do Thou, Who neither sleepest nor dost grow weary, Who art the safekeeper of Israel, bless those who take their rest under this roof, guarding them from every annoyance, so that, refreshed here after their journeys, they may resume their work restored by Thee. Grant to Thy people who come here to meet with one another and to rejoice in the graces of human conviviality and commerce, a spirit of fraternity with one another, the delight of mutual interests and prosperity here below, and the hope that, helped by their sojourn here, they may attain one day to the blessings of eternal life in the mansions Thou hast prepared for Thy people hereafter. Through Christ our Lord. Amen.

VI

Haec Studia

Excellentissime praeses, insignes cleri pontifices, prelati, ministres et doctores rabbinici; dignissimi iudices; medici periti; moderatores civitatis reique publicae magistri; auditores ornatissimi; fratres omnes, quia Almae Matris filii—salvete!

And now, out of deference to the headmaster of the English High School, let me address you in the local vernacular.

This morning in Pittsburgh I preached at a Mass of Thanksgiving commemorating the establishment, one hundred twenty-five years ago this very day, of the first school of any kind in western Pennsylvania. It was a Catholic school, established by immigrants who wished to preserve the integration of the study of religion with the study of the useful arts and the beginnings, at least, of the liberal arts.[1]

As I heard three thousand children magnificently sing the ancient Latin Mass in the Cathedral of Saint Paul at Pittsburgh, I thought to myself, these are the studies that make men holy.

But after I left the Mass, I drove by a mighty American university, with its great affiliated business, medical, sociology, and law schools. These, I reflected, are the studies that make men rich.

I passed a famed technical institute which promises to make men scientists, handy to have around, and, as long as the Communists are in their present specialized field of concentration, well worth paying the salaries that we pay technicians. These, I reflected, are the studies that make men useful.

Enroute to the Pittsburgh airport, I passed a unit of the

This address was delivered at the Somerset Hotel, Boston, Massachusetts, on April 25, 1960, on the occasion of the three hundred-and-twenty-fifth anniversary of the Boston Latin School.

United States Air Force School and one of the Army, and I thought, these are the studies that make men strong.

This evening, with a son's joy at homecoming, I return to a school, the only one in the land, that has inscribed proudly on its facade these words: "Haec studia adulescentiam alunt, senectutem oblectant, secundas res ornant, adversis perfugium ac solacium praebent . . ." and the rest of Cicero's lines, which mean: These are the studies which integrate all these other things and make them humane, tolerable, and safe![2]

These are the studies which humanize the holy; civilize the rich, the useful, and the strong; improve on all the other studies, and protect us against a few of them.

These are the studies which give strength to youth, delight to old age; ". . . secundas res ornant . . ."—they add luster to times of prosperity and security; ". . . adversis perfugium ac solacium praebent . . ."—they give us a safe harbor and a little consolation when times grow tough.[3] These are the studies that the Latin School nourishes and preserves.

I am told that there are those—some in the world of local politics, some in the world of private citizenry, some (God spare us!) even in the world of education—who question the place of this unique school in a total educational program so largely dominated at the moment by the champions of the other types of schools that I have mentioned.

There are those, I am told, who ask whether it is not a bit of medievalism or a little too precious to subsidize with tax money a Latin School and its ancient disciplines, and to maintain such a school in a democratic society where everybody should be as equal as he can be with everybody else, however much it costs him in the way of pulling himself down. It is pretended that it may be *snobbish* to pay special attention to the whims of the Latin School alumni within a public school system, or for the City to go along with requests for continued support of a school that has survived with undiminished attachment to wisdom alone three hundred twenty-five years of mingled wisdom and nonsense in American education.

As fervently as ever one prayed for preservation from any plague, I pray that we may be preserved from the danger that such shortsighted persons, whatever their posts, may have their destructive way with the values represented by the Boston Latin School.

No one who loves Boston can possibly fail to see the necessity that, in every generation, we insist over and over again on the things about the Boston Latin School which have been said here tonight. Most of you have by now lived in many cities—as I have—here and abroad. All big cities have airports. Most cities have super-highways. Nowadays there can't be any city in America that doesn't have impressive public buildings, housing projects, and other evidences of the various emphases through which we pass in our political and economic history. Many American cities have excellent symphony orchestras, libraries, art museums, and parks. There is only one Latin School like that which bears the name of Boston.

And yet, I read in the *Boston Globe*, over the venerable signature of Uncle Dudley, this frightening paragraph: "A member of the Boston City Council had the urbanity to tell the headmaster, 'Look, get this straight. Boston Latin is just another high school.' "[4]

With all due deference, in these delicate times, to the separation of church and state, and fully minded that I ceased to be a registered voter in Boston ten years ago, I venture to second the comment of Uncle Dudley on this illiterate remark. He observed that if anyone is in doubt as to what ails our contemporary society from end to end, he can find no small part of his answer in the circumstances of time, person and background to that sentence.

The United States Supreme Court recently professed difficulty in defining the concept of obscenity. I offer that politician's remark as an excellent example of what should have been in the mind of the United States Supreme Court.

No one who loves Boston should be left unaware of the

place of the Boston Latin School among the things that once made Boston the Athens of America and, however facetiously or stuffily it may have been said, "the Hub of the Universe" Boston will never be either again, in any enduring sense, if anyone can implement such talk concerning the Latin School and the values for which it stands.

No one who loves education can talk that sort of language. The Latin School has borne witness across three hundred and twenty-five years to a norm of excellence, the most recent and impressive results of which Mr. Doyle proclaimed from the platform this evening.

There are those among us who, while at Latin School and after Latin School, did not equal the academic performance of the young man whose marks the headmaster quoted to you tonight. There were many of us who merely *got by* in our marks.

But Latin School did this to us: we *knew* we just *got by*! We were never permitted to make the complacent fatal mistake of supposing that we were *tops* and we were therefore predestined, for the rest of our lives, to excel by chasms of kind those who just *get by* and yet think they are pretty good.

Latin School boys had heard Henry Pennypacker rebuke students who said, "Well, Mr. Pennypacker, say what you will, I *did get by*", with "How would you like to eat an egg that just got by?"

John Mason Brown, in his address to the Groton School for graduates three years ago, said to the boys of Groton School something that the boys of our Public Latin School understand just as well as those of Groton, Exeter, or any of the great private schools, and for the same reason. He said:

"You have had your pleasures here, genuine, zestful, and unforgettable. You have had them in your friendships, your classrooms, your sports, your extra-curricular activities, in the pursuit of your special interests, in the joy of feeling both your minds and your bodies grow.

"You have had your trials, too, because as you always will be, you have been incessantly on trial.

"But," John Mason Brown said, "compare what you now know, and more important still, what you want now to know, with what you knew when you came here, and you will get the measure not only of your own growth but the excellence of the education which has made that growth—*your growth*—possible."

Then he asked them if it had been exacting. Fortunately, yes! Count its toughness as an act of mercy, he said. The good things are not easily come by. Remember, you have been spared the unintentional cruelty of that kind of *progressive education* which misleads the young into believing that they will always be free to do what they want to do, at the moment and in the way that they want to do it. Remember, he reminded the students of Groton, that your whims are not the only orders you have to obey. They never will be. They never can be.

The Latin School taught and teaches that wisdom, as against the fancies of the *progressive education* fans who, in their folly, encourage young people to express themselves before they have anything to express. This was the blessed wisdom behind Latin School customs that made us keep bottled up our unripened wisdom until it could somehow season and mature. Hence the happy pain by which Latin School required of us *declamations* before we were encouraged to debate, forcing us to stock our minds with the lofty concepts of our elders and to taste on our lips the words of our betters before we presumed to trumpet our own small thoughts.

Hence the emphasis, too, in the Latin School curriculum, on ancient history as opposed to current events; on languages, literature, and the preludes to the liberalizing arts and disciplines which presuppose the constant reading that maketh a full man.

In a book which Philip Marston is publishing in the near future, he suggests that we are indebted for no small part of the

59

high level quality of the Latin School to the requirements once made by Harvard as the condition of entrance there—Harvard which, if only because of its primacy of time and honor in the American university world, once set the academic standards even of colleges which had other reservations in its regard.[5]

Then there came a dreadful hour when Harvard decided to *tone down* Greek, Latin, and the liberal arts as conditions of receiving a diploma which bears witness that the holder is an educated man in that sense understood by Western civilization, the language and genius of which remains so largely Latin.

There had been a time when the holder of an *Artium Baccalaureus* degree was expected to be able to translate his own diploma. He was not given at commencement, together with the A.B., a "trot translation" of the declaration that he was now an educated man.

But then came a time of playing fast and loose with the ancient controls which had accounted, in no small degree, for the excellence of our schools. In that grim period two brothers, graduates of Harvard, living in New York, addressed an open letter to the then president of Harvard in which they made what proved to be, for the moment—but, thanks be to God, only temporarily—a futile appeal for the retention and encouragement of Latin at Harvard.[6]

Among other things, these two valiant gentlemen, daring to speak for thousands, wrote to the then president of Harvard:

> You are, of course familiar with the famous classification for books made by Francis Bacon, which is as well, a classification of knowledge. Three major divisions he made, one based on Memory, one on Reason, and one on Imagination. The first was History; the second, Philosophy; the third Poetry. . . . The classification is good today for most of human knowledge which is made up of information in the various divisions, and it is good for wisdom, which is the addition to the knowledge of the parts of some understanding of the whole.
>
> Broadly speaking, all that Harvard can teach may be put under these three heads. Unless our interest in civilization is to

start at some date as recent as 1500, consider, Sir, how large and important a part of the fields of knowledge based on Memory and Imagination—which include all that is meant by History and by Belles Lettres—is played by the classics.

The most common argument advanced against the study of the classics is that the time might be better spent on the acquisition of useful information. A hundred years ago, almost to the day, a great leader in education wrote a paper on the use of the classics, aimed directly at those persons who consider the study of *dead languages* to be a waste of time. Of such persons he wrote: "Information about modern events is more useful, they think, than that which relates to antiquity, and such information they wish to be given to their children. This favorite notion of filling boys with useful information is likely, we think, to be productive of some mischief."

His argument was largely ineffective. Since that time the study of the classics has consistently been subordinated to the acquisition of *useful* information.

Do you think, Sir, that the state of the civilized world today could be that *mischief* that Thomas Arnold prophesied?[7]

They pointed out, in their loyalty to their Alma Mater, what would happen if Harvard abandoned the classical emphasis. They predicted what has, in fact, happened to colleges generally and preparatory and high schools all over America. They wrote to Mr. Conant:

More is involved in your proposal than the simple question of whether the Latin requirements be desirable. There is at stake the larger question of the desirability of classical studies as a whole as a part of what we somewhat vaguely call a liberal education. Greek as a requirement for a Harvard degree was given up many years ago. What, as a result of the colleges omitting the Greek requirement, has happened to the study of Greek in the schools? It no longer exists!

If Harvard give up the Latin requirement it takes no very great effort of the imagination to foresee a similar result in the study of this subject.

It is not an uncommon opinion that the schools from which

Harvard draws her students leave as a general rule much to be desired from an educational point of view. But while our schools may not be excellent, this, at least, must be said for them, that from the University's point of view they aim to please.

The schools teach with one primary object in view. That object is to prepare their boys to fulfill the college entrance requirements. What the colleges require the schools will teach, very little more and that none too well.

If Latin is no longer to be required for the A.B. degree, it is hard to believe that it will continue to be studied in the schools.

Thus shall we have cut off so many centuries of the world's experience, have taken one more step to confine the existing generations to themselves and their immediate predecessors; thus shall we have placed ourselves a little nearer the state we should be in if the human race had first come into existence in the year 1500.[8]

Philip Marston's present book is a record of the fulfillment of this melancholy prediction of 1935![9]

Mr. John McCormack, Speaker of the House, in his own admirable tribute to the Latin School, published in the *Congressional Record* of Monday, April 18, quotes a Latin School and Harvard man, George Santayana:

There may be older schools in other countries; but almost always they have suffered a complete change in spirit and have endured only by ceasing to be themselves. . . . But the Latin School, in its simpler sphere, has remained faithfully Latin. In spite of all revolutions and all the pressure of business and all the powerful influences inclining America to live in contemptuous ignorance of the rest of the world, and especially of the past, the Latin School, supported by the people of Boston, has kept the embers of traditional learning alive, at which the humblest rushlight might always be lighted; has kept the highway clear for every boy to the professions of theology, law, medicine, and teaching, and a window open to his mind from these times to all other times and from this place to all other places.

The merely modern man never knows what he is about. A

Latin education, far from alienating us from our own world, teaches us to discern the amiable traits in it, and the genuine achievements; helping us, amid so many distracting problems, to preserve a certain balance and dignity of mind, together with a sane confidence in the future.[10]

"Haec studia adulescentiam alunt, senectutem oblectant. . . ."[11]

No man who understands the meaning of education and of civilization will ever lay a hand on the Latin School.

No one who loves the American public school system will lay a hand on this school, which was its cradle and will remain a major norm of its excellence.

No one who loves faith—above all, religious faith—will fail to be grateful to this school, the part of which in the religious life of our civil community is symbolized by the invocation that the rabbi gave this evening, the very wording of which reminded us of how the Protestant Puritans, who founded our school and our city, took from the Hebrew Scriptures a text for their inspiration and gave it to us in the Latin of the Catholic Vulgate Bible, perpetuated in our Latin School and in the motto of our city as the rabbi quoted it.

I am prepared to speak for my own Faith when I thank the school not only for the bishops it has given Catholicism, but, what is more important, for the type of men it has placed in so many of our pulpits and our classrooms to speak the ancient Faith with an exactness and an elegance they would have never acquired save for the diligence with which they were drilled in excellence by a generation of Protestant Yankee teachers. The indebtedness of Protestant pulpits to the Latin School is a matter of familiar history; I always thrill when Max Levine speaks so warmly of the encouragement Irish Catholic teachers gave a Latin School master of Jewish faith.

No one who loves freedom will permit without protest that anyone in public office or out of it tamper with the traditions of freedom of which the Latin School is at once the symbol and the effective instrument in our community.

Make no mistake about it. It is not the technicians, certainly not the technocrats, who keep a people free. The essential method of their education, the very conditioning of their minds, makes them the easiest of men to regiment, whether they be like the German scientists whom the Russians hired or the Germans whom the Americans hired.

It is not to the mere scientist that men ultimately look for freedom. The scientist is the master of *know-how*. The liberal arts men are the masters of *know-why*. *Know-why* men are the ones who will always be distrusted by dictators, because poetry has taught them caprice, philosophy has taught them to question and to challenge on a higher level than that of mere formulae, and languages have taught them to talk. If there is one thing more than another that despotism cannot tolerate, it is informed, sensitive, capricious, and questioning talk. Yet this is made possible chiefly by the things which are taught in *"haec studia* (quae) adulescentiam alunt, senectutem oblectant, secundas res ornant, adversis perfugium ac solacium praebent. . . ."[12]

The so-called liberal arts are not lightly so named. They were originally so styled because of their function in the minds and the hearts of the genuinely educated. They are expected to liberalize the minds of those who master them and the souls of those who are steeped in a love of them. A Latin School is therefore a liberalizing force; it is an oasis of potential revolution, should regimentation come, and a focal point of freedom when all the other modern studies are subsidized, regimented, and taken over.

Some there are who tell us that such a Latin School, especially when supported by tax money, offends against the principles of educational democracy by the way in which it caters, allegedly, to the exceptional few. But democracy is well served, not undermined, when a hierarchy of values is scrupulously insisted upon and when it is pointed out not merely that some people are more excellent and some are worse, but that it is extremely important to determine why some are better and what makes others worse. It is not democracy, it is a spirit hostile to democracy, which seeks to level all persons, to level all opportunity, to reduce to least common denominators all achievement, intelligence, virtue, mastery of knowledge, growth in perfection. It is a phony democracy which promotes the insincere pretense that all schools of thought are equally valid or all schools equally worthwhile.

Not all medical techniques are equally effective. Some cure, some kill, some prolong the disease.

Not all preferences in art reflect equal taste. Some are sublime, some are vulgar, some are worthless.

Not all business procedures are equally well advised. Some lead to prosperity, some to bankruptcy, some to jail.

Not all poetry is equally inspired. Not all forms of government equally promote public welfare and freedom. Not all systems of thought have equal right before the face of truth, though they may have equal right before the law because of the metaphysical equality of persons as such.

There is an inevitable hierarchy of worth, especially in a healthy democracy. There are always some more gifted than others, more willing than others, more honest than others, more trustworthy than others, more diligent than others, more prepared than others, more generous than others, more intelligent and more interested than others. Unless there be such a hierarchy of the intellect and of the soul, then the essential equalities in which a political democracy consists degenerate and die, precisely because there are always some less prepared than others, less generous than others, less trustworthy than others, less bright and less interested in values than others.

It has been the function of the Latin School since first its door was opened to protect political democracy by promoting intellectual aristocracy, to preserve essential democratic values by fostering spiritual values which result in uneven accomplishment because of unequal effort.

It is a gross caricature of democracy to talk about reducing the Latin School, its requirements and its objectives, to the level of "any other high school" lest, perchance, it offend those who are not interested in anything but "any other high school". It is part of the proud way democracy has worked out in America that, in Boston at least, tax money has, during all these years, deliberately sought to encourage excellence and to produce leadership through the proved excellence of boys who measure up to the frankly aristocratic scholastic requirements of the Latin School.

Vigilance that these things be preserved is needed more now than it has been in generations. One thinks of the warning of Shakespeare:

"Sir, he hath never fed of the dainties that are bred in a book; he hath not eat paper, as it were; he hath not drunk ink. He is only an animal, only sensible in the duller parts."[13]

The Latin School made its students eat paper. It made them drink ink. It made them sensitive in the loftier parts and it did so, not merely for themselves, but that they might be the servants of the society that makes such a school possible. For three hundred years it has done so, and done so superbly.

Nor is the need of Latin Schools something of the past. We are daily told that we are now living in the Space Age, not in an Age of Rhetoric or Liberal Arts or Latin and Classics. But there is no reason to believe that the Space Age will be any different in its essential human requirements than any of the other ages through which mankind has passed.

A friend of mine, an editor in London, relates that one of the moments of his greatest ecstasy in this prelude to the Space Age occurred a year ago in a week of recess of the British schools, during which there was a science exhibit, featuring the Space Age, in a great London exhibit hall.

A hapless commentator for the B.B.C. showed up on the television screen one morning, following school boys around the hall as they gazed at exhibits setting forth the wonders of the Space Age: communications in the Space Age, business in the Space Age, art in the Space Age, entertainment in the Space Age, government in the Space Age, and all the rest of it. The B.B.C. commentator said to his television audience, "Let's question a couple of these youngsters. You adults don't understand all this. You still live in the Victorian age. You live in the past. These young people will be the citizens of the Space Age. Let's see what they think of these wonderful things that mean so much to them and so little to you."

So he went up to the first moppet and put the mike in front of him, saying, "Son, did you see the exhibit on science in the Space Age?"

"I did", said the youngster.

"Well," he said, "tell me, now, what is your hobby?"

The boy replied, "Stamp collecting."

The telly man looked a little crestfallen, but he tried again with the dull persistence of his type. Bearing down on a second lad, he said to him, "Well, sonny! You heard this boy's answer. But wouldn't you like to journey to the moon?"

The boy said, "No!"

"Why not?" the telly man gasped.

The lad said, "I want to stay home."

"Well," he said, "wouldn't you like to go later?"

"Yes," he said, "when some other people have gone first and come back. In the meantime I want to finish school."

Then the unfortunate commentator tackled a third kid. "What would you like to be in the Space Age? Wouldn't you like to be an astronaut? Wouldn't you like to pilot one of these things out into space?"

The kid said, "No. I would like to be a priest and preach the gospel all over the world!"

The B.B.C. man could not have been more dismayed. Such an answer indubitably violated the theological regulations of a land subject to a constitutional deity. But he made a quick recovery.

He said, "That is an unusual point of view."

"Not at all," said the kid. "A lot of boys agree with me. They want to be priests, too!"

I have a strong suspicion that the function of schools like the Latin School will be even more important in the Space Age than it was when people lived and worked close to Victorian churches, concert halls, and libraries. Those who go out into space, if they are to come back sane, will have to have something in their heads besides scientism to sustain them through the adjustments and shocks to unchanging human nature which must come with changing technology.

Men will always come back from the furthermost reaches of space as they have come back from Korea and Germany and the South Pacific to some contemporary equivalent of Horace's Sabine Farm. Sometime in the evening, they must still come home from all the competition and conquest, all the bombing and calculating and banking. When they come home, to their wives, their children, themselves, and their God, they shall need to think and to love the things we learned in the poetry, the drama, and the prose of the Latin School.

With all the building of a new world order, not to speak of interglobal and interplanetary systems, it will be well that men have once been obliged to ponder—and not in translation—the line: "Tantae molis erat Romanam condere gentem."[14] Aye, what a titanic task it was to build the Roman state! But what an even more titanic task it will be to build the organized human community and the world of the Space Age!

Therefore, I rejoice that, having made unhappy reference to what one president of Harvard did, I can now call on you to thank God for the quiet but effective support given to classics and therefore hope given to American education by Nathan Pusey.

I hold in my hand, as the late Senator McCarthy might have said, the numbers of those who are concentrating in Latin and Greek classics, with none of this "classics in translation" business, at Harvard University today. Why do I rejoice that this renaissance of classical studies should be going on at Harvard, to which, by some things I read about myself and my kin, I should be allergic? I rejoice simply because it remains true that Harvard holds the primacy, if only in time, among the universities and colleges of America and profoundly influences all other colleges ultimately, as the colleges, in turn, set the requirements for the preparatory schools, the high schools, and the Latin School.

In 1954–1955, there were [at Harvard] four hundred in Latin and Greek, which was vastly more than there were in 1940. In 1959–1960 there are five hundred and fourteen in the fall term, five hundred and nineteen in the spring term, and an encouraging increase in the instructional staff of a classics department that seemed doomed to be a casualty of World War II and the age of technology even twenty years ago.

This means, if this new interest in classics spreads by happy contagion, that Harvard will begin again to send forth men capable of faith, worthy of freedom, and prepared to serve in the light of the wisdom of the ancient world, distilled through the hardships of the mediaeval world, the Renaissance, and the adventures of modern society. But it also means that the entire academic world of America may see a new generation of intellectual aristocrats, authentic liberal arts scholars, equipped and disposed to serve democracy again as Supreme Court justices, ambassadors, learned doctors, wise lawyers, spiritual chieftains, and sensitive teachers who can help prepare America with dignity and grace, wisdom and faith, to live nobly in the good times and bad of the Space Age "haec studia. . . ."

We who love Boston wish her to play her ancient part in producing such leadership; therefore, we want the Latin School to be given encouragement to greater growth, greater glory, greater opportunities to serve.

VII

Catholic Optimism

I plan to speak to you of the quality of optimism which should characterize Catholics on every level of the life of the Church of Christ, particularly in times like these.

I think of myself as an optimist. If temperament did not dispose me to be one, Catholicism would. Catholicism is, of all the faiths by which men have walked, by all odds the most optimistic. The Cardinal Archbishop of Paris, Cardinal Feltin, shortly after the end of World War II was invited by the German Catholics of Cologne to visit their city. The French Cardinal stood in the midst of the ruins of the German city and, surrounded by the evidence of the destruction that comes from man's malice and evil ingenuity, told his German fellow-Catholics that we Catholics are, of all people, the most optimistic. We believe in the future. We know the evil of the past and we, more than any other people, are conscious of the reality and ravages of Original Sin. We are reminded in our spiritual and moral theology at every turn of the tragic fact of sin; more than most in our generation, we are aware of what sin is and what sin can do. Nonetheless, we are more optimistic than any other people because, although we recognize the evil of which human nature is capable, we are even more aware of the power of God's grace. Therefore, we are optimists.

Cardinal Feltin spoke in the tradition of the Gospels, which like the entire New Testament through the Apocalypse of Saint John, are documents of great optimism. Jesus used the words *life* and *love*, *hope* and *free* more gladly than he used any

This address was delivered at the Eighteenth Biennial Convention of the National Catholic Laymen's Retreat Conference, at the Penn-Sheraton Hotel, Philadelphia, Pennsylvania, on August 5, 1960.

other words. He spoke of sin, of course; he spoke of evil, he spoke of treason, he spoke of the other things that dismay men and frighten even the devout. But he spoke most often of those things which nourish optimism: *life* and *the life more abundant*; *love* and *the love more perfect*; *hope* and *the hope more conquering*; *freedom* and *the very freedom of the sons of God*.

All the great founders of religious orders in the Catholic Christian tradition were indomitable optimists. Had they not been, they never would have undertaken the works that they did. Saint Francis of Assisi was an incurable optimist. Saint Francis de Sales was an optimist. Saint Ignatius of Loyola was a man of profoundly optimistic temperament, conscious of what could and should be done for the greater glory of God. Saint Francis Xavier was an optimist. In every generation, the great religious founders have been optimists.

Our present Holy Father, with his radiant countenance and his clearly sanguine temperament, is a symbol of the authentic mood of optimism in the Church.

Our most typical great laymen in the history of the Church have invariably been optimists. We properly think of Saint Thomas More in terms of the merry wit with which he met disgrace and death itself; in the midst of revolutionary changes which must have depressed men of his sensitive intelligence, he was profoundly optimistic. Frédérick Ozanam, the Paris intellectual who gave such tremendous emphasis to modern lay movements of every kind, was also a man of profound optimism.

The optimism of the Catholic Christian tradition is not the voluntaristic cheerfulness of a Dr. Norman Vincent Peale. It bears no resemblance to this because it isn't a mere matter of temperament or of natural psychology, popular or systematic. The optimism of the Church is a profoundly supernatural optimism, and it is the authentic spirit characteristic of Catholicism.

Many Catholics are probably temperamentally sanguine

anyway, or, at least they like to think they are. The Irish think of themselves as being naturally and instinctively a witty, light-hearted people. As a matter of fact, there are good reasons to think them a melancholy race. Their typical comedians, like Jackie Gleason, for example, turn out to be on the melancholy side. I shall never forget spending two and one-half hours at a performance of *Harvey*, laughing heartily at the comedy of Frank Fay, only to discover afterward how grim an outlook he had. Dismal fate was at work on every side. Communists were taking over the theater. I could not see any Communists in this particular play, but toward the end of my chat with Frank, I decided a Communist must have been playing the part of Harvey; you couldn't see him, but he was there all the time! In any case, everything was melancholy!

Nevertheless, I think we are temperamentally a sanguine people. The optimism of the Church, however, has nothing to do with temperament. It has nothing to do with weather; nothing to do with the state of our nerves; nothing to do with merely natural considerations, even though such natural optimism as prevails among us may correspond to a supernatural spirit of confidence proper to and justified by the holy Catholic Faith.

Catholic optimism has its roots not in a healthy liver, nor a well-balanced digestion, nor well-functioning glands, nor any other faculty of the healthy, as the current expression has it, "well-integrated human animal". Our optimism has its roots in the gospel, in the teachings of the Fathers and theologians, and in the supernatural mood of the Church itself.

It is this supernatural optimism which accounts, under God, for the resilience, the perennial hope, the youthful vitality of Catholicism in the face of Marxist atheism and other forms of adversity. The Lay Retreat Movement should have for its principal social effect the development of a spiritual elite who, whatever their natural individual temperaments, are characterized by this optimism of the Catholic Church.[1] Retreat houses should be schools of Christian optimism in these troubled times, not a temperamental cheerfulness—I repeat—nor a psychological mood, but a spiritual outlook, a theological conviction, grounded in confident faith, ardent hope, and flaming charity; it is the theological virtues which constitute the premise of our optimism.

It is well that the retreat movement is gaining ever-deeper roots and is spreading as it is, because Christian optimism is in for some tough testing and severe trials.

Some years ago an English Jesuit made the prediction that before the end of the twentieth century we would see a substantial reduction in the numbers of Catholics in the world. He did not mean that our statistics would be cut down as a result of martyrdom, bombardment, annihilation, or persecution. Rather, he said that he suspected that our statistics on the numbers of Catholics contained no little water. We have, he argued, a lot of free-riders on the bark of Peter; we have not a few fair-weather Catholics who would drop away under any solid threat from the evils of the age. He did not think—and neither do I—that this would be bad for the Church; as a matter of fact, he thought that for the vitality and the prestige of the Church it would turn out to be a blessed and good thing. He felt that the Church would be more disciplined, more ardent, more fervent, a more impressive force in the modern world, if we were rid of our half-hearted and our two-timers, so that our statistics would reflect only those who believe and love with all their hearts.

As contrasted with our present sometimes so-impressive statistics, we might then seem a little flock, perhaps like the one that Jesus spoke of, but it might be a flock of enormously greater quality in proportion as its quantity was reduced by the dropping away of the half-hearted and the infirm of faith.

I recall the prophecy of the English Jesuit at the opening of our retreat conference because I am convinced that the well-founded optimism of Catholic Christians may be in for some

73

tough testing as we see a reduction in our statistics during the last half of the present century. And yet, it should be no source of discouragement to witness such a falling away from the Church under the pressures of political persecution or other scandal in one part of the world or another. From the very beginning, as the Gospels reveal, there were many among the followers of Christ who proved incapable of accepting His "hard sayings" and who therefore walked with Him no more. The Church must expect and indeed welcome the same fate as Christ Himself. Defections from her ranks in the face of the "hard sayings" of the Catholic creed and the hard requirements of the Catholic moral code should neither surprise nor scandalize. Some quit Christ because His dogmas are more than mere intellect can grasp. Others quit Him because they find His discipline more heroic than mere nature can support. *Mark my word: politics, human respect, dullness of perception, inadequacy of spirit will continue to account for compromises and spiritual collapse which will lose many to Christ and His Catholic Church.*

To what extent, I wonder, does lip service keep many among our statistics in times of little or no challenge, people who would drop away into easy ways of compromise in any times of trial or testing, personal or public, like those which lie ahead for the Catholic Church in the United States and throughout the world? The Anglicans like to imply in some of their magazines that many Roman Catholics, as they studiously call us, unable or unwilling to meet the requirements of the Church's moral code in marriage or even in Holy Orders, turn to the easier ways of Episcopalianism—high, broad, or low—and work out compromises with conscience which apparently give them a certain peace and sometimes a better job. Everyone knows of people who, unable to handle the intellectual tensions which occur between supernatural faith and natural reason, take refuge in the relaxed comfort of agnosticism. Agnosticism is comfortable; it's a kind of intellectual and spiritual suspended animation, and in the age of sedatives and tranquilizers, intellectual and physical, moral and medical, agnosticism has a certain lazy appeal to minds confronted with the intellectual torment of having to decide and decide clearly just how to stand with respect to the master knots of human fate.

Then there are the cynics who keep in touch with the basic sacraments and carefully remain qualified to be buried with the Church, but who are not likely to prove too strong, too prominent, or too outspoken in the total defense of the total gospel as the Catholic Church presents it for total acceptance. These have the Faith, but with the strings and the qualifications, some of them publicly expressed, some of them privately whispered around, but compromises just the same.

The effect of these on the "Catholics with a qualification" is bound to be debilitating.

Confronted with the psychological strain of trying to live in an age of secularism, easy divorce, convenient contraception, and impatience with obedience in every form, there will doubtless be many of our brethren who were baptized in the Faith disposed to say, in effect, that the *gentle Jesus* hardly expects them to live up to an uncompromising code when doing so might cost an election, or cost a job, or cost a night's sleep. Such persons find it hardly reasonable to argue that the *gentle Jesus* expects us to discharge the duties of our state in life *in times like these*; they count on Him *to understand* if each of us make his own private little concordat with the devil, our little compromise with personal conscience and with the public revelation committed by Christ to the Church.

And so the English Jesuit was, in all probability, quite right when he predicted that the ranks of the faithful may be diminished greatly in a generation when people write the Chancery Office threatening to turn Protestant if their kids are flunked in a parochial school! People without the slightest idea of what the Faith means actually threaten apostasy for reasons as trivial and unrealistic; it is a sign of the general spirit of the age, with its pretense that the *gentle Jesus* cannot really expect us to stand up and be counted in defense of conscience and of an unqualified, uncompromised Catholic creed.

Well, the Catholic Lay Retreat Movement exists to teach us the spiritual facts of life; it reminds the true elite among Catholic laymen that *Christ is not one bit gentle when it comes to the integrity of His teachings and the sovereign demands of conscience*. The Catholic Lay Retreat Movement also exists to give us, in the midst of the testing of the times, a sturdy and supreme optimism born of the confidence that Christ does not let down those who do not let Him down.

Out of such awareness of Christ and sturdiness of faith comes the authentic Catholic spirit. People who have the spirit of the world and who think of themselves as conservatives threaten to walk out on the Church whenever the Church is obliged, in the name of Christ, to rebuke the pagan excess of conservatism as Pope Pius XI felt bound to do four times in his pontificate. When certain French Catholics became so conservative, or so secular, in their conservatism that they tried to identify Catholicism with the pagan statism of Maurras, Pius XI condemned their stand. Their reaction was typical; some of them even suggested that his election couldn't have been valid! They said that if it had been, he would have seen that their *Action Française* movement was conservative and *therefore* good and *therefore* Catholic.

Another camp imbued with the spirit of the world think of themselves as *liberals*. They announce that they can no longer walk with the Church when in the name of Christ she rebukes the negations of secularism and liberalism as Pope Pius XI was obliged to do.

The authentic Catholic, whom the retreat movement exists to fortify in his faith, *is at once conservative and liberal*. He is attached to the past, but he is open to the future. In any case, he always sticks with the Church, if only because he understands, as did Saint Peter of old, that there is no other than Jesus

Christ, the Lord of history and Lord of the Church, to whom we can turn. The Lay Retreat Movement schools devout laymen in the understanding of these realities; it nourishes the optimism that enables them to face with equanimity every crisis of the Right or the Left which confronts the Church or confronts themselves.

The theme of our conference this year is *Vox temporis, Vox Dei: The voice of the times is the voice of God!* I cannot pretend to be any more a keen student of the voice of the times than anyone of you or the next person. But if the voice of the times says anything, it says this: the grounds of our optimism for the future of Catholicism, humanly speaking, are identified with the extent to which laymen understand the reasons for the traditional optimism of the Church and are prepared to make unqualified commitments to the Church. For if what we are reading about the Congo and Cuba be true; if what we are learning about South America and what the English Jesuit prophesied be also true, then humanly speaking the history and the future of the Church of Christ depend on whether our laity are prepared to bear a full Catholic witness, not merely the witness of an obedient, receptive people within the Church, but the witness of an active people, themselves speaking up clearly and confidently, intelligently and optimistically, in defense of the things that Christ has given His Church to say to our generation.

Hence the suggestion, indeed the urgent plea, that in our houses of closed retreats there be an increased opportunity for laymen themselves actively to participate in the giving as well as the making of retreats. In the liturgical life of the Church, Pope Pius XII and Pope John XXIII have now prepared us for an increased participation in the liturgy by the dialogue Mass, by increased congregational chant, by active participation by our responses in the sacraments, and by other means, particularly in the Holy Week liturgy. These two great contemporary popes have made it clear that the laity are called to be not merely beneficiaries of the sacraments and spectators at the liturgy, but actively to participate.

So, too, in the retreat movement, it would be well if men making lay retreats not merely participate in dialogue Masses and liturgical exercises, but also have increased opportunity to learn and practice the techniques of meditation. Then, even as bishops, priests, or retreat directors are prepared to give out the points for meditation, so also informed, enthusiastic, and devout laymen could give the points for meditation. Competent retreatants would not merely listen to what the priests have to say on retreats, but they would themselves be heard in suggesting and working out meditations on points intimately bound up with their daily lives as laymen, reflecting upon these according to the Ignatian method, the Salesian method, or whatever other methods have been fruitful in the lives of priests and religious. Thus will be avoided the danger that our retreats may be too passive, or that the activity of the laymen be confined only to recruiting retreatants, collecting retreat dues, or propagandizing the retreat movement.

It would be excellent if in every closed retreat at least one conference were the result of the thinking out loud of a layman in the crowd, not on political subjects, economic themes, nor the interests of this world, but on the unsearchable riches hidden in Christ Jesus.

If we are capable only of recognizing the truth when it is presented to us, then we are hardly more than animate recording tapes; it should be that many of our laymen—I dare say most of them—could so grow in the techniques of meditation that, if the need should ever arise, they could give conferences and direct retreats for the sanctification of their brethren and the strengthening of the Church.

There will, perhaps, be some among you to say that this is a little more than our people can do, but I venture to hope that they learn to do these things before the worries descend on us— the worries that have descended on other parts of Christendom.

I have in my hand an extremely interesting notebook. I have told some of you, on other occasions, about the background of this little book. When I was a young priest, I volunteered to supply in a parish of one of the so-called de-Christianized zones of France. It was in the diocese of Perigeux, one of the oldest dioceses in the Church. It had almost a thousand parishes and hardly more than two hundred priests. The parish church which I served had not had an active priest for years. It was kept attractive and clean by laymen in the town, all of them inspired by one man, a retired colonel of the French Army who from boyhood had not merely loved the Church and listened to the Church, but had realized that baptism and confirmation made him an active part of the Church. The Colonel de Corbiac had gathered the children of the village for prayer; he and his family taught the children their Catholicism. He stood up before the men and women of the parish—when they could not have Mass—and gave them a meditation.

Naturally, I lost touch with him during the years of World War II, but when I returned to the parish after the war, I met a school teacher who handed me this notebook. He said that when France fell, the Colonel became mayor of the little town in an effort to hold it together. Then when the Maquis took over, Colonel de Corbiac was thrown into a concentration camp under sentence of death. The school teacher shared the same fate. And he told me:

When I found myself doomed to live in this barrack room with one hundred and fifty men, most of whom I didn't know, until such a time as I would be led out to be shot, I thought I would die of sheer despair and disgust. My plight was the more pathetic, in a way, because I had no faith. I had given up the practice of Catholicism as a university student and had not set foot in a Catholic church in more than thirty years. The first night that we were there, in the barracks, the Colonel stood up after lights out and, in the dark, said: "How many will join me in the recitation of the beads for France and for our families at home?"

79

He was greeted with a barrage of shoes and curses. Nonetheless, he recited the Rosary together with three or four men. Finally, after a few weeks, the numbers joining him were such that he sat in the middle of the barrack's floor every night and gave meditations on the mysteries of the Rosary. Thus the ancient phrases of the faith became the last sounds we heard before we went to sleep during that dreadful time.

The teacher told me that Colonel de Corbiac's meditations were so beautifully expressed that for sheer love of their excellent language he himself began to follow them. Eventually he wrote them down. He kept in this book, in his own longhand, the meditations on the mysteries of the Rosary, on the Stations of the Cross, on the patronal saints of the churches and parishes from which the men came, as these meditations were given by a disgraced colonel, a layman, in a concentration camp where no bishop could come, a place which included no priest and which—as far as the prisoners knew—would be the place in which they would live out the rest of their days on earth.

During the months that they were in the concentration camp, better than half of the men returned to the Faith, moved by the meditations of a layman. They had heard no bishop speak and no priest preach; but they had enjoyed the blessing of having in their midst a man who for years had acquired in his own retreats the art of meditation and the ability to speak simply, sincerely, and compellingly to his brothers the truths of the Catholic Faith.

On the first page of the teacher's notebook containing these incomparably beautiful meditations, an inscription tells how each evening, in the almost complete obscurity of an overcrowded barracks cell, these humiliated and defeated men of France prayed the Rosary while one of their own number, Colonel de Corbiac, kept alive their spirits, restored their faith, and brought back Catholic optimism by little meditations— not one of them, by the way, longer than five minutes. These retreat meditations by a layman are a souvenir of nights of spiritual calm in a place which would otherwise have been hell; a souvenir of recollection and intellectual peace in a place that would otherwise have been an abyss of loneliness and of torment; a souvenir of introductions to consoling prayer in a place which, for its first few days, had been a symphony hall of cursing.[2]

You, Catholic Americans, may be tempted to say, "I'm glad that in France, when they needed him, there was a Frenchman who could give such meditations. But I am even more glad that here in the United States we have no like need!"

Let us be on our guard! There was no clause in Father Adam's will which exempted this part of his family—these United States—from the things which have happened to Eastern Europe, Asia, Spain, France; yesterday to Cuba, today to San Domingo. If and when that day comes to America, when bishops are silent and scattered, when priests are too few and hopelessly impeded in their work, we shall be still optimistic and shall still face the future with Christian confidence if the men of the American Lay Retreat Movement have been taught in their retreats not only to listen but also to speak, to speak up for Christ as did this French lay retreatant, Colonel de Corbiac, for the good of the Church, the salvation of souls, and to the greater glory of God.

The voice of the times is the voice of God! If this be true, then everything I hear about our times on the radio tells me that God wants you to be prepared to speak up for Him and His Church, whatever may happen in our times. May the retreat movement inspire and help prepare you to do so!

VIII

Temples of the Living God

It is a thrilling experience to participate, as we are all doing this afternoon, in the solemn rededication of a magnificent temple of the living God.

Many and powerful sentiments, with origins deep in the loyalties and convictions of the Catholics of Altoona and their friends, heightened the emotional, historical significance of this occasion. We think of the blessed dead, priests and laity, from the days of Bishop Garvey and, indeed, back to the almost legendary days of Prince Gallitzin and the pioneer Catholics of this region.[1] We recall that the birth-year of the Cathedral parish, 1853, was that of the City of Altoona itself; we reflect on how the progress of the civil community, as well as that of our Catholic people within that community, has been at once advanced and measured by the progress of the Cathedral itself. An occasion of this solemnity, honored by the presence of the personal representative of the Holy Father in America, prompts remembrance of the simple, almost casual ceremonies in September, 1924, when Bishop McCort broke ground for the Mother Church of the Diocese.[2] On that occasion Bishop McCort ended his brief remarks by turning to the contractor and saying, "You may proceed with the work, and may God prosper us!"

Bishop McCort's prayers have been answered through the popular generosity and prudent administration that characterized the remaining twelve years of his pontificate and the twenty-one years that Bishop Guilfoyle directed this diocese and intensified the liturgical and spiritual life of which the Cathedral was and is the center.[3]

This sermon was preached at Blessed Sacrament Cathedral, Altoona, Pennsylvania, on November 13, 1960, on the occasion of the rededication of the same cathedral.

We think especially of the inspired and bold deeds by which Bishop Carroll, fourth bishop of the diocese, undertook the titanic task of completing the Cathedral in the majestic beauty that we behold today. We reflect on the seeming untimeliness of the talented Bishop's death, the circumstances of which dramatize the ever-present mystery of Divine Providence in the relationship between the mortality of the humans who do God's work and the unchanging progress of the divine work itself.[4]

And then, no sooner do we recall the sad circumstance of the sudden death of the Bishop who had dreamed and dared the new plans for the Cathedral than we note, with grateful joy, the happy circumstance that finds the old Cathedral now completed, splendidly renewed just as the new Bishop comes to take up the old work and to play his predestined part in the spread of the Kingdom of God and the radiation of the gospel of Christ from this focal point in central Pennsylvania that is the Cathedral of the Blessed Sacrament.[5]

All this unchanging progress in the midst of human changes, this constancy in what pertains to God and His glory in the midst of mortality in what pertains to us and our part in the work, is dramatic proof that God's grace has been at work here and that God's grace has not been wasted. Thanks to that grace and to the cooperation with it of priests and people, Altoona now rejoices in its renewed and glorious Cathedral, a temple of the living God and dwelling place of His Incarnate Son in the Eucharistic Presence of the Blessed Sacrament.

A cathedral is a major means to the sanctification of souls; a temple of the living God, it is the center of the mighty work of making men into living temples of God. But the generosity and faith which have built this Cathedral are proofs that such living temples already thrive among you, or else the virtues which have made this day possible would never have been operative in your midst to produce so superb a monument of the piety, unity, and generosity of a whole diocese.

A cathedral links the city which it adorns to all the Catholic world. It makes that city *one* both with Rome and with Calvary, with the Vicar of Christ and with Christ Himself. It brings to the city within which it is built the *universal* treasures of the Holy Catholic Church. It becomes a fountainhead of *sanctity* for the people among whom it stands. The throne of a Catholic bishop is always a pledge of *apostolicity* of the Church. All the marks of the Church of Christ are recalled by a cathedral: its *unity*, *universality*, *sanctity*, and *apostolicity*. Every cathedral is the whole Catholic Church in miniature. If it were a barn or a bamboo tent, but in communion with Rome, it would be all this.

But Catholic people, appreciating the unique excellence of buildings with associations so sublime, have always striven to make their cathedrals, as you have made yours, the most beautiful buildings in the cities where they stand, vestibules of heaven itself, certainly the most superb works of the mind and the hand of man.

It was this devout desire of Catholics in centuries gone by which gave the world those cathedrals which men still journey abroad to see. Someone has said that it was the aspiration of the builders of the great Catholic cathedrals of the Old World to include all human experience within each of the temples of God which they built. All the arts associated with architecture were, of course, involved in the construction of a cathedral, but very much more was also present. The carving on the porches of the cathedrals, the paintings on the walls, the symbols in the sculpture, the pictures in the stained glass—all these summed up the science of the generations which produced them, the previous history of mankind, sacred and profane, the revelations committed to the Church and all the philosophy and theology derived from these, the visions of centuries past and the hopes of centuries to come: all were present in the great cathedrals of the ages of faith.

In those days a cathedral was a place destined for prayer, for vast assemblages of the people, for teaching and for almost every need of the cultural, intellectual, and religious life of the general community. All around the cathedral were the shops and the marketplaces. Close by the cathedral were its school and seminary; the very courts of justice were frequently near at hand; so were the hospitals and the other centers of Christian life and action.

When you visit a great cathedral like that of Saint James at Santiago in Spain you find there a thriving center of all the intellectual, administrative, professional, and devotional life of a whole people. This was once true of cathedrals like Chartres and Notre Dame in France; Ely and Canterbury in England; the cathedral churches of Germany, Austria, Hungary, and Eastern European Christendom. In such days the cathedral was a window opening on heaven, just as it still is, but it was also a mirror of all the world around it.

It was a mirror of nature and reflected everything that men knew of the universe about them: its origin and development; the beginnings of human life; the marvelous variety of races and nations; the wonders of the animal kingdom; the human reaction to these as reflected in fables, proverbs, and legends; the vegetable kingdom and the world of fruit and flowers. All these, as our ancestors knew them, may still be studied in the decorations and the symbols of the great cathedrals of the Old World.

The cathedral was also a mirror of science. It demonstrated whatever of scientific skill had been achieved, and that skill was remarkably great. It captured all the best ingenuity of the crafts and the trades. It brought together the genius of every liberal art and summed up the wisdom from at home and afar which was available to those who built it—and there was not one in the civilized community of that day who was not numbered among the builders of a cathedral.

The cathedrals were mirrors of the moral world. All the perversions of vice, all the noble possibilities of virtue were portrayed in the themes developed in a cathedral. An age which lacked books depended greatly on the instruction which a silent pilgrimage within a cathedral would provide to one pondering the problems of life.

The cathedral was a mirror of history as history came down to its builders in the Old Testament and the New, or even in the legends and the lore of antiquity.

A cathedral was a temple then, but it was also a university, a museum, a library, an encyclopedia in stone, an art gallery, a community center, a national monument, and a little universe all in one in the ages of faith. It brought together everything worth knowing and having in the world—and then it became an anteroom entering upon heaven.

This latter function is still the principal purpose of our cathedrals as, indeed, of all our churches. The discovery of printing, the complex development of science, the increasingly secular spirit of art and of learning generally, the intricate demands of modern life have all combined to account for the growth of great schools, centers of learning, and areas of action physically removed from the immediate precincts of the cathedral. The campus of the university, even among Christians, is a place apart. The guild houses of our day are even further removed from the shadow of the cathedral. So—alas, all too much so, sometimes—are the headquarters of the community administration, the halls of research, the centers of medical care and justice. I observe these facts not necessarily to lament them nor certainly to rejoice in them, but merely to state them as the facts they are.

The cathedral remains, however, the temple, the place of prayer. Sometimes it seems the only place of prayer in our civilization, since the spirit of prayer has not always accompanied those institutions and interests which withdrew from the cathedral cloisters into the farflung corners of the secular community. But to the cathedral still men turn to pray, to catch a glimpse of heaven—men of the world: doctors, lawyers, merchants, princes and peasants, workers and lords. All turn

86

back nostalgically to the cathedral when they think of heaven and feel the need of prayer in order not merely to save their souls, but even to keep their wits in the maelstrom that is their world.

It is this privileged character of a cathedral, its dedication to prayer, which powerfully appeals even to those who walk not with us, but who wistfully gaze from afar. A Protestant poet, the gentle Longfellow, loved our cathedrals as places of prayer, and wrote:

> Oft have I seen at some cathedral door
> A laborer, pausing in the dust and heat,
> Lay down his burden and with reverent feet
> Enter, and cross himself, and on the floor
> Kneel to repeat his paternoster o'er;
> Far off the noises of the world retreat;
> The loud vociferations of the street
> Become an indistinguishable roar.
> So, as I enter here from day to day,
> And leave my burden at this minster gate,
> Kneeling in prayer, and not ashamed to pray,
> The tumult of the time disconsolate
> To inarticulate murmurs dies away,
> While the eternal ages watch and wait.[6]

Also, some still turn back to the cathedrals who have long since forgotten how to pray. That is why a great architect of our generation has thus set forth the motive of his work: "My aim in designing a cathedral", he said "is to make those who enter it *desire* to pray."

This may be the principal function of a beautiful cathedral in our generation: to make those who enter it *desire* to pray. It is no longer needed or used to teach; we have our schools, seminaries, universities, and lecture halls for instruction. It is no longer used for great assemblies of the priest and people, except those of a strictly liturgical character. We have auditoriums, social centers, and great halls for such gatherings of the faithful. A cathedral is still used as the symbolic seat of the bishop's administrative authority, but this, too, is largely exercised elsewhere, as in chanceries or streamlined office buildings. All this is as it must be in a civilization such as ours.

But the cathedral remains above all else the place in which to pray, the place to which men turn who feel the need to pray. One thinks of this whenever he sees the lonely souls who wander in and out of a cathedral like Saint Patrick's in New York, for example. All day long they come and go: hucksters, actors, tourists, young intellectuals, lovers, jaded wayfarers. They walk in, they stand, and they stare. All about them are the faithful kneeling in meditation, bowed in prayer. But many of these people cannot pray; it is precisely their tragedy that they have lost the power to pray. They don't even know how to *begin* the beginning of the simplest of prayers.

But as one watches them, he finds himself first *praying* and then *confident* that here in the cathedral they will conceive at least the desire to pray. Everyone knows that such a desire must have behind it a movement of God's grace—and once God's grace enters their lives, anything can follow—anything up to and including *salvation*.

Perhaps, then, we had best build our cathedrals nowadays as places where God's grace can lurk, waiting for the souls of those who wander in, weary of the world of secular pursuits and starving for the world of eternal values. Even the architect who designs a cathedral must have such a purpose chiefly in mind; certainly this must be the sovereign purpose of the bishop who presides over it, the priests who serve in it, and the God-fearing people who build it.

This is a glorious Cathedral, worthy to be numbered among the cathedrals of the Catholic world. All our great cathedrals are glorious: Notre Dame, Westminster, Milan, Toledo, Saint Patrick's, Blessed Sacrament in Altoona. But glorious though they be, these are not the fairest temples that Catholicism builds to the honor of the living God. Our cathedrals, soaring and splendid as this one is, are merely tools and instruments for the work of the Church; that work is the adornment of more enduring temples of the living God: the souls of Christians.

If these souls be fair and beautiful, then our cathedrals of brick and stone are justified and have done their work. If the souls of Christians are drab, dirty, and despoiled, then all our beautiful cathedrals are so much rubble, nor will the beauty of their glass nor the glory of their arches conceal the perishable materials and the counterfeit perfection with which the work of man is always done.

The measure of the beauty of a cathedral is not in the skill of the architect nor in the lavish gifts of its patrons; it is in the glory it gives to God, the God Who is the God of the living, not the dead, and to Whom life means the life of a soul in the state of grace.

So we admire the beauty of the new baptismal fonts, confessionals, and pulpits, but we admire even more the bounty of God's grace at work within and around them. We rejoice in the appointments of this superb sanctuary, its altar and its rails; but we await impatiently the records of holy marriages to be solemnized here, vows to be received here, ordinations to take place here, sacrifices to be offered here. We note with interest the modern conveniences incidental to the construction of the sacristies and the other places needed for the service of souls; but the very angels of God will observe how many sinners are reconciled here, how many souls are strengthened here, how many saints are inspired here. We gaze with marvel at the exquisite splendor of the design, details of which will delight so many eyes of visitors and gladden so many hearts among the faithful; but the important question is, How much hint of the beauty of heaven will these arches and lovely lines suggest to sinners? In the answers to these questions lies the true measure of the beauty of Altoona's proud Cathedral.

This beautiful Cathedral is a temple built to the glory of God by people who believe in Him and who love Him passionately. But the purpose of their building remains unfulfilled, even now that the architect and the craftsmen have done their work, until such time as God shall have found—thanks to the truths preached here, the prayers said here, and the sacraments administered here—yet more beautiful temples in which to dwell, the temples of the living God which are the hearts of converted and convinced Christians. Millions might sit here and revel in the physical perfections of the church, and still it would be in vain until one soul has finally discovered God within its walls, discovered God and determined to achieve heaven.

Wherefore we repeat the ancient prayer of the liturgy for the consecration of the new altar in a church, together with that for the blessing of a new church's cornerstone:

> O God, eternal and omnipotent, we thy suppliants pray that through thy Sole-Begotten Son, our Lord, Jesus Christ, thou wouldst sanctify with celestial benediction this altar built for sacred purposes. And as thou didst with wondrous favor accept the offering of the priest Melchisedech, so too, receive at all times the gifts which will be placed upon this new altar. May the people who assemble in this holy dwelling of the Church be sanctified for heaven by these sacrifices, and their souls be rewarded with life everlasting. . . .
>
> May the true Faith wax strong here, and the fear of God, and the love of the brethren, that this place may be truly destined for prayer, to invoke and praise the name of Jesus Christ, Thy Son, our Lord, Who with the Father and the Holy Spirit liveth and reigneth, God, eternally![7]

And as we return thanks to God for the vision He has given the previous bishops of Altoona, together with the loyal zeal He has given Altoona's people, we offer here in His renewed Cathedral the prayer of the Church for its new bishop:

> O God, the Shepherd and Ruler of all the faithful, look down with favor on Thy servant Carroll whom Thou hast made shepherd of this holy church; give him, we beg Thee, by word and example so to lead the souls of those he serves that he may enter eternal life together with all his flock. Through Christ our Lord. Amen![8]

IX

Ecclesiastical Art and Architecture

I must begin by congratulating Father Rice, the parish committee, and the Catholics of the Immaculate Conception Parish in Washington, on the so-beautiful and so-modern provision they have made for the housing and care of the sisters entrusted with the care and the teaching of the so-beautiful and so-good children of the parish.[1] When one looks at a building designed in the contemporary, not to say, the futuristic mood of the new convent, he has the immediate momentary reaction of feeling very old. He begins to wonder if perhaps he belongs entirely to the past. One becomes so used to the styles and to the modes and manners of years gone by that it is always a little bit of a surprise, at times a shock, to find things so radically different as they clearly are in this so-modern, so-contemporary convent building. But then, he remembers that this has always been the case.

This is the seven hundredth anniversary of the consecration of the cathedral of Chartres.[2] I don't suppose there is anything in the world as traditional, as established, as familiar, and as old-fashioned as French Gothic, of which, in the opinion of most people, the cathedral of Chartres is the most splendid example. A few months ago in connection with the seven hundredth anniversary of the cathedral of Chartres, I was reading a contemporary account of the dedication ceremonies. It was written in Latin, so I shall have to translate it, and in translating it I shall abridge it a bit. What the account boiled down to was this: the eyewitness, who was recording his reactions to the then-new and superb cathedral of Chartres, expressed the opinion that in all probability most people wouldn't like it. It

This sermon was preached at Washington, Pennsylvania, on December 11, 1960, on the occasion of the blessing of the Immaculate Conception Convent.

was his considered opinion that we shouldn't change the patterns to which we have become adjusted and with which we were, perhaps, a little bit frozen.

Now, of course, the Gothic, the Romanesque, and the other traditional basic forms have become so completely familiar that when we see a variation in them or departure from them, we know that the people won't like this, and that it won't last, and that it is all very new and sometimes a little jarring. Then the true point is driven home to us to supplement the initial reaction that made us feel as if we were getting a little bit old, but the point is that we are, of course, always getting a little bit old, while the Church, the holy Catholic Church, is always being renewed, always being reborn. We all grow old like a garment, and in our tastes and our outlooks we reflect, as do garments, periods and preferences of the times when we began. But the Church, with the indestructible, youthful vitality and vision of God Himself, is continually renewed; it is forever young in every community and every town. The Catholic Church is always the most youthful institution although it is the oldest in Western history, and only we grow old, only we belong to the past. The Catholic Church is always present, always in the future, and so it is appropriate that the styles and the modalities in architecture and art of the Church should always be a little youthful and a little new, and that is startling to us as we grow old.

The Church becomes incarnate in every community, in every civilization, in every period of time, and in every place. In this she reflects her kinship with that Son of God made Man to dwell among us of Whom the holy Catholic Church is the living and indestructible presence in history. When the Son of God became Man at the first Christmas and lived and taught on the face of the earth now nineteen hundred and fifty years ago, He became incarnate among a specific people and in a specific period of time. He did not take on any vague, or universal, unqualified humanity. He became a Jew in Palestine, spoke not merely the language of His place and time but the dialect of a specific area and a specific period. He did not even talk Hebrew; He talked Aramaic. So closely did He identify Himself with those among whom He lived that had you met Him on the street you would have seen not a cosmopolitan type; you would have seen a Jew. Everything about Him bore witness to the manner in which the eternal, transcendental truth of God becomes incarnate in the temporal and place-bound circumstances of those through whom God does His work, and whom God seeks to instruct and to sanctify. The Catholic Church is, as all know, not a historical phenomenon, not a political pressure group, not a cultural society, not even a religious movement, as this phrase is used among men. It is the eternal, living presence of Jesus Christ in history; and so, like Christ, the Catholic Church becomes incarnate in every generation, among all peoples, in every place.

In one period of history it appears in Byzantine styles and speaking languages and revealing Byzantine psychological, spiritual, and cultural traits. A whole and glorious chapter of the Church's history is in Africa, where among the Ethiopians it took on Coptic color, and quality, and language, and modalities as it became incarnate among the peoples of that time and that place. In another period of time it becomes so incarnate among the French that French Gothic, French music, French styles in vestments and in piety became almost identified with Catholicism in the minds of millions. In other places it takes on the personality of Italy and reveals in music, in sculpturing, in art, in architecture, in vestments, in altar appointments the manner in which it has been incarnate among the Italians. For centuries the holy Catholic Church was incarnate among the Celts and took on many Hibernian and Irish qualities and modalities. For a thousand years the Roman Catholic Church was incarnate among the English, who gave to the world saints who made universal Catholicism so English that their language, their personality traits, their mentalities were as thoroughly Catholic and as thoroughly English as the mind and personality of Saint Thomas More or of Chaucer or of Shakespeare, those who had Catholic minds and Catholic hearts and yet who expressed these Catholic values and Catholic truths in ways which were not merely typically English but were almost the last good types of the English ways in Christianity.

Now the New World is producing its culture, and things are done and said in an American way, as in other times and places, as in other places even now, they are done in a Byzantine, Italian, German, a Polish, a Croatian, an English, a Spanish, or an Irish way. Here, too, as much at home as anywhere in the world, the holy Catholic Church becomes incarnate in American ways and American manners, and through the holy Catholic Church Christ speaks now with an American accent as once He did with an Aramaic accent. He speaks of American hopes and American visions and American realities and American loyalties and American deeds which make Him and His Catholicism as completely incarnate in America in the twentieth century or England in the fourteenth or Italy in the twelfth or Byzantine in the fifth and sixth or Africa in the fourth and fifth.

Of all these things one is reminded when he sees so contemporary, so completely modern, functional, and therefore so American a building as in the new convent that the Catholics of Washington, Pennsylvania, have built for the housing of the sisters who will teach their children the ancient, unchanging, Faith in the new and changed emphasis and accents. It is an ancient axiom descriptive of the Catholic mind and the Catholic Faith which says that in the preaching and the exemplification and the illustration of Catholic truth we offer in each age *non nova sed nove*, not new truths but the old truths presented in a new way. So the children in the schools are taught not new truths; there are none but the old truths taught in a new way in the light of new circumstances and in a manner to appeal to new preferences, new psychological outlooks—but always the old theological truths.

So the new convent is a kind of symbol not only of the way the Church becomes incarnate in every community and every

94

civilization, but it is a symbol, too, of the way in which the old truths, the old Faith, the old Creed, the old moral code continually find expression in new styles, new phrases, new enthusiasms, new emphases but with unchanging fidelity to the ancient, ever-old living truth that is the holy Catholic Faith. It is a symbol of all these things, I think, that the architect who has worked so well for Father Rice and for the parish is, I believe, not of the household of the Faith, but nonetheless one steeped in the traditions of the cultural faith so that he can remind us in a building of this kind of our own ancient truth restated in these styles.[3]

We are grateful to the architects, we are grateful to the contractors and subcontractors, who met his specifications so faithfully and so well; we are grateful above all to the people of the parish who demonstrated with new enthusiasm, new loyalty, the old generosity and fidelity of Catholic people to whatever pertains to the Faith and above all to whatever pertains to children—those who will transmit the Faith with new vitality to an age of new victories, in accordance with the old promises made to our Fathers, to Abraham, and to his seed forever.

We extend our congratulations to Father Rice for the leadership he has given and to the sisters for the opportunities for refreshed services that the new convent offers them. We express our appreciation to the civil authorities of the community who, by the licensing for the work, by granting of the exemptions, and by all their encouragements within the framework of the law and the American tradition, have demonstrated their desire to see the ancient Faith have its opportunity to serve in the New World, and to make our Christ and all His truth incarnate in this community as these have been incarnate throughout the Catholic centuries and the Catholic world.

It has been a great privilege to bless the new convent, and we end the ceremonies now by calling down God's blessing on the parish, community, and all of Washington, for the encouragement and cooperation they have given this important work.

X

Men to Match Their Mountains

"Let the mountains bring peace to the people, and the hills justice. . . ."[1]

The mountains have a special place in the history and the symbolism of Sacred Scripture. The ark, in which Noe and his kindred were saved, came to rest upon a mountain, which ever after has been a symbol of God's mercy. On a mountain Abraham, ready to sacrifice his beloved son, exemplified that self-renunciation and complete dependence on the Providence of God which made him the patriarch of all priests, the model of all spiritual chieftains forever. Moses received the law of God on a mountain, and in the mountains he came upon the burning bush from which he acquired his knowledge of the very nature of God. On a mountain Aaron died—Aaron, the type of all who are called by God to His priesthood. On Mount Carmel, Elias, the prophet faithful to the true God, entered into contest with the priests of Baal and vindicated the promises of God. On Mount Moria the Temple was built, itself the symbol of the Kingdom of God and His Church. Mount Sion became the symbol of that city of the living God, the new Jerusalem of which Saint Paul speaks in his Epistle to the Hebrews, the home and company of all the redeemed. In the prophets, above all in Isaias, the mountain is the type of Christ's Holy Catholic Church.

It was to the mountains that Mary fled in awe of her own vocation and to bring Elizabeth the news of the Incarnation. From a mountain the Son of God preached His Beatitudes and the saving precepts of His revelation. On a mountain Christ was transfigured that we might discern the glory of His

This sermon was preached in Denver, Colorado, on January 4, 1961, on the occasion of the episcopal ordination of the Most Reverend David M. Maloney.

humanity and the power of His divinity. On one mountain, that of Olives, the final stages of His Passion began; on another, Calvary, the work of redemption was consummated and salvation was assured. From a mountain Christ ascended into heaven; and to a mountain, great and high, the spirit of God took the apostle Saint John that he might behold the vision of heaven, where "there shall be no more accursed thing, but the throne of God and the Lamb shall be there and the servants which serve Him forever."[2]

And so mountains fire the devout imagination of the people of God as symbols of the powers of heaven and of the aspirations of earth. They speak to the faithful of God's majesty and yet His mercy, His eternity, and His Providence. They symbolize man's immortal longings, his desire for reunion with God and for salvation, his hunger for eternity. All the things that God can do and all the things that men most need are suggested in Scripture under the symbolism of mountains. But so, too, are the obstacles between men and God. Above all, the obstacles to the preaching of the gospel unto men's salvation and God's glory are typified in terms of mountains that must be brought low and hills that must be made into highways for the coming of the Lord.

It was the vocation of the prophets of the Old Law, it is the duty of the Catholic bishops of the New Law, to do the divine works and serve the human needs symbolized by the mountains and to level the mountainous barriers between men and God, between men and men.

The peoples who settled in this part of America early developed an intensified understanding of the symbolism of the mountains. Their deepest desire, expressed in a line of popular poetry, was that God would give them *men to match their mountains*. By this they meant, on the spiritual and religious level of their lives, men equal to the task of over-coming the obstacles to the gospel in a new world of pioneers so bold and so disposed to live dangerously that they might easily have become strong in their own conceit. Devout people have wanted men of God mighty in those qualities, divine and human, of which the mountains are the symbols and to match in their virtues and their works the majestic heights of the mountains.

Give us men to match our mountains was not merely a cry for physical giants of brawn and mere natural strength; it was also a religious call for spiritual men of prophetic depth and magnitude, mighty men of God who would preach Christ's gospel and build *here* His Church even as brave pioneers of great natural prowess were already building here a great human city and spreading the mighty political and economic empire of the American West.

The Catholic Church has given this part of these United States *men of God to match its mountains*, just as the nations of the world have given it their sons and daughters to match the challenge of Colorado's heights. The Catholic Church has given to God's people pioneer priests who have endured in the face of the obstacles to the gospel and present-day priests who have reproduced in themselves and in their people those qualities, divine and human, of which the mountains are dramatic symbols. These priests have been led by great prelates—bishops and archbishops—who in these mountains have borne the witness to the mercy of God that Noe did on Mount Ararat; to the majesty of God that Abraham did on Mount Moria; to the authority of God that Moses taught from Mount Sinai; to the exclusive rights of God that Elias vindicated on Mount Carmel; to the glory, the clemency, the compassion, and the sweetness of God to which His Christ, the Good Shepherd of the New Testament, bore witness on the mountains of the Holy Land.

Such a bishop for three decades, such an archbishop for a score of years has Denver's stalwart Metropolitan—truly *a man to match Denver's mountains*—proved himself to be.[3] Such a priest and such a bishop has our Holy Father—ruling God's Holy Church from the hills of Rome—found in these mountains to serve as the auxiliary to Archbishop Vehr, to be an elder brother to the exemplary priests of the Archdiocese of Denver, a father in Christ and bishop of souls to the Christian flock so loyal to the Faith of their fathers and so compactly united to the Church of Christ here in the mountains and valleys of Colorado.[4]

All who know, as do his lifelong friends, the priestly patience, the broad range of humane interests, and the spiritual stability of Bishop David Maloney know that in him the Catholic Church is giving this part of these United States another bishop who is a *man of God to match its mountains*.

We took our text this morning from the glorious psalm which scholars attribute to King David, the model Israelite ruler, the ancestor and type of the Messiah, the foreshadowing, in so many ways, of a bishop of the Church of Christ. The seventy-first psalm is both a prayer and a prophecy. It is a prayer for the qualities that the king of Israel desired in himself and in his royal line, the qualities which the Church desires in her bishops: "Give to the king Thy judgment, O God; and to the king's son Thy justice: Let him rule Thy people with justice and Thy poor with equity. . . . Let him guard the lowly among the people, and save the children of the poor and bring low the oppressor."[5]

And the psalm is also a prophecy of Christ and, therefore and at the same time a prophecy of the truly Christlike bishop who, with a special sacramental dignity, perpetuates Christ's office and performs His work:

> For He shall rescue the poor man when he cries out, and the afflicted when he has no one to help him. He shall have pity for the lowly and the poor; the lives of the poor He shall save. From fraud and violence He shall redeem them, and precious shall their blood be in His sight. . . . For him they shall always pray, . . . His name shall be blessed forever.[6]

It is from this psalm that the liturgy takes the verses which describe the Christ of Epiphany; from this psalm come phrases for the Mass of Christ the King. The psalm speaks in symbols appropriate to the consecration of a Colorado bishop, an episcopal envoy of the Messiah, for it tells of how it would be from mountains that would come the peace that Christ came to give, and from the hills the justice that Christ's bishops are called to teach, to administer, and, please God, to exemplify.

"Let the mountains bring peace to the people, and the hills justice!"[7] It is now almost two thousand years ago, in the very days between Christmas and Epiphany that we are presently commemorating, that the peace desired by God's people and the justice for His people decreed by God began to radiate from the mountains of Judea where the Messiah came and where the shepherds and kings acclaimed Him. And now, today in Denver, Colorado, the mountains again bring peace to the people, and the hills justice, as the Church consecrates another of her good priests to be a bishop acting for the Messiah and as the Catholic people of Denver hail him with the joyful affection of God's people for the king and the king's son.

"Behold upon the mountains the feet of Him who bringeth good tidings and that preacheth peace!"[8] The same good tidings that the angels brought to the hills of Judea, and the same peace—these the Catholic Church brings to the mountains of America. She does so through her bishops and through the priests and people who proclaim the Faith of Christ and praise the glory of God in unison with their bishops.

May the contemplation of his native mountains give the new Bishop David that strength that King David of old found when he looked up to his mountains of Israel! May the supernatural gifts that come with his consecration prepare this Colorado man of God to match the mountains among which he serves, both in the majesty of his priestly work and in the mightiness of his battles against whatever stands between the people and their God. Thus, in good truth, shall the mountains continue to bring peace to the people, and the hills justice, through the ministry of the bishops of the Holy Catholic Church, the men of God called to match the mountains of this world.[9]

XI

The Loving Obedience of Free Men

Ours is an age in love with liberty and with learning. Love of freedom is undoubtedly the most powerful motive to which to appeal in any effort to awaken the ideals and rally the energies of decent men in our day; eagerness to learn, to explore and master all mysteries, is the dynamic behind the zeal and sacrifices responsible for the mighty, costly venture that is contemporary education.

It is not strange that freedom should be so universally, so passionately, beloved. Human liberty complements that freedom of will with which we were created; it is God's most precious gift to our nature, according to Dante, since by it we are made happy here below as men, and happy as gods hereafter.

So persuaded are men of the truth of Dante's concept of the dignity and worth of freedom that the valiant will gladly accept death itself rather than renounce liberty. They understand perfectly the warning of the poet that "Life can be no charm for him who lives not free."

The burning desire for knowledge, the love of learning, is not less urgent and understandable. The earliest commentary on human nature is that passage in the Book of Genesis which tells of how our built-in human hunger to know all things, to rival God Himself in knowledge, proved our undoing in the Garden of Eden; it was to pride of intellect that the Tempter appealed when he flattered our first parents, saying, "Ye shall be as gods, knowing good and evil!"[1] And yet there was a well-founded basis of sound truth in Satan's seductive argument, for knowledge is truly godlike, and it is precisely in the

This sermon was preached at Saint Michael Cathedral, Toronto, Ontario, Canada, on May 31, 1961, on the occasion of the episcopal ordination of the Most Reverend George B. Flahiff, C.S.B.

intellect, in the power to know, that we are made in the image and likeness of God.

But for all the burning convictions of mankind concerning the dignity of liberty and the divine power of knowledge, there is suggested by this morning's ceremony something even more noble than freedom and knowledge, more admirable surely than either liberty or learning alone; something more positive in the perfection of the human personality and more constructive in the building of human society, whether civil or sacred. That something is the obedience of free and learned men, the dedicated, consecrated use of human liberty and intellectual gifts for the service of others and the glory of God.

A truly humane City of Man always acknowledges that obedience to law is liberty and that true wisdom consists in the knowledge of how most nobly to use learning. The City of God proclaims that no freedom is so great as that of the children of God—those who, being free, nonetheless bind themselves by the perfect law of love preached by Jesus Christ; it proclaims also that no knowledge is so great as that spiritual knowledge by which we grow in the divine truth that makes and keeps men free. "Ye shall know the truth, and the truth will make you free!"[2]

It takes courage, but it is relatively easy for men to die for freedom. It takes greater courage to practice, day in, day out, the loving obedience of free men. It is natural to love freedom; it is impossible for the normal man not to crave it; but it takes supernatural grace truly to love obedience and to rejoice in the noble excellence of the obedience of free men.

Such is the obedience of every good priest, and in this obedience he acquires his share in the unique glory of the priesthood of Christ. Christ was a priest not in His divine nature, but in His humanity where He "accepted an obedience which brought Him to death, death on the Cross. That is why God has raised Him to such a height", Saint Paul tells us.[3]

It was not by His majesty, then, nor by His power, nor by

His other kingly titles that Christ was made a priest. It was by His obedience. So, too, it is not by any personal talent, or genius, or other gifts that men are made priests of Jesus Christ. It is by their obedience, the only gift they can possibly offer to that God who is the source of all that they are and have.

This is the key to the certain special excellence of the religious life in the Catholic scheme of things. That life involves the particular solemnity of vowed obedience which in turn includes pledged willingness to go without question wherever one is sent, in order to contribute to the building up of the Kingdom of Christ. Herein, too, lies the merit of a rule of life under which religious—like the Basilians—so forswear external honors that it is even under obedience itself that a priest is brought to accept such an episcopal consecration as that which this morning rejoices the family, the friends, the students, and the colleagues of the new Archbishop of Winnipeg, Archbishop George Flahiff.

The discerning will perceive in the personality and work of a religious like Father Flahiff, a prelate like Archbishop Flahiff, how the perfect freedom of a scholarly man and the praise-worthy obedience of a learned priest are blended by the grace of God in order that the work of God's Kingdom may be accomplished on earth. The Archbishop was born of a people whose every tradition speaks of the love of liberty and of learning. His name proclaims him the descendant of a people for whom freedom is almost an obsession and desire for learning has been a hunger more intense than any other craving, save only that for heaven itself. He was trained in schools where devotion to freedom is intensified by every lesson taught.

George Flahiff's eagerness to learn manifested itself in his early graduation from high school, when he was too young to enter the University of Toronto. His love for the things of the mind brought him academic distinction at Kitchener, Toronto, Strasbourg, and Paris before and after his profession as a religious and ordination as a priest. His intellectual quality and his basic good taste account in no small degree for the substantial part that the Congregation of Saint Basil—the Basilian Fathers—has played in the intensification of intellectual life and the lifting of the level of artistic taste in the places where his influence in Canada and the United States has been felt.

And so Archbishop Flahiff has used his freedom and dedicated his intellectual gifts during the years of his priesthood in utter obedience to the will of God as that will has been revealed to him in the assignments and responsibilities he has received from those in the Church of Christ who speak to him with God's authority. His consecration as an archbishop, a captain commissioned to command in the army of the Lord, will inspire and edify those who understand that—as Thomas à Kempis observed—no man surely commands but he who has learned to obey.

The priestly career of Archbishop Flahiff demonstrates—and this morning's ceremonies dramatize—a truth which is the strength of the Holy Roman Catholic Church, a truth which the City of Man, with all its proper passion for liberty and love of learning, must early and urgently learn. It is the truth of which Jacques Maritain wrote: that the virtue of obedience is an exalted virtue, eminently reasonable; it is not in the least servile or blind, but requires on the contrary the greatest freedom of spirit and the strongest discernment. By the obedience of free men, free men with cultivated minds and gifted personalities, the world is made civilized and strong; by this obedience the Church of God is made holy and indestructible. Freedom without orderly obedience and learning without the reasonability that comes from a sense of stewardship easily become nuisances to society and menaces to civilization; but disciplined liberty and dedicated learning are the foundations of decent civilization; they are the best hope of democracy and the guarantees of the freedom and faith which make men truly like to gods.

It is entirely fitting that we recall these lessons of the dignity of obedient freedom and the nobility of consecrated learning as, here in Saint Michael Cathedral, a Cardinal of the ancient Roman Church consecrates a learned Basilian religious to do the work of a modern archbishop in Canada. It is timely that we speak of the correlation of liberty and the obedience of free men, of the interplay of learning and religious obedience in the human accomplishment of the will of God. For Canada is playing a major part in the exemplification of the power and the appeal of liberty in our generation, and Canada is giving timely and impressive example of the intelligent and equitable encouragement of learning on every level of her educational system and of her truly democratic government. The Church owes it to a nation devoted to both liberty and learning, as is Canada, to give Canada prelates loyal to her hallowed traditions of liberty and sympathetic with her healthy aspirations after learning.

The Church serves the interests of religion, but she also contributes mightily to the common good of the democratic society when she raises up prelates, as in Archbishop George Flahiff she does for Canada, who by the spiritual obedience of free men and the consecrated use of learning adorn and strengthen the liberties of democracy and the faith of Christianity. Such prelates are needed more now than ever, needed for the good of the Faith, needed for the good of the free society. For the appointment of such a man to the important See of Winnipeg, the Catholics of Canada and Canada itself, civil and religious, owe Pope John their fervent and grateful appreciation.

At the dawn of the century, a sensitive prelate of the Church in my own country described the need of the Church and the desires of North America in what pertains to the quality of our priests and prelates. Bishop Spalding said:

> We need men whose intellectual view embraces the history of the race, who are familiar with all literature, who have studied all social movements, who are acquainted with the development of philosophical thought, who are not blinded by physical

miracles and industrial wonders, but know how to appreciate all truth, all beauty, all goodness. And to this wide culture they must join the earnestness, the confidence, the charity, and the purity of motive which Christian faith inspires. We need scholars who are saints, and saints who are scholars. We need men of genius who live for God and their country; men of action who seek for light in the company of those who know; men of religion who understand that God reveals Himself in science, and works in Nature, as in the soul of man, for the good of those who know and those who love Him.[4]

Had Bishop Spalding added that our need for men thus endowed by nature and grace, but also generously disposed to the obedient use of their freedom and the dedicated use of their learning to perpetuate the faith of their Church and to promote the freedom of their country, then he would have given the complete description of the type of man whom, in George Flahiff, Canada gave the Church; whom in Father Flahiff the Basilians gave the priesthood; and whom in Archbishop Flahiff the Roman Catholic Church now gives back to Canada, to serve as a spiritual shepherd. He is the type of those men who, as religious, give an example of the obedience of free men to a society that alternates between forced obedience and freedom without responsibility. He exemplifies that love of learning which sees in learning the noble means to an even more noble end: the service of men and the glory of God.

May the Lord preserve Archbishop George Flahiff and give him strength! May his years be many and fruitful, to the great advantage of this growing, mighty nation and the fair repute of this Holy Roman Catholic Church!

XII

Monsignor Vincent J. Rieland, 1898–1961

What can one possibly say at our leave-taking of this so extraordinarily good and manifestly great priest?[1] How can we possibly pretend that we do not bless God for taking him to Himself? Must we not say that precisely because we loved him and so admired him we rejoice that his sufferings are done and that he stands in the presence of God, before the dispensations of whose Divine Providence he never once murmured and in the service of Whom, as an exemplary priest, he ended his days? With the end of his days came the end, as all know and as must be uppermost in the thoughts of one and all, of twenty long years of physical disfigurement and pain, of psychological anguish and spiritual desolation that would have broken anyone who was not as Monsignor Rieland was—all man and all priest.

During those twenty years he not merely kept all his priestly friendships; he multiplied them. They were his great strength, as he was assuredly that strength to his friends. He identified himself, more than many who are completely at ease in society, with every type of civic affair, and where others would have seen a legitimate, an unchallengeable, excuse to put aside the burdens of priestly work and civic responsibility and the humiliations of mingling with people, he mingled more than ever during his twenty years of disease.

Without any touch of morbidity, or self-pity, or complaint, or question, he cooperated with doctors when they thought they could help. But at all times he cooperated with the grace of God and worked to the fullest extent as a priest. By entering

This eulogy was preached at Saint Mary Church, Beaver Falls, Pennsylvania, on June 7, 1961.

community affairs as he did, he made the Holy Catholic Church loved by people who saw her beauty in him.

All during his priesthood, this remarkable man attended everything. I tried to think yesterday if I could remember any single major diocesan event or convention for whatever aspect of the life, work, or interests of the Church, that he didn't attend; I couldn't think of one in the time I have known him, and I have known him during these last tortured months of his life.

He particularly loved and was good to the children. The priests told me that the only hint he ever gave that he regretted, even humanly speaking and in passing fashion, the cross that he carried was when he met new school children for the first time. But he learned that very soon they came to see his true beauty and to love him as did we all.

He taught all the lessons and all the truths that any priest, any prelate, any good Christian tries to teach, but he taught a host of others. What particularly did he teach during these two decades of Purgatory that he endured so courageously and with such supernatural spirit? Perhaps this is the time to raise a question to which his sufferings may give an answer: Did you ever think that if the good, the holy, are called by the merciful, loving God to suffer some of the things that they do, how can the rest of us dismiss so lightly, as we sometimes do, the reality of Purgatory?

These lessons he taught as a living and constant priestly rebuke to those of us who are forgetful—sometimes for years, certainly for seasons—of how we too are called to fill up those things which are lacking in the Passion of Jesus Christ. It is a troubled thought to compare the contribution any of us make to filling up what is lacking in the Passion of Jesus Christ when we contrast and compare ourselves to this holy priest, this great and good prelate.

We are taught another thing, too. It is almost indelicate to mention it, but in the case of a man who was so great, so unashamed and so confident before people because he was so constantly in the presence of God, it is in order that we mention it. Speaking of the priesthood, a German poet, Gertrude Von le Fort, wrote in one of her poems in *Hymns to the Church* a line that is worth meditating. She wrote: "The priest at the altar has no face." Listen again: "The priest at the altar has no face!" By this she meant, of course, that at the altar of the Holy Roman Catholic Church there are no considerations of nationality, none of color, none of majesty, and none of humble estate. So incidental is the priesthood of the earthly ministers of Christ that it doesn't make much difference who they are when they stand at the altar. So all-sufficient and so totally operative is the priesthood of Christ, the sole priest of the New Law, that when we kneel in church for Mass, when we are present before the altar for the liturgical services, it is almost empty and idle to ask which priest is at the altar. It is always Christ. It is always Christ! The priest is there only to provide Christ with hands and a voice; that is all. The priest at the altar has no face, and our people have never been attracted to the Church or to the altar, they have never been kept in the Church or kept at the altar, by any personal considerations bound up with a human priest.

The priest at the altar is not brilliant, and he is not dull; he is not tall, he is not short; he is not German, he is not Irish, he is not Jewish; he is not black, he is not white, he is not yellow; he is not sick, he is not well; he is not handsome, he is not disfigured. The priest at the altar has no face! And when he is—as *this priest* was—aware of this, and in his humility so subordinate to the priesthood of Jesus Christ that it wouldn't cross his mind that it mattered who stood at the altar—ah! then he can take anything, and he can do anything, for all his life he preaches the unicity and the uniqueness of the sole and sufficient priesthood of Christ in the Catholic understanding of that concept.

Monsignor Rieland had that concept. He knew what a priest

109

is. He knew that a priest is not a personality, he is not a glamor boy, he is not an ecclesiastical huckster; the priest is an instrument, a tool in the hands of Jesus Christ. So long as he does the work for which God manufactured him in the hour of his ordination, then any considerations of pleasure or pain, embarrassment or joy, are ultimately nonsense. Monsignor taught this to us, but he taught it first of all to himself; then he was in a position to teach it persuasively to the rest of us, as only they can teach who have learned the lesson well themselves—who have accepted it, loved it, and lived it, finding no fault with it. Monsignor Rieland had a perfect understanding of the nature of his cross, and the greatness of his cross, and the significance of his cross; he also had a perfect understanding of himself as a priest, and so he bore this cross with magnificent resolution and absolute serenity.

All of us who have worked with the chronically sick, particularly in hospitals for the chronically ill, know that good Christians, all people who love God, and even some stoics who don't know anything about God, can bear crosses, physical disfigurements, intense pain with a certain calm; but I don't think it is illusory to say that the good priest can bear these things better than anyone else. This is not the time to grade the heroism or the sanctity of others. It is simply to say what Dorothy Thompson once said very eloquently about another kind of cross. Immediately after she went as a representative of the newspapers to visit the concentration camps in Germany, she talked with thousands of people who had been in these dreadful hells. She talked with people of every race and religion, every class and background. And when she came back she wrote an article on what she had learned about the concentration camps. One of the things that she said about the camps is recalled by the heroism of Monsignor Rieland in the way he bore his suffering. Thompson asked the people who survived the concentration camps which people, which groups, had stood up best under the humiliation and the horror. And she said that all to whom she talked, Jews and Christians, Frenchmen, Italians, Russians, Germans, all said: *the Catholic priests*. The Catholic priests stood up best under humiliation and horror. Well, that would disappoint no one, and it should surprise no one. Monsignor Rieland's parishioners and friends saw for twenty years an example of why it is true—because of the understanding that a good priest has of the place of humiliation and of pain and disfigurement in filling up that which is lacking in the sufferings of Jesus Christ.

At Eastertime he sent me from the hospital in New York a very beautiful note. Again it is indelicate to mention it, but how can we talk otherwise than like this about such a man and under such circumstances? I had published in the diocesan paper some meditations on the Passion of Christ under the title *Words in Pain*, and he was kind enough to say that they had brought a little solace to him.[2] Then he added wittily: "Bishop, I hope you will be able to say the *words* for a long time, and I know that I will have the *pain!*"

That's the solidarity of the priesthood. And the message is perfectly clear: the words of all of us are a consolation to each of us, and the pains of each of us are a strength to all of us. Monsignor wanted his pain to give strength and grace to me and his other fellow priests, and he was grateful when our own words solaced his pain.

Monsignor Rieland loved the poor, the burdened. I have mentioned his love for children. They are going to miss him!

He loved the Roman Catholic priesthood, and he was particularly attached to the Serra Movement because Serra means the love of laymen for the priesthood. Serra constitutes a pledge of our hope that there will be many priests. Reflect on this: having suffered so many years in his own priesthood, Monsignor Rieland might easily have been tempted to say, "I wonder if I should seek to bring boys into a life that has been, over so many years, so difficult for me?" But he spent a major part of his time in the work of Serra—zealously, ardently, actively, passionately seeking young men to take his place in that which he found so glorious, so consoling, so beautiful: the priesthood of Jesus Christ.

To his family, our thanks and admiration for the consolation they brought into his life, and our sympathy in the loss of a great and good brother.

To his two assistants, here in the parish church, a special word of gratitude from all their brother priests and their bishop for the magnificent manner in which they worked with him and for him and in imitation of his spirit. They were privileged to learn at firsthand what a priest is, but they also showed that they were deserving of that privilege.

And now, with great confidence, we can assert that Monsignor —who walked by faith all his years—now sees God face to face and beholds the majesty of God. And God, gazing at him, sees in his soul and in his transfigured face the shining beauty of the Catholic priesthood.

XIII

Catholicism: An Unknown Quantity

It may strike the uninformed as a curious fact, but it is none-theless true that Catholicism sometimes seems an unknown quantity in the American community. Despite the considerable publicity which Catholicism and things Catholic receive in the popular press, the movies, and other media of American information, Catholicism is in many ways the least well, or, at least, accurately known of the myriad religions whose names are familiar to Americans.

Dean Willard Sperry, of the Harvard Divinity School, demonstrated this strange truth some years ago when he wrote his book *Religion in America*. The dean wrote in response to an invitation from the Cambridge University Press to contribute a volume on American religious life to a series of books prepared to help the English public understand certain American institutions. Dean Sperry undertook to explain in a general way all and in a particular way many of the two hundred and fifty-six religious groups in America, their nature and their place in the community. He obviously could comment knowledgeably and objectively on all the religious traditions in the American community, from Adventism to Zoroastrianism practically, all, that is, save one. That one was not a recent importation from the Orient nor a passing fringe-form of any obscure cult in the hills of the South or the exotic towns of the West. The one exception was Catholicism.

Dean Sperry himself confessed, with disarming humility, his inability to interpret Catholicism in America to his English readers. He clearly appreciated how embarrassing this inability

This address was delivered on September 10, 1961 to the Peoria Council of Catholic Women in Peoria, Illinois.

was, especially since, as he admitted, he had lived all his life surrounded by large numbers of Catholics and in a community where Catholic institutions are not only many, but long-established and quite public. And yet he avowed that his own knowledge of their understanding of themselves by his Catholic neighbors would be only that of *the average Protestant householder*.[1]

The knowledge of Catholicism possessed by such a person is thus described by Dean Sperry:

> The average Protestant householder knows Catholicism only outwardly: by its substantial churches; by the crowds pouring from its doors at the end of a Mass; by the police directing traffic at such a time—an attention seldom given to a neighboring Protestant congregation and, if the truth be told, not always required by its smaller numbers; by the arrangements which must be made to allow maids to attend Mass; by the early dinners in Lent or during a Novena preaching mission (by the way what is a Novena?); by vague rumors that the *Index Librorum Prohibitorum* is not observed on the news stands or in bookstores; by disgruntled comments in conservative clubs at the growing strength of the Irish vote; by the loyal patronage which parish priests accord professional baseball games; by the intransigence of the Church in the matters of birth control and divorce, and its scepticism as to the *noble experiment* of prohibition. In all these respects we look at Catholicism with mixed emotions of envy and perplexity. Its customs are not ours, the two ways of life do not always *mesh* like well-oiled gears. There is, however, one thing we cannot do: we cannot ignore that which we do not wholly understand. The massive fact of American Catholicism is too considerable to be dismissed by studied indifference.[2]

And so, in order to be fair and to complete his picture of religion in America, the dean adopted a device that was clever but revealing. He chose to let the mysterious Catholics speak for themselves. However, in the hope that their spokesman might be someone with a mentality somehow approximating that of himself and of Protestant readers generally, he selected a convert to Catholicism, Mr. Theodore Maynard, to interpret the Catholics to him so that he in turn might present American Catholicism to his English readers. He boiled down Maynard's *Story of American Catholicism*, being careful to attribute almost svery proposition to Maynard, referring to him as *our chronicler*.[3] Writes Sperry: "I shall refer to the author as *our chronicler*, and shall introduce my own comments by the gambit *one* or *we*. In this way I shall hope not to make the author himself chargeable for my Protestant second thoughts."[4]

Thus by a combination of courtesy and caution Sperry could conscientiously describe some thirty million of his American neighbors with something like accuracy and at least attempted understanding. Mormonism, Christian Science, Vedanta, and Rosicrucianism would seemingly have presented no comparable difficulties!

It is this astonishing confession by an urbane and friendly critic which prompts the contention that, for all the publicity it receives, Catholicism is almost an unknown in large areas of the American community. Perhaps even more distressing is the fact that the place of Catholicism in the American community is largely unknown to Catholics themselves.

As a practical conclusion from this initial fact, the relatively unknown part of Catholicism in the national life, one is tempted to suggest a self-study by Catholic Americans themselves in order that they may discover their own heritage in America. Their complex contribution to the national community is much more intimately identified with the American reality and ideal than they or their neighbors usually suppose, and their impact on the minds and customs of their fellow citizens is considerably greater than seems to be understood at home or abroad.

In recent years it has again become almost a stereotype to speak of fear of Catholicism and to take it for granted that

Catholicism is disliked—or held suspect—by large numbers of American citizens. The response to Paul Blanshard's lectures and books warrants the suspicion that Catholicism is an object of a certain misgiving in large areas of the American community. So do some of the articles and editorials which appear regularly in typical non-Catholic religious periodicals, even literate ones like *The Christian Century*. So, finally, and notably, do anti-Catholic attacks as the hurtful article which presumably a responsible writer like Joseph Harsch wrote in the *Christian Science Monitor* at the time of the McCarthy hearings, an article purporting to give *reasons* why Catholics are allegedly given special treatment in Washington investigations.

It is important to analyze the roots of these mixed sentiments of fear and fury which cloud up discussions of Catholicism in the American community. Such analysis reveals that most of our difficulties stem from almost the same circumstances as do our advantages. I mean that the very factors which, from one point of view, make us so readily American, apparently operate, from another point of view, to make many Americans nervous about us.

For example, the Catholic Church in America is probably still thought of as an *immigrant* church. To be sure, the other religious traditions in America are also importations from abroad except for a half-dozen denominations which have sprung from the native soil and which, oddly enough, are not usually thought of as being particularly American. Everyone, I think, knows the sense in which Protestants, even when relatively close to their European origins, can be nativists, while Catholics are frequently thought of as *immigrant*. The distinction between nativist and immigrant is arbitrary, but it is a clear and fairly widely accepted practical distinction, even if sometimes ridiculous.

I might cite a personal example. My mother was born in Boston. So was her mother before her. Yet a Swedish lady who lived near our house when I was a boy and who came to this country when she was already married, used to speak of my mother, with great neighborly affection but heavy Swedish accent, as "the little Irish woman with six children".

This alien air which has surrounded Catholicism in so many American neighborhoods has resulted in many short-range disadvantages, but it should be a long-range source of strength to the Church in a nation which is, in its roots and idealism, itself entirely *immigrant*. The hierarchy of the Catholic Church in America illustrates, at least in its ancestral origins, how similar to the American civil pattern is the make-up of the Catholic spiritual community in this country. Catholicism in America has been served by bishops who, by origin or descent, have been the sons of just about every national group represented in the national life: Austrian, Belgian, Canadian, Cuban, French, English, Dutch, German, Hungarian, Luxemburger, Irish, Italian, Mexican, Polish, Scottish, Spanish, Swiss, and Eastern European. One of our bishops blended Negro and white blood in his veins.[5] To the extent that America herself has been made strong by a plurality of racial strains, the Church in America has certainly shared the elements of that strength as well as of the genius of America by reason of her parallel diversity. One feels that this may prove of great significance both to the Church and to America in the future, especially if any effort be made to splinter the unity of the American community.

Perhaps related to this first point is a second of even greater significance. There is a sense in which the Catholic Church in America has been from the beginning and is still *proletarian*. Rural America has been and remains largely Protestant, with exceptions which prove rather than violate the rule. To the extent that this is true, any peasantry which we have in America is Protestant rather than Catholic. Catholicism has been largely identified with the working classes and the cities, though not with all the cities, of course. Perhaps the word *proletarian* is not the happiest or most exact word to use in this context; all I mean is that Catholicism in our country is a religion with deep roots and powerful support among the so-called *working classes*.

This also is illustrated in the hierarchy of the Church. One should not exaggerate the significance of this fact, but it remains interesting nonetheless that, as Archbishop Cushing pointed out in a talk to a C.I.O. Convention, the *democratic*, not to say proletarian, roots of our bishops are dramatically exemplified in the family backgrounds whence they come. Of all the bishops, archbishops, and cardinals in the history of the Church in America and down to the moment of writing, not one is the son of a college graduate. Not one comes from what people would consider a *privileged class*.[6]

Our bishops and our clergy are the sons of farmers, mill-workers, coal-miners, dock-hands, day-laborers, tradesmen, shopkeepers and other types of working men, including *white-collar* workers, but in each case *workers*. It would seem, then, that if this is the century of the *common man* in any Christian and democratic sense, the Catholic Church, both through its spiritual chieftains and through the broad masses of its devout working people, should have a congenial place in the American community and should make a powerful contribution to the spiritual direction of a community so largely industrial in its character.

There may be a reflection of the truth behind these same truths in the interesting coincidence that the most recent Democratic administration and the Republican administration of the national government have both found it somehow appropriate to name Catholics to the post of Secretary of Labor in presidential cabinets from which Catholics are otherwise too often strangely absent.

A corollary of this *proletarian* character of the Catholic body in the American community is that our people are, as we have noted, chiefly urban in their background and interest. This fact, too, may well account for some of the prejudices against Catholicism.

Catholicism is largely urban, but America is not. Rural America's suspicion of the city *slicker* is a favorite subject of caricature and comedy, but it corresponds with something quite real in rural American character. Anyone who watched the telecast of the investigations in which Senator Tobey of New Hampshire pursued with righteous wrath the people involved in *big-city* political scandals must have noted the clear inability of Senator Tobey to comprehend how God could permit situations to develop in a city of five million which do not occur in a New Hampshire town of five hundred—or do they?

In any case, recent Congressional hearings revealed a tension between rural and urban America. To what extent this antagonism carries over, however falsely or inappropriately, to the relations between *urban* Catholicism and *rural* Protestantism, it is difficult to estimate. It is a point worth notice, however, in any study of Catholicism in the American community.

On the other hand, Catholics themselves obviously feel completely at home in the American community. They have not merely come to terms with the basic postulates of that community but have been accused of undue attachment or at least uncritical devotion to some of the practical corollaries and by-products of these postulates. On this point Dean Sperry writes with sympathetic insight. He says that the people of no church are more vocal in unqualified affirmation of their one hundred percent patriotism than the Catholics, and he makes it quite clear that these protestations are completely sincere and justified by events. However, he observes that in matters of national policy the Catholic Church in America sometimes seems to many Protestants too uncritically patriotic. He considers that our *instant loyalty* to the federal government is in part a vote of thanks for the opportunities which this country has given the Catholic Church, and he quotes utterances of our clergy which say as much. "What one misses, perhaps, in these utterances", the dean observes, "is a strain of sober, critical second thought upon all of our American institutions."[7]

Catholicism has played one part in the American community which distinguishes it from all other religious traditions, and yet which has also given it an authentically American characteristic. It has perpetuated strong strains of many of the national cultures of the Old World, while reconciling them with one another in the pattern of the New World. It has done this work of reconciliation without eliminating anything valid and of value. If it be true, as is sometimes said, that Catholicism in America has as yet produced relatively little by way of an indigenous Catholic culture, it is also true that precious cultural heritages have been preserved in the United States by Catholic peoples, who take their own spiritual goods and share them for the considerable enrichment of the American community. Not long ago a non-Catholic doctor, who grew up in a Maine town, remarked that the French-speaking Catholic priest of his native town was the only intellectual companion with whom his father had felt at home in the Yankee town. He remembered the priest as the representative not only of Catholicism in his community but also of a rich cultural heritage to which his own travels had introduced him.

Nor has this broadly cultural influence of Catholicism been limited to the influence of a few gifted individuals. Catholic people as a group have exercised a more refining and spiritualizing influence on the general traditions of the community than they themselves ordinarily realize. The American observance of Christmas and of other sacred seasons is a case in point. For example, Theodore Maynard reminds us in his book *The Catholic Church and the American Idea* that the observance of Christmas was proscribed in Boston as late as 1856 precisely because it was looked upon as a Catholic aberration. Christmas Day was studiously made a work day; even in 1870 any pupil who stayed home from school on Christmas Day was severely punished or even expelled. The family of Emily Dickinson was suspected of being secretly Catholic because they observed Christmas in Amherst.[8] We owe it to the influence of the Irish with their family and parish observances, the Germans with their Advent wreaths and Christmas trees, that these prejudices were eventually eliminated and that Catholic observance of Christmas became so typically *American*. The late Cardinal O'Connell used to tell of being rebuked by one of his grammar-school teachers who lost patience with him for speaking of "Good Friday". "Every day is good", this Puritan schoolma'am insisted.[9]

We fortunately need not assume responsibility for some of the more recent development in the American observance of Christmas and Easter, but the manner in which these festive seasons presently loom so large in the American imagination we owe in great part to the Catholic influence.

It is only fair to note that occasionally persons outside the household of the Faith regret that our influence along spiritual lines is not even greater. Here again Dean Sperry proves a friendly critic when he writes that many miss in American Catholicism any wide concern for the contemplative life. We Americans are too practical, he asserts, too much given to action without reflection. He contends that Catholicism might have been expected to correct American culture at this point.

It is never difficult to think of embarrassing examples of the uncritical patriotism of those who forget or cannot understand that our country, much and properly as we love it, is not the only country in the world; that it is part of the family of nations and is subject to the judgment of God and the law of conscience; that *my country, right or wrong*, can easily be a pagan cry. For Christians, as for sincerely patriotic Americans, there is always an awareness that many things in our country can and should be made better. The part of our country in world affairs must always be motivated by humane considerations arising from the nature and claims of the human community as well as by self-interest.

Catholics, especially, should understand this. And yet whenever super-patriots begin to organize in some strange movement to impeach Earl Warren, a disturbing number of Catholics are almost sure to be caught up in the movement in the name of *patriotism*; when cranks are going about seeking support for the idea of getting the United Nations out of New York, too many Catholic cranks are found in the ranks of the nervous; more Catholics than Protestants, proportionately, seem susceptible to joining letter-writing campaigns *investigating* foreign policy associations, international discussion forums, and efforts to promote the peace—as if *all these* were necessarily Communistic and anti-patriotic!

It is reassuring, moreover, to detect in the catalogues of Catholic publishing houses a very remarkable increase in strictly spiritual literature, most of it derivative from the Catholic traditions of other countries, but not a little of it revealing the native genius of our own land. It is noteworthy, too, that the Catholic Lay Retreat Movement is continually extending its numbers and its influence, and that days of recollection are now conspicuous in the calendar of present-day Catholic institutions, clubs, and parishes.

Catholic scholarship in the American community is a subject of frequent analysis and debate. So many recent studies have appeared on this point that there is probably no need to discuss it here. The most recent of these are marked with a forthrightness and objectivity which argue well for the prospects for reform or improvement where these may be needed. They justify the hope that we are beginning to come into our own, little by little, in the world of scholarship, despite the real disadvantages of a financial kind under which most of our educational institutions do their gigantic work.

It must be confessed that, except for a few familiar names, the authors who have most impressively related the best chapters of our cultural history in America have often been friendly neighbors rather than our own writers. One thinks of Francis Parkman, Willa Cather, even Longfellow on occasion.

At the moment it is difficult to deny that our place in the

American community is under attack. The numbers of those who join in the attack and the permanent significance of what they have to say are open to question. The *fact* of the attack and the lines it follows are clear; the latter are new in their direction.

A century ago the attack on the Catholic Church in America was essentially pornographic. The creeds of Blanco White and books like *Maria Monk* remain fair samples of American anti-Catholicism in the last part of the last century.

Today the attack is largely political, or at least pseudo-political. There is a professed misgiving in some circles as to what use we could make of political power if we became a majority in this country, and there are even charges that our professions of fidelity to the Constitution and to American political idealism involve an *interim ethic* which we might put aside should we acquire greater numbers and sufficient power.

It is exasperating to be perpetually issuing assurances that Catholics are sincere sharers of the constitutional and other American traditions—which we consider ourselves to have helped establish—indeed, to have inspired in no small degree. It is idle to plead the evidence of our support of America and her institutions by the same means which others employ in the support of these. It is beneath our own dignity to argue, as we so often do, from the statistics of our representatives in the Armed Services and in other posts of trust. These considerations are received with cynicism by any who need such arguments.

On the other hand, there are undoubtedly many things Catholics can do to persuade others (and perhaps ourselves!) of our major and beneficent place in the American community. For one thing, it is well that we keep clear the rather obvious fact that we are here in America to stay. This basic premise is by no means as well understood as it should be; the points we have considered concerning the immigrant air attributed to the Church would indicate as much.

Then, too, we would do well to extend the influence of our good works, our corporal and spiritual works of mercy, in the widest possible measure. It is very difficult for essentially good people to resist the logic of goodness in others. The work of Catholic religious sisters frequently dispels more prejudice than could be handled by more hours of speeches than we should care to give or hear. A recent book by the Jewish father of a cerebral palsy child quotes the illuminating remark made by a non-Catholic doctor when he was obliged to tell the parents of their child's unfortunate condition. "Try to place the little boy with Catholic sisters", the doctor said, adding that thus the parents would be doing all that their hearts could desire to protect the little boy. It is an eloquent testimony to one side of Catholicism which has favorably and powerfully impressed most members of the American community from the beginning.

Finally, we can perhaps be a little more conscious of the need that we develop certain potentialities of Catholicism in this country which, rightly or wrongly, many people think have been neglected. Our mightily organized activities and impressive organizations will lose nothing from more frequent emphasis on the organic nature of the Church. Perhaps the present flowering of the Trappist and other contemplative communities in our midst, together with a new American interest in spiritual literature, closed retreats, and vigils before the Sacrament, will both increase and emphasize those mystical resources of our people which they themselves occasionally underemphasize and their critics so frequently forget. In this connection the Liturgical Movement is making a special and providential contribution in America.

Those who love the Church will pray God to prosper the intellectual apostolate among us. The difficulties of the intellectual vocations in the service of the Church are many and familiar; they are the same in America as they are elsewhere. Good works are usually much more easy than the long, hard road of study, consecrated learning and dedicated defense, by written and spoken word, of the truth taught us by the Divine

Intellectual, the Incarnate Word of God. The traditional temperament of the typical American, a willing doer of the Word more often than a rapt listener, has helped make scholarship a neglected field among us.

It is through the intellectual apostolate that, please God, we shall best increase and intensify the international ties and interests which increasingly operate among us as counteractives, sometimes badly needed, to our American isolationism and as corollaries of our Catholic supranational idealism. On the level of good works Catholicism in America had a remarkable record of authentic Christian world-mindedness; the Catholic American part in the support of missionary work and the characteristic generosity of Catholic America to world relief appeals are impressive evidence that we have not acquired any nationalistic spirit so narrow that it leaves us unmindful of our brothers' need.

Perhaps we are not always equally mindful of the need in which we stand, a need for inspiration and even instruction by our Old World kinsmen in the Faith. The liturgy and the love of the saints have always served to keep us somehow close to the lands whence we came. But now there are heartening indications that on the level of scholarship and the various areas of the intellectual life, Catholic America is making new international friendships and associations. Nothing could be more constructive for America or more consistent with the spirit of Catholicism.

XIV

Perseverance in the Seminary: Problems and Remedies

The problem of perseverance during the years of seminary life varies from place to place and, no doubt, from generation to generation. Remedies effective in one place are frequently worthless in another; so, too, approaches to the question of perseverance which may be valid in one period of history appear to lose effectiveness with the changing patterns of passing time. *Autres les temps, autres les maux à conjurer.*

The Sacred Congregation of Seminaries has conducted a survey on the problem of perseverance as on every other aspect of vocations in the contemporary Church. The replies from four hundred dioceses in every corner of the world confirm the a priori conviction that the problem is not alike in any two places. Just as the reasons for an initial lack of aspirants differ widely as between Switzerland and Sweden, Belgium and Brazil, North America and South America, or even Pittsburgh and Miami within the same nation; just as the problems testing the virtue of the ordained priest differ markedly in the land of Bernanos' *Journal d'un Curé de Campagne* from those in the land of Canon Sheehan's *My New Curate* or Willa Cather's *Death Comes for the Archbishop*, not to mention Edwin O'Connor's *Edge of Sadness* or Guareschi's *Don Camillo*, so the problems of perseverance in the seminary present inevitable differences as between the Grand Seminaries of France, Maynooth in Ireland, the colleges and universities of Rome, the seminaries of the United States, and those of Latin America.

This address was delivered at Rome, Italy, on May 22, 1962, during the first International Congress on Ecclesiastical Vocations.

Many of the problems which impede the recruiting of vocations and which beset the lives of the ordained complicate also the question of perseverance within the seminary. We shall concern ourselves in this conference not with the peculiar difficulties special to particular places but rather with the general problems which all but universally present themselves nowadays as obstacles to perseverance in ecclesiastical vocations.

As we have noted, some of these difficulties relate to the problem of the initial shortage of candidates for the seminary. One such difficulty is the general decline in the sense of vocation itself. Perhaps the awareness of the Providence of God is less sensitive in our mechanistic and secular civilization; perhaps even the Christian's consciousness of individual destiny and personal significance is less sharp in our so frequently collectivist, standardized, and impersonal civilization. In any case, not merely in what pertains to the idea of vocations to the priesthood, but in all walks of life there appears to have been an eclipse, please God temporary, of the awareness that *every life* involves a special call under the Providence of God; that *every life* involves a stewardship for which an account must be rendered to God; that *every life* is a mission. The basic sense of vocation which once gave meaning and direction to all walks of life has been a casualty of collectivism, existentialism, and secularism, three of the moods induced by a widespread practical atheism that, forgetting God, undermines the significance of the person and destroys the sense of individual vocation, whether to marriage, to a career, or to the priesthood.

By unhappy contagion this aspect of our civilization undoubtedly *debilitates* the sense of vocation even of many who enter the seminaries but who, in the inevitable crises of the long years of study, fall by the wayside because not fortified by the powerful motivation that comes from intense awareness of having been called by God as was Abraham, or Aaron, or Moses, or Paul.

Accordingly, it must be an objective of all our teaching and preaching, on every level of the life and action of the Church, to restore the *basic sense of vocation*, lacking so universally among men to the great hurt of family life, personal growth, society, and, specifically, ecclesiastical vocations. Only when a lively sense of the Providence of God and of the reality of individual vocation provides clarity, confidence, and purpose can we look for heroic responses to the needs of the time, whether in the Church or in civilization.

Some of the special problems of perseverance in seminary years arise from difficulties within individual persons. Questions of physical health are obvious enough, but not so widespread as to call for extended comment; much more serious and even common in our generation are those psychological difficulties of a subtle kind concerning which contemporary psychiatric and psychosomatic studies have made us so conscious.

This is a delicate, even dangerous, field and some of us are tempted to consider that there has already been too much attention paid to psychological testings, their data and alleged significance. One shudders to think how much of the color, the accomplishments, and the mightiness of the things that God has done "through the weak and foolish things of this world"[1] would have been lost to the Kingdom of Heaven on earth had earlier generations of Church history been bogged down by psychometric requirements and the seeming naturalism of intensive psychological screening!

On the other hand, sober studies of the problem of perseverance through seminary years warrant reference in this discussion to certain psychological difficulties which might well be anticipated by prudent testing or might well be solved by psychologically sound counseling of students who have personality difficulties after entrance into the seminary. The Most Reverend Bishop of Monaco, Monsignor Barthe, contributes a discerning preface, well documented from Canon Law, pedagogy, and common sense, to Professor Paul Grieger's book *Caractère et Vocation*, a study of the place of psychological considerations in handling the problems of vocations, those of perseverance included.[2]

A reading of Professor Grieger's book suggests that we may lose many candidates during the years when perseverance toward ordination is under trial simply because of our failure to use *constructively* the psychological sciences, not merely to discover individual defects but especially to remedy these. In all this, of course, the ecclesiastical sense will put one on guard against naturalism or any mere *psychologism* that might downgrade the essential place of divine grace in vocations and especially in perseverance. An ecclesiastical vocation, completely and properly understood, comes from God; it involves a divine grace which in turn involves the *complete* Christian in the realization of some plan of Divine Providence. The essential element of a vocation is linked to divine election and therefore to grace, as well as to a personal choice and cooperation with grace. But the *criterion* of a vocation, so far as the Church and the aspirant himself are concerned, depends on analysis of certain aptitudes and qualities, physical, intellectual and moral, which render a candidate acceptable. So Pope Pius XI emphasized twice at least in his encyclical on the priesthood; so would all agree.[3]

The proper recognition of the place of psychological considerations—a study of temperament, basic character, and mental structure, in determining the presence of a vocation or in meeting certain problems of perseverance in a vocation—need not be inconsistent with recognition of the essential place of divine grace in both. Cardinal Verdier used to warn against inordinate or, rather, heretical dependence on God's grace in this connection; he used to say, by way of jest, that the grace of God might well turn a violin into a good violin or turn a trombone into a good trombone, but that it would never turn a trombone into a violin!

Hence the pertinence and the need of helping students acquire sound psychological self-knowledge, just so interest in this does not become a species of psychological hypochondria but is a prelude to self-discipline and a means of avoiding drop-outs among students who might persevere if they knew the true nature and proper remedies of their psychological difficulties. They are most likely to persevere whose self-knowledge is clarified by sound psychology and whose self-discipline is the more exact and efficacious by reason of such self-knowledge.

It is on the psychological level that questions of nature and grace meet to solve or complicate one another according as prudent direction is present or indifference and neglect. This is the heart of many psychological difficulties in seminarians: the lack of proportion between *supernatural maturity* and *natural maturity*.

Such natural maturity consists in a normal adult condition and control of the body, the mind, the will, and the emotions. It means the mastery, in due stages and on their several levels, of natural faculties and human instincts so that these function in integrated equilibrium. Such an equilibrium expresses itself in responsible, intelligent, and effective responses to reality.

Supernatural maturity is characterized, above all else, by an *adult faith*. Such adult faith involves a familiar paradox, the paradox pointed out by Our Lord ("unless ye become as little children. . .") with the thoughts of Saint Paul ("Keep the innocence of children, with the thoughts of grown men").[4] The thoughts of grown men in a truly adult faith center with dogmatic accuracy and fullness on the Person of the Risen Jesus; as Father Sauvage, Superior of the Grand Seminary, Lille, points out: such thoughts embrace, man-fashion, the Paschal Mystery. They place the mature believer in the line of Abraham, whose God was able to raise the dead; they make the mature believer seek the source of sanctity and the pledge of resurrection in the Risen Christ; they prompt him to manly reliance on the sacraments, above all the Eucharist; they give him insight into the mystery of his own identity with Christ, both dying and resurrected, and his own consequent part in bringing to pass the identity between Christ and humanity, all in the Church.

In a word, the ecclesiastical student of adult faith is a man who perceives by faith and resolves by grace to achieve what God has made him and calls him to become; who perceiving this, receives through the sacraments of the Church the dynamism of grace from the death and Resurrection of Christ and brings this to the service of the Church, all with informed faith and disciplined resolution.

How achieve such an adult faith and blend it with natural maturity to produce supernatural maturity in our seminarians? How overcome the individual and personal, community and sociological impediments, not to say resistance, to such maturity? How help the seminarian put away the things of childhood—the *egocentricity* which makes the child value things only in the measure that they serve or protect him, substituting for this egocentricity the Christocentric Faith and cult which make Christ rather than self the measure of all things? How bring to maturity the childishness in faith which keeps a student excessively dependent on those who initiated the Faith in him, but whose tutelage he can and must outgrow if he is himself to be capable of the spiritual paternity that is the privilege of priesthood? All these difficulties are weighed by Father Sauvage in "Maturation Humaine et Surnaturelle, Problèmes de Grands Séminaires", in the review *Vocations Sacerdotales et Religieuses* for October 1961, an article analyzing that *spiritual immaturity*, the lag of supernatural behind natural maturity, which, of all psychological problems, probably accounts for most failures in perseverance.

Somehow the very *content* and *manner* of the teaching of our *dogma* classes must play the principal role in overcoming immaturity in faith and the consequent supernatural lag behind merely natural maturity. Properly related to ascetics and to spiritual motivation, dogma accomplishes this by what it teaches concerning Christ and what it teaches concerning priesthood. What better remedy for the disturbing sense of inadequacy which so often causes failures of perseverance? It is ironic that this sense of inadequacy should frighten away otherwise fit candidates, since a humble and wholesome sense of personal inadequacy is the first condition of the indispensable acknowledgement of the total part of Christ in the works of the priesthood. It is not only the apprehensive student who suffers from feelings of inadequacy, but also the saint who asks the question that causes so many to drop out: *"What can I possibly offer or do, given the sublimity of the priestly office and my inadequacy?"* The answer is always and certainly: *Nothing*! If this were the end of the matter, there would be nothing further to be hoped either by the anxious student or by the ardent saint. But this is only the beginning of the matter. Robert Hugh Benson sets forth the saving truth that our dogma classes must inculcate in students if they are to have the intellectual premises of a disciplined will to persevere:

As, therefore, the priest in the pulpit cries, "I say unto you": so in the confessional he whispers "I absolve you", and at the altar "This is My Body". . . . This, then, is a second, and an over-whelmingly awful thought, yet essential to be understood, if we are to realize in what manner Christ is present in his priest.

First He is present in him when he delivers, it may be more or less mechanically, the message with which he is entrusted. The Divine Prophet uses human lips to "utter knowledge", and to declare truth. But when we reflect that the Divine Priest uses human lips to effect sacerdotal purposes, we see that the Presence is far more intimate than that of a King in his ambassador. For the ambassador is practically *in no sense* his Master. He can dictate the terms of a treaty, but he cannot finally conclude it: he can plead with those to whom he is sent, but he can only in a very limited and representative sense reconcile them to his King. Yet these Ambassadors of Christ, in virtue of the express commission which they have received in such words as "This is My Body . . . do this for a commemoration of Me." "Receive ye the Holy Ghost. Whose sins you shall forgive they are forgiven them"—are empowered to do that which no merely earthly ambassador can do. They effect that which they declare: they administer the mercy which they preach. . . .

Here, then, we can say in reality, that Christ is present in His Priest—present, that is, as He is present in no saint, however holy, and in no angel, however near to the Face of God. It is the priest's supreme privilege, as well as his terrifying responsibility, to be, in a sense Christ Himself. He says not, "May Christ absolve thee"; but, "This is My Body." It is not then merely the utterance of the lips which Christ employs, but Christ Himself for the moment must sway the Will and Intention; since it is a Divine Act that is done . . . by the union of [the priest's] free-will and free intention with that of his Creator.[5]

Psychological, too, but not without strong moral overtones is a further cause of drop-outs from the seminary, particularly in the sometimes arid years of long, long study. One fears that it is frequently almost an unrecognized sin, but it can be fatal to perseverance. It is the fault from which Paul Claudel prays to be delivered in his prayer at the Seventh Station:

It is not a stone underfoot, nor a tight-drawn halter,
But the soul that all on a sudden begins to falter.
Oh, scorching noon of our life! Oh, fall deliberately made!
When the magnet no longer has pole and faith sees no Heaven displayed.
Because the road is long and because the end is afar,
Because one is quite alone where no consolations are!
Oh, straggling aeons of time! Secret disgust, not withstood,
For this unbending commandment and this companion of wood!
That is why one flings out both arms like a swimmer losing his pace
And falls—no, not on one's knees, but blindly, full on the face!

The body falls, it is true, and the soul gives instant assent.
Save us from the Second Fall when *boredom* wakes wilful
    consent![6]

Of all the explanations of the mystery of non-perseverance
in a vocation, this bored *acedia*, certainly on the moral level, is
among the most frequent. This *melancholy loss of taste for things
of the spirit* is akin to the tedium and ennui that begets a certain
repugnance and characteristic fear in the face of the effort
needed for the fulfillment of one's duty. The Scripture describes
the *accidioso* when it speaks of the slothful man who treats
remote contingencies as if they were present, imminent dangers
excusing him from action: for the slothful man there is *always*
"a lion in the way, and a lioness in the roads".[7] Anything to
excuse action; anything to avoid work or even decision; such is
the boredom of *acedia*.

To meet the tedious ennui of the long years between the first
fervor and springtime of vocation and the eventual joys of
ordination, many means, natural and supernatural, are useful.
The examples of the saints, the encouragement of spiritual
directors, the development of strong supernatural motivation,
and conscious, enthusiastic cooperation with the daily graces
of the sacraments—all these are basic. *But important, too, is the
keen intellectual stimulation that comes from access to good libraries,
the opportunity at every stage of study for appropriate apostolic
works, and, of course, wholesome recreation.*

In his conference to the Third Meeting of Italian Seminary
Superiors and Professors, Monsignor Ugo Cavalieri has made
some pertinent observations concerning libraries in seminaries
and the development of personal libraries by future priests. A
powerful antidote to the dangerous boredom of *acedia* as well
as an important stimulus to intellectual growth would follow
from the full application to seminaries of the apostolic counsel
of Pope Pius XII:

> But for the encouragement of study, which is not infrequently
> made impossible for priests because of the meagerness of their

financial resources, it is most desirable that the local Ordinaries, in keeping with the ancient and excellent practice of the Church, should restore to their former dignity libraries which were formerly attached either to the episcopal residence, or to Chapters of Canons, or to the parishes themselves. . . .

These libraries should not be regarded merely as store-rooms for discarded books, but rather as something living, and should be equipped with suitable facilities for study. Above all, these libraries should be organized to meet the needs of our times, and be provided with publications of all kinds, paying special attention to religion and the social sciences, so that teachers, pastors, and especially newly-ordained priests, may draw therefrom sufficient enlightenment to enable them to preach the truths of the gospel and to refute errors.[8]

If seminary libraries are living centers of proper priestly interest, as easily accessible and as regularly frequented as the refectories and gymnasiums, only less loved than truly devotional chapels, *acedia* will be a less likely peril. So, too, participation in programs of the Confraternity of Christian Doctrine, hospital and prison visiting, corporal and spiritual works of mercy, liturgical conferences, etc.—all proportionate to the maturity and capacities of the seminarian—will at once serve the apostolic action of the Church and nurture the lively zeal of the future priest.

Another possible cause for failure to persevere can arise from the very nature of some seminary physical surroundings. In this connection Pope Pius XII raises an important point when he speaks of the need for prudent balance between Spartan simplicity and luxurious ease in seminary buildings. The discouraging effects of inadequate or squalid physical circumstances are obvious enough; but not less perilous to perseverance are the "palatial houses and luxurious ease and comfort" against which *Menti Nostrae* warns.[9] The most desirable candidates may fail to persevere in such sumptuous surroundings precisely because they will be spiritually uneasy in an environment which corresponds neither to that of the ordinary people of God whom they prefer to serve nor to that of the meek and modest Christ in Whose spirit they wish to serve. Moreover, the less sensitive, who remain untroubled in palatial houses, acquire therein tastes which may later be disenchanted, with the result that they are unprepared to persevere in the less-easy circumstances of their eventual missions and assignments. We may well ask, then, if mere comfort, when it is in excess of normal, manly requirements, is not itself a hazard to perseverance; the remedies for this difficulty are obvious!

An urgent question is suggested by Father Sauvage as to the extent to which a certain *institutionalism*, uncongenial to personality and itself easily remediable, may contribute to that lack of vital maturity, natural and supernatural, which we have seen to be a cause of failure to persevere. Certainly excessive *institutionalism* fails to correct such a lack, and therefore we do well to be on guard against any stereotypes that might become fixed institutional patterns. Father Sauvage quotes a description of one such which may not be typical but is, one fears, recognizable, with its atmosphere "faite de petits cancans, de susceptibilités, de petites preoccupations, médisance et autres mouvements d'opinion futiles. . . . Atmosphère rapetissante, peu propice à une maturation de la foi et de la vie spirituelle."

The Sacred Congregation for Seminaries, in the admirable report of the conferences on *Menti Nostrae*, has provided an example of the alertness of Italian seminary superiors and professors to the contemporary needs of the seminaries in their nation if these are to be organically sound, free from sterile institutionalism, and forming a mature clergy. It would be well if each nation were similarly to explore the mind of *Menti Nostrae* against the background of its own institutions for training clergy.

The militaristic tinge of modern nationalism indubitably accounts for not a few of the problems of perseverance on the part of certain candidates for the priesthood. Compulsory peacetime military service, so trenchantly described by Cardinal

Gasparri as the cause of so many and such great evils for more than a century ("la vraie cause d'une multitude de maux qui ont affligé la société") has taken its toll of perseverance in seminaries. The evidence of some nations where universal peacetime conscription has become engrained suggests that the disorders of subsequent marriage date from moral results of peacetime barracks conditions; the destruction of fitness for priesthood and of the virtue of perseverance, *inter alias*, seems not less certain a result of moral factors bad enough in all military situations involving the young, but fatal in a setup of permanent peacetime conscription.

But even in less militaristic civilizations, there is a subtle temptation that saps the strength of perseverance in many ecclesiastical students during a period of history marked, as is ours, by frequent wars. Where ecclesiastical students are bound to military service, the dangers to eventual perseverance in a priestly vocation are already clear; where they are not so bound, the subtle temptation to which we allude asserts itself— and its effects may in some cases be even more disastrous than would be a straight call to service. The normal young man, normal in his virility and in his patriotism, may not be at ease in the cloistered security of the seminary when his kinsmen or contemporaries are risking their lives in response to their country's call. Patriotism is a form of piety with powerful emotional overtones, and in time of crisis it can dull the claims of other pieties. Patriotic, virile young men—and such our seminarians generally are—do not like to be thought of as shirkers, much less as shirkers from the danger that is a duty for their brothers in the world. This is a problem at the moment, a common one, in my opinion; it consists in the desire to perform one's military service, even though not obliged, before completing one's ecclesiastical studies, indeed even at the risk of forfeiting them by interruption. The remedy can only lie, again, in heavy emphasis at every level of preaching and teaching on the full concept of piety; the hierarchy of obligations in piety; and the manner in which priestly piety, perfectly performed, contributes supremely to the patriotic good, the common good of the brethren, more than any other form of piety and at a sacrifice far from less heroic than that of the soldiers of Caesar. Somehow we must make clear and cogent to our young men the ringing thesis of Cardinal Suhard: "That man who dies so his brothers can live, who washes the world in the blood of Christ and makes it acceptable to the Father, that minister of unity and peace, can anyone say he is a deserter?"[10]

Broader than the misgivings arising from questions of military service, there are like fears, not so likely to be present in the youngest aspirant for the seminary but gradually manifesting themselves with the passing years. Strong in a period of revolution like the present time is the fear of being a curious character among men; a museum piece in one's civilization; irrelevant, however holy and admirable, to the cultural interests, political preoccupations and common strivings of one's generation.

This fear has probably always been present in the priests of a people bound by their very faith, as are Christians, to be pilgrims and strangers on the face of the earth. It is a fear that is, in fact, well founded in the very nature of the priesthood, a fear which will less often cause men to faint and fail in their perseverance if it is faced honestly and its premise seen for what it is—i.e., a reason for a *greater*, not a *lesser*, sense of relevance to the needs and worries of our times. In his luminous pastoral *Priests among Men*, Cardinal Suhard treats of this *irrelevance* of the priest to our civilization, the paradox of the seeming futility of the most indispensable men, but putting the matter in a proper theological perspective which, clearly perceived and profoundly grasped, will help keep men of sound judgment faithful to their strange but sublime vocation:

> Civilizations come and go; nations spring up and disappear "with their might and their glory"; the priesthood does not

138

pass. It perpetuates itself on earth, in humility in its outward appearance, with nobility of a royal dynasty which has never known an interregnum. The priest is a strange man whom his contemporaries consider archaic but who is always modern and new. He is accused of being reactionary. The truth of the matter is that he is ahead of his time. He looks ahead. He prognosticates. He prepares for the future. He anticipates. He goes beyond all progress and humanism by constantly showing men Christ, the *new Adam*, and begetting them into His transcendent life. But because he speaks the language of eternity he is not considered worth listening to.

People think he is removed from them because he breaks through ordinary conventions. They think he is indifferent because he keeps quiet and is given to meditation, whereas, in fact, he *considers the whole world as his parish*. The ungrateful city ignores the fact that he watches over it. It is unconcerned about the custodian who protects it during the night. It is not grateful to him for giving it life.

This is the eternal paradox of the priest. He is a study in contraries. At the price of his own life he reconciles fidelity to God and fidelity to man. He seems to be poor and weak. And indeed there is nothing weaker than a priest. He has neither political power nor financial resources nor the strength of arms which others use to conquer the earth. His strength consists in being unarmed and "able to do all things in Him who strengthens him." It consists in going, with an independence which his detachment makes possible, to those who suffer, those who are ignorant, those who fall. There has been nothing more belittled, nothing more misunderstood, nothing more attacked in all history than the priesthood. Yet it is only before a priest that people kneel. Well do they know it, those who would banish God's Church forever from the world! Until the end of time the priest will be the most beloved and the most hated of men, the most incarnate and the most transcendent; their dearest brother and their arch enemy! Until the end of time his mystery, which remains a holy enigma even to himself, will outlast world events and civilizations and be the great witness of the invisible kingdom. Priests know that when they go up to the altar for the first time.

139

They are not ignorant of the fact that until death they will be the "sign of contradiction", a light for the children of light, darkness for the sons of the night.[11]

Once again, therefore, the solution of a major problem impeding perseverance, that of a false understanding of the sign of contradiction that every priest must be, depends on how *solidly* but also how *profoundly persuasively* our *dogma* is taught—"ut quae salutariter edocentur, intellectu capiant, corde retineant, opere exsequantur." Wherefore at every stage of studies Christ and the dogmas concerning Christ must be the focal point of attention and the heart's core of love. *Solutio omnium difficultatum Christus*; perseverance is born of great love for Christ—but here, too, the axiom is valid: *nihil amatur quin prius cognitum*. How early, how intimately, how profoundly do our students come to know Christ—as Paul knew Him, or as knew Him that renowned French preacher who said from the pulpit of Notre Dame: "Since first I came to know Jesus Christ, I have never felt seriously the power of any rival to him!"

Yet it is precisely the rivals to Christ, competing for the heart of our students, that explain the failures in perseverance in His footsteps. Those rivals explain most of the internal crises and individual tensions to which we have directed attention. Basically, they stem from the spirit of the times, and especially from these problems born of that spirit:

1. *Problems of contemporary education*, so secular in its mood, so exclusively technological in its scientism, so negligent of humanistic studies (so little Latin, less Greek, scant philosophy), so indifferent to contemplation and to the teachings of revelation—and therefore so inadequate to give us students prepared to delight in theology, Scripture, and the sacred sciences, and therefore to persevere in their pursuit;

2. *Problems of contemporary morality and moral atmosphere*, so tainted by pansexualism, all-pervading in its evil spell and

debilitating the power to persevere even of the strongest and the soundest—an atmosphere that prompts many to ask if all virtue, but especially perseverance in vocations, might not be strengthened if the age of confirmation were more closely related to the age of dawning susceptibility to sensualism and if, also, a more efficacious appeal could be made to maturely deliberate profit *ex opere cooperantium* from the *strengthening* and *maturing* power of *confirmation*—that sacrament which, par excellence, should be the *sacrament of vocations* and of *perseverance in* them;

3. *Problems of contemporary civilization and cultural values.* First, our civilization places a new and paralyzing emphasis on *security*: social security, health security, job security—*everything is insured*. In the face of such a cult of guaranteed *security*, there is less disposition to take a chance with one's life, to gamble on the Providence of God and to make unqualified offerings of one's self to the unknown and unquestioned will of God. There is less walking blind into Damascus, less uncalculating heroism. But suddenly the evidences of youthful generosity in Papal Volunteers, in Peace Corps, in Catholic Action apostolates of youth, in missionary adventures remind us that generosity and idealism still flourish in youthful hearts and can be directed into persevering vocations.

Then our civilization fosters a sometimes-misleading concept of *democracy*, the egalitarianism of which destroys the sense of a spiritual elite, so necessary to the nourishing of true democracy and so essential to perseverance in a vocation to pursue the *optimam partem* and to resist reduction to dead levels of virtue and least common denominators of excellence. Not only does the egalitarianism of false democracy produce the cult of mediocrity which is hostile to perseverance in pursuit of greater perfection, but the libertarianism of a civilization forgetful of the freedom of the sons of God can also prove a pitfall in the path of perseverance. Among the *great possessions* of the young men who turn sadly from the call of Jesus today, the greatest is probably their sense of *personal liberty*. The initiates know well how consistent with the fullest human liberty is the grace of God, including the grace of perseverance in vocation; but many conferences and questionings reveal that the fear of loss of liberty is a greater contemporary obstacle to perseverance, as also to initial response to vocation, than are even the difficulties of the senses and instincts of flesh.

So far has this mistaken concept of liberty interfered with the normal Christian attitudes toward vocations that even devout parents and sensitive spiritual directors stand in terror of seeming to bring *pressure* by even prayer or persuasion on those who might seek or attempt to persevere in an ecclesiastical vocation. Monsignor Renard does not exaggerate when he puts the present problem of misconceived liberty in these words: "In order to be sure that we give a young man the liberty *not* to be a priest, we take away from him the liberty to be one!"

Here, obviously, is a problem to the correction of which prudent parents, enlightened educators, and wise spiritual directors must bring, all and severally, the remedy that can come only from an early and accurate understanding of what liberty is and what are its most noble and rewarding uses. Here, too, the early and accurate knowledge of Jesus Christ is essential, Jesus the Lord of Life freely choosing to die; the Lord of Majesty made, freely, obedient unto death—that freedom itself might be saved and sanctified.

Finally—and perhaps most pertinent of all—our civilization tends, by reason of the rewards and consolations which it exalts, to ignore or downgrade the *joys* of the priesthood. The result often is that even the devout, perhaps even priests, certainly some pious writers, speak too much of the *sacrifices* of the priestly life and too little of its *joys*, its *intense satisfactions*, and its *sweet consolations*. Perhaps there is too much emphasis *even among us* on the yokes, the burdens, and the renunciations of the priesthood. And here also the remedy lies in the rediscovery of Jesus Christ, every day, every year of progress through the seminary—of Jesus Christ and the encouraging, life-giving words by which He insists that His yoke is sweet, His burden light.[12] If our dogma professors, our teachers of every discipline, our parents and priests will make clear again the true *glory* of the cross and *joy* that comes from its glad embrace, then will more young men take up that cross and follow Christ—perseveringly, enthusiastically, all the days of their lives!—*usque dum vivant et postea!*

XV

Social Morality and the Christian Intellectual

You have asked me to discuss how the Church counts on the collaboration of university men and women in putting the social doctrine of the gospel into practice.

I assume that we are here discussing some mandate to intellectuals generally, not to university men and women in the particular terms of the duties of their respective states in life as a result of their academic or scientific specialties. Accordingly, I shall not attempt to spell out what the Church expects specifically of the engineer, the philosopher, the journalist, and research student, the doctor, the lawyer, the social scientist, or the members of other learned professions. Suffice it to recall that the Church counts on all these specialists to use their individual God-given talents or university-trained skills in the mighty work of social reform which demands the specialized contributions of every occupational and professional group, all in full measure and each according to its gifts.

But I address myself this morning to university students and alumni without reference to your specialties and on the broad premise of your general social vocation as Christian intellectuals. Both words in that proud yet holy title *Christian intellectuals* are significant, and I emphasize both.

As Christians you are one with Christ and one with one another by virtue of your baptism. By baptism you were not merely made eligible for redemption yourself; you were caught up in the mighty work of the salvation of all mankind, all for whom Christ was born, worked, suffered, died, and rose again from the dead. You share with all Christians the responsibility for preserving in yourself and sharing with others

This address was delivered at Montevideo, Uruguay, on July 30, 1962, during the Twenty-Fifth World Congress of Pax Romana.

the graces of baptism; these responsibilities flow from your basic Christian relationship to Jesus Christ and to His brethren.

As Christian intellectuals you have a special work to do because you have a special relationship to Jesus Christ. All Christians manifest in their particular callings and make good in their special ministries one or another aspect of the many-sided but single incarnate Son of God. Christians who hold authority acquire a special relationship to Christ the King; their contribution to the Kingdom of God is conditioned by their special vocation, and they are called to pattern themselves on the majesty yet humility of Christ the King. Christian citizens have their exemplar and their inspiration in the Christ Who shed His tears of predilection over Jerusalem, the capital city of His nation. Christian workers should understand their privileged place in the building up of the Body of Christ on earth because they conform to Christ the Worker, Christ Who was reputed to be the carpenter's son and Who plied the trade of his foster father. The Christian patriot, the Christian internationalist, the Christian priest, the Christian judge, the Christian king or statesman, the Christian friend—all these have a special relationship to the Kingdom of God because of the particular manner in which Christ, the total and unique Redeemer, provides for them a special pattern of excellence in the work that they are called to do.

So it is with the Christian intellectual. As Christians you share in the grace of God and take your place among His children, all the baptized. As intellectuals you are called to a special resemblance to and collaboration with the Divine Intellectual ". . . Christ Jesus, in whom are hidden all the treasures of wisdom and knowledge".[1] Just as your special relationship to Christ among Christians derives from your vocation as intellectuals, so your contribution to the cause of Christ, to the spread of His Kingdom and the salvation of the souls for whom He died must also involve you precisely as intellectuals.

As intellectuals you are concerned with ideas; you are called to be idea-people in our civilization. This gives you, potentially, a sublime similarity to that Christ Whom I have called the Divine Intellectual because He is the Infinite Idea, the *Logos* of the Father, all Divinity summed up in one subsistent Idea and then made Man.

You study *words*, and *words* are the tools of your work as intellectuals; Christ is the Incarnate Word of God. See, then, the many parallels between your vocation as intellectuals and the vocation of the Incarnate Word of God. Consider how Christ-like is the function of the Christian intellectual, called to imitate Christ by making incarnate in each generation and in each human culture something at least of the treasures of eternal wisdom and knowledge, the divine ideas summed up totally and perfectly in the Person of the Son, the *Logos*, the *Verbum (quod) caro factum est et habitavit in nobis*[2] that men might see His glory and be guided by it.

The Church, then, counts on the collaboration of university men and women in putting the social doctrine of the gospel into practice by expecting not only that your specialized professional and scientific skills will be used for the glory of God and the good of souls, but that you, precisely as intellectuals, will conform to the pattern of the Divine Intellectual, the Incarnate Word of God. She counts on you to bear the special witness of an intellectual in the midst of a world which is unregenerate, but called to redemption; a world already redeemed by the thought and action of Christ, but still requiring the application of the fruits of that redemption by means of the thought and action of Christians, instructed and inspired by you.

How shall you learn to do this? The first and most effective answer is in terms of the saints. One of the chief functions of the saints is to provide us other Christians with proximate living examples of how Christ would apply His thought and action to the specific circumstances of our several vocations. A saint like King Saint Louis of France bears vivid witness to kings as to how they must think and act if they aspire to conform with the pattern of Christ the King. A saint like Thomas More of England does the same for statesmen; so does Benedict Joseph Labre for beggars, the Little Flower for cloistered nuns, Don Bosco and Vincent de Paul for workers with the poor, Francis Xavier for missionaries, Saint Monica for mothers, Dismas for thieves. This is the sacred pedagogy for which the Church uses her saints.

And so to answer in more lively and cogent fashion our question of this morning: *How does the Church count on the collaboration of university men and women in putting the social doctrine of the gospel into practice?* (which means: *how will you as intellectuals best reproduce the thought and action of Jesus Christ in the social order of the day?*), we do well to meditate the examples of those saints who shared your human vocation as intellectuals and whose divine vocation as Christians you aspire to share.

There are many examples in the world of the university to which I might appeal in seeking an answer to our question concerning the Christian intellectual's part in the renewal of the face of the earth and in the temporal reform, as well as the spiritual salvation, of society; these are saints of every century, every nation, every intellectual specialization. The example I choose is not a canonized saint, though we are encouraged to pray for his beatification, and millions do so daily. I choose him in part precisely because he is not canonized and thus seems the more close to you and to me in our pursuit of sanctity. I also choose him because he is close to our times; close to the patterns and problems of our civilization; close to the great debates, the interests and the atmosphere of contemporary universities; close to the revolutions which fascinate and challenge us; close to the contemporary statements and practice of the ancient Catholic Faith which he shares with us and we with him.

I urge you to take the nineteenth-century Sorbonne student

147

and professor, Frédéric Ozanam, as the uncanonized patron and exemplar of the manner in which the Christian intellectual, precisely as such, conceives and accomplishes his social vocation.[3]

Next year, 1963, will be the 150th anniversary, the sesqui-centennial, of the birth of Ozanam. I ask you to reflect on how close this saintly Christian is to most of you in the patterns of your lives as Christians. Ozanam was the son of a university man, a medical doctor. He was himself a lawyer as well as a student of history, a professor of literature, a lecturer and writer on philosophy. He was a lonely voice of Christian culture in the dominantly secularist and indifferentist halls of the Sorbonne of his day, yet Frédéric Ozanam was obviously at home in the world of the university and in the company of intellectuals. I urge him as a modern exemplar for university people who, worthy of their baptismal salt and taking seriously the apostolic mandate that came with the oils of their confirmation, seek to play their part in the divine renewal of human society. Specifically, he provides personal dramatic illustration of the answer to the question: How, over and above the dedicated use of their special disciplines and particular professions, should university people, precisely as intellectuals, play their Christian part in putting the social doctrine of the gospel into practice?

I am, of course, aware that there were many young intellectuals active in the ferment of the nineteenth-century Catholic revivals in England, throughout Europe, and in the Americas, the ferment out of which were destined to be distilled the emphases on faith and freedom which characterize and explain the power of twentieth-century Christian Democracy. All must acknowledge the major part in this ferment of faith and freedom played by great prelates, Italian, German, and English, and, at their head, the Roman pontiffs, including, as Professor E. E. Hales has demonstrated, Pope Pius IX as well as Pope Leo XIII.[4] This rise of Christian Democracy was the work of many priests, notably among the French; of thousands of working men and women, and of not a few conscientious industrialists. If I choose as your exemplars a single group of laymen and name one from among them, it is because they are typical of the spirit of the others and they are most akin to yourselves as university students and alumni. Moreover, most directly and pertinently, the intellectuals gathered about Ozanam addressed themselves to the question that engages the attention of your Congress, i.e., *how translate into practice the social doctrine of the Church?*

To repeat, the circumstances of Ozanam's French university days paralleled those common in many parts of the world to-day. Positive atheism and negative agnosticism, supplemented by an anti-Christianity that dominated the press, schools, and forums, welcomed any doctrines which could be called *liberal*, whatever their title to that worthy name; under the July regime full play was given to every form of free thought and party passion. The university was taking full revenge for any disciplines under which it had groaned during the Restoration. The Sorbonne was particularly aggressive. Young Catholics with the spiritual vitality to react strongly against movements were in a minority. Discouragement was general even in the leadership of the Church in France. With timid silence on the one hand and aggressive error on the other, what could a handful of students accomplish against the voice of the acknowledged masters of learning and eloquence, the holders of academic power and popular prestige? And yet Ozanam and his friends decided to oppose their speech to the spoken word of the anti-Christian, and to do so face to face, on the same ground, at the same moment, to the same audience that the secularists dominated.

In a letter dated February 10, 1832, some four months after his arrival in Paris, Ozanam gave the following account of his plan of campaign against the anti-Christian teaching at the Sorbonne:

> We have in our growing ranks young men of noble disposition who have given themselves up to this great work. Every time

that a professor raises his voice against Revelation, Catholic voices are raised in protest! Many of us have agreed to do this work. On two different occasions I have taken my share in this noble work, by sending in my objections in writing to the gentlemen with those contentions we disagree. Our replies, which are read out, have had the best possible effect both on the professor, who all but retracted, and on the class, who applauded. The most striking result is that we are showing young students that it is possible to be a Catholic and to have common sense, to love religion and liberty at the same time. It serves to withdraw young men from religious indifference, and to make them used to discussion of serious matters.[5]

Thus as university students these heralds of a devout democracy prepared themselves for the witness they would later bear as university professors and members of their respective professions. The case of Ozanam himself is preeminent, but typical. In his eventual university lectures and conversations, Ozanam urged the necessity of Christian Revelation against the naked secularism of his day, even as we must against the related and progressive secularism of our day. He did so in his trenchant critiques of Saint Simonism, but also and notably in his lectures on Dante.

Ozanam discovered in the Florentine patriot-poet an advocate of the concepts of democracy as Christians understand it. However, he sharply distinguished Dante's Catholic Guelph democracy from the strictly secularist democracy that craves to be *without God or Master*. Ozanam made that distinction with eloquence:

Dante did not deify humanity by seeking to make it self-sufficient, with no other source of inspiration but reason and no other law than its own will. He did not confine humanity within the limited circle of an earthly destiny. . . . He saw that humanity is not complete here below, and he looked to the next world where the final appraisement of the Last Judgment awaits mankind. Standing on Truth, which men are bound to believe,

150

and on Justice, which men are bound to do, he weighs their works with the measures of Eternity. . . . Thus morality, the norm bound up with an eternal destiny, enters into History; Humanity, humiliated by the law of Death, is elevated by the law of Duty; true, a fallacious, fraudulent apotheosis is denied mankind by Dante's Christian concepts, but by them men are lifted forever from the lot and the level of the beasts of the field.[6]

In his Dante lectures as in his philosophical discourses, you will note the emphasis of Ozanam on the law of duty as distinguishing the man from the beast and as providing the basis of human worth in the Christian intellectual's understanding of democracy. This is not to say that the Christian democrat is unaware of *rights* or insensitive to them, his own rights or the rights of others. But it is to say that he does not share the contemporary impatience with obligations and duties, recognizing, as he does, that although rights are the foundation of the decent society, duties and their conscientious discharge are the cement that makes firm that foundation and strong its walls.

Ozanam did not see in duty a dull, regimented, loveless, and enforced conformity; he saw in it the highest expression of freedom, not only human freedom but the freedom of the sons of God. He said:

Our Lord makes us ask in His prayer that His will be done on earth as it is in Heaven; not as it is in Hell, where it is done of necessity, not among men, where it is often done with murmuring, but as it is in Heaven, with the love and joy of angels.[7]

This spirit of loving joy doubtless explains the manner in which Ozanam was able to be the militant apostle of Catholic truth and yet able to say near the end of his days: "One of my greatest consolations in the decline of my career is the certainty that, while defending truth with all my might, I have never offended anyone."[8]

This same spirit gave him and his co-workers their authentically Christian attitude of optimism toward their discouraging times. It was an attitude like to that of Pope Pius XI, who, surrounded by revolution and contradiction, rejoiced to live in an age which he said made it impossible to be mediocre. Ozanam expressed it this way:

> Ah! my dear friend, what a troubled, but what an instructive time is that through which we are passing! We may perish, but we must not regret having lived in it. Let us learn, first of all, to defend our belief without hating our adversaries, to appreciate those who do not think as we do, to recognize that there are Christians in every camp, and that God can be served now as always. Let us complain less of our times and more of ourselves![9]

This spirit, too, impelled Ozanam to make the choice that must be yours and mine as to what will be our attitude toward nonbelievers as we seek to present the Catholic creed and moral code to their attention. Ozanam once wrote that he and his friends noted among Catholic intellectuals two directly opposite schools of thought, both desiring to serve God with the pen in our times. One, he pointed out, claims for its leader, M. de Maistre, whom, however, it exaggerates and misrepresents. This school selects the most violent paradoxes, the most controversial theses, provided only that they irritate. It presents truth, not in a form that attracts, but in a form that antagonizes. It seems motivated not by the idea of bringing back unbelievers, but of inflaming the passions of believers.

The other school he describes as seeking to find in the human heart, even of the unbeliever, any secret links which bind it to Christianity, to develop in that heart the love of the true, the beautiful, the good, and then to proclaim those ideas in revealed faith toward which every decent soul aspires. This school is motivated by the idea of winning new souls to the fold, thereby increasing the number of Christians. Ozanam remarked: "I must say that I prefer to belong to this second school. I cannot forget the saying of St. Francis de Sales that more flies are caught with a spoonful of honey than with a ton of vinegar."[10] M. de Francheville was congratulated by Ozanam on the fact that he had "chosen the poetry of love in preference to the poetry of anger", i.e., that he preferred the apostolate of loving persuasion to the polemic of indignant denunciation.[11] So must we, you and I.

One thinks of Ozanam's friendly, conciliatory attitude toward the persons and opinions of others when one reads in Pope John's encyclical on the social questions this timely and genial paragraph:

> In the exercise of economic and social functions, Catholics often come in contact with men who do not share their view of life. On such occasions, those who profess Catholicism must take special care to be consistent and not compromise in matters wherein the integrity of religion and morals would suffer harm. But likewise, in their conduct Catholics should weigh the opinions of others with fitting courtesy and not measure everything in the light of their own interests alone. They should be prepared to join sincerely in doing whatever is naturally good or conducive to good. . . .[12]

Such will be the mood in which you address yourselves to the social questions of the hour if you are to be intellectuals in the pattern of Frédéric Ozanam and in accordance with the paternal counsels of Pope John. You will devote your intellectual energies, as did hzanam, to the discovery, the exploration, the defense and the propagation of the Christian intellectual heritage. But you will early recognize that, in an age of preoccupation with social questions, the intellectual apostolate by itself is not an adequate contribution either to civilization or to the cause of religion.

In this recognition you will again parallel the experience and profit from the example of Ozanam, who wrote:

> When we Catholics, in our relations with unbelievers, deists, followers of Saint Simon, Fourierists, architects of the new moulding of society, when we sought to direct their attention to

the benefits conferred by Christianity, we were met with the invariable answer: "You are right when you speak of the past; in former times Christianity worked wonders; but what is it doing for humanity today? Even you, who pride yourself on your Catholicism, what are you doing to show the vitality and efficacy, to prove the truth of your faith?"[13]

Ozanam was much affected by that challenge. So must you be.

Then with humility but with determination Ozanam added: "If our efforts have not succeeded, is it not because something is lacking to the supernatural efficacy of our teaching?"[14] He thought so, and he perceived clearly what it was: "Yes, one thing is wanting that our apostolate may be blessed by God— *works of charity*. The blessing of the poor is always the blessing of God."[15]

Thus became manifest to Ozanam as it must to you, the *two-fold apostolate* that Christ, the Church, and humanity itself expect of university students in our times, the *double apostolate of truth and action* exemplified by Ozanam and mandatory for every Christian intellectual. Ozanam was an *apostle of truth*, a student and spokesman of the Catholic truth which he always undertook to defend. At the age of seventeen he was immersed in the intellectual apostolate and deep in the studies by which the Church counts on intellectuals to prepare to apply her social teaching. At eighteen he opened his intellectual attack against Saint Simonism; at twenty he raised the standard in the Sorbonne against the anti-Catholicism of Jouffroy; at twenty-one he waited on the archbishop of Paris to appeal for up-to-date preaching in Notre Dame; at thirty he enthroned truth with eloquence in a professional chair in the Sorbonne. He devoted himself to the defense of truth up to the last breath of his body.

But Ozanam was not less, indeed even more, an *apostle of charity*. At twenty years of age he inaugurated with a few students the first Conference of Saint Vincent de Paul with his historic call: "Let us go to the poor."[16] From Paris, from Lyons, he extended his apostolate of works to France, later to both hemispheres: "I wish", he said, "to enfold the whole world with a net-work of charity."[17] Before closing his eyes in death he could count two thousand centers of the Vincentian charitable works he had dreamed. As his studies nourished the seeds of these works, so the works made fruitful his studies.

The almost casual personal social program of Frédéric Ozanam may strike you as hardly relevant to our so organized and collectivist society. And yet Pope Pius XII, analyzing how the Church counts on all her members to collaborate in putting the social teaching of the gospel into practice, makes the general observation that the Church has never preached social revolution; but always and everywhere, he says, from the Epistle of Saint Paul to Philemon down to the social teaching of the popes of the nineteenth and twentieth centuries, she has worked hard to have more concern shown for the human being than for economic and technical advantages, and to get as many as possible, on their part, to live the Christian life, a life worthy of a human being. The same luminous pontiff put his finger on what he called the great temptation of an age that calls itself social, an age when, besides the Church, the State, the municipality, and other public bodies devote themselves so much to social problems. That temptation, he argued, is that when the poor man knocks on the door, people, even believers, will just send him away to an agency or social center, to an organization, thinking that their personal obligation has been sufficiently fulfilled by their contribution in taxes or voluntary gifts to those institutions. Thus personality and persons fade into annihilation; the helper is not a person, but an organization; the helped is not a person, but a *case*, a problem.

Ozanam and his Christian intellectuals guarded against this temptation and guaranteed the spirit of the gospel by the principle they set for their practice when Ozanam wrote:

> The knowledge of social well-being and of reform is to be learned, not from books, nor from the public platform, but in climbing the stairs to the poor man's garret, sitting by his bedside, feeling the same cold that pierces him, sharing the

secret of his lonely heart and troubled mind. When the conditions of the poor have been examined, in school, at work, in hospital, in the city, in the country, everywhere that God has placed them, it is then and then only, that we know the elements of that formidable problem, that we begin to grasp it and may hope to solve it.[18]

So it is with every other problem in social morality. The precept and example of Jesus Christ, the faithful imitation of Christ by Ozanam and by the saints, the mind of the living Church all inculcate the lesson that social legislation and massive social programs are never by themselves the complete answer. They all will depend ultimately for their efficacy on day-by-day, face-to-face personal relationships, above all of Christian friendship, among those estranged. Such personal contacts dissolve, as can nothing else, the walls of division that create and perpetuate problems in social morality, problems like anti-Semitism, xenophobia, segregation, class conflicts, and the cold, cruel isolation between those who *have* and those who *have not*. There is no substitute for personal friendliness as the solvent of social problems.

Nor can the Catholic intellectual limit his personal friendships only to individuals or to a milieu that he finds sympathetic and congenial. This is an obvious temptation and one which has frequently paralyzed Christian social action, above all in interracial, intergroup, interclass conflicts. Ozanam stated the problem in extreme terms and answered it exactly as must you:

> As we grow up and as we see the world more closely we are grieved to find it hostile to every ideal and to every sentiment that is dear to us. . . . When one has been reared in a devout family, such a reaction fills the heart with disgust and indignation, and one is tempted to protest and to condemn. *But the Gospel forbids that; it places before us the duty of devoting ourselves entirely to the service of that same society that repels and despises us.*[19]

Ozanam described our service of the poor and the alien in terms not only of friendship but of our voluntary servitude in behalf of those less privileged than we. Indeed, he once declared himself bound, as a Christian intellectual, to the service of Jesus Christ in the persons of the poor even to the point of *martyrdom*, the ultimate proof of our perception of the truth and loving acceptance of all its practical corollaries. His description of his understanding of such martyrdom is well known; he wrote:

> The world has grown cold, it is for us Catholics to re-kindle the vital fire which has been extinguished. It is for us to inaugurate the era of the martyrs, for it is a martyrdom possible to every Christian. To give one's life for God and for one's brothers, to give one's life in sacrifice, is to be a martyr. . . . To be a martyr is to give back to heaven all that one has received, wealth, life, one's whole soul. It is in our power to make this offering, this sacrifice. It is for us to select the altar at which we shall dedicate it; the divinity to whom we shall consecrate youth and life; the temple where we shall meet again; at the feet of the idol of egotism, or in the sanctuary of God and Humanity.[20]

There is something alive in the very air today that appears to inspire men to be *martyrs* in the radical and original sense of *active witnesses* to the gospel of Christ, to the majesty of God and the worth of man. Perhaps this something reveals itself on the fringes of Christianity in the widespread ranks of those who, abandoning the very name of Christian and the Faith of Christ, wish to be known as *Witnesses—Jehovah's Witnesses*. Perhaps this same something explains the sometimes narrowly secular but warm idealism of the growing numbers of youthful volunteers to programs like that of the Peace Corps; it even seems present in the heroism and endurance, worthy of disciples of Christ, of so many of the young partisans of a revolution they intend should be godless, though what may yet be God's purposes for their revolution and His final judgment of some of them remains to be seen. Within the Church, this *something in the air*, surely not disassociated from the Spirit that breathes where it will, must account for the new hopes for religious vocations on every side, the shining sense of supernatural witness they bear who bring to human love and marriage such profound mystical insights and an idealism so fresh and so sublime. It reveals itself, too, in the rehabilitation among Catholic writers and speakers of the very word *witness*— a word we almost lost to our Protestant brethren, but which has recovered its primitive apostolic force for a generation that serves the gospel and the Church better by *positive witnessing* to the truth than by *negative defense* or *polemic*.

Valiantly witnessing to truth, the devout intellectual who seeks to discharge his social duties, beyond the obvious duties of his state of life in a given profession, will not have to seek far to find his opportunity. *Whatsoever thy hand findeth to do, do it!* In the daily business of life the social duty of the Christian intellectual is usually as simple and as close to him as that line of Sacred Scripture suggests. *Whatsoever thy hand findeth to do, do it!*[21] This is clearly the sum and substance of the social philosophy of Ozanam. He did not seek causes to champion; he set to work immediately upon the need, the opportunity, and the task closest at hand. His social morality never merited the condemnation which Chesterton gave the amorphous, ineffectual humanitarianism of people who love the human race, yet ignore the man next door, a social philosophy which is truly globaloney as long as it neglects the needs of the neighborhood and leaves one uninvolved in the worries of one's own parish, one's own street, one's own neighbor. *Whatsoever thy hand findeth to do, do it!*

A similar sense of immediacy and of practicality will prompt the Christian intellectual, working in the spirit of Ozanam, to note carefully the passage from Pope John's *Mater et Magistra* which seeks to put social philosophy debates among Catholics in their due place. There is no great theoretical debate about what should be the response of the generous hand to the immediate need for a cup of water, for the sharing of bread, the encouraging word, the place of shelter; not merely the example of Ozanam and the saints but the unqualified command of

Jesus Christ makes clear the answer. But on the wider level of social theories and philosophy there is a certain place, even need, for debate and perhaps even hesitation. Pope John states the problem and gives the practical solution when he writes:

> However, when it comes to reducing these teachings to action, it sometimes happens that even sincere Catholic men have differing views. When this occurs they should take care to have and to show mutual esteem and regard, and to explore the extent to which they can work in cooperation among themselves. Thus they can in good time accomplish what necessity requires. Let them also take great care not to weaken their efforts in constant controversies. Nor should they, under pretext of seeking what they think best, fail to do meanwhile, the good that can and hence should be done.[22]

There is, as all know, a parallel debate concerning the relationship of the Christian social ideal to historical reality, concerning whether a Christian society is ever attainable here below and in what sense or in what degree. The *Harvard Educational Review* carried recently a timely debate between two devout Catholics, one of whom sees in the writings of Professor Christopher Dawson grounds for the contention that certain cultures and civilizations may be cited as specifically Christian, the other of whom rejects the contention. But such debates as to whether the ideal Christian order has been, is now, or can be attained anywhere within the historical order are strictly academic debates, at least to this extent: *all will agree that none of the positions which any of the devout hold in such debates excuses the Christian intellectual from his obligation, here, now, and always to strive for the realization within himself of that full image of Christ to which he is called—and to seek to diffuse by word and deed,* in opere et veritate, *the sweet and saving influence of Jesus Christ by whatever professional skills may be his and whatever personal witness he can bear or deed he can do.*

To accomplish this social vocation of the Christian intellectual, not far-flung and complex organization is needed so much as dedicated, Christ-like personal action in the pattern of Ozanam and his associates. Once again, I ask you to reflect on the extent to which the thought and action of these mid-nineteenth century university people explain the providential presence and strength of Christian democracy in France, Italy, and Western Germany at that very moment in the middle of the twentieth century when the end of World War II found anti-Christian thought and pagan political social programs so totally discredited, so disastrously bankrupted.

I ask you to ponder the historical parallel for the future implicit in the recent past, and I ask you to make that parallel the pattern for your present thought and action. The conditions which surround many of you now are precisely parallel to those which surrounded Ozanam and his friends just over a century ago; if you are faithful to the formulae of faith, hope, and charity which Ozanam and his friends followed in the last century, we may confidently expect that the fruits of your witness and works will parallel in the future the fruits which today flourish from the seed sowed by these Christians a century ago. If you share their insight into a layman's true place in the life of the Church, if you are their collaborators in the perennial task of building the Body of Christ as you are their colleagues in the intellectual vocations of university men and women, they you will play equal part with them in the hallowing of history, the regeneration of society, and the diffusion of the divine influence of Jesus Christ. For this not only the Church but civilization itself will one day be grateful, as both must be grateful today for the values of religious faith and political freedom which, however sometimes feeble and sometimes compromised, survive today in Europe because of the thought and action of the Christian intellectuals, a handful in numbers but a host in spiritual influence, of which Frédéric Ozanam was typical.

Why did these men attempt the things they did? How did

they accomplish the holy, humane, and positive things which have so contributed to the transforming of the face of the earth? Was it because they were university men? Alas, their universities then were steeped in secularism, as morally paralyzed by indifferentism as so many universities are now. Was it because they were young and therefore eager for ideals and new directions? Ah, you well know the answer to that question: even the young early come to terms with the evil in the world, and new directions, especially when they call for heroic idealism, readily yield to old and easy patterns of indolent neglect. Most of the contemporaries of Ozanam were caught up in revolutions, to be sure, but, then as now, they were often revolutions hostile to the disciplines of divine faith and to the humane use of freedom which must characterize the sons of God. Was it because they were French or the sons of traditionally Catholic families, or *modern* in their interests? But there were scores of others as *modern* as they; there were thousands from devout families, Catholic in a certain narrow and rather tribal sense; there were millions of other Frenchmen, but all these did nothing. Ozanam and his university associates did what they did because they were Frenchmen who loved their civilization and understood its debt to and dependence on Christian Revelation; they were Catholics who saw in the Faith not a personal preserve, a mere family heritage like the inherited titles of their fathers or the jeweled trinkets and ancestral brocades of their mothers, but a fire let down from heaven to purify them and be spread by them; a leaven entrusted to them in order that, thanks to them, it might energize the full mass of human society; a pearl of price greater than any known in the shops of Place Vendome or the ballrooms of Versailles, a pearl for which one risks all and with the luster of which one can illumine the lives of millions, enriching their ideas, loves, and strivings.

Finally, they accomplished what they did, and we who cherish faith and freedom are forever in their debt, in no small part because they were fortunate in their spiritual directors. We cannot overemphasize the part of intelligent and dedicated priests in arousing Ozanam and his friends to their intellectual and moral responsibilities. Some of those priests were later open to justified criticism because of certain extravagances that came to characterize their preaching as, in their passionate love for the Church and zeal for souls, they sought to bring about the triumph of the gospel in the hearts of their contemporaries. When they erred, it was on the side of the angels; Mother Church has never so criticized their doctrinal contentions as to obscure her appreciation of their personal merits and their apostolic aspirations.

Neither can we exaggerate our indebtedness to the prelates who, like the Archbishop of Paris, gave their personal encouragement and official patronage to university students eager to translate the social doctrine of the gospel into practice. Above all, modern times are indebted to such prelates for the pastoral care with which they placed effective priests where they could work with university students. If there is example for lay intellectuals in the thought and action of Frédéric Ozanam and his friends, there is also example for the hierarchy in the thought and action of those prelates and priests who instructed, encouraged, and supported the efforts of Ozanam and his associates to be intellectuals in the pattern of that Incarnate Word of God Who debated in the Temple, argued in marketplaces, recreated with the children, tarried with the sick, suffered with the imprisoned, consorted with the sinners, worked with the saints, made Himself at home with the poor, gave Himself to the rich and died with the outcast—all that He might bear His witness both by the word of truth and the act of the generous hand, *in opere et veritate*.

Not long ago one of the most thoughtful of the men in the United Nations, the spokesman of a nation poor in material resources but rich in wisdom, spoke of the need of the hour if civilization is to survive and to prosper. He addressed himself

162

to the *great powers* who were then, as always, seeking to impress one another with the inventories of their respective physical forces. He ventured to describe other resources which must ultimately be put into play if the good society is to be any more than a mirage, a *douce chimère*. He said, in summary effect: Material force by itself, no matter how overwhelming, is interesting and important only insofar as it may prove a means to bringing about a condition in which spiritual and intellectual values can begin to operate again; otherwise it is of no significance. Sooner or later, when you have finished your bombing, your armament production, and all your marshaling of physical forces, there must be a penetration of minds by minds and spirits by spirits. This means that the future belongs not to those who have the most trains or the most machinery, but to those who have the most ideas. It means that over and above your stockpiles you must have a cultural and spiritual message so profound, so true, so universal that it will satisfy the souls of men everywhere and make them forgive you your rich supplies and your privileged resources.

The question, therefore, which confronts us is not who has this bomb or the other, but who can develop a type of person who will sum up in his character such qualities of understanding and of humility, of truth, of humor, of moral stature, of strength and resourcefulness of mind, of pregnant ideas, of universal sympathy, of capacity for friendship and love that he will be admired and respected even by those who might otherwise have every reason to hate him.

This is a description of the kind of intellectuals that Frédéric Ozanam and his friends aspired to be. It is a description of the kind of men who do promptly whatever good deed their hands may find to do. It is a description of university men and women who do not dwell in ivory towers and are not the prisoners of their own privileges, but who understand and implement the double vocation of the Christian intellectual, the aspect of *intellectual truth* and the aspect of *charitable action*, the truth of *faith* that motivates effective action, the *works* without which faith is dead and all teaching is vain. It is a description of university men and women in Ozanam's pattern of the Christ Who came into the world "to bear witness to the truth", but Who is described by Scripture as One Who "went about doing good". I pray God it is a description of you and of your generation of intellectuals; the future of both faith and freedom demands that it be.

XVI

The Place of the Laity in the Church

This is the Silver Jubilee Convention of the Women's Retreat Movement. It is, therefore, twenty-five years that the retreat movement has been serving the Church by preparing women to understand their proper and effective place in the life and the action of that supernatural society in which the Spirit, breathing where it will, prepares us for eternity, the destiny of free, spiritual beings.

Against the background of this Jubilee and of the part retreats play in preparing the laity (and the rest of us) to understand and discharge our duties in the life of the Church, it is good for us to consider the role of the laity in the Church and the relationship of the lay retreat movement to this question.

The place of the laity in the life of the Church is a theme on many lips and on the pens of many writers at the moment. It is a phrase behind which there is tremendous hope for the Church, the Kingdom of God, and also for human society, influenced as society *must be* by the laity—and influenced for the better as society *will be* when the laity have understood and accepted their full place in the life and the action of the Church.

Some of the debate about the place of the laity in the life of the Church may be out of focus. If the Church were a sociological phenomenon or a debating society, a cultural movement or a political entity, then much of this debate might be valid. But one finds scant justification for the suggestion that the Church is notably any of these. The Church is, as a matter of fact, a *theological* entity. It is a spiritual society, a supernatural

This address was delivered at the Hilton Hotel, Chicago, Illinois, on August 17, 1962, on the occasion of the Twelfth National Congress of the National Laywomen's Retreat Movement.

force at work in history; therefore, presumably, it is governed by different laws and standards than those which govern sociological movements, cultural patterns, or political societies. I would like to see the debate about the place of the laity in the life of the Church based on a solid premise of the theology of the matter.

When theology again becomes the center of the present debate, when the laity is playing a part, well-grounded on theological premises, in the Church's essential work—the work of witnessing to Jesus Christ teaching His truth—then, only, will debate about other matters come into proper focus.[1] In the meantime one is, of course, gratefully aware of the enormous part played by laymen and laywomen in the *organized* action of the Church within history. However, without the *organic* life of the Church, even the organized action can become mere action—merely sociological, merely cultural, merely temporal—and in grave danger of lacking eternal implications or eternal fruit. We could be wonderfully organized, wonderfully active, and yet accomplish little or nothing enduring and supernatural, though we would all be holding the places to which we had been appointed or elected and the organization, the sociological structure, would be intact— intact but mechanical.

It is only when we relate our thinking about the place of the laity in the Church to the concept of the supernatural nature of the Church—its spiritual mission, its relationship to eternity, therefore, its theological aspects—that we begin to get Catholic lay action and all the work of the Church in proper focus.

First of all, we have a few words to define. The immediate word is *role*. Role means a task or a function. *Church*: Church *means* that historic body of living people, baptized and professing the Faith, who are in communion with the organization established by Christ and the organism that derives from His very life. *Laity*: this is the most difficult of all to define; but in its common usage, it refers to those people who are neither clergy nor religious.

Now let's go back to the concept of *the Church*. What is the Church for? The Church was instituted by our Lord and Savior Jesus Christ to continue the work which He did while He was here on earth—the work of *teaching*, the work of *guiding* (which has slid into the word *ruling*), and the work of *sanctification*. In other words, the Church is the extension of the Incarnation. That is why Saint Paul refers to the Church as Christ's Body. It exists to maintain and to spread the teachings of Christ in the world, and to safeguard and use those means to salvation which Christ provided.

It must be obvious from even so elementary a definition of the Church that knowledge of religious truth, life lived in accordance with that truth, plus the sacraments to fortify our efforts, are the means of grace whereby men are saved. What matters then for everlasting life is not so much that one is a priest, a nun, a brother *or* a lay person, as that one is a member of the Church—a baptized Christian who receives and puts to work, nourished by the sacraments, the Faith revealed in, through, and by Jesus Christ, preserved and communicated by His Body which is the Holy Catholic Church. There is no essential difference, so far as being a member of the Church is concerned, between one member and another.

Perhaps we would get a further understanding of the role of the laity in the life of the Church were we to ask: *What is the role of the clergy in the life of the Church?* No one seems to run into any difficulty or obscurity here. Their role is in a special way *to serve*. The bishops, in union with the pope, have as the successors of the apostles the duty of teaching the Christian Faith; they have the duty of governing the Christian flock, and they have the duty of sanctifying others and themselves by their ministry at the altar and in administering the sacraments. Note this carefully: The role of the clergy in the life of the Church is what we would call in TV quiz shows a *service role*. If their role is understood in any other way by anybody, especially by themselves, they are misunderstood and to that extent they are distorted.

Now there are certain clerical functions, certain service functions, which the clergy perform and which are of divine origin and depend on divine *orders*. Others are not. For example, the celebration of the holy sacrifice of the Mass requires holy orders. Other functions do not; they are historical developments. But even the specially reserved and ordained functions are not meant to separate the clergy from the laity in the Church; it is simply a question of *functions* and vocations being separate.

The pope and the bishops in union with the pope are teachers in the Church by divine appointment. This does not mean that every bishop is a learned theologian. As a matter of fact, it is perfectly possible and desirable that lay people be accomplished theologians. Wilfrid Ward, one of the members of the remarkable Ward family in England, was a professor of dogmatic theology at a leading English seminary, Saint Edmund's College, for years. He was also a layman. The fact that laymen *could*, *should*, and—it is my hope—*will* increasingly know as much theology as they can study does not alter the fact that it is the business by *divine appointment* of the bishop to *teach*, even if he personally has to consult first with theologians who are not bishops (as he would often be well advised to do in order to exercise his divinely appointed function intelligibly and intelligently).

Knowledge of theology is not essentially for the clergy only, any more than holiness is for the clergy only. The pope is called the Holy Father for reasons associated with his office as the custodian of the Church, as the chief shepherd of the Church through which holiness is dispensed. But this does not mean that *my* father is supposed to be unholy. These phrases do not touch the heart of the matter so far as *membership* in the Church is concerned.

These reflections on the role of the clergy should throw light on our understanding of the role of the laity in the life of the Church. The Church is a *unity* consisting of a single Body. In apostolic times Saint Paul told how among the members of the Church there was diversity of operations, a diversity of offices, a diversity of ministries, but one single Spirit at work in all. This is the *theological* fact. We should have a deeper, more aware consciousness of our being members of the Body of Christ than we have of our special functions or roles (either as laity or clergy) in that Body.

So this discussion might well center on the *sacraments* because it is not a degree from college, nor an election to a parish committee, that gives us our place in the life of the Church—it is *baptism*. *It is baptism which gives us our life in the Church.* The sacrament of holy orders gives us a place in the life of the Church different from the place matrimony gives us, for example, but the place that matrimony gives us is a very real place in the life of the Church. Confirmation gives us an enormously important place in the life of the Church. No one can even comprehend, let alone state, the place given us in the life of the Church by the Eucharist worthily received.

Since the Church is a supernatural society, no one who understands the full implications of the effects of baptism, confirmation, Holy Eucharist, and the sacrament of matrimony can take as supremely important discussions on the place of the laity in the life of the Church that center on matters which are secondary and subordinate operations of the Church in the community; for example, who sets this policy, who buys this piece of real estate, who does this or that other service.

It is clearly more important to have been baptized than it is to have been ordained. Baptism should have such an over-whelming effect that we should be aware of it all the days of our lives—aware that we are Christians, baptized in Christ. The glorious fact of having been reborn in Christ should color all our concepts of the Church and our place in it for the rest of our lives. We should understand that nothing happening to us subsequently could be of greater significance than that moment of baptism. No bishop in his right mind would suppose that his consecration to *do* a job was more important than the day of his baptism to *be* a Christian. It is more important *to be* than it is to be something particular, and baptism is the sacrament by which *we are*—by which we acquire *being* on the level of Jesus Christ. Have you some aspiration beyond the level of Jesus Christ? Could a pope? Could a Dame of Malta?

We began to be in the Church when we received the sacrament of baptism. From then on we took on functions. All our jobs have their radical significance from the effect of that initial baptism. If one's subsequent calling is that of a housemaid and she discharges her duties, under the influence of her initial baptism, better and in more holy a fashion than he discharges his calling who had the office of a bishop, who will be the one more likely to be saved? Who will have the more perfect place, the more certain place in the Church Triumphant for which we are all preparing or we are not alive in the Church?

We might say then that every member of the Church has a twofold calling. He has his calling as a Christian and then has his works—that of being a farmer or a farmer's wife; a mechanic or a mechanic's wife; a jockey or a jockey's wife; a lawyer, a housekeeper, or a housekeeper's husband; a nurse, a secretary, or a secretary's boss; a priest, a bishop. When he is a priest, when he is a bishop, when he or she is a religious, there is a clear relation between these two vocations. But so also work done in the world, for the layman or laywoman, the second calling should be intimately bound up with the first; it is the role that God wants one to take in the history of our times, and in the sanctifying of our society, and in the building of the Kingdom of God on earth. So we should talk of the *many roles* of the laity in the Church, not *the role* of the laity in the Church. One layman has the role of being premier of France and as premier of France has had a role in the plans of God. Who will say whether that role is greater or less, eternity-wise, than the role of a specific clergyman somewhere in France? Another has a role as a mother. Is there anyone who has so lost sight of the heart of the matter that he does not understand the titanic place in the life of the Church played by that convert from Methodism who was the mother of the Vaughans?

She wasn't on any diocesan committee. She didn't wear the cape or medal of any order of chivalry. But she gave the Church a cardinal, an archbishop, a Jesuit son—and she gave the Church, in addition to these, other holy people among her other sons and daughters and those whom they in turn influenced.

Would you say that she was merely a passive participant in the life of the parish? She was never made to feel intimately identified with the administration of the Church. She was never consulted on points of policy. The prelates never knocked on her door to discover what she thought on one of the great issues of the hour. There was no democratic consultation of her rich experience in the planning work of the Church. What was her place in the life of the Church?

Or take the place of Thomas More, a layman in the life of the Church. Can you imagine seriously debating whether the place of Thomas More in the life of the Church would have been greater if there had been an election held in the parish or the diocese so that he could be closer to parish policy or closer to diocesan administration! Do you know any prelate, any priest, who seriously thinks he has a greater place in the true life of the Kingdom of God on earth than Thomas More—a layman? The call, the basic call, is the one which Jesus uttered in these lines, "Be you therefore perfect."[2] This is addressed to drugstore clerks, to astronauts, to bishops, to housewives, parents, and lay brothers.

There are, thank God, many laymen and women who feel called to take a yet-more-active part in the apostolate, the organized life and work of the Church as, for example, writers, school-teachers, Catholic Action workers, lay missionaries, lawyers, consultants on matters of technical nature. This is good, holy, and necessary—but it is all *over and above*; if people

171

view such activities as *that which* gives them their true place in the life of the Church, then they are wide of the mark as to what should be their basic relationship to Christ. That we are in the Church is of far greater importance than any post we hold in the Church. That we are children of the Church and members of one another, vivified by a single spirit, is of far greater importance than what we do on the secondary level— the temporal and historic order of one or another specific task.

When you hear talk about clericalism and anticlericalism, you are hearing talk that is symptomatic of the fact that the sense of Christian community has broken down, and it is important to find out why. The unity which should constitute the single Body of Jesus Christ is somehow and somewhere missing. When I say therefore that we should approach this question of place in the Church *theologically* instead of *administratively*, *culturally*, or *politically*, I don't mean that we should necessarily study more about the Faith. Learning more about the Faith means, for most of us, that we should buy more books and get more information. That isn't the point at all. The point is that we should be aware of the basic theology of our baptism and the consequences of it; our holy orders, if we have those; our matrimony, if we have that; our confirmation and the mandate that came with it; in the absence of either holy orders or matrimony, the Eucharist and the specific sacraments by which we are sustained to keep the promises which were ours in baptism and to respond to the calls to perfection, whatever our walk in life, which have come to us since.

Sometimes we hear, "Well, I think I understand all this, but I want the voice of the laity to be heard more, and I want the voice of the laity to be considered on many matters on which it is not now consulted."

That's fine, provided that clergy and laity alike are functioning within that single spirit of which Saint Paul speaks, and provided that their activity is based on the theological premise of the true nature of the Church, and their true relationship to it.

Membership in the Church is itself a sacred state. Christians,

172

precisely as Christians, belong to a sacred order. There is the reason why so much of this talk about men in sacred orders and the laity can be misleading even when true. It seems to be implied that men in sacred orders are the only ones in a sacred state, and the laity are purely secular. The importance, the self-consciousness, of being a baptized Christian is the concept we must get back into focus. Then there will be plenty of time to talk about the sociological, the cultural, political, and administrative problems.

To sum up: Let us stop arguing about which *jobs* or functions in the Church are important and focus on the great work of Christ in which all, clergy and laity, must play a united part. The Church of Christ is a single, living organism. It has its organization, and within this organization there are different functions. Saint Paul, as we noted, called these a diversity of ministries and of offices, but he insisted on the single unity of all who make up the Church.

When people are more conscious of their function than they are of the fact that they are identified with Jesus Christ through baptism, the basic and essential sacrament, then someone is missing the point. The contemporary excessive self-consciousness of being either a layman, a clergyman, or a religious has an unhealthy element to it. We should be so conscious of being baptized members of Christ that we see all our diverse functions and offices within the Church as secondary and subordinate, however high or low they may be; otherwise, we will prove worthless in our particular works.

It is more important on the last day to have been a member of the Church, worthy of our baptismal salt, than to have been elected or appointed to any specific place in the hierarchy or "lower-archy".

And I submit that the Lay Retreat Movement is the most important single organization preparing all of us—bishops and batboys—for a Christian understanding of what it is to be a member of Jesus Christ *in any capacity*—the sublime dignity of being a member of Christ in the Church.

173

XVII

The Place of Work in Religious Life

In view of the fact that we are concerned with the formation of sisters, who in increasing degree will be concerned with the formation of yet other uncounted thousands of people who, in their turn, will be concerned with no small part of the formation of the image of the Church itself within and beyond the limits of our country, as the Church will be concerned with the formation of civilization—in view of all this, what we say here is of ricocheting significance.

According to your own formation of outlook and motivation, and of patterns consistent with both, so will be the formation of hundreds of teachers; according to their formation, so will be the formation of thousands of students; according to their formation, so will be the formation of a segment of the Church and of a period, perhaps, of civilization. It is well, then, that we address ourselves only to *essentials*, to basic principles and to basic problems.

I cheerfully take it for granted that one so skilled in the arts of formation as is Father Gambari has focused your attention on the essential *principles*. I should like this morning to address your attention to two basic *problems*.

The problems can be stated in terms of two words around which they swing. I state these two words in the conviction that the issues and questions which revolve about them are the essential problems of religious life in our time—in all probability, the stumbling blocks on which the success of the work frequently stumbles. In any case, they are the points on which we must focus attention if we are to do what God and His

This address was delivered at Mount Mercy—now, Carlow—College, Pittsburgh, Pennsylvania, on August 20, 1962, at the Sisters' Formation Workshop in Spirituality.

people expect of us in this particular moment of history and in this part of the world.

The two words to which I direct your attention are the words *work* and *person*. We shall speak of the first in this present conference, and of the second at the eleven o'clock conference.

First of all, the *work*. The great problem connected with the work at the moment is the problem of how we will match *spiritual* progress and maturity with *intellectual* progress and maturity in the education of religious. Stated in terms of the work, this becomes, I think, the following problem—perhaps one of the great unresolved problems of almost all our religious orders, certainly of all religious orders founded prior to the twentieth century. The problem may be stated in these simple terms: How will those charged with the formation of our religious personnel inculcate and encourage that *personal involvement in the work* which is indispensable to its being effectively done and, at the same time, preserve that *detachment in the work* which is indispensable for the salvation of the soul of the religious?

We can state this problem the other way around; it is a problem that runs both ways, and stated either way it is equally true. How will we develop a spirit of religious *detachment in the work* while at the same time inculcating and encouraging that *professional involvement in the work* without which the work will not be done as it must be done in our civilization and against the competition that we have?

This is the problem of the *work*. If it is not clear to you, as a religious superior, that such a problem exists, then I ask you at your earliest possible convenience to resign your present post because you are standing in the way not only of the progress of your community and of its work, but in the way of Jesus Christ. I repeat the problem: How can you inculcate and encourage *professional involvement in the work* to be done, and at the same time inculcate and preserve *religious detachment in the doing of the work*? Or, to state it the other way around for those

175

who think that by placing something first you therefore give it a priority of importance: How can you inculcate and preserve *religious detachment*, as all are agreed we must, and yet at the same time inculcate and encourage *professional involvement* in the work—which involvement is indispensable if the work is to be done with the excellence and the competence required if we are to meet our competition and to do what Jesus Christ expects of us in this generation?

How to inculcate, how to encourage professional involvement in the work, whether it be hospital work, whether it be teaching, whether it be the teaching of a specific subject, whether it be social work, whether it be retreat work, whatever it may be—and yet preserve religious detachment? Here is the central, the basic, problem confronting all religious communities in our time. The problem has revealed itself in many different ways; most of us were still young when we first noted that it was revealing itself. Those of us educated under some great religious communities detected, even when we were young people, the sometimes cruel effort to keep a dichotomy between these two objectives—competent *involvement* in the work, and *detachment*.

When it occurred to us as students that some of our professors were teaching subjects simply and only because assigned to them under obedience, the reaction of many was "What a hideous way to treat *learning!*" As we grew older and began to have some idea of the mind of the Church, we began to say, "What a hideous way to treat *obedience!*" As years went by, one said, "What a tragic waste of talent and appalling waste of good will—*both* the gifts of God", and one began to think "What a hideous way to treat *God!*"

One remembers, sometimes with tears, teachers admirably prepared to teach religion, Latin, poetry, history, or science but assigned to teach other subjects than those for which they were prepared—and sometimes merely on a misreading of the spiritual principle *agere contra*. What dreadful waste! Even—let's

176

put the proper word on it—*sinful* waste. The fact that the work was done under obedience doubtlessly removes the element of sin from the worker—but does it from the superior? In all charity, one can only hope so!

So, to resolve this first and basic problem, a problem we all share, dioceses as well as religious communities, suppose we begin by agreeing, as I hope we will, that the most important question with respect to the work is that the work—precisely as a work—be well done, be in itself, as nearly as we can make it, a tribute worthy of the God for whom the work is done, a work consistent with the fullest possible realization of the God-given talents and aspirations of those by whom the work is done. Only when we agree on this will we not be afraid of encouraging personal involvement in the work, of emphasizing how important it is that the work be well done.

To do this, we must be on guard in our spiritual direction against any misreading of phrases in our rule and customs books which may have had meaning in the eighteenth century when many of these were first written. When, for example, a whole class of ardent, dedicated, God-inspired religious in the course of a profession ceremony announce, "We rejoice to be dead to the world", what does that phrase mean? "Dead to the world. . . ." When we were children, my mother used to tiptoe upstairs in the evening to see if the younger children had fallen off to sleep. She'd come down to say, "They're all right—they're *dead to the world*!" Is that what we want? Would we really rejoice if we had X number of sleeping sisters on our hands? If so, the grounds for rejoicing are limited!

Now you and I know what this phrase means; we know exactly what it means. But it is asking too much of human nature to expect that citizens of the civilization around us are going to know what it means. They will try by every means at their disposition to render themselves immune against people who are suspected of taking *seriously* what superficially, at least, the words seem to mean. One is not asking that the words be dropped; one is not suggesting that the meaning of the words is out of order, or heretical, or wrong. But it must be understood and made clear that they are paradoxical, at least as pledges of espousal to Him Who said, "I am come that they may have life and have it more abundantly."[1]

I am only asking that the planning of the work be done on the assumption that although *dead to the world* our religious are *alive* to the work of the Kingdom of God. They are dead to the world, as Jesus died, but very shortly later that He might rise to a new and much more glorious life, a transformed and glorified life, a life that, once dead, dies no more. It is important, then, that our concept of the religious life not end on the note of *death*. To the *work* there must be brought *life*; to the *work* there must be brought *love*; to the *work* there must be brought *commitment*, as the contemporary phrase has it; to the *work* there must be brought *involvement*—intense involvement. Wherefore, the traditional mystical phrases must be given meaning within the context of the need that the work be *alive* and *loving* and *dedicated*.

But this, too, can be perilous. When we become involved, when we become personally and professionally engaged, there is the danger that we may lose the detachment necessary to the life of a religious. Every superior, every bishop, every provincial knows this—or knows nothing. What to do?

The time-honored formula by which the rules and customs of religious life in the Holy Catholic Church protect us against involvement becoming *ivory-towered* and against engagement becoming eccentric is, of course, summed up in the word *detachment*. Perhaps, then, the key to the problem lies in a refreshed understanding of what we are to mean by the word *detachment* and hence the responsibility of those who, in the early years of the religious formation of future sisters, must school them in *detachment*.

This need not be done by inhibiting the desire to excel, which is essential to competence; nor by eighteenth-century talk about *contempt of the world*—including in this, presumably, contempt for the work that they are themselves doing in the world—but by a positive understanding of what we mean by *detachment*. We must inculcate *detachment* as it has been understood perennially, so that we mean the same thing by *detachment* that Jesus Christ meant, as revealed by what He *did* and by what He *said*.

What, then, in this context, do we mean by *detachment*, the detachment which we must nurture in our religious if they are to be protected in that professional involvement which they must have if they are to be worthy of the work and if the work is to be worthy of God? I submit that the most effective understanding of detachment will be found in positive, rather than negative, terms. That understanding is not suggested to any girl born in this century by words like *contempt of the world* unless such phrases are carefully explained. The phrase *contempt of the world* is an easily misleading translation of the original Latin; there is not the same overtone of *contempt* that is now present when we say that a thing is *contemptible* or that So-and-So is a *contemptuous person*. The word must be understood in terms not of disdaining exclusion, rejection or repudiation, but in terms of a *hierarchy* of values.

This concept of detachment that we must develop in ourselves and seek to communicate to others is set forth admirably by Ida von Coudenhove in *The Nature of Sanctity* and by specific example of her book on Saint Elizabeth of Hungary. In the essay on *The Nature of Sanctity*, Ida von Coudenhove points out that detachment does not consist in destroying the capacity for love in one's heart—that is, love for whatever is good, true, and beautiful. It does not consist in *inhibiting* knowledge or love; it certainly does not consist in these when what a religious loves is the *work* or the *skills* needed to do the work competently and well. Detachment consists not in diminishing the enthusiasms or talents one may have; it can consist, rather, in developing these in full and healthy measure—and then having

179

a love for God that transcends all measure. It consists in loving the work to the very limit and top of my heart, and then loving God with a love that overflows my heart; but it does not consist in attempting to live the fallacy that can only lead to a schizoid spirituality, the lie that I must *love* God but hold His *work* in *contempt*. This is a fraud, and the fraud is not sanctified or redeemed by dressing it up in pious talk.

Detachment should consist in loving the work—every minute of it—and in desiring to do it ever more perfectly precisely because it is the work that God gave me talents to do. It should consist in seeking perfection in the doing of the work and in one's self as the doer of the work, but in recognizing that the work, though sublime, is, of course, less sublime than God.

But the work is not, on that account, *contemptible*. It is glorious because it is the work of God, and it merits my enthusiasm because it is work God called me to do; the spread of His Kingdom may depend on how well and competently I do it; for even though, of course, the eternal Kingdom of God transcends any temporal work that I do, nonetheless by my work I become a *part* of the eternal work of God! Thus understood as a sublime means to an even more sublime end, the work calls for performance with all my heart, while recognizing that I do it contingently, contingent on the pleasure, the will, and the Providence of God.

Consider in this connection what was the essence of the sin of our first parents. Was their guilt in that they failed to *despise*, to hold in *contempt*, the Garden of Eden in which God placed them? Not at all. They had been called to stewardship over all the things of the earth and were commanded to bring the things of the earth to even greater perfection in the service and glory of God. The sin of our first parents was not that they loved the things that God gave them, the gifts that they had. Their sin arose from the fact that they forgot from Whom they had their gifts. They were *ungrateful* for the gifts which they had received, and they failed to use them in accordance with the purposes for which God had given them. Their sin began with *ingratitude*, the sin suggested by the phrase of the serpent: "You shall be as gods"; that is to say, you should use all you have as if they were all from and for yourselves. [2]

Now, had they used the delights of the Garden of Eden, the Garden itself, with *detachment*, that is to say, with full appreciation of all the wonders which were theirs but with constant reference in gratitude and humility to the God from whom they had them, they would have them still—and we, too, would have them.

It would not have been *detachment* for our first parents to pretend that they did *not* possess their privileged powers, if they had said, falsely and hypocritically, "We are creatures more stupid than the ass, more crawling than the serpent." But it would have been *detachment* to use their gifts gratefully, fully consistent with the purpose God implanted in the things themselves.

And so *detachment* consists in *loving* the work, in *perfecting* ourselves to do the work with excellence second to none, knowing more Latin than the Latin teacher at the corresponding secular school, writing poetry more sublime than the poet in the nearest beatnik coffee-klatch, studying or teaching whatever it may be our talent to study or to teach to the full limit of our ability. *Detachment* would result in our differing from the secularist, not in competence, God forbid, nor in the desire to excel, but in our having a love for Almighty God and a dedication to His purposes so transcendental that however excelling our love for the work be, it would seem *relatively* as nothing. We don't *think* it's nothing, but our love for God should be so great and our dedication so great as to make anything else immeasurably less.

Our need, then—it is also a great need of the age—is the development of the *Christian humanism*, or *humanism of the Incarnation*, which, avoiding any false dichotomy between love for God and love for the work, as if these were Cartesian parallels which never meet, tries to recognize that these fuse in Jesus Christ and in a hierarchy of values within which all things take on, in addition to the natural value they have as creatures of God, a new and greater value by being caught up in the eternal and supernatural purposes of God.

Within such a hierarchy of values we can talk cogently of detachment because within it we can talk of the life that does not die and of the life that is merely transient and which we must therefore use fully while we have it, lest by neglecting it we lose also the life that does not die. But talking of the one as *life* and the other as *death*; talking of the one as *alone* to be desired, instead of *supremely* to be desired, and of the other as *contemptible* instead of as a *great good* needed to achieve a *greater good*, is obviously misleading. Such talk may have had, in the mentality of the eighteenth century, some meaning, but what that meaning may have been is largely a recondite footnote point in the history of spirituality and of culture.

Living in other times and cultures, we must weigh the implications for our own generation of phrases like those. When we ask our novices and postulants to hold *anything* in contempt, let us go to the trouble to tell them the history of the word; after all, they may take us seriously; then you will have depressed cases on your hands! They may decide that they are themselves contemptible; then it may cost you twenty-five dollars an hour for them to talk it over with a psychoanalyst who will try to get them back to the moment before they first decided they were contemptible. But an analyst cannot teach them the value they have; however, you *can* and *must* teach them their value when you teach them why sisters are so important to God's work, so significant to His purposes, so eager for excellence professionally as well as spiritually.

Our *detachment* will be sound and positive if we remember that "God so loved the world that He sent His only-begotten Son".[3] Thank God *this* was written when it was, and not in the nineteenth century! God held the world in no contempt. He

182

thought it "no rapine"—how shall we translate that wonderful phrase of Saint Paul?—He thought it no *violence* to Himself but entirely worthwhile to *empty Himself* in order that He might redeem this world which we sometimes pretend must be held in *contempt* or considered as naught.[4]

An example. Was there ever given a spiritual conference on the vanity of work which did not tell the story of Saint Thomas' final (alleged) evaluation of his own work for the Church? Consider the magnitude of that work, the passion with which it was done. Remember all his years of teaching at the University of Paris, all his goings about to talk at the learned meetings. But when Saint Thomas was dying, he said, "*I count it all but straw.*" Well, as contrasted with eternity, no doubt. Then, too, he was dying, and he was terribly tired. He had worked hard, and he had a right to talk with battle fatigue on the threshold of eternity. And whatever he said, *we* know that it *wasn't* straw. It's the straw which, with the books of Revelation, built the foundations of Christian civilization. It is not mere straw—whatever he said on his deathbed, on a hot day in Italy, in the late hours of the afternoon. If he had thought it straw in the novitiate, there would have been no Saint Thomas Aquinas, and where would you Dominicans be now?

It was not straw! But oh, the way that line has been misused! Another example: one often deplores the way that the poor Curé of Ars has been used in some seminaries as if it were desired that the boys be stupid because allegedly the Curé of Ars was. Altogether too much has been made of the alleged incompetence of the Curé of Ars. One wishes all stupid people worked as hard as he did! It would be a great cheer if all those who take pleasure in his supposed stupidity heard confessions as effectively and for as many hours as he did. Moreover, he was not all that stupid; I went to Ars once upon a time and I saw not only his confessional but also his library. I wish every priest coming out of the seminary had a proportionate library!

But my point is only that superiors must be careful about

any effort to make holy capital out of examples or remarks that are irrelevant to the basic call, a call that we be saints, of course; that the Lord God be first served, of course; but also a call that we be competent, that the work be beautifully done, proudly done, done with holy pride—albeit with detachment, the detachment of people who love the work quite as much as the children of the world love the work, but who have another Love that purges, sanctifies, redeems, motivates, energizes, and perfects that lesser love with which our work is done—please God, to His glory and to the service of His people.

XVIII

The Human Person in Religious Life

During the brief intermission between our two encounters, some religious were kind enough to bring to my attention some lugubrious phrases from their ceremonies that I did not mention but against which we should well be on our guard. I would like to underscore that Providence has impartially distributed among them the number of misleading phrases in the rituals of our religious; they are not limited to any single tradition. As a matter of fact, there has been a certain holy rivalry as to who could come up with the most misleading phrases, and it is an open question as to who has won!

We speak now of the second great problem in the effectiveness of our religious communities in the middle of the twentieth century. We are, of course, limiting ourselves to discussion of two problems only because we are limited to two talks. We are not pretending that these are the *only* two problems; nor are we pretending that we have *only* problems. We are aware of the heroic accomplishments of religious in the middle of the twentieth century. Indeed, were it not for their tremendous potential and actual accomplishments it would not be worth our while to talk about the problems that stand in the way. We are underscoring two problems which our religious communities share across the board with one another and over the board with religious communities of men, with dioceses and the universal Church. Indeed the Church shares them with everything functioning in the middle of the twentieth century. This is particularly true of the second problem.

This address was delivered at Mount Mercy—now, Carlow—College, Pittsburgh, Pennsylvania, on August 20, 1962, at the Sisters' Formation Workshop in Spirituality.

The first problem, you will remember, was how are we going to promote the *work* which, when each of us is dead and gone and all of us are judged, is the thing which will have mattered. We decided that we will best protect the work if we inculcate at one and the same time professional *competence*, the desire to excel in the work, the aspiration to do the work excellently, on one hand, and, on the other, *detachment* understood in positive terms which inhibit nothing but sin. The latitude thus allowed is wide indeed. It is not true, as the Jansenists supposed, that the vast majority of things which the decent wish to do are somehow touched with sin and that professional competence and a consciousness of being competent are necessarily a sign of or conducive to depravity and damnation.

Our second problem is concerned with the *person*. We live in a civilization which constitutes an open conspiracy against the survival of personality. We Americans like to point out that the rest of the world has fallen victim to regimentation, to collectivism or totalitarianism or other depersonalizing forces which subordinate the individual person to the collective entity, whether it be the class, as in communism, or the state, as in fascism—fascism of the black shirt of Mussolini, the brown shirt of Hitler, or whatever color shirt the Spanish Falangists wear. We like to talk as if collectivism were the disease of other parts of the world and as if we who live in a democracy do not suffer from it at all.

Directly opposite my office downtown, as if to provide me with a permanent reminder that we may not be as immune to depersonalizing as we suppose, they are now building an IBM machine building. The IBM machine (with all its other and undeniable advantages) may be a bit of a symbol of the extent to which our civilization, too, can, in its mechanism and standardization, *depersonalize*! Someone not long ago wrote a facetious essay in which he pointed out how many *numbers* a child has by the time he enters college. The only conclusion one could draw from the article is that most men, if they wish to survive in our civilization, are better advised to remember their numbers than they are to remember their personal *names*. Now their names they received as *persons* in baptism, although even in the Holy Catholic Church, if they live in highly organized parishes, they have numbers from baptism on. When they are old enough to get one of the children's collection boxes they have a number. They enter school with numbers, and the description of them is reduced to numbers, including their I.Q. A singularly pathetic paragraph in one of those horrible news stories about the tragic end of Marilyn Monroe said that all her beauty and personality had suddenly been reduced to six numbers on a tag that the coroner tied on her foot. She was case number such and such, she was in coroner's box number such and such, on slab such and such, tier such and such. He seemed to think that there was something particularly tragic about this. Well, it's the tragedy of everybody in America. They all have social service numbers; they all have draft-board numbers and numbers of every conceivable species so that they can be processed conveniently through IBM machines without any reference to personal considerations. The least important thing about anyone now is often his name; the increasingly important thing is where he fits on punched cards.

Not long ago I was worried about the *case*, as we say, of a singularly attractive and talented little girl who came to my attention through a diocesan institution. To get the background on her and to see how I could be helpful, I called the agency which had referred her to our institution. I asked if they would send me the file on this girl. The top paper in the file looked like those notices I get from the bank telling me that I am overdrawn. It is punched with holes; some places are black or grey; some patterns went one way and some another. With it came a note that said, "This you will be unable to decipher." (It is now so controlled that only a couple of experts know what it is.) "You will be unable to decipher this report on Joanne; however, our worker will be very happy to interpret it for you."

Something like the *Book of Mormon* or Mrs. Eddy's *Science and Health*—you cannot make head or tail out of it if you read it yourself, but if you get one of the adepts, he can tell you what it means.

I couldn't imagine anything I cared to know about that child that could possibly be in that confounded record. It takes an IBM machine for the filing of these records according to their categories, but it was very important to get this child out of a category to find out what made her significant and possibly find out what God had in mind when He made her.

Now you and I are guilty of the more terrible sin when we go along with this hideous business. Because, of course, we tell the children that God had a particular purpose for making every single one of them. If this be true, then why are we so eager to standardize them? Why do we settle so readily for these median groupings, percentiles, and similar scientific categories dreamed up by people, frightened of immediate contact with persons, who prefer to work with formulae, statistics, and abstractions as well as *abstracts*?

It is, then, of the first importance that we, in an age of regimentation by fascism, by collectivism, totalitarianism, and emphasis on race, class, nationality, and *types*, reaffirm the *person* as more significant than any of the categories in which persons may be classified. The problem of the survival of persons in a society so regimented and so codified is so general that I am sure that no one will misunderstand or take offense if one says that perforce in religious communities there is a kind of double-barreled danger to personality. Often the very genius of our religious patterns might lend itself to the conspiracy against the person; this is something that we early begin to detect. Sometimes the great teaching orders aspire to turn out a girl who will be recognized immediately as the product of their particular religious tradition. One has to be very careful in this connection, by the way, because one is talking about his best friends!!! So how shall we word this safely? Is there any community that bears the name of—all the good and wonderful names appear to have been exhausted—Sisters of the Holy Flag, for example? If there be, then you may be certain that their great aspiration is to turn out a typical and lovely little Holy Flag girl who will be known immediately as a Holy Flag girl wherever in the world you meet her. Holy Flag girls in Germany, Holy Flag girls in France, wherever you meet them, you can tell them: they are Holy Flag girls and nothing else. They are to bear scant resemblance to other Catholics. They are to stand out like sore thumbs.

Happily, most of the students have *beat the system*. The majority of the religious who taught them have beat the system, too, and though they were trained by the Holy Flag Sister, they remain American or Canadian but, above all, Catholic Christians. And more than they recall *the Order*, they remember Sister So-and-So. If they were really educated, somewhere a personality shows through. The most effective teacher may have been a religious, but she was a *person*.

Sometimes we get a little paranoid about this point. We think that the religious habit depersonalizes. Priests wear *uniforms*; so do army officers, so do mailmen, so do cops, so do the members of the College of Cardinals; all these are reduced to least common denominators by *habits*, by rubrics, by protocol, by rule, by a thousand things. Yet among these you remember some persons so real that they shine through it all, and you remember the person more than you remember what he or she wore. Cardinal Merry Del Val was one of these. It is easier to remember that he was a person than that he was a cardinal; I mean an ordinary cardinal. If you ever saw his picture you remember that it is impossible to find a hue of crimson so brilliant that it would tone down the luster in his eyes.[1]

So you who have the formation of sisters who will be teachers, nurses, social workers are obliged, of course, to inculcate in them the ideas of your specific community and tradition and, therefore, to impose a certain pattern; but do be careful that these are not destructive of personality. It is not the least heretical to say that there is no religious order in the world as important as a *person*. How could there be? Because there is nothing in the world as important as a person. All things in the world exist for the perfection of personality: the Church, the state, every society, secular and sacral, comes into existence for the perfection of human personality, to serve the person. You remember Saint Paul's wonderful development of that thought: "All things are yours, for you are Christ's and Christ is God's."[2] See the hierarchy of personality involved: Paul said everything belonged to the one to whom he was preaching. Cephas belongs to you, Apollo belongs to you, all belong to you. All things eternal and temporal, God Himself in a certain sense. Isn't it so?

So Saint Paul, so the Church, teaches the children. We even say, "If you were the only one who existed, the Incarnation would have taken place for you." We teach that. Is it merely talk? Everything exists for the development of personality in the pattern appointed by Christ and expounded by Saint Paul—not to make America great, not to strengthen Peru, not to promote nor even to preserve any organization for its own sake, but only as a means to the great end of the hallowing and perfection of the person.

This is not always our mentality, though it is always the idealism that gave us our original existence. Every religious founder or foundress was preoccupied with *persons*; but often we become *institutionalized*, which is probably all that is meant by the otherwise vicious remark "Every religious order should die with its founder." Can you imagine Saint Vincent de Paul giving a hoot about what anyone thought of his organized Vincentians as he went, day and night, looking for abandoned babies because each one of them was a *person*. True, he organized the congregation, the society. That's a tool. It isn't a person. It began to be at a given moment, and it will end when all of them do; but the *person* is immortal. He wrote a rule of life because that is a means to an end, an end bound up with *persons*, persons here below whom we serve, persons in the infinite and incomprehensible Godhead of Whom one became man to dwell among us so we might have driven home unforgettably and with infinite relevance the significance of a *person*.

We are made in the image and likeness of God, but it is in personality that we are the *like* of God. Pope Pius XII, so luminous on so many subjects, was especially luminous on this. What a dreadful job his was, being carried in on that portable throne, in front of fifteen, twenty, twenty-five thousand people. Now, fifteen thousand is a mob. Yet one had the feeling, not without warrant, that he was more aware of *persons* than he was of the *mob*. He would reach out to a child in the crowd, as the child is more important than the crowd. He hoped that everyone in the crowd would see in the gesture a reaching out to every one of them. He took the trouble to ask, "And from where do *you* come?" because he recognized that each one thinks it important to come from his particular place. So he went, up to within fifty hours of the time he died, still walking up and down and saying to them, "Where did *you* come from? How many children do *you* have?"

I will never forget when I had the opportunity to bring in my own father and mother. He met the fathers and mothers of ten thousand priests a year, I suppose, but I am certain that each one to this day thinks he or she respectively was the only one he ever met. He had the gift of making each person feel significant.

By way of example, and not merely of precept, Pope Pius XII spoke about the dangers to personality in much that passes for charity and social service at the moment. You can adapt this to anything else you want. You can adapt it to education, specifically. The mere size, not to say spirit, of so many colleges makes it impossible now for any teacher to know students personally. Our teachers knew every one of us by our names; they knew our good points, knew our bad points, knew our brothers, our sisters.

Today, alas, the trend is toward the college also becoming a faceless mob, a mob processed, increasingly, in and out of college by Remington Rand or IBM machines. Students do not even flunk under their own names now. Each has a number! So do hospital patients. Some years ago I was going down a corridor of a hospital, and I heard a *noise* saying to one of the nurses, "See what is troubling 605." Now, she didn't mean what I understood. But isn't it a symbol? 605 could have been known as *Nora* or *Mrs. Jones*. *"See what is troubling 605."* You almost wish they wouldn't bother, that they would just let you filter out like any old process and be done with it.

Pope Pius XII spoke of this in terms of personal service in sociology. He said that the great temptation of an age that calls itself social, when besides the Church, the state, municipality, and other public bodies devote themselves so much to social problems, is that when the poor man knocks on the door, people, even believers, send him away to an agency or social center, to an organization, thinking that their personal obligation has been sufficiently filled by their contribution in taxes or voluntary gifts to these institutions. The result is that *personality* and *persons* fade into annihilation. The helper is not a *person*, but an *organization*. The helped is not a *person*, but a *problem*.

And this, I think, brings us to our second big problem. There is a terrible danger that we *institutionalize* our religious, rather than *personalizing* them in terms of what spirituality has to offer to the perfection of personality. We may easily suck out of *personality* everything that will make the *institution* flourish. Somewhere there has to be a happy balance between

192

the two. The *institution* must grow great as a *means*, but the *persons* must remain vital both *as an end in themselves* and then *as a living means* to the service of other personalities.

No institution serves personality. No one is grateful to U.S. Steel. No one is grateful to the Red Cross. In a certain sense, which all will understand who keep their theology straight, no one is grateful to the Catholic Church, and therefore certainly no one is grateful to the ancient and honorable Congregation of the Holy Flag. People are grateful to *God*, grateful to *Mother*, grateful to *Dad*, grateful to *Eisenhower*, grateful to *Jesus Christ*, grateful to *Francis of Assisi*, grateful to *John Bosco*, far more grateful to the *Little Flower* than to the Carmelites. Why not? The purpose of the Carmelites is to give us the Little Flower, but not only one—*many*!

Persons are terribly important at the moment because of the trend of the times. The mechanistic, highly organized, impersonal ties make all our institutions and commissions, despite their necessity in organized society, less important than organic, dedicated, individual persons. These are always the strength of the Church.

History proves it. We remember the builders of Catholicism in America not as the Roman Catholic Archbishop of Boston, Inc., or the Roman Catholic Archbishop of New York, Inc., or the NCWC or the Bishop's Commission for the Spanish Speaking or anything of the sort. We remember them as *John Cheverus*, *John Lancaster Spalding*, *James Gibbons*. Weren't they terrific? They were persons. Archbishop Cushing, who has done a little work in his day, asked me one time with obvious envy, "How do you suppose a person like Mother Cabrini ever got so much done?" He answered, "She came over here, she didn't know the language, she didn't know the country, she didn't have any friends, and look what she did. What did she have that I don't have?" I felt like saying (but I couldn't; I was his secretary) that the only thing she had besides the grace of God was, in fact, what he himself has, *personality—*

personality that breaks through mere patterns, upsets out-moded patterns, sometimes a little disastrously but to the enormous advantage in the long haul of the work.

And that brings us back to the work. Work is done by persons, and persons exist to do the work as long as it is the work of the Lord. So we solve these two problems: how we will keep the *work perfect* and remain *detached* so we can give it up to go to another assignment (or to die, which is another assignment!), and how shall we keep alive *personality* so that our *institutions* will be *strong* as means to an end? Let our traditions be creative and powerful; let the personalities they nurture justify the institutions, congregation, and the traditions by the *works* they do. It's that easy—and that hard!

XIX

Interview with Gereon Zimmermann

Zimmermann: Why did Pope John call the second Vatican Council? Is the Church at a crossroads?

Wright: Like every Christian, the Church is always at a crossroads.

But probably the crossroads that confronts civilization itself prompted him to call Vatican Council II. We must choose between human unity and fratricidal division. It is not merely the old problem of *One and Many*, with its political, military, economic, and cultural corollaries. It is the question of whether civilization can survive the bitter divisions by which the *Many* are driven even farther apart and by which the realization of the *One* is impeded.

As far back as January, 1959, Pope John linked the plan for the Council to the gradual achievement of an ever more perfect reunion of Christians. Even when he has spoken of more immediate objectives of the Council, the Pope has always linked these objectives to the hope of the reconciliation of the divided brethren of Christ as a means of making a spiritually strong Church the *soul of the world*.

Zimmermann: Where will the meeting of the Council be held? In the Vatican?

Wright: The plenary sessions will be held in Saint Peter's Basilica, sometimes called the Vatican Basilica, the largest church in Christendom

This interview was published in the October 23, 1962 issue of *Look* magazine.

and probably the only one in which more than two thousand and five hundred bishops and an indefinite number of consultants, functionaries, and onlookers can gather.

Important to the freedom of the Council, the Vatican State comes under the political sovereignty of no modern state; it has its own radio, cable, and post office, and, above all, sovereignty. Historically, many Councils were forced to wander about from place to place in order to avoid or escape the rival pressures of political states. Vatican Council II should be preeminent among the Councils of all time in its freedom from political, economic, and similar pressures.

Zimmermann: What principal matters might come before the Council?

Wright: Some idea of how impossible it is to give a satisfactory answer to this question—or to a like question on how long the Council will last—is gleaned from the fact that the Fathers of the Council have already been given one hundred and nineteen booklets containing the matters presently scheduled to come before the Council. These booklets add up to two thousand and sixty pages and represent a distillation of the efforts of more than one thousand men, aided by computing machines, working for three years to give a summation of the principal matters that have been suggested for discussion in the Council.

The preparatory commission has announced eleven projects as having been prepared for major discussion, typical of many others: the nature and contemporary relevance of Revelation; the bases of the moral order; the content of the Faith committed to the Apostles; what precisely we mean by *the Church*; what is the place of the Mother of Christ in the Church; how best can the organizational work of the Church provide for the modern care of souls; how should we meet problems of apostolic personnel, teaching the Faith to so many with so few to do the work; how shall we profit from new knowledge in improving ancient customs; by what means may the sacraments be made more pertinent to and more efficacious in our times, especially holy baptism, confirmation, holy orders, and matrimony; the great question of liturgy; what does theology require of the laity in the life and action of the Church on every front?[1]

Zimmermann: Has one Council ever reversed the decisions of another?

Wright: No Council has ever reversed a decision reached by a previous Council and subsequently ratified by the pope. It must be remembered that conciliar decrees have no permanent and obligatory force unless they are confirmed by the pope and promulgated by his command. The decrees of twenty Ecumenical Councils have been ratified in full; those of eight so-called Ecumenical Councils were entirely rejected; those of one, neither approved nor rejected; those of six, partially approved. Even in the case of the twenty Ecumenical Councils, a clear distinction must be drawn between matters definitely decreed and matters merely subjected to discussion and perhaps even to a vote of the Fathers of the Council.

It is true, of course, that subsequent Councils have more than once supplemented or clarified questions incompletely treated in previous Councils.

Zimmermann: Have laymen been active in the Council's preparations?

Wright: There were no laymen serving on the traditional commissions organizing the Council agenda. This is not particularly surprising, if only because of the procedures of previous Councils and the highly specialized nature of the work.

However, there has certainly never been a preparatory period for any Council in which there was so much solicited and unsolicited (but generally welcomed) expression of opinion by the laity. Catholic newspapers have run miles of columns setting forth the hopes, fears, recommendations, and reservations of lay writers, Catholic and others. The Cardinal-Archbishop of Montreal and the Cardinal-Archbishop of Vienna are but two of those who systematically consulted the laity as they prepared to make their own suggestions for the agenda of the Council. Around this present Council, many see developing a healthy, historic, and valid *public opinion*, largely lay, cited by Pope Pius XII as increasingly important to the Church.

Zimmermann: Will *national mentalities* prevail in the Council?

Wright: *National mentalities*—and this phrase is difficult to define in the space age—may have been factors centuries ago in Ecumenical Councils. In some of the early Renaissance Councils, the bishops voted by nations. This will not be the case during Vatican Council II. Actually, I believe *national mentalities* are becoming as secondary as the narrowly national interests in a commercial, cultural, or military order, in these times of the European Common Market and growing international consciousness. The authentic spirit of the Church is reflected in what the American bishops said recently: "To conceive of [the American bishops] as mere delegates of the Church in the United States would be to misunderstand the constitution of the Church, the function of a bishop and the nature of an Ecumenical Council. An Ecumenical Council is not a sort of congress or parliament made up of delegates elected to represent various churches or parties or interests. It is a solemn meeting, whose members are divinely constituted to bear witness to the contents of Divine Revelation, the Deposit of Faith, and to enact disciplinary regulations for the Universal Church. . . . The attending bishops will represent precisely what they are —successors of the Apostles gathered together in solemn council. At the same time, they are expected to bring to the Council the benefit of their experience and discernment as religious leaders in their own lands. Hence, the bishops of the United States may be expected to bear witness in the Council to the elements which, under God, have led to the remarkable growth of the Church in the United States, and to its generally flourishing condition, and to make known their judgment on whatever further development or reform appears to them to be advantageous for the Universal Church."

Zimmermann: Some say that the Italians, so close to Rome, and the Americans, so young in the Church,

	are less likely to be independent in their thinking than other nations. Is this true?
Wright:	This is eyewash. Christian independence is not a matter of geography or of relative antiquity in the Faith. Any man with independent intelligence must be able to perceive how equally loyal are the differences of opinion among the prelates of any given country or given time where discussion is free and difference of opinion is part of the way in which truth is finally attained. I have never been able to understand the glib talk about the supposed unthinking compliance of Americans or the conspiratorial compliance of Italians. Perhaps it is a symbol that the two who voted against the decree of papal infallibility in Vatican Council I were an American named Fitzgerald and an Italian named Riccio! The two bishops, having courageously recorded their opposition, no less courageously acknowledged their assent when due process had decided against them.
Zimmermann:	Can this Council be compared to any previous Councils?
Wright:	A like age of inquiry, exploration and revolution confronted the Council of Trent (1545–1563). Moreover, a certain spirit, eager for unity, was manifest then as it is now. At the time of preparation for Trent, overtures were made to those in England and Germany who were later to become firmly Anglican and Lutheran, respectively. The legate of Pope Hadrian VI spoke in terms of humility and sympathy—we call it *ecumenism* today—when he sought to secure the presence of Lutheran parties at Trent. Cardinal Pole's address, as a presiding prelate, is called the *Trenikon*, because

	it was so conciliatory and intent upon reunion. I thought of Cardinal Pole when I saw the photographs of Cardinal Bea in London.
Zimmermann:	The climate of Vatican Council II seems different from that of Vatican Council I. Why?
Wright:	Well, take the attitude of America in 1870. Thomas Nast drew for *Harper's Weekly* a cartoon that showed the pope floating dizzily in a wooden tub almost submerged by waves. The tub was labeled "Ecumenical Council", and the waves (you guessed it) were labeled the "Holy See". Other publications viewed the Council with similar defects of insight and charity.

Today's climate is markedly different. The 1962 coverage on the Pope and the Council reflects deep sympathy with the hope expressed by John XXIII, and so shared by millions, that this Council will be the prelude to *the sudden flowering of an unexpected spring*.

The British Catholic writer Hilaire Belloc remarked that the grace of God is in courtesy. There is no telling what mighty movements of that grace may have seed in the recent courtesy visits to the Holy See by the Archbishop of Canterbury, the presiding Bishop of the Episcopal Church in the United States, the Lutheran Bishop of Berlin, the Moderator of the Church of Scotland—and even personalities like Dr. Shizuka Matsubara, the first Shinto priest recorded to have visited the pope. In any case, they exemplify a new spirit.

Zimmermann:	Hopes for the *unity of all Christendom* rose with the first announcement of the Council. Have these hopes waned?
Wright:	I don't think so. The word *ecumenical* has been

an *in* word for about five years; we would do
well to pray that it not be *out* from misuse by
next season. Perhaps the word itself causes
false hopes because of its many different
senses.

One involves a certain ecumenical hope that
has always been the consolation of a divided
humanity; derived from Hebrew prophecy,
this vision of the peoples of the earth living as
brethren under the blessing promised Abraham
is confirmed in Christian Revelation. Recent
events have sparked that hope anew.

Divided Christianity has yearned for unity
since the waning of that nationalism which
was so much of the dynamic of denominationalism. For almost one hundred and fifty
years, the ecumenical movement has been at
work in Protestant Christianity. It has already
resulted in the World Council of Churches.
Catholics have abstained from it because of
their own understanding of the nature of the
Church, but on that account they have not
been unsympathetic or indifferent to it. They
recognize that the grace of God is at work
here.

More realistic second thoughts may afford
more substantial basis for ecumenical hopes
today, after the exuberant first impressions of
1959. The Ecumenical Council is specifically a
Catholic gathering; it is truly *ecumenical* because it brings together from the ends of the
earth the successors of the apostles, even
though it cannot yet expect the acceptance and
presence of all who are Christians. Realistically,
there will be no new heaven and no new earth

	after the Council. But there will be the more abundant grace of God with which men of goodwill on all sides may work.
Zimmermann:	What of Protestant observers at the Council? Can they vote?
Wright:	Only bishops in communion with the successor to Peter vote in the Council. As for the American Protestant observers, they include Methodist Bishop Fred Corson, Dr. Jesse M. Bader of the World Council of Disciples of Christ, Dr. Frederick Grant, an Anglican representative, Dr. George Lindbeck of the World Lutheran Federation and Dr. Albert C. Outler of the World Methodist Council. The noted Lutheran scholar, Dr. K. E. Skydsgaard of Denmark, has been studying the Council's work from the very beginning. Most of these men are far from strangers in the Eternal City, and the rise of the *religious dialogue* has brought them, and many such men, together over the recent decade. Cardinal Bea's Secretariat for Promoting Christian Unity has become a major channel for the exchange of views.

The Archbishop of Canterbury, Dr. Arthur Michael Ramsey, made this statement when he announced the three appointees of the Anglican Lambeth Conference: "The Vatican Council will not be concerned with negotiations for reunion. Arrangements are being made for the observers from the non-Roman Catholic churches to be present at the public solemn sessions of the Council and also at its closed general assemblies. In addition, the Vatican Secretariat for Promoting Christian Unity is to hold special sessions for the observers so that the deliberations of the Council can be fully discussed. This will enable the observers to follow closely the working of the Council and be accurately informed on all matters of interest. It is fitting that we of the Anglican Communion should accept this invitation from our fellow Christians in the Roman Catholic Church."

Zimmermann: What caused the schism with the Orthodox Church of 1045?

Wright: Politics, mostly. Once, the politics of Eastern and Western emperors used religious division, or even fostered it. Now, a world divided by the Iron Curtain helps to perpetuate ancient grievances and foment new resentments. Orthodox prelates in the Soviet Union, for example, seem less generous in their judgments about Vatican Council II than do their brethren in free societies. The reason for this is obvious.

A new mood characterizes our times again. In 1869, the Ecumenical Patriarch, the Orthodox Archbishop of Constantinople, appears to have been indifferent to the overtures of Pope Pius IX. But clear ties of personal esteem—indeed, friendship—exist between the present Ecumenical Patriarch of the Orthodox and the Patriarch of the West, Pope John. Few have spoken more prayerfully of the Council than has the Patriarch Athenagoras. It would be idle to pretend that reconciliation between the Orthodox fold and the Catholic world is easy, given the traumatic memories left by politics and the confusions that still arise from cultures frequently so different. But more and more people understand nowadays the words of the Orthodox Greek Bishop of Chios, the Metropolitan Panteleimon, who said in 1952: "Between the Orthodox and the Catholic Church, it is fanaticism alone that has emphasized the insignificant differences that were never serious, that existed in former times without bringing about a schism. The two most ancient churches, the Orthodox and the Catholic, should fall into one another's arms, weep over their past and then, purified by the tears of contrition, appeal to the Divine Power and, through their reconciliation, give their peoples the joy of the Lord."

Zimmermann: What are the long-range effects of the Council likely to be?

Wright: Who knows? For the Christian, the effects of an Ecumenical Council may be meager or even disappointing in immediate terms. What God's purposes are may take a long time in becoming clear to all of us.

But generally, the long-range effects of a Council are not the expected effects. Vatican Council I affords an example.

Its principal action was to define the special place of the pope in the infallible teaching mission of the Church. However, men like French Bishop Dupanloup were hardly enthusiastic about the terms and timing of the definition; in America and Britain, non-Catholic communities felt the Council's decree placed another *unbridgeable chasm* between Protestants and the papacy. In Germany, the followers of Döllinger promptly called themselves *Old Catholics*. The governments of

Prussia, Bavaria, and Austria labeled the decrees a danger to the state. Prime Minister William Gladstone spoke out against the tenet in Parliament, and he was echoed in the press.

Since Vatican Council I, however, the popes have governed with unprecedented love within and esteem outside their own fold. How much of this modern prestige of the Holy See under Leo XIII, Pius X, Benedict XV, Pius XI, Pius XII, and John XXIII is due to the providential but widely resented decrees of 1870?

Zimmermann: Will the Council condemn specific doctrinal or moral errors?

Wright: It is rumored that some five thousand proposals were submitted to the Council. Most, doubtlessly, were concerned with *heresies* (such as the absence of metaphysics in the works of Jean Paul Sartre or the absence of clothes in beauty contests). Archbishop Felici's commission had the finger-breaking job of sorting all of these proposals, and he groaned, "They have sent enough material to Rome to supply ten Councils with agenda!"

Like presidents, popes have *styles*, and Pope John has a manner that is positive and pastoral. Hotspurs who wanted only more denunciation of atheistic, totalitarian Marxism in his encyclical *Mater et Magistra* were chafed. He gave instead a blueprint for titanic hard work that scares the daylights out of those Christians who would be comfortably grateful for a mere thundering to which their response need be only a fervent "Amen".

Christianity does not need a million campaigns against a million heresies so much as a timely statement of its own first principles.

Zimmermann: Will the Council be a *rubber-stamp* session?

Wright: It is said that only one of the most violent thunderstorms in Roman history was able to drown the arguments of Vatican Council I.

Fierce arguments and much *withstanding to the face* have occurred in the major Councils. Catholic historians would be bad historians if they pretended all has been peace and easy compliance.

Everyone speaks of the fair according to how his horse made out. Some applaud the bold positions of Cardinals Pacheco and Madruzzo, both Spaniards, at the Council of Trent. Others admire the firmness of the presiding officers during those sessions. But no Christian with perspective will regret the debates—or the absence of the *rubber stamp*. The historian Hubert Jedin says that an assembly of "yes-men would be a distortion of a Council of the Church".

Zimmermann: Thus, will there be any statements of new doctrine?

Wright: "Not new things, but in a new way" (*non nova, sed nove*) is the expectation for the Council. The pope has spoken of the need for a vigorous and pertinent statement of the basic Christian principles. The Council will probably not introduce new definitions, but seek to make relevant the wisdom of Christ, whom Saint Paul described as "yesterday, today, forever the same".

Zimmermann: What contributions can all people make to the Council?

Wright: Whatever else it may be, the Ecumenical Council is an event in sacred history. It brings together men, and not angels; diplomacy and

scholarship will play a human part in its success, but nothing is needed more than the
plain, powerful prayer of contrite hearts. That
is why Pope John has so repeatedly begged the
prayers of all who know what prayer is. That
is why, of all the pronouncements on the
Council by our fellow Christians, none has
been more heartwarming or more welcome
than that of the Presiding Bishop of the
Protestant Episcopal Church in the United
States. Bishop Arthur Lichtenberger gave an
example that we hope others will follow when
he asked his people to repeat privately, and in
their churches, three beautiful prayers that set
forth the purposes of the Vatican Council. In
the midst of prayer so universal, the very
voice of God should be echoed in our times.

XX

Vocation and Virtues of the Scientist

Our intentions at the altar this morning include in a most special way the work and well-being of all the scientists represented by the several thousand delegates to the Convention of the American Association for the Advancement of Science presently meeting in Philadelphia.

We pray particularly for those who, affirming their love at once for the Faith and for the disciplines and rewards of science, are present as members of the Albertus Magnus Guild.

Two excerpts from Sacred Scripture—"subdue the earth" and "all things are yours, and you are Christ's and Christ is God's"[1]—form at once the charter and the mandate of the devout scientist. Around these two texts, the first from one of the earliest chapters of the Old Testament, and the second almost a summary of the New Testament, Pope Pius XII used to weave, as around the point and counterpoint of a musical theme, his luminous conferences on the vocation of scientists in human civilization and the part of modern science in the building of the Kingdom of God on earth.

All men are at all times under a vocation. As Cardinal Newman observed, we are called not once only, as in youth, but many times; all through our lives God calls us, again and again, to sanctity and to service, but also to accomplish, in accordance with our talents and opportunities, His purposes as these are linked to the works He empowers us to do with our gifts of nature and of grace.

Those who live in a spirit of faith are keenly conscious of

This sermon was preached at Saints Peter and Paul Cathedral, Philadelphia, Pennsylvania, on December 30, 1962, before the American Association for the Advancement of Science.

their vocations, whatever may be their careers. When, as happens to all scholars and thoughtful people, such persons have forcibly brought home to them certain truths which they did not know before or had not fully perceived, they tend to see these truths, even when abstract or seemingly remote from the daily concerns of life, as involving duties for them and impelling them to works bound up with their own perfection or the service of the good of their neighbors and the glory of God. In moments of such awareness of new truth and of its implications, devout scientists are strengthened in their sense of vocation, of being called by God Himself to the pursuit of *truth* and to the accomplishment of the *good* which the knowledge of truth makes possible.

There need be nothing necessarily miraculous or extraordinary about circumstances in which such a call from God is thus heard. God can and often does reveal His will to us through our natural faculties and the normal conditions or even the accidents of our daily lives and work. Still, as Cardinal Newman again reminds us, what happens to us in the ordinary ways of God's Providence may be in all essential respects like to what happened to those to whom Christ spoke with His living voice when, addressing them directly and in audible words, He bade His followers do specific works for Him. Such biddings involve vocations; so also the insights and truths which come in his daily work to the devout scientist may involve a divine call to a destiny appointed by Providence.

In his allocution to the 1954 International Convention of Geodesy and Geophysics, the late Holy Father spoke of the modern scientist as being manifestly and before all else a man *faced with a destiny*, called to a mighty vocation, and he spoke on a few of the many virtues which twentieth-century scientists, certainly those represented before the altar of God at this Mass, exemplify in their response to the vocations which they share.

I suppose that scientists, like us all, whatever posts we hold, are marred by their inevitable personal limitations and are guilty of manifold professional defects of omission or excess. I have neither time nor taste to speak of the inadequacies or the sins of the scientists; there is never any lack of people who feel competent and called upon to take care of these. One prefers the positive attitude of Pope Pius XII, an attitude of generous encouragement of worthy objectives and of honest gratitude for great good accomplished; the Pope's attitude typified the authentic disposition of the Church, as distinct from that of some of her nervous children, toward scholars, scholarship, and science.

The authentic mind of the Church recognizes and rejoices in the vocation of the scientist. That vocation, in its contemporary demands and opportunities, is complex and manifold. On the moral and spiritual side it includes, however, a noteworthy part in the easing if not the resolution of a major tension which plagues our civilization. It is a tension which is perhaps inevitable in a finite order where nature and grace, the mystical and the earthbound, the spiritual and the material, reason and faith, experience and speculation, know-how and know-why, even body and soul, are too often seen as total *antinomies*, in mutual and irreconcilable conflict, rather than as correlatives within a single, unified plan at work in disparate material causes but all converging on final causes under a supreme and overriding divine purpose.

These conflicts—including conflicts in the moral and intellectual universe which appear to be symbolized and paralleled by conflicts in the material universe—are keenly felt by our generation. Pope Pius XII, protesting against the pessimism of existentialist and other reactions to them, spoke of them at length in his last Christmas message. That message has been published under the significant title *Modern Technology and the Divine Law of Harmony*. It is a tract for the times. I urge its careful rereading by scientists and by all who would understand how truly the qualified spokesman of the authentic mind of the Church must welcome and applaud the indispensable work and witness of the scientist. Specifically, it suggests the important part of the scientist, especially the scientist who seeks God's will, in reconciling seemingly opposed or unrelated forces encountered in rival fields of study and of harmonizing the conclusions from seemingly contradictory phenomena.

Pope Pius spoke of how modern man is torn between an ecstatic admiration for the world of nature, which he is exploring to its furthermost reaches and its deepest recesses, and a bitter uneasiness brought on by his own chaotic existence. He described the strife and tension of a human condition never better described than in Saint Paul's phrases about "fears within and conflicts without" but never more tragically verified than in the neuroses and cold wars of the present. He observed that a resultant pessimism sees little in the world but a vast ocean of cruelty and of sufferings afflicting individuals and whole peoples, frequently, indeed, as the direct or indirect result of our external progress itself.

Then he spoke of the work of the scientist as he lays bare the harmonies that underlie the conflicts in the universe and reveals laws that are at work in creation, thus enabling technology to put these to work in the service of mankind and unto the reconciliation of the facts and the forces that so often bewilder modern man. To an age of "fears within and conflicts without", the scientist brings the steadying influence of the truth that he discovers and the saving example of his own characteristic virtues in the mastery of truth.

Of the many virtues of the scientist, permit me to recall but three. The first is associated with the sheer joy in knowledge that constitutes no small part of the reason which impels keen minds to wish to study and to know. The intellectual delight that comes from the mere joy of knowing the secrets of creation is not just the joy of conquest or of feeling one's own power; as a devout French scientist has noted, it includes the joy of doing one's job competently and therefore as God would wish, as well as the joy of being useful to mankind, an instrument of God in skillfully mastering and beneficently using the secrets of nature. *But it also includes* an element of joyful gratitude to God and joyful admiration of His majestic power.

Undoubtedly pleasure in one's own knowledge or skill can be complacent; the sense of joyful satisfaction that comes from *praxis* and technological triumphs can be stated in Marxist terms. But these can also be stated, and much more fully and consistently with the historic dynamic of the Western world, in the religious terms of Benedictine service and Franciscan joy, as Professor Alfred North Whitehead appears to have understood and as all will recognize who understand, as do Christian humanists, that the scientist need not be in Promethean contempt of the gods but may well be a willing steward of God's wonders, serving the sons of God in a spirit of holy joy.

The second great virtue of the typical contemporary scientist, above all the man of faith, is the virtue of patience. An Italian writer has given an intriguing title to a somewhat less interesting book. He speaks of *La Pazienza della Verità* and, whatever the merits of the book, the title proclaims a timely, instructive thesis: the need for the patience that comes from truth.

A poet once wrote, perhaps a little cynically, of "the wint'ry smile upon the face of truth"; one would speak more accurately of *the patient smile upon the face of truth*. It is that smile, patient and wise, with which the informed, competent scientist reacts, calmly and compassionately, to the vexations, the violence and, on occasion, the vituperations of those who, preoccupied with personal considerations, grow nervous or fret in the face of the challenges and changes which come from the discovery or progress of truth.

Those who are intent on truth for its own sake are patient in the face of contradiction, being resolved to profit from adversity as much as from advantage in discovering yet more of God's

213

truth. Those who are troubled with status, position, prestige, or the superficial appearances of things, above all the things that pertain to themselves, are unduly downcast or excessively ecstatic according as matters turn out in terms of their subjective hopes and preferences; those who love objective truth, as scientists tend to do, are much more mature in the Godlike virtue of patience.

Scientific centers of patient study and persevering research, like cloistered places of spiritual retreat and religious meditation, resemble the "little bay" of Coventry Patmore's verses:

> Here in this little bay,
> Full of tumultuous life and great repose,
> Where, twice a day,
> The purposeless, glad ocean comes and goes,
> Under the high cliffs, and far from the huge town,
> I sit me down.
>
> For want of me the world's course will not fail;
> When all its work is done, the lie shall rot.
> The truth is great and shall prevail,
> When none cares whether it prevail or not.[2]

Such sublime patience comes only from the possession of the truth. It is the secret of the patience of God. It explains the historic patience of the Church. It is exemplified by the special patience that is the characteristic virtue of the scientist.

I mention last, but with warm admiration, the refreshing humility that renders so attractive all the other virtues of so many contemporary scientists. By and large, twentieth-century scientists must be acknowledged among the most humble of men in the soundest and most spiritual sense of the holy word *humility*. The French author whom I have already quoted cites in this connection a distinguished research scientist, the leader of a team which has contributed to the increase of our knowledge of cosmic rays and the new particles. Bearing witness to the virtue of humility, as well as solicitude, that he finds in the contemporary scientists with whom he works, this Christian scholar reminds us that between Christian and non-Christian scientists in our times there is a common denominator, composed of the corpus of knowledge, of all the qualities that must be developed if research is to be undertaken, and the attitude to be adopted toward the results of research and as regards science itself . . . an attitude of humility, of concern and anxiety, which is in singular contrast to that of the nineteenth century. For those who have faith, it is written into their faith itself and at a very deep level. Yet it is equally present in those scientists who are not Christians. This is why you get on perfectly well together. There is a sense of brotherhood, which certainly did not exist in the nineteenth century, between those scientists who have a religious temperament and those who have not. In the past there was a certain stiffness, an abrupt, unyielding, proud attitude which raised formidable barriers between you. But this is no longer the case. You discuss together the problems of life and death. These discussions are genuinely friendly, and you genuinely respect one another's convictions, because you share the same forward-looking spirit and the same anxieties in the face of the way the world is going.

If it be true, as I take it to be, that the virtue of humility is increasingly a virtue of modern scientists, men made sober by the awesome mysteries at the edges of which they work and in the face of the terrifying problems which science may solve but can also woefully complicate, then we are less likely to hear in the future of conflicts between religion and science and more likely to hear of how religion and science, reason and faith complement and lend aid to one another. The moving humility of the twentieth-century scientist, every day more conscious of the immensity of creation, to say nothing of eternity, is in sharp contrast with the not-infrequent attitude of nineteenth-century scientists who were sometimes so impressed by new learning that they became forgetful of ancient wisdom. It is significant that the admirers of nineteenth-century science so often spoke to us of *the history of the conflict between Religion and Science*; it is not less significant that the distinguished twentieth-century scientist who addressed you last evening in the general convention spoke, I am told, wistfully and with reverence of the spirit of the Christmas season in which we meet and of its lesson for our times.

All this is reassuring to those who count on faith and reason, divine grace and human virtue, the things of God and those of man, to be allies in the saving of our happiest heritage and the realizing of our holiest hopes. It is good for civilization, a blessing to the City of Man and a joy to the City of God, when scientists are sensitive to their own divine vocation and when scholars exemplify the virtues which we other mortals so urgently need in these troubled times.

XXI

Interview with Donald McDonald

McDonald: Is there something, Bishop Wright, that can be defined or even described as American Catholicism? If so, what do you consider to be some of its most characteristic elements?

Wright: I don't like the term American Catholicism, as I do not like the terms French Catholicism or Spanish Catholicism. It seems to imply a nationalization of that which should remain universal and transcendental. However, everyone knows what you mean by that term. You are asking whether there are characteristics of Catholics in America by which they are individualized, perhaps, in the practice or in the quality of their Catholicism. So understood, the term has a valid signification, just as we may speak, for example, of an Irish way or an English way in sanctity, without on that account restricting or changing the essential and universal aspects of sanctity.

American Catholicism has been characterized from the beginning by a profound spiritual loyalty to Rome. In no small part this has perhaps been because so many of the immigrant Catholics came to America precisely as a result of their religious loyalty to Rome. I think, for example, of the Germans who came here at the height of the *los von Rom* movement in Bismarck's day; and of the Catholics of Eastern Europe, where

This interview was published in *Religion* (Center for the Study of Democratic Institutions) in January 1963.

the very hallmark of the Faith for centuries has been fidelity to Rome in contrast to local autocephalous and national Orthodox traditions. I think particularly of the English Catholics who settled here; passionate loyalty to Rome has always been characteristic of English Catholics in their homeland and here. The Irish have never forgotten Saint Patrick's plea that they be Romans precisely because Christians: wherever else Gallicanism may have flourished, it has not been among our Franco-Americans in what pertains to the pope.

The American Catholic's loyalty to Rome is an almost mystical thing. It is strictly spiritual. It has little or no political overtone; it isn't always matched, perhaps, by equally unanimous understanding of such matters as, for example, specific social developments in the papal encyclicals. Yet it does reveal profound love for that Rome of which, as Dante said, Christ was a Roman.[1] It has nothing to do with the Rome of the Risorgimento or nineteenth-century Italian nationalism. The Roman loyalty of American Catholics constitutes a supranational commitment of which we have been proudly conscious. People in the community around us have been very much aware of it, too, but sometimes they have been either uncomprehending or unsympathetic.

McDonald: You say there are other characteristics of the American Catholic?

Wright: Yes. Another, I think, is an energetic and generous disposition of the American Catholic for the performance of good works; the prosperity and flourishing of good works among us is no accident. The appeal of programs like the Vincent de Paul movement, the manner in which American Catholics will rally for the building of charitable institutions, even when they may not be equally interested in institutions for intellectual or contemplative purposes—this is characteristic and is, I think, a trait we share with Americans generally.

A third and like characteristic of American Catholicism is its heavy emphasis on moral rather than dogmatic theology, on moral consideration rather than doctrinal speculation. This appears also to be something we have in common with the non-Catholic American community. Their genius, as ours, has been heavily practical and moral. This characteristic, in my opinion, has arisen from the very geography of our country and from the circumstances of our history; the stern and rockbound New England coast left little time for philosophical speculation among the New England Protestants, and the pressing practical problems of survival which confronted our immigrant peoples inevitably influenced their cultural development.

There are three of the most obvious characteristics of American Catholicism in contrast with certain European patterns. For example, Spanish Catholicism is heavy on speculation, short on social programs; French Catholicism, in some chapters of its history, reveals a Gallicanism quite unlike the great awareness of Rome in the American pattern; in German Catholicism the genius, again, is more often for dogmatic and speculative theology.

McDonald: European visitors to the United States frequently comment on the fervor and devotion of Ameri-

	can Catholics in their practice of the Faith. Would you include this as a characteristic note of Catholicism in this country?
Wright:	Yes, and this, too, may be partially the result of precisely this characteristic moral preoccupation of which we have been speaking. Then, too, it has been our *practice* that has revealed us as Catholics, whereas in other traditions it has rather been the *ideas* and *outlooks* of people that revealed them as Catholics. Think, for example, of France and men like Charles Péguy. Péguy was weak in practice, but no one could be under the illusion that he was other than Catholic; all that he said and thought reflected the intense Catholicism of his mind and heart. Among us, however, faithful, even scrupulous practice of the obligations of the Faith became the familiar outward sign of our inward conviction, even when or if we weren't always particularly felicitous or articulate in other expressions of inward convictions.
McDonald:	American Catholics are said, on the one hand, to be virtually indistinguishable in their behavior from non-Catholic Americans. And, on the other hand, American Catholics are also said to be rather separatist, *non-engaged* or non-involved with much of the ongoing work of our society, whether it be in the political, social, or cultural order. One manifestation, perhaps, is the proliferation of specifically Catholic organizations which, in many instances, parallel the work of non-denominational organizations in the areas, say, of scouting, rural life, civil liberties, and all the rest.
Wright:	I am one of those who believe that a principal

explanation of the proliferation of specifically Catholic groups duplicating or overlapping other groups in the community is that, unfortunately, for a long while we were left out of the original organizations and movements, especially in some communities. And so, in many cases, we plowed ahead and did like things under our own auspices. It's the old problem of *which came first?* In this case, was it the exclusion of Catholics by others, or the voluntary withdrawal of Catholics from the company of others? Alas, all too often I fear it was the first.

McDonald: Would you care to make a judgment of the extent to which American Catholics are now involved in the mainstream of American life, regardless of the causes for their involvement or non-involvement in the past?

Wright: I think they are now deeply involved in American life and action. By this I do not merely mean the areas always mentioned in this regard, e.g., the Army, Navy, Air Force, though the Lord knows they are heavily *engaged* there! I mean that they are deeply engaged in the American scene, and, American fashion, are engaged on every side in the divided camps that comprise America. Perhaps this is one reason why we fail to give a united and characteristically Catholic witness in some areas. Certainly in political matters American Catholics function in a highly divided fashion; they bear a deployed and varied witness, and I see no reason to regret this.

McDonald: In what areas or on what levels, then, has there been a specifically and solidly Catholic witness in American life?

Wright: It seems to me that we have borne such a witness,

again, on the moral front. Some years ago the Protestant publisher of a New England newspaper told me that during the years of his publishing career he had observed the processes by which two communities changed from nineteenth-century American communities of largely Protestant complexion to mid-twentieth-century American communities of largely Catholic complexion. He mentioned three things that seemed to him to characterize the Catholic contributions to the communities. At the beginning of his career, he said, the lads working on the docks and railroads were mostly Catholic immigrants. He had seen them transformed by the temperance movements (the Father Matthew Society among the Irish, the Jean-Baptiste among the French) from a people who, in their economic discouragement, had been in danger of chronic alcoholism, into a temperate people. This was accomplished by spiritual and moral means that bore no resemblance to the pressures of the largely Protestant Prohibition movement or Carrie Nation crusades. It had been accomplished in the confessional, in parish missions, and by patient religious programs.

The second thing he mentioned was speech. He said that the foul-mouthed language of desperately poor workers had, in his lifetime, disappeared, chiefly under the tremendous and beneficent influence of the Holy Name Society. Then he remarked that he, a Unitarian, had observed that out of the ideal Catholic family and school situation there came a recognizable type of girl and woman, a type that reflected typically Catholic influences and a Catholic

222

witness. He considered this type of girl (and corresponding types of men)—the persons so often described as good Catholics—as exemplifying a major contribution Catholicism had made.

McDonald: What has been the effect, do you think, of the nineteenth-century decision by American Catholics to resolve the problem of education by establishing their own school system rather than, as some Catholics then advocated, entering fully into the public school system? How has that affected the character of American Catholics and the extent to which they are engaged in the work of the general community? Has it taken them automatically and inexorably out of a large part of the mainstream of community life, and if so, is this a significant factor?

Wright: Perhaps it is, but not in the way that is sometimes feared. Indeed, I sometimes think it will prove a significant factor in enriching the authentic American tradition in a way that may never have been expected, certainly not in the way that I once expected. I am in a peculiar position on this matter. Not only did I go to public school, but I am very happy that I went to my specific public high school at the time when I did, because I fear it would no longer be equally worthwhile to go there now. It has changed, as have all things else. Now I find myself believing, and passionately believing, that a principal contribution of the Catholic school system to the American educational tradition may be as a means and instrument for the preservation of the very freedom of education. I am not paranoid on this matter, but I have talked with people involved in it often enough to be aware of the forces in the land that are bent on establishment of a single public school system, a monolithic educational system under state, even federal, control.

As of a couple of generations ago I might have wished we Catholics had gone, in the nineteenth century, fully into the public school system. Now I consider this would have been an unmitigated political and educational disaster. Let's face it; totalitarianism is present, seed fashion, in every purely secular government as it would be in any theocracy; the moment you say that ours is a purely secular state, at that same moment you provide a basic formula for one or another form of totalitarianism, and you come perilously close to Mussolini's concept: "Everything within the state, nothing outside the state." The separate school system is a major and healthy obstacle to such a situation.

McDonald: There can be a third form of political society, can there not, which is neither *purely secular* nor *confessional* in nature?

Wright: Yes, there can be, and our American society bade fair to be a good example of such, but it is dubious whether it could have survived, especially if we had made a different educational decision in the nineteenth century and had not established our own school system. The forces for secularism were already at work, and they were destined to gain momentum with the passing years. Some of this momentum was gained directly from secularism itself; some came indirectly from groups not, perhaps, intent on the establishment of secularism but made the

224

de facto allies of the secularists by reason of their own special interests. For example, whatever mutual understanding had been worked out between Protestants and Catholics in the Christian community, there was always in some degree and recently in great degree the pressure of the insurgent group of the secular humanists.

But not less important than the political and sociological problem is the educational question. Many things that some of us look upon as indispensable parts of education were doomed by the educational forces that were to develop in American education. One may write all the articles and dissertations one wishes in the effort to establish that John Dewey didn't really hold what John Dewey obviously held about the nature and purpose of education, and/or that his words admit of other interpretations. But the fact remains that his contentions were understood in a specific sense by universities, textbook writers, school associations, and above all, teachers' colleges all over the land. I do not find the net result in American culture such as to make me wish we had abandoned totally our independent educational witness.

McDonald: Then you don't think Catholic presence in the public school system would . . .

Wright: Would have changed it? No. Water seeks its level. The constant temptation of our people would have been to say, "Ah, well, this is education, not cult or creed", and we would have gone along with the reduction to dead levels of standardization. As a matter of fact, even in our own schools we have too often conformed to standards and requirements set by other schools.

I often fear that we have been able to retain only a minimal part of our heritage in our own schools. There are too many Catholic schools all over America where one finds scant trace that they are in the living stream of the worldwide, historic communion of saints, except, perhaps, in the names of the schools, which are often accidental and not infrequently turn out to be names like *Our Lady of Lincoln Highway*, which, all by itself, is as local in inspiration and as lacklustre as P.S. 282. Yet even with half an hour of religion in the morning and a few memories of the saints and of the Christian centuries in the school week, there is still a free, independent witness that is essential to religion and healthy for America.

McDonald: Is this purely a cultural difference in American Catholics that you see?

Wright: It is cultural, moral, and social. I think of the men who came out of my old college in the days when it was frankly a small Catholic college. They were typical of a whole generation. It is not a question of whether they were *better* than others; the point is they were *different*, and their differences contributed mightily to America. Moreover, one feels that more often than not they were probably *better* than the standardized Brooks Brothers suit man. It isn't that this fellow is incompetent; it is simply that he isn't significant. He has no specifically Catholic or other personality worth notice.

I think, too, of the Yankee doctor who once told me he would have died of boredom in his little Maine town had it not been for the presence there of a Catholic priest who had studied in

Rome, who was of French descent, and who became his friend. In that lonely Yankee town, with its built-in conformities and cultural limitations, the priest, whose Faith the doctor never accepted, kept him in touch with a whole world that he had come to know and love in the year after he had graduated from Harvard and made the grand tour with his father and mother.

I think, too, of Worcester, Massachusetts, and the jewel of a Gothic cathedral that had been built by Father John Powers from Boston sixty years before the diocese was established. He had studied in a Catholic tradition, and he brought into a nineteenth-century mill town some of the things he had seen, learned, and loved elsewhere, things that were specifically Catholic and that would have been lost to love or even to memory in a monolithic educational system.[2] The pastor of Saint Paul's in my time was an old man, Father Mike Kavanaugh, who had gone to Rome as a young student some sixty-two years before. He had studied at the old Scandinavian college in Rome and had become an authority on the medieval saints about whom Sigrid Undset was later to write. Father Kavanaugh was also a great Latinist. He read the classical authors and watched for boys who gave a hoot about such things.

Here in Pittsburgh I find what might have been a drab industrial city alive with traditions and color because of Eastern European memories kept strong in the midst of labor and struggle by groups like the Tamburitzans, flourishing around families to be sure, but greatly encouraged by our schools.

In Pittsburgh, too, I find the magnificent

monument of Sacred Heart Church, lifting the
level of courage and vision—undoubtedly unconsciously—of thousands who went home
every night exhausted from the steel mills. They
were kept sane as well as saved by the beauty
found in the church built by Father Coakley.[3]
We will have fewer such men and will make a
poorer contribution to the national life to the
extent that in our own schools we conform to
least common denominators of a cultural and
educational kind. And so, bleak as the picture
sometimes is, our schools are the only contact
we still have with what some of us still mean by
a humane civilization.

McDonald: Theoretically, at least, educational diversity is
possible within a single school system.

Wright: But historically it does not sufficiently work out
that way, not any more. The great public school
system which grew up in the early nineteenth
century was in fact diversified. There was the
old Latin school, or classical school. There was
the mechanics-arts school. There was the high
school of commerce. But now every little district must have all the departments within it. In
Worcester the last class that will ever graduate
from a classical high school was graduated last
year. The classical high school will now be
closed, and all students who want to study
classical subjects can take them, as incidental
electives, in the local district high schools. But
many subjects they will take with the boys and
girls who wish to study no subjects and who are
merely complying with the compulsory school
attendance law. At the moment this is almost an
American, indeed a *democratic*, ideal, and it can

yet mean that our land is headed for dead levels of performance and interest, human nature being what it is.

The seeming fate of my own school, Boston Latin School, illustrates the problem. From 1635 until certainly World War II, though supported by tax funds as part of the public school system of Boston, it taught only boys who wanted to study Latin, Greek, ancient history, and the pre-liberal arts humanities and who had the privilege of doing so under masters who delighted in these subjects. Now an unholy concurrence (probably fortuitous) between the theories of some educators and the political interests of some politicians jeopardizes such schools as no longer *useful*, relevant, or, forsooth, *democratic*. It may be an encouraging sign that one thousand and seven hundred boys of the school signed a petition demanding that the school committee leave Latin in the curriculum; but are those boys the temporary end of a tradition?

McDonald: What social or cultural impacts do you think Catholics have had on the American character or the American community?

Wright: To the extent that we may look upon the American community as enriched by certain of the great liturgical holy days of Christendom, the mysteries of which played so powerful a part in the development of Western culture, there is obviously a substantial Catholic contribution to community values. I never see a decorated Christmas tree, even in the most commercialized circumstances, without remembering that we are indebted to the German Catholic immigrant for no small part of the element of our national life of which the Christmas tree is the symbol. And even when I see a candle in an absurd penthouse window on the top of a hotel, I remember that we are indebted to the Irish Catholic for the candles at Christmas time. The midnight services in Boston Congregational churches on Christmas eve show the effect the Catholic French Canadians have had on New England Puritanism, the *Minuit Chrétiens* and the *crèche* they brought into our tradition. Emily Dickinson was suspect of being a Catholic convert because she *kept Christmas* in Amherst! I think these things are but hints of a considerable influence on the national culture.

There are other things, too, some of them hardly more than subjects of light-hearted conversational banter, that reflect the Catholic factor in our observances as a people, as, for example, when people plan a dinner and are glad to remember that the So-and-So's don't eat meat on Friday; one thinks of all the corny but friendly little jokes about Al Smith getting up for Mass at early hours of the morning or leaving *important* business to say his prayers! These are all signs of contradiction but also of assimilation; they give local meaning to phrases like a good Catholic or a bad Catholic, and suggest how these have influenced American thought and values.

McDonald: Do you think that American Catholics, by and large, are conservative? I'm not speaking in terms of the familiar liberal-conservative tensions and arguments, but more generally. Aren't they for the most part conservative in their theological thought, political and social thinking and action, cultural and artistic life, intellectual life?

Wright: Why are they so? I think American Catholics, by
            and large, tend to be conservative on most sub-
            jects. The moment we say that, we have to make
            immediate exceptions; we have to point out, for
            example, that Catholics have been up to their
            necks in the trade union movement as they are
            now up to their necks in the New Frontier, at
            least those who are Democrats. But why are
            they so often conservative? I think they are
            conservative because any people with a proud
            tradition tends to be eager to retain it—the first
            families of Virginia, the Plymouth Rock people,
            for example. So ours are a people with im-
            memorial traditions to cherish and defend.

            This fact is also bound up with our moral
            preoccupation. Moral considerations weigh
            heavily with a conservative people. It is fre-
            quently, but too facilely, assumed that the people
            with strong moral emphasis in their thinking be-
            come the advance guard. The progressive people,
            the liberals and revolutionaries, are more often
            those whom a dream hath possessed. Dreams
            possess those interested in speculation, philo-
            sophical and intellectual, rather than those who
            put their chief emphasis on morals. Moral con-
            science goes along with speculation, of course,
            but the emphasis is quite the other way. We
            American Catholics are not so much a people
            whom a dream has possessed; we are more
            often a people whom memories haunt—holy
            memories, happy memories, perhaps, but mem-
            ories of the past rather than dreams of the future.
            We are a nostalgic people. Our typical nationality
            groups tend to be people with long memories,
            many of them melancholy, many of them sweet,

many of them proud, but, again, memories. The Irish are characteristically nostalgic; the Poles, the Franco-Americans, the Slavonic peoples have long memories. So have the Latins.

Not only is there this nostalgic characteristic, but not a few people have the tenacity of those who have only lately acquired what they have of this world's goods. Those, for example, who seem most fiercely to oppose social legislation, like Medicare, are not infrequently doctors who are just beginning to be able to educate their children on the scale that America has taught them should characterize professional men, men who are of a certain social status. Status people are much more nervous about losing their status if they have not had it long. European nobility take their status rather casually as contrasted with recently arrived Congressmen.

McDonald: Something that I have always been struck by is the contrast between the progressive thinking of the Holy See (which, according to its institutional character, one would think would be conservative in all things) and the excessive caution and static quality in so many areas of American Catholic life. I wonder whether the transmission processes, say the Catholic press, fail to convey the advanced work from the modern popes with clarity and vigor. Perhaps this accounts for the contrast in the thinking of the Holy See and that of American Catholics on so many matters, social, cultural, spiritual.

Wright: The Holy See is resolute for theological and spiritual reasons, but, let's face it, it can be sure of itself even psychologically, too. It has been there for almost two thousand years. It has survived so many destructions, so many crises, so many upheavals, and so many catastrophes that there is a sense in which for it to be morally courageous is no longer psychologically difficult. There is little sense of risk. Why did Queen Victoria never look behind her to see if the chair was there when she sat down? She knew right well the chair was there. It was *always* there. On the other hand, when a people first move into society, they instinctively tend for a long time to check on whether the chair is there.

So it is, *mutatis mutandis*, for American Catholics, including your editors, the majority of whom may not have the social and psychological sense of security of those who see history the way the Holy See so easily can. They do not have it, as we were saying a while ago, because the sense of history is not sufficiently in their education. A characteristic question among us is, "What will happen if we try this and it doesn't work?" Those who are schooled in older traditions less often ask that question. They are more likely to say, "The last time we tried that, this is what happened. The last time we failed to do this, that is what happened. For example, in the case of Napoleon, *this* is what happened. In the case of Hildebrand or Barbarossa, *that* is what happened." On the other hand, we in America, including, alas, Catholics, often reveal no such sense of history, and so we say to ourselves, "Dear Lord, what will be the reaction if we use the word *socialization* instead of such-and-such? What will be the effect on the circulation of our paper? What will be the effect on our Protestant neighbors, who mustn't be scandalized?" Etc.,

etc., . . . In its best moments, the Holy See is more likely to say, "This is what we must do or say because this is the direction of history; *vox temporis, vox Dei*: This is the manifest requirement of the hour."

They don't look behind them to see if the chair is there; they know it is there. We do look. The editor may even look behind him every morning to see if it has been removed from under him during the night. There are spiritual values involved here, but there are also cultural, psychological, and educational influences. It comes back, therefore, to the reason why our educational system should be not merely American and Catholic in its moral emphasis, but also Catholic, even papal, in its doctrinal and historical content. We cannot possibly teach our children too much about Pope Saint Leo the Great, Pope Hildebrand, Pope Pius VII, and all the indestructible saints.

McDonald: You seem to assign great importance to the educational and intellectual in your estimate of the character of the Catholic tradition or of any tradition.

Wright: The intellectual element must always be *basic* to a society. The moral element is essential, integral, indispensable, but not enough. When you have only moral motivation for social action, it may tire very early in the fight. When Edna St. Vincent Millay writes that there is no man dies in Capri but she dies, too, she may be talking sentimental rubbish unless her moral idealism is firmly rooted in a philosophy or dogma concerning *man* and, indeed, *death*. It is only a powerful doctrinal consideration that compels a

Vincent de Paul to pursue the poor, not with poetry but with exhausting *work*, seeking out fallen girls and guarding their babies not in Capri, but next door as well—which is more difficult and more rare, but also more to the point. He lives a moral life and leads a social revolution in accordance with the dynamic that comes from his *dogma*. He doesn't get up in the morning asking himself what the sensitive moral conscience should say about the problem of his underprivileged contemporaries. Rather, a consuming *dogma* makes him seek the image of Christ in every place, person, and problem. There is and must be a doctrinal foundation for the action he performs, or he grows perfunctory in the action. The very nature of the human beast requires that in the last analysis we be moved to act by *ideas*, not by *codes*. It is not enough that noblesse oblige, unless those obliged have clear ideas of why noblesse obliges and of what noblesse is. Here could and should be the potential and social kind. Otherwise we fritter away our moral heritage and fail our proper vocation as people of faith. Sometimes we seem perilously close to such a default now. We are living on a moral heritage which in point of fact has survived for several centuries without sufficient dogmatic renewal. Herein lies an embarrassment for religion in America and a peril for America herself.

McDonald: It has been said that American Catholic theologians are sometimes more concerned with textbook theology problems than they are with some of the pressing issues of the day such as the morality of nuclear warfare, a theology of work or a theology of toleration, the whole Church-and-State issue, and so on. Whether or not there are theological *solutions* to all of these things, do you think there has been, from the Catholic side in this country, any theological illuminations of the discussions and dialogues that are going on in these areas?

Wright: On the obliteration-bombing question we have, I fear, an example in the general community of the precise kind of moral preoccupation without robust doctrinal premises that underlies the problem of culture that we have been discussing. I think that many people who are worked up about "the Bomb" are merely appalled at the prospect of everybody being killed at once, though some of them could take in stride the elimination, one by one, of a whole generation if only it be done *decently* and by some less physically horrible means. The Christian, on the contrary, is appalled by the killing of even one man, one fetus, or one baby born imperfect. The emotional drama and logical fallacy of massive numbers killed by "the Bomb" are both irrelevant to the moral issue.

Another item: in *McCall's* magazine, for June 1962, I find an article on the childless marriage by a Dr. David R. Mace. The doctor raises the question of how we are going to provide children for unfortunate couples whose marriages have been infertile. In the midst of the discussion he naturally comes to a discussion of artificial insemination. He says that, admittedly, it presents certain psychological problems. However, he considers that it may be desirable for the following reason, and on the cultural and moral

236

implications of this sentence I ask you to meditate in terms of girls now of school age. "If at some future time our contraceptive techniques are so perfected that the supply of children conceived outside marriage and available for adoption falls off sharply, then it will be inevitable that there will be a greatly increased demand for artificial insemination."[4] In other words: Should we finally bring things to such a level of *perfection* that contraceptive devices will be easily obtained by the youngsters who now get into the *trouble* that brings them to unmarried mothers' homes, then we won't have any babies for adoption, and *this* will leave many couples childless, so that we will have to have increased artificial insemination! So long as sentences like that are read (and written) blandly in family magazines, I reserve judgment about the depth of the *moral* fears or indignation about bombing expressed elsewhere in the same or like circles.

McDonald: Nevertheless, do you think American Catholic theologians are paying adequate attention to the bomb and other such questions?

Wright: I submit that the things on which theologians are prepared to talk in 1962 are those on which they did their homework in 1932. I argue that such work must be done this patiently and even, in a sense, quietly if it is to be done worthily and lastingly. I am deeply persuaded that the homework is being done in 1962 on what we will eventually be able to say the more clearly and cogently on these other questions. It is being done here in America; it's being done all over the world. There is an enormous amount of searching of the Scriptures and the other sources,

237

rational and revealed, on these new questions, on new formulations of old questions and problems.

There is not, by the way, a single new worry, including the obliteration-bomb, that involves totally new moral concepts even when they do involve staggering new dimensions. I would be made suspicious—as a matter of fact, I would be discouraged—by any sudden show of brilliant clarity on the part of our theologians in matters so complex. I would fear that whatever they might have to say so glibly would be as un-impressive intellectually and unimportant his-torically as what I find being said on these questions by others, Catholic or non-Catholic, who have spoken too soon and with what seems brashness.

McDonald: Are there any even tentative manifestations of the homework that is now being done on some of these large-scale questions?

Wright: Yes, I think so. On the bomb question, a good series appeared in *Commonweal* a few months ago. The Catholic Association for International Peace convention was taken up totally with the ethics of modern war a few years ago. At that time many people said of Father John Courtney Murray's paper on the subject that they were glad he hadn't tried to be too final on this so-delicate issue. Some were kind enough to say the same thing about my own paper at that time.[5] Father John Ford has being doing much work on this question. It took John Ford years before he put down his thoughts on depth-psychology and its relation to certain moral problems. I don't think that a truly Christian sense of urgency expresses itself on the intellectual questions of the hour by rushing forward with the final answers. Spontaneity is possible and obligatory in the performance of the works of mercy; you give the glass of water right away because it is here and now needed. But moral philosophy is not so spontaneously worked out.

McDonald: Then, as a matter of your own personal conviction on this question of American Catholic theological speculation, you are not . . .

Wright: Dismayed or disturbed? Temperamentally I chafe with impatience at the slowness with which it is done, but in my better moments I know why study is slow, particularly when I read what emerges from the offhand solutions by others of long-range worries. Moreover, I think it an unduly narrow statement of the question to ask what *American theologians* are doing on these problems. This carries an implication which is un-Catholic, the implication born of a tendency to overemphasize the *American conscience*, the *English conscience*, the *German or French conscience*. The problem is one for the *human conscience* and/or the *Christian conscience*.

So it is important to ask not what is being done in any single national tradition, but what is being done in the Church everywhere and anywhere. I should hate to think that we would ever be so dependent on whatever American theologians might think out by themselves that we would no longer continue to profit from the enormous thinking of the French theologians or the Germans, or others who are at work on the formation of a Catholic Christian moral judgment of the new problems. But even with that said, I still feel that many American theologians are doing no little patient groundwork on the great issues of the hour, particularly in the area of moral theology.

McDonald: In recent months there have been a great many articles, news stories, editorials, and talks with regard to the place of the layman in the life of the Church. One bishop has announced that laymen will be participants in his next synod; another has appointed laymen to his archdiocesan school board. In Montreal, Cardinal Léger has turned over an entire Catholic college to lay administrators. Do you think the American Catholic laity are acquiring a new, deeper maturity? Will this be a significant new factor in the history of American Catholicism?

Wright: Undoubtedly. But, once again, the discussion we have been hearing is often in terms that are reductively sociological, political, and merely historical rather than sufficiently in terms most relevant to any discussions of the Church, namely, *theological*. We should be on guard against our American tendency to think in terms of organization, with scant reference to organic realities. This could be easy and fatal in talk about the place of the layman in the life of the Church. Is he going to be heard, for example, on school boards? Is he going to be heard on the question of how many collections should be taken up on Sunday and whether or not we will continue to have seat money? Well, I would hope he will be heard on all these things, but I hope that these peripheral questions of a policy and purely organizational kind are not made the measure of a baptized Christian's true place in the organic life of the Church. And this brings us back to the question of the appalling need in which we stand of a greater knowledge of theology, above all dogma, if the place of the Church in American culture is to be vital and the place of the layman in the life of the Church is to be worth talking about.

A refreshed theological understanding would make us gratefully aware that we all have our place in the life of the Church not as a result of an election or an appointment but as a result of baptism, confirmation, holy orders, matrimony, and Eucharist, sources of a dignity greater than human. How many laymen have the slightest glimmer of the theological realities behind their dignity as baptized persons, as confirmed persons, as persons who receive the Eucharist? Can you imagine discussing the place of the Blessed Virgin—a member of the laity, by the way—in the life of the Church in terms of her influence on the appointments made by the apostles?

McDonald: You think, then, that theological formulation, among other things, must precede full, organic participation of the laity in the Church?

Wright: Yes. The Church is not a purely human society. It is not a merely historical phenomenon. Like Christ, it is not of this world. This means that it is a theological phenomenon, and this, in turn, means that to appreciate it or our places in it we must become a people with a theological sense. I don't mean only lay people; I mean that the bishops and clergy and religious, all of us, must continually refresh our dogmatic insights, the theological roots of all that we are and are yet to be. Unless we do, what difference does it make, with or without laity on the administrative boards, if nobody knows or cares about the organic realities? Would the incomparable place of Thomas More in the life of the Church have been enhanced had he been on the board of administration of some English diocese in his day? Would the beneficent influence of Frédéric Ozanam in the Church have been greater if the archbishop of Paris had consulted him in the purchase of real estate?

McDonald: There are some things, however, that distress Catholic parents and do not fall into the category of the merely organizational aspects of the Church. The quality of some of the textbooks, for example, and how they can approach the problem of replacing inferior texts with good ones, assuming that some are indeed inferior. I think a good many of the laity are not concerned with getting in on the administrative or organizational activities of the Church, but they are concerned with the quality of the intellectual and spiritual formation of their children.

Wright: Agreed—and they are frequently quite right. In any case, they doubtless need and deserve far greater voice in such matters. It would be good for the Church. But my point is that such administrative and organizational problems do not sufficiently involve what should be our profound understanding of the *place of the layman in the life of the Church*, and I am afraid the present debate on that place is in danger of becoming merely an argument on such *relatively* superficial levels.

McDonald: To the extent that lack of theological formation of the laity exists, doesn't this reflect the quality of their Catholic education?

242

Wright: I am afraid so. The Catholic educational system, with all its substantial accomplishment, still owes it to the Church and to America to correct a situation in which so many thousands of boys and girls can come out of it so little able to tell us about Dante and his profoundly theological thought—or Saint Paul, or Thomas More. They have read too little by far of these men—and without these they cannot possibly catch for themselves or communicate to others the social, historical, and cultural implications of the Incarnation. It is not enough that our students be merely prepared to tell us things they would have learned equally well had they gone to strictly secular schools. There is an impressive argument for our *holding on* to our schools, not only for the preservation of our own religious tradition but also for the spiritual witness that is essential to the national culture.

McDonald: You said that the American Catholics' response to most of the social and political problems of our times will be adequate or inadequate according to how clear their understanding may be of the implications of the Incarnation, the fact that God assumed human nature in the person of Christ. If American Catholics sometimes do not seem as fully committed to the legitimate work of the temporal and earthly order, can this be due in part to a defective understanding of the incarnational aspects of Christianity?

Wright: Perhaps we are faced here, again, with the defect of a virtue, that is, the heavily moral emphasis of American Catholicism. But, alas, any moral code is predestined to be superficial unless it has deep roots in the inexhaustible doctrinal riches of Christ of which Saint Paul teaches. A people who had anything like a due understanding of the implications of the Incarnation would be a people with commitment and passion in their humanitarianism, as well as in other things, far greater than any with which we are ordinarily familiar. The proof of that is the saints. Saint Vincent de Paul, Saint Francis of Assisi, Saint Joan all were distinguished by a passionate intuition into the nature and corollaries of the Incarnation, which took place precisely because God Himself so loved the world as to send His very Son. The saints are relevant to our discussion because the contribution of Catholicism to America, as to any other nation, should be the raising up of saints. Our embarrassment may well be the extent to which we have not done this more fully, though, in all truth, I often suspect our contribution of hidden but saving sanctity has probably been rich.

McDonald: Do you think that as a matter of fact one of the great problems of the Christian is how to come to terms with both the temporal and spiritual sides of his nature? He is confronted with this dualism and tension, and how he works it out will determine to a great extent his attitudes and his actions in both orders, the temporal and earthly order and the spiritual and supernatural order.

Wright: Yes. And perhaps our gravest deficiency (a failure that would have been even greater, I feel, had we gone the way of the nonhumanistic education that threatens to dominate secular education in America) has been the failure to date of American Catholicism to produce a persuasive Christian humanism in our land. This is all the more lamentable because, as I have intimated, in the nineteenth century I think we were well on the way to producing such a humanism. However, to the extent that we abandoned or neglected our specifically Christian humanistic heritage, as Catholics, we have let America down. America desperately needed a truly devout humanism. We were in the process of bringing such an emphasis to America; we may yet help bring it. Unless we do, I don't know who else will; any other humanism that is apt to find substantial following in our land suffers from the pernicious cultural anemia of secularism.

McDonald: People like Father Walter Ong say that some American Catholics seem to be looking back to Europe too much, that they ought to be more concerned with forming and developing a distinctive American tradition.

Wright: Agreed, but with one qualification. Just as it would be dated for us to be looking back to Europe in terms, let us say, of nineteenth-century Europe, or early twentieth-century Europe, so Father Ong's point of view, too, it seems to me, reflects a bit of a cultural lag if it fails fully to consider the fact that the world is becoming ever more close-knit in its unity, so that for new reasons we must not so much *look back* but *look over* to Europe, even as Europe, indeed, must *look over* to us. Human affairs are constantly becoming more interrelated and interwoven. It is not a question of looking back to dated things, as, for example, to a romantic medievalism, but of moving forward, together with Europe and all the human family. The

Common Market is simply the most recent symbol, on a rather lowly level, of the trend that has long been developing on other levels, scientific, literary, and religious. Our culture, more and more, will be neither European nor American, but *human*, and, I pray, *divine*. Hence the relevance of the Incarnation to our cultural problem, national and cosmopolitan.

McDonald: In a lecture on the historic role of the American Catholic bishops you stressed the fact that the hierarchy has always been close to the laboring man and to his aspirations, and that American Catholics in general have been strongly identified with the laboring man and the labor movement. Was that identification primarily an economic rather than an ideological one? Have American Catholics ever worked out, say, a theology of the working class? In the absence of such a theological or ideological conviction about labor and the laboring man, have American Catholics abandoned their identification with the laboring man as they have moved up the economic ladder in recent years and have taken on the attitudes of the middle class?

Wright: This is probably true, but it doesn't alter my essential point in the lecture. What made the hierarchy close to the working people is secondary to the fact that they were. And that this was good both for America and for the Church was the point I was making. Whatever the reasons, even if merely economic or social, it was historically a blessing that the clergy were, in fact, so close to the workers. It spared us from the anticlericalism that marred the life of the Church elsewhere. Also, this closeness of the clergy to the workers brought into the organized labor movement a saving influence, even a certain conservatism, that kept it from going to the extremes of socialism and ideological materialism which hurt so many nations elsewhere. I think, too, that it has a beneficent effect on the family sense of the American workingman. Probably nowhere in the world has there been so great an emphasis on the rights of the workingman precisely as the head of the family. I see in this a result of the religious influence.

Conversely, the fact that we were a working people, in the main, has colored, more often for good than otherwise, the quality of our Catholicism. If one revisits the older sections of most American cities he finds an interesting illustration of what I mean. In almost all of them there is a great church of a religious order—the Gesù in Milwaukee, the Immaculate Conception in Boston, others of the Jesuits, for example, in New York, Philadelphia, St. Louis, Baltimore— and invariably alongside of them is the first college that our people built in each of these cities. More often than not, the college itself has long since moved, but note well how early it was founded and that it was founded precisely in working-class areas. It represented the dynamic of our people, as Americans in this land of opportunity, to see to it that their sons went to college. Moreover, these colleges, humble when they built them, were, if I may so put it, darned good ones. In the things that matter to me, in the humanistic branches and in the realms of religion, they were sometimes better than they are now.

I remember Francis Rogers, then Dean of the

Harvard Graduate School, speaking at Assumption College in Worcester and reproaching us because at the moment our colleges are doing the things done elsewhere, but often are doing them less well. He lamented that we are not keeping alive in the intellectual community of America those values for which we established colleges a century ago. I subscribe to that. When our colleges and universities were founded, they had a clear commitment both on the cultural level and on the religious level. For a long, long time they met that commitment, courageously and competently. They are not always equally clear about their commitment now, and that worries me. If they clarify their commitment, religiously and culturally, they are more likely to provide the spiritual philosophy of labor, of family life, and of other human values that you properly ask of them and that their devout and patriotic founders dreamed would be their contribution.

McDonald: Are there any other specifically Catholic influences you can discern so far as the American character is concerned?

Wright: Oddly enough, I think the Catholic influence has produced some of our most constructive revolutionaries, or, at least, people identified with our most constructive revolutions. Many of our nationalities happen to be involved historically in revolutions, which is one reason why we happen to be here. It is interesting to me that many people quite outside the household of the Faith, when they relate the stories of their part in America's typical progressive movements, tell of their indebtedness to specific Catholic priests for encouragement.

248

McDonald: And yet, wouldn't you say that one of the characteristics of American Catholics is the intransigence with which they cling to the articles and content of their Faith, a certain resoluteness in matters of Faith?

Wright: No doubt, and I am glad that this is so. I also think that American Catholics are, if I may use the word, the *prayingest* people in the world. Constantly on the lips of our people are phrases asking or promising prayer—prayers for the living and for the dead. Throngs of people at noontime and at odd hours of the day drop into our city churches habitually to pray before the Blessed Sacrament. This is a strictly voluntary, almost mystical, characteristic of American Catholics. It involves no species of conformism or legalism. It is impossible to believe that this enormous fact of constant and universal prayer is not without tremendous effect and repercussions in our national life, especially when we add this massive force of popular lay prayer to the daily treasury of prayer and meditation in our contemplative houses, monasteries, schools, and churches. Heaven knows, whatever else we may be, we are a people who pray. I think it is important that this witness of prayer be thought of whenever we are talking about how a religious group influences the nation.

McDonald: The Supreme Court recently ruled that a prayer prescribed for voluntary recitation in the public schools of New York State was unconstitutional. The State Supreme Court of California last year threw out as unconstitutional certain local ordinances and laws governing narcotics traffic, pornography, prostitution, and the like. Do you think the moral climate of our nation is deteriorating and that the courts are perhaps hastening the process by accommodating the law to what they think is the majority viewpoint on morals?

Wright: This appears to me, as one among many, to be ground for grave concern. We tend at the moment, I think, to be too facile about the overly sharp distinction between what is legal and what is moral. Sometimes the Supreme Court seems almost too eager to say that it cannot define concepts like blasphemy or obscenity and so cannot rule on questions involving these concepts. True, our generation, by and large, considers morality a private affair, but one cannot help feeling that moral liberalism so extreme neglects the intimate interrelationship between law and morality, even though the formality of conscience and the formalities of legal obligation differ. So wide a distinction between legality and morality as that which aggressive secularism demands leaves us open to a dreadful harvest. It will require much more than the new electronic devices to catch income-tax evaders and other scofflaws if the glib dismissal of any moral implications in the areas of legal obligation becomes the permanent pattern of our national law.

It is unquestionably true that the realm of moral conscience and that of civil law are often distinct in their premises and in their sanctions; frequently in history both religious and political freedom have depended on the due distinctions between these, not only in pluralistic societies but everywhere. But the exclusions of the secularism that is so aggressive at the moment are quite another matter; they forget that unless the

Lord build, they labor in vain who strive to build the human city. I fear that as excesses of authoritarianism historically led to extremes of libertarian reaction, so the present extremes of libertarianism will lead to a conservative reaction, even a reactionary conservatism.

McDonald: Something you said early in our discussion about the theoretical possibility of a third kind of political society which would be neither purely secular nor confessional or sacral reminds me of something Father John Courtney Murray once said in his description of America. He called it a *lay state*, which, he said, should not be confused at all with a *laicized state*.

Wright: Yes, and we had the happy makings of that, the makings of an entirely unique political society, before the recent drive of secularism. We had, in a sense that Cavour and his crowd never dreamed of, *a free church in a free state*. We may not much longer have it. We had it in the sense of a free church which enjoyed a certain favor of the law within the free state. And we had a free state which enjoyed the full blessing of the free church. That was an enviable situation. It did not entail an establishment, either of religion or of a church, but it gave the favor of the law to morality, as certain things may have the favor of the law without on that account being part of the government. Certain decencies enjoy the favor of the law. That favor was reflected in tax exemption of charitable, religious, and educational work. It was reflected in the attitude of the Northwest Ordinance toward religion, virtue, and piety. It was reflected in many ways. It was, in point of fact, the reason for the enormous system, unique

251

in America, of chaplaincies in the Army, Navy, and Air Force, in mental institutions, poorhouses, and elsewhere. Such favor of the law did not mean an establishment of religion by the state.

By the same token, there was and still is no place in the world where the Church is so eager to be positive in its approach to the civil institutions and secular traditions as it is here in America. We do well to pray and to work that this tradition, so uniquely American and so favorable to both civil and religious progress, is not lost to us under the pressures of sheer secularism, anticlericalism, or clericalism—home-grown, or alien.

XXII

Patriotism, Nationalism, and the World View at the Editor's Desk

I choose to talk tonight about a question very much at issue in our generation and pertinent to people who are writing, particularly those who are editing publications which increasingly reach international reading audiences. We can state this question in terms of two questions: *For whom do you write? From what angle do you write?*

Some write for a local audience, and from a local angle. These every year are increasingly fewer. Some write for a national audience and from a national angle. Even these are increasingly fewer every year. The emphasis is nowadays on internationalism, international points of view, international developments, international interests. True, there are not a few momentary crises of tension between traditional nineteenth-century nationalism and the new insurgent twentieth-century internationalism. But the dynamic of the future appears to be on the side of those values, those visions, those interests, which are *supra-* or *inter*national.

We do well, however, realistically to note the momentary conflicts. For example, just as Western internationalism seemed to be in full ascendancy, there has emerged on the world scene an entirely new continent. It was always there, of course, potentially rich and politically powerful, but I think no one, no one in 1920, no one as late as 1930, or even as late as 1940—less than twenty-five years ago—seems to have realized that Africa would loom as large in the last decades of the twentieth century as in point of fact Africa will. And Africa at the moment is a

---

This address was delivered on February 7, 1963, in Pittsburgh, Pennsylvania, before a gathering of Pittsburgh's Associated Editors' Society.

seething furnace of intense nationalism—nationalism which is throwing out the ancient imperialism and colonialism, British, French, Dutch, Belgian, Spanish, Portuguese, and Italian.

This twentieth-century nationalism is very real and in the case of Africa may even be healthy, if only because it is a stage in the coming to maturity of peoples who must pass through all the adventures through which the European nations passed before they could be ready for the internationalism that is only now beginning to characterize them. When you read in the newspaper of dreadful things happening in Ghana and just south of Ghana in that miniscule nation that raised so much rumpus last week; when you hear things that are happening in the Congo, Angola, and elsewhere, you think how savage all this is. In all the best clubs you hear discussion about "these savages at the U.N.", meaning the men there from the new nations of Africa. This may be the reaction if all you read is the newspaper, but if you read a history book with anything like attention, it occurs to you that the new nations of Africa are going through the same growing pains through which passed England when the men of Kent and men from East Anglia, Northumberland, and other tribes were forging the nation that was, after many centuries, to become England. You are now reading about African nations what you might have read about England in the days of King Alfred. And Africa will presumably recapitulate in each nation something of the history of England from King Alfred to the first Elizabeth, under whom the full flower of English national unity and English national sense revealed itself.

But then the nations of Africa will doubtless pass through the refining influences through which England passed until the English became a people willing to talk in common terms, in world terms, and little by little voluntarily to do the magnanimous things that Britain has done as she changed from the empire, so gracefully, into the commonwealth of nations and from that into whatever is coming out of the present crisis.

One thought of all this at the Ecumenical Council when one saw what a tremendous power Africa has become in the Catholic Church. Anyone like myself—born in America, educated in America, subject to so many American influences, but with memories such as all Americans have of the European nations to which one is particularly indebted—went to a meeting like the Ecumenical Council curious to see the successors in 1962 to the great archbishops who had dominated the previous ecumenical councils in the history of the Catholic Church. Cardinal Montini, the Archbishop of Milan, for example. There's a diocese 1800 years old, with a succession of great saints that goes all the way back to and beyond Saint Ambrose. You wanted to see the Archbishop of Milan, the Archbishop of Vienna, the Archbishop of Munich, the Archbishop of Cologne, the Archbishop of Madrid, the archbishops from England, the Archbishop of Dublin.

But when you went to the Council you looked around and you couldn't see these. Each was lost as any one man would be amidst twenty-seven hundred men all vested exactly alike. But you did see—and saw with amazement—men whose faces made them shine out of the white vestments—the great group of bishops whose skin is black. Every now and again you pick up a newspaper and read that the pope has appointed *two* bishops in Africa, then *one* in Africa, *six* in Africa . . . you lose count. But when you sat down that first day of the Council and saw black faces every place you looked, you began to realize the many-colored complexion of the future. When the business of the Council began it soon became clear that among the most competent Latinists present was a tall, thin Negro cardinal from Africa, so lordly, so conscious of his dignity and his prestige in the twentieth century that the Italian newspapers never described him without using the adjective *signorile*, aristocratic. Just over fifty years old, he had been born in a mud hut near the shores of Lake Victoria; his mother had never seen a mechanical instrument as complicated as an alarm clock, never seen a typewriter or a telephone. Such a man stands up in the middle of our century, in the midst of several hundred North Americans, Europeans, and others and speaks "in the name of the bishops of Eastern Africa, of Madagascar, and the African Islands". The future is with him and his peoples.[1]

So India! One day early in the Council the Cardinal of Bombay[2] stood up and explained that he and some of his brother bishops from India must leave. There were serious incidents on the border between India and China, and so back they go by jet to India; six days later they're back to tell us the situation has eased and they now can resume the business of the Council. We read about India in the papers, and we say, "Ah, India, with its exploding population and tribal wars. We must get the Ford Foundation to do something about straightening that place out. It's like Africa; when will they stop murdering one another?"

But here, too, it's all as France was when Clovis was King and *they* were on their way up. It's as Germany was when the Teutons had not yet developed the sense of their significance and their historic importance. It's as Ireland was when Patrick went there, and England when Augustine went there to do the best he could to civilize them. These men of India and Africa, sitting in the Council in the middle of the twentieth century, are the spiritual chieftains of sometimes strange because new nations; they are *now* what once were the great men of fifteen to nineteen hundred years ago whom *now* we revere as the spiritual founders of the great nations of Europe: Cyril, Methodius, Patrick, Augustine, Clovis.

Note carefully, then, the fact of African nationalism; it is big with importance to those who intend to write pertinently in the middle of the twentieth century for our generation in the area of business, religion, science, or the arts. Nor is nationalism limited to the new nations. We are sometimes prone to suppose that nationalism is over in the western world, but every now and then we get reminders that it isn't yet over by any manner or means. We got a dramatic reminder the other day when a man stood up who twenty years ago was a symbol, in a way, of the *international* forces abroad in the world, as were the *maquis*, the World War II groups of Resistance and especially the Free French of whom De Gaulle was the head. He was on *our* side—the side of the universal and international values—wasn't he? He was the very symbol of those who were putting Pétain and the men of Vichy to death, which was so odious because it was so nationalistic. He was then a symbol of the new internationalism—and the other day he appears to have emerged as a symbol of the ancient nationalism. Some see in him a cultural, political, emotional, or intellectual throwback across several centuries, as if he had said: "Not the English. They were the same English we threw out in the days of Joan of Arc. They are the ones who lined up against us with Blucher and Wellington against Napoleon. They are the ones who in 1870 we had to court against the Germans. Not the English."

But is he not, at least for the Germans? Yes, but perhaps for nationalistic reasons, by the way, which he probably spelled out several months ago in a speech in Germany, a speech the significance of which was missed by most editors and apparently by our State Department, who profess once again to have been surprised. He stood before the German people and told them in German (he knew that their own nationalism is so intense that if they heard him, even as a friendly visitor, talking French in the middle of Cologne, his mission would have been ended) in effect: Many things have divided our two nations across the centuries and these things have brought us frequently to war with one another, but some things unite us. And then he suggested a few. He invoked the memory of a name around which the part of Germany in which he was talking could rally as could most people in France—Charlemagne—a man buried at Aix-la-Chapelle (the Germans call it Aachen) and who ruled in the days when both sides of the later boundary were but one people. They were one people who included many *gentes*, but "not the English".

257

In some of your companies you may hear of this, in different ways, before many months have gone by. It may be that if he carries the day, if he sparks any romantic throwback of a nationalistic kind, we may find some of the mills that your companies built, in order to avoid national taxes here and national labor rates here, *nationalized* abroad as national regimes in Europe have a disagreeable habit of doing every now and again, without reference to the vote of the board of directors or the stockholders. When someone is starting a nationalist movement in Germany as Hitler did, in Italy as Mussolini did, in France as Maurras tried to do, one of the first things they do is point out the wisdom of nationalizing the industries so that the proceeds may remain where they are.

We have had another bit of nationalism insurgent this week in Canada. The present crisis in Canadian-American sentiment involves nationalism. Did you ever suppose that in your lifetime and mine we would find mounting up in Canada the kind of tension that as recently as today's five o'clock broadcast on the Canadian Broadcasting System revealed the reasons why Mr. Diefenbaker feels that he can brazen it through and perhaps get himself reelected on an anti-American platform? Those reasons are strictly nationalistic. Fifty years ago we were used to the idea of Canada being almost subdivided between the French-speaking part and the English-speaking part, each with a nationalism all its own. But now in Canada there is a nationalism that may hamper the unities we thought the twentieth century would see so strong.

Meanwhile, in America's own ranks there is also a powerful nationalism at work, especially in those states where the graph is on the way up. The old places, the tired places, have relaxed, but in California, notably in some place like San Diego, nationalism is likely to be feverish and universal values likely to lack appeal. Make no mistake about it: the troubles we have in the South are reductively a form of nationalism.

So also in the Cuban crisis; though the hidden forces are

beyond doubt Communist, the present emotional appeal is nationalist. The vast majority of the Cubans who are cheering for Castro can't spell Khrushchev. But they can spell *Cuba*! They have a strong sense of what it is to be *Cuban*, and the dynamic behind Mr. Khrushchev is not yet international revolution; it's nationalism: Cuba, *sí!* All else, *no!*

For that matter, consider Russia itself. The Russian regime purports to be a triumph of an *international* revolution. I wonder. You will remember that when the first astronaut gave an account of his adventure he said that as he started to come back to earth, he recognized the beautiful farmlands of—where? The hills of home. And the other two astronauts who rode in space in separate but coordinated rockets, symbols of modern international science and of the Communist internationalist revolution—do you remember what they did when they passed within communications distance of one another? They sang *Russian* poetry . . . little bits of *Russian* songs.

And yet there *is* this new internationalism, as well as this lingering powerful nationalism. You must take account of both in everything you write. You must serve and try to promote the national interest, but you must also play your part as architects of the balanced sane and saving international sentiment so greatly needed as well. In this latter task you may expect help from the level of science. When scientists meet there is ordinarily no divisive nationalism present. I had a dramatic reminder of that at Christmas time. For years, I've made a hobby of collecting things pertaining to Saint Joan of Arc; friends all over the world, knowing this, have sent me things in any way associated with Saint Joan.[3] As a result some curious things turn up. A French astronomer, for example, discovered a new asteroid, a minor asteroid, and he registered it with the International Astronomy Society under the name of Saint Joan. A priest in the astronomical observatory at the Vatican told me about this minor asteroid, somewhere out among the millions of stars, that bears the name of Jeanne. He, an American, gave me a photo of the corner of the sky where Jeanne is located. He told me it rarely shows up to the naked eye but promised to let me know when it might. This Christmas I received a letter from him. He said that the International Astronomers divide up among the different nations responsibility for publishing yearbooks about different types of celestial bodies; it turns out that the Russians are responsible for keeping track of the minor asteroids. In preparation for 1963 the Russians had printed and distributed to astronomers all over the world a list of the asteroids that will show up this year. Saint Joan will show at a given hour of the night of October 30, I think it is.

In any case, it is a reminder of how on the level of science all these things are so shared in common that there is no such thing as a *national* scientist, if, indeed, there ever was. Science, like every form of truth, has always been a bond among the nations, but never has this been more true than at this moment. So are the arts, all the arts. Only in moments of the most fierce nationalism do we ask, "What *nation* produced this music?" In World War I, it is true, the cosmopolitan people of Boston fired the conductor of the Boston Symphony because he was a German; one also remembers the difficulties certain opera singers had in World War II because they were Germans, or they had sung for Germans, or said they liked to sing for Germans, or something of the sort. But when you go to a symphony performance in normal times, no matter where and nowhere more than here, you are reminded what a force the arts are for internationalism. How non-national is the authentic, cultural heritage of music. How many and irrelevant are the nationalities of the musicians, the nationalities of the composers, the nationalities of the directors. Who would like to have a steady diet of nothing but American music, played by nothing but American musicians, directed by nothing but American directors?

So, even as is science, so art is on your side as you help build the forces of internationalism or supranationalism and as you try to focus attention on these. Isn't it interesting that the very moment that finds us on the verge of a highly nationalistic row with Mr. De Gaulle also finds us duly in the art museum down in Washington to gaze for eight seconds each at the Mona Lisa? Has there been anything intellectually stranger and yet more significant than the performance of the National Administration showing up hushed and humble in the presence of one painting, by one Italian who in point of fact turned out hundreds of paintings, and this one surrounded by an honor guard, armed to the teeth, as it hangs in solitary grandeur in the museums which borrow it—though it hangs on the wall of the Louvre with a dozen other paintings in the same room? Yet silly as the whole performance has been (one wonders if De Gaulle sent the thing over so that his smile could travel on the face of Mona Lisa as she looks out at us all standing there), it is also a reminder of the universal bonds. Huntley and Brinkley were rather amusing as they ended their program the other evening telling how the Mona Lisa rode from Washington to New York along the New Jersey pike, and as it did it passed a truck going in the opposite direction bringing to Washington, so it wouldn't starve culturally for the week, Whistler's portrait of his mother.

So all the arts are equally at home in any of the civilized countries. Whistler's portrait of his mother is as much a focal point on the Louvre walls as is the Mona Lisa. The one is the work of a cosmopolitan Italian, the other the work of an expatriate American.

Robert Frost's death last week recalls the same truth. One of the most intelligent gestures of the National Administration was, indubitably, the decision to send Robert Frost to Moscow so that he could stand before Russian audiences at eighty-five years old and, as he says, *speak his poems*.

So, too, is the Ecumenical Movement in world Protestantism. We no longer hear so much of Protestantism in the language of nationalism, at its beginnings so strong a force in its development, since the rise of Protestant denominationalism tended to identify with the rise of European nationalism. There will be less emphasis in Protestant circles on the Church *of* Scotland, the Church *of* England, etc., and there will be more on the church *in* Scotland, the church *in* England, etc., as the World Council of Churches has its influence and as the new ecumenicism asserts itself.

If, as editors of journals serving industry and business on various levels and in varying degrees of international interest, you are going to do your job intelligently and well in such a moment of history, you will have to draw and appreciate sharp distinctions between *nationalism* and *patriotism*. Patriotism like religion is a moral quality.[4] Indeed, moral theologians describe patriotism and piety as twin virtues. They have the same root in affectionate gratitude toward our origins, religion linking us by piety to our spiritual origins in God, and patriotism linking us by certain sentiments of piety to the land and traditions that perfect us. Patriotism is a virtue. It involves elements of emotion and morality. It is a noble sentiment, perfectly consistent with sound universalism, balanced cosmopolitanism, and Christian internationalism.

Patriotism is a tie with our roots, with our ancestors, with the land out of which we came, with the language which was our maternal tongue. Indeed, men speak of their native land in terms which indicate their relationship to it is a filial one. They speak of the German Fatherland, Mother India, and the like. Nationalism is another matter. Modern nationalism is a politically fomented development of patriotism which makes it a divisive principle. It sets us off from and frequently against other people, as patriotism does not.

Modern nationalism has attempted to make the political state or the nation itself the object of our all-out loyalty and all our love. Patriotism never did that. Patriotism made us love our native land, or our land of adoption, with a preferential love, but a love that was perfectly consistent with a wholesome participation in the affairs and the destinies of others. Patriotism has inspired poetry, music, art. Nationalism tends to absorb all our sentiments and our loyalties and to subordinate to it all other sentiments and loyalties, as it did in National Socialism, as it did in the nationalism of Fascism, as it does in Spanish Falangism, and as it does in American nationalism when that runs riot, or French nationalism, or any other unbridled nationalism.

I would like to conclude by speaking of a specific form of patriotism which has not been much discussed in the last few centuries, so preoccupied as they have been with nationalism— British nationalism, Irish nationalism, French nationalism, German nationalism, Italian and American nationalism. In the days when patriotism was a virtue, finding more pure expression, there was a powerful patriotism and loyalty that linked people to their cities. Nationalism is always on the march toward imperialism. British nationalism speedily became British imperialism. Italian nationalism became Italian imperialism. French nationalism became the Napoleonic empire, and German nationalism we know from three wars.

But patriotism is close to home, close to local things, and so patriotism has always included a strong love for one's own city. Italy is interesting as a study of this. Prior to 1870 when Italian nationalism took over and laid the grounds for eventual Fascism, Italy was a peninsula in which there was little nationalism but much local patriotism. Most of the older Italian people, whose memories go back to that period, rarely thought of themselves as Italian. They said they were Neapolitans, Sicilians, Genovese, or Venetians. Once I heard a girl answer "Naples!" when asked what was her country. Some people are Parisians more than they are Frenchmen; this is going to be one of De Gaulle's problems. So within French nationalism there are local patriotisms which remain strong. There are people who are loyal to France, for civic reasons, but they love Paris for personal reasons. Not long ago a shrewd writer commented that it wasn't so much Al Smith's religious loyalty to Rome that defeated him and made him seem alien to the American Bible Belt. It was his sentimental attachment to New York. It never occurred to his campaign manager that people in Iowa and Oklahoma didn't like to hear "The Sidewalks of New York". It was *his* patriotism, and it was enough to make them sick.

We all know people who would rather be from Dublin than from Cork. I know people from Galway who would almost consider it a mixed marriage if their son married anyone from Cork. Some people think more of London than of England, some people think more of Quebec than of Canada; there are any number of people who will join in criticism of the United States, but if you say anything about Texas or Brooklyn, or the South Side, you'll be in trouble.

There are, then, local patriotism and local loyalties. It is extremely important that people who deal in ideas and shape public opinion always be aware of these if we are to have a harmonious balance in discussing international values, national values, local values. These are not mutually exclusive; they are strands in a single strong cord; if any one of them is missing, the person who lacks that one is somehow defective. Anyone who is so nationalistic that he despises the rest of the human race is unbalanced. Anyone who is so cosmopolitan that any place he hangs his hat is home sweet home to him is basically unreliable. He has no roots, no deep loyalty in the social order.

Once upon a time the love of a city was the thing that made cities great. The name of Athens will endure as long as civilization lasts, and it will endure because the people of that one city, the Athenians, so loved the place, so made it the object of their patriotism as to give it a dynamic toward greatness, which after these twenty-five hundred years makes us still admire Athens. The love for Athens was expressed by the great citizen Pericles in an oration which schoolboys still studied when high schools still gave an education. Pericles spoke of the things by which her soldiers had enriched the Athenian spirit; spoke of what they were fighting to save, and listed the things that Athenians loved and that these boys thought were menaced, so that they would rather die resisting than live submitting.[5] That mood is dying among us. It's the "better red than dead" thing in reverse. The Athenians knew better!

Our American cities need the patriotism of Athens. It is not a patriotism that any longer leads to militarism; cities no longer wage armed warfare. But it is a patriotism that leads to pride, to planning, to unity and prosperity among citizens. Pittsburgh shows no little local patriotism; but it could stand a little more.

I conclude, then, by making this plea to you. Some of your work will suggest the wisdom that you emphasize the international implications and interests of whatever branch of business claims your talent. Some of the problems of the hour will require that you write in terms which foster the national well-being. But at the same time I would hope that you who work and write here in Pittsburgh have in mind what made Athens great, so that you will nurture in yourselves and communicate to others a local patriotism, a love for this city. People of this city should be glad to die resisting rather than live submitting to whatever would cause the degeneracy of its values and the scarring of its proud, beautiful face. This is patriotism because it involves things that are close to home.

You must play the editor's part in the defense of national interests. You must play a part in encouraging internationalism and worldwide human interests, because everything everywhere touches on everything here. But in the midst of your national loyalty and international endeavor, I urge you to keep alive local loves and local patriotism.

XXIII

The Real Aim of Education

The austere elegance and disciplined beauty of the chapel, library, and other new campus buildings which glisten in this morning's so-radiant sunshine make unmistakably clear the sense of the text I have chosen for our reflection today. Those words are taken from Saint Paul: "For all things are yours, whether it be Paul, or Apollo, or Cephas, or the world, or life, or death, or things present, or things to come; for all are yours. And you are Christ's and Christ is God's."[1]

In Pope John's thrilling encyclical *Pacem in Terris* there are many things to warm the hearts and to give fresh, firm direction to the thinking of all who seek a City of Man somehow worthy of the children of God.

Especially inspiring to those in the battle for social reform in accordance with humane philosophy and Christian principles is the Holy Father's clear, positive emphasis on the person and on personality as the center and norm of all sound theory.

Such an emphasis has important corollaries for the education of the citizens who must be at once the beneficiaries and the builders of the good society. Reflection on these points is therefore much in order during the ceremonies which rejoice the friend of Mount Saint Joseph and all Cincinnati today.

Pope John opens his new encyclical with a brief but powerful affirmation of the infinite majesty of God and the marvelous created dignity that God has given His chief creature, man. Then he goes to the very heart of the moral universe of which man is at once a part and yet, by divine appointment, the steward and, in a sense, the master. He points out that this

This sermon was preached at Mount Saint Joseph College, Cincinnati, Ohio, on May 1, 1963.

moral universe demands among men a well-ordered and prosperous society and that this in turn presupposes as its very foundation and first principle *that every human being is a person*. In this fact resides the innate dignity of men; from this fact flow their universal, inviolable and inalienable rights; by this fact, the Pope argues trenchantly, the image of God Himself is mirrored in men—for God created man in His own image and likeness, endowing him with intelligence and freedom, bidding him rule over the works of God's hand. "Thou hast put all under his dominion."[2]

The analogy between the human person and personality in God parallels and proceeds from the analogy between being in man and being in God. That is why Maritain can say that the notion of personality thus involves that of *wholeness* and *independence*.

> To say that a man is a person is to say that in the depth of his being he is more a whole than a part and more independent than servile. It is this mystery of our nature which religious thought designates when it says that the person is the image of God. A person possesses absolute dignity because he is in direct relationship with the realm of being, truth, goodness, and beauty, and with God, and it is only with these that he can arrive at his complete fulfillment. His spiritual fatherland consists of the entire order of things which have absolute value, and which reflect, in some manner, a divine Absolute superior to the world, and which have a power of attraction toward this Absolute.[3]

By virtue of his being a spiritual person, though individuated in the material world—a creature with the senses and instincts of the animal body as well as the reason and will of the spiritual soul—man is, Maritain reminds us, *a horizon in which two worlds meet*, and this fact, the effect of his being a person, determines what must be the content as well as the intent of his education. It also provides the permanent case for Christian education and makes the Christian gospel more-than-ever relevant in an age of humanism.

Again, Maritain is a convenient guide. The chief aspirations of a person are aspirations to freedom. I do not mean that freedom which is free will and which is a gift of nature in each of us; I mean that freedom which is spontaneity, expansion, or autonomy, and which we have to gain through constant effort and struggle. . . . It [involves] the desire for inner and spiritual freedom. In this sense Greek philosophy, especially Aristotle, spoke of the independence which is granted to men by intellect and wisdom as the perfection of the human being. And the gospel was to lift up human perfection to a higher level—a truly divine one—by stating that it consists of the perfection of love and, as Saint Paul put it, of the freedom of those who are moved by the divine Spirit.[4]

Wherefore, Christian humanism adds to the Greek ideal—*Know thyself*—and the Roman ideal—*Rule thyself*—a third formula. It gives a dynamic purpose inculcated by the teaching and patterned on the example of Jesus Christ. It is: *Give thyself*, the highest exercise of freedom and the most perfect expression of personality.

With its developed projection of the primacy of the person, under God, the recent encyclical becomes a timely, indeed urgently needed, statement of a Christian social premise that is by no means novel, as Pope John is the first to point out. It corresponds exactly to the constant papal teaching that in God's holy Providence all society, religious and civil alike, and all traditions, both of authority and of liberty, exist for the perfection of human personality. Thus must be understood the magnificent implications of the doctrines which Pope Pius XI wonderfully summarized:

> It is according to the dictates of reason that ultimately all things should be ordained to man as a person that through his mediation they may find their way back to the Creator. In this wise we can apply to man, to the human person, the words of the Apostle: "All things are yours, whether it be Paul or Apollo, or Cephas, or the world, or life, or death, or things present, or things to

come; for all are yours; and you are Christ's and Christ is God's."[5]

But the new encyclical explicitly relates this general social teaching to the specific place of women, precisely as persons, in the good society. It touches, by unmistakable implication, on the problem of the requisite education of contemporary women to play their full part in the building of a humane social order and to enjoy their abundant share of the good common to that order. The words of the Pope are succinct but rich in points for meditation; they might well be carved on the gates of this modern campus as the purpose of all the buildings and the justification of every sacrifice required to erect them. This is what the Pope wrote:

> It is obvious to everyone that women are now taking a part in public life. This is happening more rapidly perhaps in nations of Christian civilization, and, more slowly but broadly, among peoples who have inherited other traditions and cultures. *Since women are becoming conscious of their human dignity, they will not tolerate being treated as mere material instruments, but demand rights befitting a human person both in domestic and in public life.*[6]

Here again the Holy Father's emphasis on *personality* and on the *person* corresponds with a social and educational truth once crystal-clear but now often in need of rediscovery. *We, the people* were the original architects of the state's competence and of society's concern—not *classes* of people, not *majorities* with special powers nor *minorities* with special rights, not *native* people, nor *foreign* people, not people colored white nor people colored any other color—but *We, the people*. All *persons* were the beginning and the end of social philosophy.

So also it was (or at least it was ideally) in the philosophy of education. Before schools and colleges, even ours, became confused by the categories of people and the special but subordinate needs of such *categories*, education was thought of not in terms of professional *groups*, cultural, social, or political

269

types, and similar mere *categories*—but in terms of *persons*. Hence the definitions of purpose, so lucid that they perhaps seem over-simple, which used to appear in catalogues of at least our colleges: *Education is the complete and harmonious development of the faculties distinctive of a man*—not of an American *citizen* only, not a French intellectual, nor a Britisher gently born, nor of any other *type*—but a person—*an image of God*, as God shone forth in Adam and Eve—unfallen, primeval, self-conscious, God-fearing persons.

There are heartwarming evidences that such is the motivation again of a growing number of campuses, especially those of women and, one prays, of those campuses which, since they are called *Catholic*, should above all be characterized by emphasis on the universal, the truly human, and should be in constant struggle for the emergence, in all grace and truth, of the image of God in the persons they seek to produce.

For the purpose of education is not to produce the mere useful worker; not the mere good citizen; not the mere thinker; not the mere mystic. It is to produce the full *person*: the person trained to be useful, disciplined to be loyal and cooperative, intellectually stimulated to be thoughtful, spiritually awakened and motivated to be prayerful; but, above all, the *person: homo economicus, homo politicus, homo intellectualis, homo mysticus*, but all integrated in the total *person*, the creature composed of body and soul and made to the image and likeness of God.

That is what Maritain means when, rejecting the *biological* and *sociological* formula for education of philosophers like William E. Hocking, he insists that education has for "its real aim . . . to make a man. . . . Education should essentially aim not at producing the type but at liberating the human person."[7]

Hence the content and the purpose of the educational program pursued and encouraged here at Mount Saint Joseph. That program is in the tradition of the Christian humanism the educational elements of which Saint Paul in our text this morning spells out almost in terms of the curriculum of the students privileged to share it: *All things are yours:* teachers, friends, administrations (Paul, Apollo, Cephas); science and everything in nature (the world); art and all that lives (life); all the mystery that surrounds us and impels us to work (death); history and current events, the riches of culture and civilization (things present); prophecy, theology, the joy of planning the future, eternity included (things to come); humanism (all things are yours)—but *Christian* humanism (for you are Christ's and Christ is God's)!

This heritage of Christian humanism is as old as the gospel, its natural foundations older still, being deep in the history of human striving after whatever is being and good, and beautiful and true. In every period of Christian history it has been nurtured by saints and scholars of every race and clime and condition, all bringing their gifts of reason and of faith to its adornment and its flourishing. In our own times it has been well served by generous scholars, priestly and lay as well as religious; Christian humanism has, moreover, enjoyed the full favor and patronage of the supreme shepherds and teachers in the Church—Pope Leo XIII, who gave it powerful impetus by his luminous precept, patronage, and example; Pius X and Benedict XV, who defended it from attack—the first from *intellectual* undermining, the second from the devastation of social upheaval and militarism; Pius XI, who defined it so eloquently and exactly; Pius XII, who enriched it with keen insights in wholly new areas and gave increased dynamic to it by venturesome directions; and now Pope John, who would have us bring it to the emancipation of the person, the perfection of personality, and the consequent building of a human society acceptable to God because worthy of persons.

For all persons are called to be brothers and sisters of the Incarnate Second Person of the adorable Trinity—Christ Jesus, thanks to Whom all human persons are crowned with honor and glory to rule over the works of God's hands. It is by His Incarnation that a Divine Person enters history and that human personality is called to the supernatural perfection which Christian humanism proclaims and promotes, the perfection of those persons to whom Paul said what John echoes: "For all things are yours, whether it be Paul, Apollo, or Cephas, or the world, or life, or death, or things present, or things to come; for all are yours. And you are Christ's and Christ is God's."[8]

XXIV

The Education of Women Religious

I had supposed that I would probably not in this lifetime see anything more ecumenical than the presence of various kinds of Protestants, various kinds of Orthodox at the Ecumenical Council in Rome, but I must confess that this coming together of sisters from various religious communities is even more miraculous. As a simple public school boy, I had never expected to see the lions and the lambs lying down together and the ecumenical spectacle of the daughters of so many religious traditions, each unique and far better than all the others, brought together in order to study together the wonderful works of the Lord and to grow at one and the same time in knowledge and in perfection.

Well, unity is the passion of the hour and the dynamic of our moment of history. The movements which tend toward unity come under different names: ecumenical on the religious level, international and global on the political, scientific, social level. The big word at the moment, however, is *integration*. The heavy emphasis in the present use of the word *integration* is on a sociological splintering. The fragmentation of our society is in the name of race, with overtones sometimes of class, but nonetheless it is sociological, and therefore it is superficial and in all probability is merely a symptom or a symbol of a deeper fragmentation, a much more profound splintering which forms the object of your preoccupation and mine as builders of the kingdom of God. The superficial sociological problem—economic, political—with which the term *integration* is presently so heavily associated is a heartbreaking problem. It is charged

This address was delivered at Marillac College, Saint Louis, Missouri, on August 24, 1963.

273

with emotion, and it has complications and potential for great harm against which we are constantly being alerted; but it remains superficial and, I repeat, symptomatic or symbolic of much deeper problems of more profound significance.

So the integration of which we read in the daily papers in connection with the sociological problem is a symbol of integration which is underway, please God, on much more essential levels and in areas of values where there have been scandalous splits, schisms, dichotomies hurtful to human culture and, therefore, hurtful to the Kingdom of God and its coming, which depends so on the work of nature and of civilization refining, all of which add up to culture. On the level of culture, there is a grave need for an integration to take care of a dichotomy, a split which has grievously wounded Western civilization.

Last month at a sesquicentennial observance at Colby College in Maine, Mr. Frank Stanton, of the broadcasting industry, spoke of this deeper dichotomy which calls for integration, and in his talk he recalled how Sir Charles Snow, the novelist, scientist, dramatist, had been speaking in England and the United States during the 1950s and to date on a theme summed up in the title of one of his books, *The Two Cultures*.[1] Snow voiced deep concern because, not just in the English-speaking world but throughout our Western civilization, the one great single stream of learning has been split into two smaller ones, which have been rapidly diverging and which are now far apart. One is the stream of technological, scientific learning—scientific humanism—and the other, a kind of varied stream, with motley swimmers in it, is all the rest of learned people. Snow called these latter people, for reasons of convenience, the literary humanists or the literary intellectuals. So he saw our civilization split into the followers of scientific humanism and the followers of literary humanism—Bachelors of Science and Bachelors of Arts—but never speaking, and having very little influence on one another.

274

Snow also suggested in his lecture that, of course, the technological or scientific humanism was definitely in the ascendency and that it was giving the color and tone to our contemporary civilization. He expressed it this way. He said that in the days when our education was largely classical and literary, if you wished to find out if a man were educated you said, "Have you read such and such a work of Shakespeare?" But now if you wish to know if a man is educated, you ask if he can describe the second law of thermodynamics. If he can, he belongs. If he can't, he is a medievalist. Or, in any case, he is one of the motley crowd swimming in the stream of literary humanism.

And Stanton made a plea (at Colby College) that you and I would be inclined to sympathize with, for the rephrasing of all this, so that it could be recognized that it is just as important to know what Newton was up to as it is to know what Shakespeare was up to. And he made his plea for the integration of scientific or technological civilization, but he called it humanism and literary or philosophical humanism. He found it interesting that both these geniuses, Newton, more or less the father of technological humanism, and Shakespeare, a symbol at least of literary humanism, lived in the seventeenth century. And he suspected that the great split either began or gained momentum then.

You and I, as Christian humanists, will wish to integrate these two disciplines in terms of a third and will wish to blend the contribution of Newton and that of Shakespeare, to use just two type names, in terms of Jesus Christ. We will wish to know and wish our students to know what Shakespeare was up to, but we must also find out what Jesus Christ was up to and what He had to say about us, since it is only in terms of us—human nature—and what He had to say about us—the potential of human nature—that either Newton or Shakespeare becomes relevant, and it is only through these that Newton and Shakespeare and their respective traditions can be integrated.

275

But this work of integration reaches into areas other than that of the cultural, to much more profound depths of the human experience and divine plan. The dichotomy, the divergence which has driven technological humanism so far out from literary humanism, and both from religious or Christian humanism, is but one more form of a split the origins of which we must explore and to the healing of which we must bring some kind of philosophical and spiritual integrating influence and force. The theory of love has been the victim of this disintegration, fragmentation, polarizing at extremes. Everyone has seen the famous painting that hangs in one of the Roman art galleries of sacred and profane love—sacred way down at the end of the park bench, profane way down at the other end, looking in opposite direction, presumably concerned with mutually exclusive spheres. This is a fragmentation, a very ancient one, pre-Christian, but reasserted in terms devastating to Christian civilization and Christian spirituality, in the Renaissance, out of which the painting comes.

The concepts bandied about in discussions of legal philosophy at the moment—sacral civilizations and secular civilizations, sacred concerns and profane concerns—these very words and certainly the antinomies they seem to suggest imply a fragmenting and a dichotomy to which there must be brought some sort of integrating influence. The very extreme emphasis on the apparent contradiction or antinomy again between nature and grace, as apart from the very valid and necessary distinction between nature and grace—the manner in which nature and grace, necessarily distinct, seem to be pitted against one another, even in theological discussions of these, let alone on the level of psychology and sometimes psychiatry and on the level of culture—this is another disturbing sign of fragmenting and of dichotomies to which some species of integrating influence must be brought—which, especially in the nineteenth century but still now, in no small degree, there was thought to be an antithetical conflict between religion and science, between reason and faith.

In the Vatican Art Museum there are two famous paintings by Raphael, which ever since student days have been symbols to me of this tragic dichotomy which our civilization sees as existing between reason and faith. In one glorious panel Raphael has painted all the great thinkers, all the great philosophers of the ancient world and of later civilizations; that painting is called *The School of Athens*. And then on the other side of the doorway, in an equally glorious painting, Raphael has brought together all the theologians and all the mystics and some selected saints to talk about the Faith, and that is called *The Dispute about the Sacrament*—the debate about the nature of the Blessed Sacrament. On one side is the picture of all those who know by reason and on the other side all those who know by faith and there is a door between them and a couple of angels to make sure that none of the scholars are found too close to the sacraments and that none of the saints are caught in the library. It's a symbol, isn't it? You look forward to the day when some more enlightened painter of equal skill will mix them up a little bit, so that there will be a scientist or two over there saying his prayers and not as a compartmentalized part of the life of a devout scientist but as part of the dispute about the Sacrament. And we would like to feel that a few of the saints would be at home, as indeed they would have been, over in the School of Athens talking about some of the metaphysic bound up with the dispute about the Sacrament and a little bit of the poetry, in which the wonder of the Sacrament has been expressed quite as well as it has in the questions and answers of the catechism and the theology book. Thank God.

And then there has been the dichotomy or the fragmentation calling for some specifics of integrating influence to which Cardinal Suenens has directed attention in that wonderful and disturbing book of his, which should never be in the hands of anyone but a mother superior and then only if she is likely to do something about it and act in the light of it.[2] The dichotomy that he points out between the forced dichotomy and between Martha and Mary—the dichotomy bound up with the perilous, excessive separation of intellectual development from spiritual formation, in the case of sisters and priests and bishops and lay people and the sisters-in-law of the presidents or dictators of Asiatic republics—this, of course, is a problem to which Marillac College has addressed itself, providentially, a problem in regard to which it has recognized that the work of the religious on the professional or academic or intellectual level and the prayer of the religious—the meditation, the spiritual formation of the religious—are not rivals. Certainly not enemies, not two separate forces which have to be mutually placated, but two which must be integrated and reconciled. Cardinal Suenens, we said, has had a little bit to say on this as on so many other matters. Speaking of the novitiate, he points out how the Church wants her future religious to be Mary before being Martha so that later she can better be Mary and Martha, together in one vocation. This is a recognition that Mary and Martha are not merely two sisters in a single family; they are two aspects of each single, complete person. There is much of Mary in all of the Marthas, and unless we plan to be bankrupt there must be a good deal of Martha in each Mary.

This is the sort of thing that Pope Pius XII, that wonderfully luminous man whom I beg you never to forget, had in mind when speaking of sisters to religious superiors. He stressed that they provide the sisters with good preparation and intellectual training. And he instructed the superiors to give the sisters all they need, especially books. Especially books! I don't know whether technically that's an infallible pronouncement, but I would wish it were. Especially books, so they can follow, even later, the progress made in their subjects and be able thus to offer the young a rich and stable, balanced harvest of knowledge. This is in conformity with the Catholic concept which accepts with gratitude all that is naturally true, beautiful, and good since it is the image of Divine Truth, Goodness, and Beauty. That is the Catholic concept, but it is not the concept among all Catholics, because of a fragmenting and departmentalization, as well as a dis-integration between the intellectual and spiritual, between the things of the mind and the things of the heart—this dichotomy between intellectual excellence and spiritual perfection still persists. All of these are symbols of the dichotomies, the segregation, and the antinomies, call them what you will, which have plagued our civilization and our personal spiritual lives to the point that many students of civilization and of culture find themselves with a consequent polarity that results in a tragic diminishing of the witness of Christians and of the influence of that Catholic understanding of things concerning which Pope Pius XII spoke.

Well, how integrate, how reconcile, how blend values which we have seen to have been thus departmentalized and fragmented, placed in such antinomy, such dichotomy to one another? It is necessary to form some rough idea of the origin of the basic dichotomy behind it all. And here it is possible to be overly simple, to be overly pat in pointing to a specific incident or person or teaching or event in history. But still in rough truth, I think we can link at least the modern form of this antagonism between learning and sanctity, between reason and faith, between science and literary humanism, between the Church and the world, to Descartes and to the Cartesian method.

Descartes gave us a method, and the method created a mood, and the mood has inspired a civilization. Now, we warned ourselves that we must not be overly simple about this. It did not all begin with Descartes. There was body and soul and a certain tension between them long before Descartes. There was psyche and eros long before Christianity and, therefore, long before Scholasticism, against which Descartes was in revolt. And there was Manichaeanism and all species of dualisms in the ancient world and in the early Christian world. But the devilish part of Descartes was this. He elevated to a theory of knowledge and a system for mastering knowledge this split between the things we know from reason and the things we know from faith. And so he played into the hands either of rationalists, who, enamored of intellect, would despise faith, or into the hands of fanatics, who, enamored of spirituality, would despise intellect. And so we do owe the current form of the antagonism in no small degree to Descartes, remembering always that there were people before him, Abelard, for example, to name no others.

But nonetheless Descartes did set the pattern which became disastrous in latter nineteenth-century and early twentieth-century modernism, with its idea that there were not only carefully departmentalized realms of knowledge dominated on the one hand by reason and on the other by faith, but there were two ways of knowing these were utterly segregated. So that by the time of Loisy and the great modernists, we had two Christs; the Christ of history and the Christ of faith—the object of mystical, fideistic, and believing knowledge. This had spread its disintegrating poison everywhere, even in the Church, and therefore it is no surprise if it has created a discord between the Church and the world.

But nowhere has it shown up more than in sister formation: the keeping of the library a long way from the chapel, and the chapel a long way from the library. Shown up not only in the formation of sisters, it has shown up in the formation of priests. In the seminary in which I attended, by all odds the best in the world, by definition, the chapel was always open and the library was always locked. I managed to get into it, in my deacon year, by the simple technique of suggesting to the rector that it be used as the place where we had movies once a week.

There are popular things which indicate how this has worked out: "Be good my child, and let who will be clever", as if these were irreconcilable attributes, as if the holy need to be necessarily stupid and the bright predetermined to damnation. But this has been a common misgiving. It has been the feeling behind the gleeful latching on to the alleged intellectual dullness of the Curé of Ars by spiritual directors, who certainly wanted us to be holy, but who were militantly on their guard against our becoming intellectually proud. The Curé of Ars has been the victim of some dreadful distortions. Once I visited Ars and I found, to be sure, that his confessional had all the signs of constant wear, which indicated that he was a saint and a saintly confessor. But imagine my scandal, after the spiritual conferences which I had heard about the beauty of his stupidity, when I discovered that the Curé of Ars had a sizeable library! Not only that, but a rather shocking library which may have played some small part in enabling him to be a sympathetic confessor. I don't know, but in any case he had all the Latin classics there, and they were as well thumbed as his confessional was well kneeled. And after that I always brought a pinch of salt to the chapel with me when the spiritual director was talking to us about "Don't you fellows mind about the degrees and all that stuff. You be like the Curé of Ars." And I thought to myself, "You bet I'll be." But I didn't say anything out loud because that was before the Council.

But in any instance the trend today, or almost all, is the other way. The basic unities are making felt their power, and their cohesive pull is being felt all over the world. The basic unities beneath the unities, beneath the diversities of the superficial level of phenomena, the unities of a human kind, the unities of a divine kind, the unities of a spiritual kind—all these are making felt their power and their cohesive pull. There is familiar experience of this in the ecumenical movement in the area of religion, in the One-World Movement, thoroughly resisted by all those brought up on the un-Catholic mentality of Descartes and of others. It is being felt in the political world—the Christian humanism movement at work to pull together the two cultures, the fragmentation of which into technological humanism, scientific humanism so worried Snow and Frank Stanton. This is the valid part behind the intuitions of Father Teilhard de Chardin. His theology may well be

281

disastrous. Whole areas of it certainly are woefully inadequate and incomplete. But nonetheless, the anthropologist in him made him sensitive to whole areas of unity, unduly fragmented by racism, by nationalism, and by other *isms*. And the poet in him made him sensitive to unities unduly fragmented on the level of culture and of semantics. And so he may be a theologian imperfect enough, well to merit the reserve that is prudently suggested by the Holy Office in his regard, but he is, nonetheless, a witness to unities, the unities that underlie the diversities of the phenomenal world that we merely see and merely hear.[3]

How is this great integration to be achieved, the integration on every level which you and I as Christians must permeate with the leaven of the unifying gospel? Well, first of all, obviously, it must be achieved in a person, in persons, and this achievement must be the result of clearer knowledge of the unity of the human person. It is precisely as a person that I, that you, reflect the image of God; and here, too, all and seemingly utterly parallel distinction between body and soul is being rethought as we perceive in an age of psychosomatic medicine what a psycho-physical unity mankind offers us in each person. Into this, theology throws great light, and not the least by the theology concerning the Resurrection. More and more it has been understood, or is beginning to be understood, that, contrary to what men have tended to believe and believe greatly since Descartes, we have but one heart. We don't have a heart for sacred love and a heart for profane; with that same heart with which I am called to love God, I love the things that God has made; and, conversely, with that same heart that I love the world which I see, I am drawn to the love of the invisible world of which the Preface in the Christmas Mass sings.[4] I have but one heart. We do not have two hearts. We have but one. It loves on many levels, and it loves in different directions, and it loves diversified things, but it is but one heart. I have but one mind. That one mind knows by reason some things, and it knows by faith other things, but it is one mind. I am but one psycho-physical unity. I am but one person. And so the reconciliation can and must begin with that one person. And in that one person. And it can be achieved by one person, and that one person you and I well know—Jesus Christ, who reconciles within Himself all antinomies, those which I as a human reconcile in mind and body—the love of time and eternity—but also reconciles within Himself the extremes of infinite and finite, created and uncreated, God and man, earth and heaven, bringing all into oneness.

So the integration must begin and be perfected in the person, in each person and by one person, by assimilation under the personality of Jesus Christ. And as every religious understands, this assimilation, this integration in her person by a person must be expressed through the work. To the work we bring our natural talents, poor talents at best but ours to give, nonetheless; and to the work Christ brings the part of His grace, the supernatural force of His charity. Sometimes pious writers, victimized by the dichotomies of which we have been speaking—often, I regret to say, even religious and spiritual directors—have tended to despise or have seemed to tell us to despise intelligence as being merely natural, talent as being merely human, skill or other personal gifts as nothing, certainly nothing as contrasted with God's grace, God's power, God's supernatural order; but the contrast has been unduly forced, and the dichotomy does not come from the teaching of Jesus Christ. It comes from Descartes and from Manichaeanism and from other dualisms, which were never intended to have such weight in a Christian scheme of things, never intended to be divisive, so exclusive. It was intended that divine grace and human powers, however limited, should be blended to the glory of God and the good of souls, and the proof of that is the Incarnation. It is not only the proof of it but it is the pledge that we, cooperating with the graces of the Incarnation, can achieve the integration of which the Incarnation is the exemplar.

Another proof is the sacramental system. So is the life of the religious who brings talents, joyfully trained and generously given, to the life of grace.

Saint Bernard illustrates this well enough, to conclude with him. In commenting on the mystery of the marriage feast of Cana, Saint Bernard puts this searching question to which Marillac College helps to provide no small part of the answer. Saint Bernard asks, "Why did our Blessed Lord command that, before He would give them the wine that they wanted, they must bring water?"[5] Anyone who knows water and who knows wine knows that there is no earthly connection between the two. None whatever. It would be far easier to produce a bucket of good wine out of thin air than out of a bucket of the best water—make no mistake about that. Well, what was the point of lugging in all the water? In order to provide the wine. The Lord had no headstart toward wine when they brought the water. None at all. Then why the water? Saint Bernard says the point is this: the Lord wished to teach us that He will not waste His grace on a vacuum; that we must bring the best we have on the level of nature, before by His divine power of grace it will be transformed into the best that God needs and that we want. In the measure that we bring the mere water of our intelligence, our skill, our love, our training, our capacity to serve, in that measure we will have wine back. But wine isn't water. And the water isn't wine. The distinction between nature and grace is carefully kept, but the measure of our giving is related to what God does to those who thus give. Well, this is a long way of saying what the scholastic axiom said all along: "Gratia non tollit naturam, sed perficit et supplet defectum naturae."[6]

Grace elevates and ennobles nature and perfects it, but the work of nature must be done first. You can pour all the holy water you choose on a stupid person; at the end she's holy but stupid. The work of nature must be done first. And when it is done, then the Lord is not working in a vacuum, but we have brought Him the stuff with which His transforming power can renew—us first, and the face of the earth. An American poet means something close to this, I think, when he bids us thank God for the gifts and opportunities He gives us, and then give ourselves for everything which is natural, which is infinite, which is Yes. The Church needs no less of you in this predestined century. She needs of you everything which is human and natural, ours to give. Everything which is infinite and divine Christ has given. Everything which is Yes, Yes to history, Yes to mankind, Yes to our best desires, above all, therefore, Yes to God.

XXV

Monsignor Daniel A. Lawless, 1875–1963

"See [said God] that thou make all things according to the pattern which was shown thee on the mount."[1]

These words which God spoke to Moses and which Saint Paul applies to the priest of the New Law, I associate for many reasons with the magnificent prelate of whom we take leave today.

First, there is the obvious possibility of linking to Saint Paul's words the fact that Monsignor received his priestly formation at the *Mount*—Mount Saint Mary's, in Emmitsburg, and the not-less-obvious fact that he remained through so many decades of priesthood faithful to the sacred pattern which was shown him in the spiritual direction and teaching there. He remembered the *Mount*, his seminary, always; he spoke of it lovingly and went back there gladly, with special joy and pardonable pride on the occasion when it honored him in 1951 with its Doctor of Laws for exemplifying so well *the pattern which was shown [him] on the mount*.

But I begin with Saint Paul's words also because the text suggests the true source of this priest's truly mountainous strength and endurance, his faith and greatness. The mount in Sacred Scripture is always the symbol of Christ. For Christian spirituality, Christ is the mountain up into which the devout person must go to find the pattern that God had in mind for him when He called him into being at creation and called him into service by his vocation, whatever it may be.

As a mountain seems to be the meeting-place between earth and heaven, the place where the arch of the sky meets the

This eulogy was preached at Saint Paul Cathedral, Pittsburgh, Pennsylvania, on December 23, 1963.

world—so Christ, as this Christmas season reminds us at every turn, is the meeting-place of God and man, of Divinity and humanity. Any man wishing to know God's plan for him, God's pattern and work for him, must constantly return to the mount—as Moses to Sinai, as Monsignor Lawless to Christ.

When Jesus walked the earth, all manner of people went to Him as up into a mountain to see God's pattern for them and their lives. *"Lord, what wouldst Thou have me to do?"* The rich young man asked this, and when he saw the pattern God demanded of him, he turned away sad and went away to failure. Peter asked it and, inspired by the pattern shown him, turned from a fickle man to the very symbol of rocklike fidelity. Mary Magdalen asked and became a saint in the pattern Christ revealed to her. Judas asked, rejected the pattern, and died in despair. Pontius Pilate asked and averted his eyes in cowardice from what he saw.

Every man who came to Jesus saw in Him the image of his own best possible self, the pattern of what he could and therefore should be. Many lost heart at the sight of their pattern and went their way to be not what they could be, nor what they should be, but what they, in self-defeat, chose to be.

Daniel Lawless saw his pattern decades ago and unswervingly kept to it all his life. It was the pattern of Moses; this is the third reason I choose for him the text that recalls God's words to the Old Testament chieftain of God's people.

The phrases which describe the mighty man of God, Moses in the Old Law, aptly apply to the mighty priest of the New Law to whom today we bid our affectionate farewell. The memory of Moses, the Hebrew leader, lawgiver, prophet, and historian, has ever been one of *isolated grandeur*. Bossuet says that all the prophets who followed Moses in the Ancient Law prided themselves on being his disciples. He always spoke as a master; what he said invariably had a clarity and conviction of unequaled majesty, and yet an artlessness that was winning and endearing.

287

Such was also the case with Monsignor Lawless. He had no awesome tongues of fire, as did Moses, to impose reverence on the people, but he had a majesty and a granite-like quality. Yet he was tender and gentle, almost childlike in his simplicity. I shall never forget the day that he came into my office with a slip of a girl who needed the shelter that Roselia Hospital could best provide. He felt that the bishop should meet and encourage the young girl before she went to the unknown mysteries of the maternity hospital. The somewhat stern man had his massive hand clasped over that of the frail young unwed mother; he could not have been more gracious or kind as, all man and all priest, he introduced her as if she were a princess. Majesty and mildness equally contributed to making a frightened girl grateful to him.

Let me read to you from Monsignor Knox's translation of the Book of Exodus a description of a day in the work of Moses among God's people:—

> Now Moses took his place each day deciding disputes among the people, who stood there from morning till evening waiting for an audience with him. . . . They come to me, said Moses, to find out what God's decision is. . . . [And Jethro said to him]: It is beyond thy powers to sustain this office all alone. . . . Thy part is to be the representative of all these people with God, referring all their affairs to him, prescribing to them rites and observances, customs to be kept and duties to be done. Meanwhile, choose out here and there among the people able men, Godfearing, lovers of truth. . . . Put these in charge of a tribe, or of a hundred families, or fifty families or ten. . . . Share thy burdens with others. . . . It will leave thee free to carry out God's commands and endure the weight of all His claims upon thee. . . .[2]

Does it not sound like a description of his life at the Point? Does it not recall the long, busy years when the Point was the base from which he directed the Missionary Confraternity? Finally he, too, chose from here and there among the people, all over the diocese, the able men and women, "Godfearing, lovers of truth", who undertook the instruction of families, in various numbers, gradually brought together in instruction centers which eventually had 22,000 children enrolled in religious classes in 202 missions with 902 lay teachers, all under the direction of this modern Moses.

Let me read another description of the relationship of Moses to his flock as their captains fought the battles which were their lot and which were bound up with God's purposes for His people:—

> At Raphidim, Amalec came and waged war against Israel. Moses, therefore, said to Josue, "Pick out certain men, and tomorrow go out and engage Amalec in battle. I will be standing on top of the hill with the staff of God in my hand." So Josue did as Moses told him: he engaged Amalec in battle after Moses had climbed to the hill with Aaron and Hur. As long as Moses kept his hands raised up, Israel had the better of the fight. Moses' hands, however, grew tired; so they put a rock in place for him to sit on. Meanwhile Aaron and Hur supported his hands, one on one side and one on the other, so that his hands remained steady till sunset. And Josue mowed down Amalec and his people with the edge of the sword.[3]

This was Monsignor Lawless' relationship to the city that he loved and to the men whom he trusted and admired in their fight for that city, its triumph over the ancient evils that seek to destroy every good city and its prosperity in the battles that the cities of men must constantly wage against forces that make for decay. His was a truly and authentically priestly part in those battles. He never entered or *played* politics; but, like Moses on the hill of Raphidim, he kept aloft his arms in prayer while those he trusted fought in the arena of public life. This was his part in the life of the great Pittsburgh mayor and Pennsylvania governor whom he so admired as a friend and a Christian, Governor David Lawrence.

The things that God said to Moses, He also said to Monsignor Lawless, and Monsignor Lawless made them the pattern of his life and the unchanging theme of his preaching.

"And the Lord spoke to Moses, face to face as a man is wont to speak to his friend. . . ."[4]

> The Lord spoke to Moses, bidding him give the whole company of Israel this message: You must be men set apart, as I am set apart, I, the Lord your God. . . . When thou reapest the crops on thy land . . . leave something for the poor men and wanderers to glean; remember what God you worship. . . . Do not pervert justice by giving false awards, taking a man's poverty into account, or flattering the great; give every man his just due. Do not whisper calumnies in the public ear . . . the Lord hears thee. . . . Thou shalt love thy neighbor as thyself; thy Lord is his. . . . If an alien comes to dwell in your land, and settles down among you, do not treat him disdainfully; welcome him as if he were native born, and do him kindness as if he were one of yourselves, remembering that you were aliens once. . . . The Lord your God remembers. . . .[5]

All who came to his door discovered how well he understood these words. Priests who shared his table, no matter how alien, always felt at home there. He who speaks certainly did.

> . . . There will not be wanting poor in the land of thy habitation: therefore I command thee to open thy hand to the needy and poor that liveth in the land.[6]

And so, through plagues and trials, through periods of want and flood, through the temptations of poverty and sometimes the temptations of prosperity and softening well-being, Monsignor Lawless has led the people of our city even as did Moses—in the pattern of Moses, say better, the pattern of Christ. It was the pattern Daniel Lawless had learned on the *Mount*.

And even as Moses died in a land in which he had not been born—and among people whom he had made not merely God's but also his own by powerful ties of affection, reverence, and gratitude—so has Monsignor Lawless died. He will, I regret to say, be buried elsewhere. But the description of the death of Moses is in many ways the description of Monsignor's death among us:

> There, then, in the land of Moab, Moses died, the Lord's servant, still true to the Lord's bidding. . . . And when he died, still his eyes had not grown dim and his vigour was firm. There was never such another prophet in Israel as Moses: whom the Lord knew face to face.[7]

May God grant him, this modern Moses, who worked so long, so stoutly, in our midst, his share of that Promised Land which alone matters, which alone he sought![8]

XXVI

Reflections on Conscience and Authority

Saint Paul tells us that it is a fearful thing to fall into the hands of the living God.[1]

So it is, no doubt.

But it is no joke to fall into the hands of Mr. Dan Herr.

The way I did—this time, at any rate—is a long story. Dan wrote me and asked if, under suitable conditions, I would give the lecture that brings me to Chicago this afternoon. I replied that I would. He then told me that if I worked hard on the lecture he would give me a medal.[2] I said I would. He invited me to stop in Chicago one morning at about one o'clock, and he then gave me, together with scrambled eggs and marmalade, the subject of my lecture. Thereafter, he wrote me from time to time asking me what progress I was making; he checked the veracity of my replies through an elaborate system of espionage which included, on several occasions, the editor of my diocesan paper and, on at least one occasion, in violation of all the decencies, my private secretary.[3]

In September I went to Rome, in connection with some incidental obligations, to a minor ecclesiastical event that is being held there.[4] In Rome I found letters waiting for me from Dan Herr, reminding me that I was to talk here today in the vernacular. At intervals of a week, I received further communications designed to keep my mind sharply focused on the lecture. Finally, on Thanksgiving Day to be exact, I received a letter from the editor in a New York publishing house informing me that Mr. Dan Herr had told her I was writing a book and could she publish it, please.

This address—The 1964 McGeary Foundation Lecture—was delivered at Chicago, Illinois, on February 9, 1964, during the twenty-fifty anniversary celebration of the Thomas More Association.

I wrote her that I was, in fact, preparing a lecture; that Mr. Herr had told me that it should not be longer than an hour; that it would be a rather measly book and that there must be some mistake.

However, subsequent letters from the publisher made it clear that I had been brought into the world precisely to write a book of reflections on conscience and authority and that instead of the lecture becoming the book, the book should become the lecture.

And so, my reflections this afternoon will outline the book that I shall write if God so abandons me as to let me sign any contract drawn up by the editor, at the behest of Dan Herr, to catch me unaware as I wander in my fragile barque o'er life's tempestuous sea.

But meanwhile I am under contract to compress my proposed book into one imposed lecture the timing of which may now begin.

If I were to write a book of reflections on conscience and authority, I would confine myself to the discussion of these powerful and sometimes conflicting moral forces as they operate within the Holy Catholic Church.

I would do so aware, of course, that conscience and authority are also at work and in conflict in the general society, in the family, in professional life, in the university world—wherever there are persons in societies of whatever kind of origin. I realize, moreover, that the most bitter arena of conflict between conscience and authority in our century is probably the modern State, which, in all its forms, tends to be characterized by a certain absolutism which creates grave problems for even the natural conscience but tormenting antagonisms for the consciences of those who believe in a supernatural order transcending and subordinating the claims of secular authority.

But I would write of the concepts of conscience and authority within the Church because when these concepts and their mutual relations are clear, when a Christian conscience is soundly formed, a model is proposed for all other societies and

Christians are the better prepared personally to face up to parallel tensions elsewhere and socially to contribute to the easing of these in their other forms and areas of conflict.

I would note carefully, in thus limiting my discussion to the Church, how Pope Pius XII could distinguish sharply between the spirit of authority in the Church and the spirit of *authoritarianism*. I would recall his careful distinction between the structure of authority in the Church and that in totalitarian regimes, insisting, as he did, that these latter "can claim no point of resemblance to hierarchical constitutions of the Church", precisely because of the respective attitudes of these and of the Church toward "the clear and incontrovertible dictates of conscience", "the laws of individual and social living written in the hearts of men", and "the freedom and improvement of the human person".[5]

I would probably develop this point at some length, having in mind the confusions, already widespread and now intensified by writers like Mr. Paul Blanshard. I would seek to bring to American readers some of the reflections of their European Catholic brethren on the point made by the Auxiliary Bishop of Rouen at a 1961 Anglo-French symposium on problems of authority in the Church:

> The hierarchical government of the Church will always be radically different in its innermost nature and in its visible manifestations from the hierarchical government of a human society of secular type. It is only to the extent that sin corrupts the hierarchy by depriving it of the God-given sense of its organic function in the Church, and developing in it a *will to power* that knows no limit and has no religious purpose, that the Church becomes that *huge sociological beast* which used to terrify Simone Weil (and many others in good faith after and before her time).[6]

Jean Cadet, more positively, emphasizes how the use of pastoral authority in the Church is necessarily different from the use of authority in any secular society, since *justice*, at best,

294

is the object of secular authority, whereas the whole juris-dictional order of the Church must be the servant of *love*. This is a point which I would develop greatly in my book; I mention it now because it cannot be too soon emphasized in any discussion of conscience and authority, or of anything else within the Church.

My first chapter would have to include a pointed explanation of one reason why there is no much seemingly tentative and even hesitant talk about the relations between conscience and authority. In fact, the problem is relatively modern in time and not even now universal in its geography, the contemporary statement of the problem of conscience being linked to recent and regional claims with respect to the sovereign independence of the individual person. In clarifying the implications of this fact, I would depend heavily on Jacques Leclercq (*Liberté d'Opinion et Catholiques*), who contends that citizens of the Western world suffer from a certain optical illusion when they adjudge the sovereign independence of the individual person to be one of the major themes of human literature, political, moral and other.[7] On the contrary, this theme, including its statement in terms of conscience, is even now almost confined to Western Europe, North America, and Great Britain, plus some contiguous and scattered zones influenced by ideas transplanted from these.

In the Western world, however, the theme of the supremacy of conscience, in a valid sense and also with some exaggerations, Leclercq can compare to a steadily expanding river, flooding in all directions; it has become an *idée fixe*, a master theme, perhaps *the* master theme of Western civilization. People have become accustomed to link, somewhat over simply, its origins to controversies arising out of sixteenth-century religious and political disputes. However, as in the case of other great ideas, it is possible to dig up from the more distant past precursor statements at least of the problem surrounding the idea. Those who read history persuaded that there is nothing new under the sun—or that, as Marie Antoinette's milliner put it, there is nothing new except what has been forgotten—find some earlier affirmations of the supremacy of conscience in Greco-Roman antiquity (drama, philosophy, and eloquence) and even in the literature and ethic of the Far East.

Whatever of this, the theme of the sovereignty of conscience, validly stated and otherwise, like that of the supremacy of the person, has chiefly developed in Western Europe and in relatively modern times. The controversy passed from the religious to the political arena in the seventeenth century, largely reaching its first high political plateau with the French concepts of the rights of man in the eighteenth century and pressing forward thereafter in politico-social movements inspired by the idea of liberty, above all personal liberty, and thus becoming associated with movements and points of view that came to be called *liberal*.

The orderly development of my subject would require that my second chapter concern itself, perhaps, with the history of the concept of conscience. This could be a book all by itself; indeed, many books have been written on the concept of conscience in different times and places, even on the great changes in the concept of conscience within the Christian tradition from New Testament days down to our own times. I would point out that *conscience* is one of those words which everyone uses readily enough and which most think of as not only basic but also very simple, though an invitation to define it usually reveals confusion and embarrassment. Fortunately, it is easier and, indeed, better to have a good conscience than it is to define one, as Thomas à Kempis pointed out about compunction.[8] People can feel very strongly about conscience and be quite fierce in asserting its claims, while being little prepared to say what it is, even though, as they might point out, "everyone *knows* what it is". It is something like a spiral; everyone knows what a spiral is, but when pressed for a definition, most helplessly wiggle their fingers in the air.

In seeking to define conscience, some do so in inspirational terms, like those which little George Washington used when he wrote in his copybook, "Labor to keep alive in your breast that little spark of celestial fire—conscience."[9] Others still speak in the more negative terms of the so-called *accusing conscience*, that stern, tormenting voice that speaks to you only when you have done something wrong and which many suppose to be the only true sense of conscience. This, I think, is what people usually mean when they use phrases like *a New England conscience*, which, under study, often means the guilty recognition that you have spent too much money or that you are likely to be found out in some indiscretion and to find your name in the paper, or, what is worse, to have forfeited your credit in the local bank.

This chapter could be extremely long and singularly boring except to those interested in semantics or the historical development of philosophical concepts. And so I would simply invoke some dictionary definitions which seem to do justice to the general concept of conscience and would then throw in some bibliographical references to more precise definitions and hasten on to the more imaginative considerations which stimulate me most.

Most would probably settle for the definition in the *Century Dictionary*; published in the period 1889–1911, it reflects the notion that is probably uppermost in the mind among those who speak of conscience with positive commitment still. For it, moral conscience is

> the consciousness that the acts for which a person believes himself to be responsible do or do not conform to his ideal of right; the moral judgment of the individual applied to his own conduct, in distinction from his perception of right and wrong in the abstract, and in the conduct of others. It manifests itself in the feeling of *obligation* or *duty*, the moral imperative "I ought" or "I ought not"; hence the phrases the "voice of conscience", the "dictates of conscience", and the like.[10]

This dictionary definition reflects a heavily individualistic concept basically consistent with the personal element present from the beginning in the Christian doctrine concerning the idea of conscience but adding a certain exclusiveness and debatable autonomy, with overtones discordant to the Christian ear, from post-Reformation, Renaissance, and Enlightenment times. Nonetheless, it is a working definition for our purposes, as are also some of the descriptions of conscience with which Victorian philosophical literature abounds. A good example is that by Sir William Hamilton, the nineteenth-century Scottish philosopher (not to be confused with the husband of Lord Nelson's mistress, they having the same name and overlapping dates but somewhat different preoccupations):

> Man, as conscious of his liberty to act, and of the law by which his actions ought to be regulated, recognizes his personal accountability, and calls himself before the internal tribunal which we denominate *conscience*. Here he is either acquitted or condemned. The acquittal is connected with a peculiar feeling or pleasurable exultation, as the *condemnation* with a peculiar feeling of painful humiliation—remorse.[11]

Such definitions or descriptions leave us with several unsolved problems to which we shall have to devote later chapters of our book. The first is the problem of the relationship of the dictates of internal conscience, so understood, to the demands of external authority, the heart of our present reflections. Another is that of how and whence such a conscience derives its knowledge of the law by which its actions are to be regulated; in a word, how is such a conscience formed or illumined? What norms, other than its own *ipse dixit*, does it have?

On this latter point my second chapter will have to evaluate many different speculations. Protestant Christian theories include explanations often bound up with illuminatism or even direct divine inspiration, if not revelation; others, more often in the eighteenth and nineteenth centuries, relate (as did Sir William Hamilton and the even greater Sir William Blackstone) the concept and function of conscience to the concept of Natural Law, a source of knowledge of God's will which a solid Protestant tradition once exalted much higher than any Catholic doctrine of Natural Law exalts it, since the interpretation of Natural Law for Catholics has always been within the context of the mind of the Church where revelation serves to illumine, to purify, and to warm areas of Natural Law which are otherwise obscure, harsh, or unduly rigorous.

For the development of the Catholic Christian understanding of the concept and range of conscience I would refer my gentle reader to a standard treatise in moral theology. The choices are many, but for the purposes of my book, which I would seek to relate to contemporary problems and to infuse with the spirit in which these problems can best be met, I would suggest the first volume of Father Bernard Häring's moral theology for priests and laity entitled *The Law of Christ*.[12] There my reader will find a more-than-adequate survey of the concepts of conscience from the pre-Christian days of Epictetus, Seneca, the Stoics, Chrysippus, and Ovid (whose definition of conscience as "God-in-us" is a remote ancestor of little George Washington's copybook phrase) through the Sacred Scriptures, which are eloquent on the power of conscience but not entirely clear on the definition of its nature, to the development of moral conscience in Patristic writings (especially Saint Augustine and Saint Jerome) and the great scholastic philosophers and theologians.

These latter, Father Häring will point out, offer divers theories regarding the nature of conscience, while agreeing on its claims and its power. The theories of Albert the Great and Thomas Aquinas are intellectualistic; those of Alexander of Hales and Bonaventure are voluntaristic. Both are consistent with Father Häring's own contention, typically Catholic as distinct from *direct voice of God* concepts of conscience, that God is indeed at work in the depths of conscience, at work as a person *who calls and invites, a judge, living, absolute, the source of the summons and the law*, but that we ourselves contribute out of our natures something which must be trained to play its part in the decisions of conscience. Even if we Catholics do not acknowledge the dictate of conscience as being the direct voice of God, as some others tend to do, we do speak of conscience as including somehow the voice of God. *It is the voice of God, but in the sense that we must contribute something of our own in the formation of the decision of a conscience which is right in God's sight. Error is possible in our decision, but we are able to trace it to its source.* That source, and it operates commonly, is in ourselves, not God, and it is, of course, the presence and perils of it which so complicate the discussion of conscience itself and its relations with authority.

This is particularly true, as my chapter will point out, when there is talk of the freedom of conscience as that further concept is debated in our day. *The fact is that, contrary to a general but loose impression, conscience binds far more than it loosens.* Conscience is not something by which I am set free from obligations so much as it is something by which I am bound, controlled, and on occasion sternly rebuked. It is necessary to get this unpleasant fact (if it is unpleasant) in clear focus at the outset of any discussion of conscience. This is, of course, what befogs much discussion, outside the Ecumenical Council, of the progress of the debate on religious liberty as an aspect of freedom of conscience; it also makes extremely delicate the debate on freedom of conscience in the Council itself.[13]

Bishop De Smedt, whose magnificent address introducing the draft on religious liberty was universally applauded at the Council, was painfully aware of the widespread confusion on this point not only among possible critics of his position but also among some who have no idea what he is talking about and might, in fact, reject it if they did, but claim him as their champion.[14]

Hence De Smedt cannot safely as an honest Christian nor prudently as a competent debater leave his case on the apodictic assertion of Pope John, namely: "Every human being has the right to honor God according to the dictates of an upright conscience, and therefore the right to worship God privately and publicly. . . ."[15] He is obliged to shoot at enemies from half a dozen directions, those who wish to scuttle his ship and who clamber over its prow in the honest effort to sink it and those who are scampering aboard in the aft section and all around the sides in an effort to sail under his banner into harbors for which De Smedt is not destined and of which he wants no part.

And so he is obliged to devote whole sections of his Council speech to explaining what he is *not* talking about, since what he *is* talking about is highly mysterious to a generation which talks passionately of conscience, but often to the confusion of the cause.

Accordingly, my chapter on conscience will quote at length from Bishop De Smedt's speech to the Council beginning with the section in which he says:

> When religious liberty is defended, it is not asserted that it is proper for man to consider the religious problem according to his own whim without any moral obligation and decide for himself according to his own will whether or not to embrace religion (religious indifferentism).
>
> Nor is it affirmed that the human conscience is free in the sense that it is, as it were, outside the law, absolved from any obligation toward it (laicism).
>
> Nor is it said that falsehood is to be considered on an equal footing with truth, as though there were no objective norm of truth (doctrinal relativism).
>
> Nor is it admitted that man in any way has a quasi-right to maintain a peaceful complacency in the midst of uncertainty (dilettantistic pessimism).[16]

Then I shall return to the *Century Dictionary* definition, adding a word or two about the positive claims of conscience as these are set forth in Saint Thomas Aquinas and in a very brief but very forceful phrase of the Fourth Lateran. The

Lateran Council said that anyone who acts against conscience does so to his damnation. Saint Thomas specifically considers the possibility of conflict between the dictates of conscience and those of authority in many passages, one of which will suffice:

> Therefore conscience is more to be obeyed than authority imposed from outside. For conscience obliges in virtue of divine command, whether written down in a code or instilled by natural law. To weigh conscience in the scales against obedience to legal authority is to compare the weight of divine and human decrees. The first obliges more than the second, and sometimes against the second.[17]

Wherefore my next chapter must, obviously, concern itself with the concept of authority. I shall be the more eager to write this chapter because the concept of authority in the Church, like that of conscience, involves difficulties which are everywhere encountered in the contemporary ecumenical dialogue. Moreover, the concept and fact of authority are not merely widely discussed at the moment; they are also universally threatened. Within the family, within political society, in the world of teaching and philosophy, in the realm of morals and religion, authority is of all concepts the least popular. On the decline in the prestige of authority and in the recognition of the constructive and noble elements of the virtue of obedience, another whole book could be written. I think it unlikely that any editor will be clamoring for it, and I gravely fear that even the Thomas More Society will not confer a medal on the man who writes it.

However, as you all know me to be a plain blunt man, I shall spell out some basic truths about authority, relying once again on the doctors of morals, dogma, and laws *utriusque* to point out the premises and develop the corollaries of the Christian and human case for authority. I shall be grateful, of course, if the Ecumenical Council, plus the literature surrounding it, so speaks about the nature, limits, and claims of authority as to make these more persuasive to fallen and capricious human nature, always allergic to authority, particularly in an age of democracy and, perhaps, in the land of youth and freedom beyond the ocean bars, where the air is full of sunlight and the flag is full of stars.

However, authority is not just a word; it is, as John Todd sagely notes, a *fact* whose manifestations everybody accepts or endures.[18] I shall follow, in this connection, Yves Simon in recalling that in every society, political and religious, public and private, necessary and voluntary, authority is essential as a cause of united action even in the smallest and most compact community; it is necessary also for the very volition, let alone the attainment, of the common good. Considered in its essential functions, therefore, authority is neither a necessary evil, nor a lesser good, nor a lesser evil, nor the consequence of any evil or deficiency. It is, like nature and society, unqualifiedly good. Even Bertrand Russell, without theological premises or preoccupations of any kind, develops the pragmatic but significant contention that a healthy society requires both central control and individual initiative; without control there is anarchy; without initiative there is stagnation.[19] It will be my task in this chapter to suggest that without certain metaphysical and even theological realities beyond these superficial correlative forces, neither the individual initiatives nor the central controls are likely to stand up very long.

In accomplishing my task I shall be grateful to many authors, particularly to Romano Guardini for a brilliant essay in which he questions the radical possibility of authority in an atheist scheme of things.[20] I shall not, of course, even mention Guardini in my chapter, hoping that no one will translate his article until after I am dead; but I shall share with the reader the things that I shall have stolen from it, particularly those which indicate how authority is bound up with the origins, divine and human, of our being and how contempt of the authority of parents, as all other human sources of what we are, grows fatally in proportion as our recognition of the mystery of creation and the fact of God grows more and more agnostic, however sentimental, and finally atheist.

But I shall develop this important point by borrowing again from Father Bernard Häring, who, writing of the mutual interplay of conscience and authority, points out how conscience instinctively seeks the guidance of authority and presupposes its existence, even as genuine authority by its very nature postulates the existence and freedom of conscience; authority cannot exist, function, or accomplish its divinely appointed purposes save in a moral universe where conscience is alive and at work.

And so I shall use John Todd's introductory essay in *Problems of Authority* for points for meditation on the origins of authority. He reminds us not only that both authority and obedience presuppose conscience, but that both are related to the most intimate and profound notion of *being* itself. Todd, perceiving that the being of creatures is itself relational, traces the nature and claims of authority from the very origins and authors of our being, finding that the ultimate meaning of authority is to be found in the reality conveyed by the word *author*.[21]

This is the same point, philosophical and semantic, that Romano Guardini makes. It involves the mystery of creation and the meaning which that mystery gives to the authority of God; it suggests the limited but analogous nature of human authority, limited because all human authority is devoid of that character of absolute authorship which belongs to God alone; analogous, however, because men can be the *authors* who increase or develop (*augere*) the *growth* of that to which God has given *existence*.

Creation does not mean for many of our fellow men what it does for us in the Church; neither, therefore, does authority. But for those in the Church, the concept of authority on whatever level we encounter it will be shaped and hallowed by the mystery of creation, directly and fully in what pertains to

God, analogously and proportionately in what pertains to anyone less than God. Christian doctrine will bring us to see that human authority is a phenomenon and service whose origin is in God's creative act. Everyone who exercises authority is invested therewith by God and will have to answer to God for the use he makes of it.

For this reason, it is established Christian doctrine that one who holds authority stands to his subjects in the place of God. But this must be understood in its most positive and fruitful sense; it must not be limited to meaning that the superior, natural or religious, represents the authority of God in only a merely negative or inhibiting sense. Understood as God (who works through the constitution of nature and the dispensations of grace) must intend it for the building up of His Kingdom, authority, communicated to others by God, must mean that he who holds it represents divine love not less than divine authority, divine mercy not less than divine justice and, in sum, the *life-giving* power of God, as Father Corbishley puts it.[22]

This means that authority is not only established to regulate, to order, to control, and, on occasion, to forbid, all in analogy to God; it means also what is usually much more important and urgent, namely, that authority is given to inspire and to encourage the initiatives of others, as does God by His grace; to coordinate the purposeful lives, strivings, aspirations, undertakings and energies of others, to press forward, leading, directing, and challenging others, as God, by His grace and through the voice of conscience, is constantly calling to new levels of excellence those subject to His sway and responsible to His authority, even as He sometimes, by a grace or a rebuke of conscience, dissuades, prohibits or overrules them.

Human authority needs always the spiritual disciplines and moral restraints that reason and revelation both inculcate; those who hold authority must, for their own salvation's sake, be mindful that they are, in themselves, not only the equals but the least of the brethren: "Each of you must have the humility to think others better men than himself, and study the welfare of others, not his own. Yours is to be the same mind which Christ Jesus showed. . . ."[23]

But while humility is essential to the salvation of one who holds authority, it is not enough for the achievement of that perfection of individuals and society for the service of which authority is given. These divine purposes require that human authority be not only Christlike in humility but somehow Godlike in its full and positive use of office to lead; Christ emptied Himself and became the equal of slaves, not that they might remain slaves, but that by adding His powers to their deepest desires, He might lift them to a level a little less than the angels, crowning them with glory and honor, giving *them* rule over God's handiwork.[24] This, not contradiction and restraint only, is the purpose and office of authority.

At this point we should note how the modern popes have clearly conceived their office as involving authority not merely to rebuke error and admonish the erring, but to proclaim truth and to inspire all who seek it. They have seen authority as obliging them to provide intellectual leadership, spiritual direction, effective example, and indefatigable challenge to all who acknowledge Peter's authority and depend upon it for positive leadership as well as negative guidance in the battles for truth and goodness to which their consciences summon them. Father Congar can, as a result, happily write:

> In the nineteenth century, Romanticist literature, and often history also, had spread the idea that power and the holding of very high office offered an opportunity for greater enjoyment, for complete freedom to do as one liked and for helping oneself. The popes of the nineteenth and twentieth centuries and with them, the whole body of the bishops, have stood before the eyes of the whole world as men for whom power is responsibility and authority service.[25]

Nor can it be otherwise once it is recognized, as it must be, that authority in the Church is always a relative thing, a means necessary, under the present dispensation, to an end which is Love. Indeed, it is only in the Church that we can speak of authority as the servant of Love, rather than Justice, of which authority must elsewhere be the instrument. This is what Monsignor Journet means when he writes:

> The order of jurisdiction, necessary and of divine origin though it is, is not the noblest or most divine thing in the Church. All its greatness is derived from its purpose, which is to be the servant of Love. Did not our Lord himself say that he had come to serve? When then the pope declares that he is the servant of the servants of God, he is telling the truth. But the Church is greater and nobler than what exists for its sake. The papacy is for the Church, not vice versa. It is therefore true that the pope is not a master but a servant, and that the Church, absolutely speaking, is more excellent and nobler than he, although, from the standpoint of jurisdiction, he is her head.[26]

Not for nothing did our Lord link his conferring of jurisdiction to Peter's threefold declaration of love for Christ and *therefore* for the flock that he must serve. Not for nothing must the pope, the Sovereign Pontiff, sign himself the servant of the servants of God.

By this time, my gentle reader will require of my book a chapter explaining how it came to pass that conscience and authority, the concepts of which are so interrelated and the functions of which appear, theoretically at least, so harmoniously reconciled in Church doctrine, have often grown so far apart as to find themselves so often antagonists, almost antinomies, in so much history, literature and private speculation.

This chapter will require a review of the political, cultural, and scientific forces which have influenced, for better or for worse, the minds of Christians and altered sometimes the accent, if not the voice, of the Church herself through the centuries since Christianity came out of the catacombs and entered the mainstream of human history. Then our chapter will seek to reconstruct, if not the history of the primitive

Church, at *least some recollection of what must have been its mood when it was still so close to the unifying person of the Risen Christ that its unity was still that of brethren in a close-knit family community of which God was the Father, Christ the elder Brother, and the Church, whose prototype is Mary, was the intimately known and loved fostering mother.* In such a family-community, compactly one, personal conscience would rarely have been the starkly individual, lonely, sovereign, and even defiant thing that we find it to be, almost by ideal, in and after the sixteenth century. Authority, too, must have seemed quite different in such a Christian community from what it doubtless came to seem when the princes of God's people began to dress, to talk, and often to act like the other princes of the Renaissance world, the ideas and values of which were so little related to those of the primitive Christian community, or, indeed, the Church itself at times.

Perhaps as our liturgical practices and theological concepts begin to express, with refreshed clarity, the ancient Catholic attitudes and insights on other levels, there will be a renewed understanding of the interplay of conscience and authority and a moving away from the starkly individualistic concepts of both conscience and authority which have developed in recent centuries. In history there is no bringing back the past, but in the case of the living Church it is always possible and is, indeed, a duty to strip away the dead accretions of the past to reveal the essential timeless nature of the Church herself.

Such a stripping away reveals in the early centuries of Catholicism a vision dominated by what Saint Augustine called the *Christus Totus*. Christians are in essence and always a community; *then* they even lived as a community, wrote to each other as members of a community, were martyred as representatives of a community, prayed as a community. The very fact of being constantly subjected to possible outbreaks of persecution reinforced this sense of the community; it should still. Even their failures in the moral problems of life were principally failures to maintain the *concord and harmony* of the community; they should be so seen still. In such a community the conscience of the Christian early acquired a formation which preserved it from individualism and moral solipsism.

On the side of authority, also, the situation was (and essentially is) such that Father Congar can write:

> In the early Church authority was that of men who were like princes in a community which was wholly sanctified, *plebs sancta*, and overshadowed by the Spirit of God. The Church leaders were all the more conscious of their authority in that they saw it as the vehicle of the mystery of salvation which God wishes to accomplish in his Church. They wanted to be, and knew that they were, moved by the Spirit, but they also knew that the Spirit inhabits the Christian community and in the exercise of their authority they remained closely linked to this community.[27]

But consciences, too, were moved by the same spirit; the formation of conscience was accomplished by a single spirit through the shared teachings of the single Mother Church, and this with the result that although conscience was warmly personal, as the Christian conscience must be, it was never sharply individualistic, as later influences have made the human conscience and most things else.

To suggest briefly how the sense of Christian community deteriorated, to the great hurt of concepts of conscience and of authority alike, I shall refer to a stimulating recent book by Theodore Westow, *The Variety of Catholic Attitudes*.[28] It sketches what happened to early, authentic Christian communal and organic concepts of every kind: doctrinal, social, liturgical, and moral. It reveals, for example, that by the eleventh century, though the feeling was still common that Christendom was still one and that the Catholic Faith was still the universal foundation of society, nonetheless there were already many symptoms pointing to new, sometimes promising, sometimes disastrous, developments.

You and I do not have time this afternoon, as my reader will have, to analyze all these, but we can note swiftly the significance of the feudal rivalries which prefigured national rivalries and independence. We can observe the effect of these on the Christian community, even on the deep levels of its doctrine, liturgy, and morals. We can imagine how the gradual replacement of a land economy by a money economy intensified each individual's instinct for personal independence. We shall not, then, be so startled when we begin to find the sense of community growing weaker and weaker in the religious literature of the Middle Ages, so that finally the whole accent of expression between, roughly, the eleventh and sixteenth centuries, falls increasingly on the *first person singular* when we ordinary people are speaking and on the first person plural when a person invested with authority is speaking—a very significant shift, indeed, from earlier usages.

Westow cites a typical paraphrase of the Creed, written in the eleventh century, and already set forth in the form of a highly individualistic prayer from which, significantly, the article about the Church is completely omitted! Small wonder that even spiritual life by this same time began to abound in individualistic forms of spirituality, visions, revelations, and mystical experiences. All this prepares us for the later tendency to emancipate conscience itself more and more from the formative influence of anything but one's own insights, separate graces, and private judgments.

Westow acknowledges, of course, that this fuller expression of the individual as distinct from the communal side of the human person is not without good effects in the development of human culture and of those divine purposes by reason of which all things turn out for good for those who love God. But the passing evil out of which came the permanent good was sometimes evil indeed; it was particularly hurtful to profound devotion, to the authentic image of the Church, and to Christian concepts of conscience and authority. Medieval and Renaissance developments gave impetus to new branches of dogmatic, moral, and mystical theology and inaugurated discoveries in psychology which uncovered intimate facets of the human person as an individual; this period in our history made contributions both sound and lasting. But Westow rightly argues that it was unfortunate insofar as it overconcentrated on the individual, overstressing the importance of purely individual experiences and emotions and leading to an individual sensitiveness, with complications unsettling to the delicate balance of society as well as of the person.

All this threatened to dissolve the sense of the human community; it had already weakened the very sense of membership in the Church, tending as it did to turn religion into a wholly private affair. It made the ordinary man chafe under the guidance of authority, and it tempted him to excessive confidence in his own spiritual strength apart from the Communion of Saints in the company of the Church. *In terms of conscience, it accounts for the total difference between the Catholic position of Saint Joan, even as late as the fifteenth century, and the completely Protestant position of Luther only a century later.*

What happened in later history explains the dismay of a present-day Anglican scholar over what has happened to the New Testament concept of conscience not only in modern society, but in the Church as he knows it. In his book *Conscience in the New Testament*, the Kaye Prize Essay for 1955, Professor C. A. Pierce contends that it is one thing to teach that conscience is inviolable and that no authority would be justified in overruling it when it speaks out against an action or command which alerts it to protest, but that it is something quite different to suppose that conscience is infallible. He protests that when the Church offers men no better guidance than *act according to conscience*, she is abdicating the office to which she is appointed and is apostate to the first article of her Creed, i.e., Jesus is Lord. He contends that the word *conscience* has been so torn out of its Christian context that in any conflict between conscience and Christ Himself, the modern opinion would make Christ come out second best![29]

Reflection on this aspect of what has happened to the concept of conscience in modern times adds depth to the contention of Lord Acton that the Reformation turned out to be, in many respects, a movement against freedom of conscience. It left conscience subject to a new authority, the arbitrary initiative of a prince who might differ in religion from all his subjects, but also it left the individual conscience without other rudder in a turbulent sea of multiplying moral crises which have shattered in the name of several *Christian consciences* the moral consensus of a Christian community already shattered by the princes of this world in its social structure and therefore doubly removed from the original *Total Christ* who ruled the consciences and refined the authority of the original Christian.

As a result, not all the rhetoric which has extolled the sovereignty of the modern individual conscience can cover the pathetic moral state in which it has so often left individuals. This rhetoric has, however, blinded us to the ugly face that exaggerated sense of the autonomy of individual conscience can give those whose consciences become not only the norm of their own moral lives but also their putative title to dominate the lives of others. I think it likely that, as a matter of relative statistics, there have been more hearts broken and hopes frustrated by the demands of someone else's *righteous conscience* than by the demands of public authority, especially when that someone else, in the name of conscience, demands his way (or her way) rather than permit sons or daughters to do what every other voice of God and nature suggested that they do.

I have seen the look of implacable refusal or unbending rejection on the face of duly appointed authority; I have seen it in the movies and in the paintings which tell the tragedies of those who have suffered for conscience's sake at the hands of authority. But in none of these have I seen colder fanaticism or more corpse-like absence of the living breath of charity than that which I remember on one face, typical of thousands, the lips of which hissed at me, in the name of conscience, all the reasons why its owner could not permit his daughter to marry

312

a man whom only he despised, for reasons which he alone could perceive. But how, in the climate of our times, could a mere bishop urge considerations of humanity or experience, of the mind or heart of the Church, let alone of romance, against the self-righteous declaration: "Bishop, will you dare to tell me that the Catholic Church expects me to change a decision I have made in the light of my conscience?"

So, too, when we are told that a man in public office will follow his sovereign individual conscience, heedless of any other voice, when making decisions affecting public policy and the lives, deaths, or coming to birth of millions, we do well to remember the effects that like lonely consciences have had in history. One of the greatest exponents of the *I and God* sense of conscience was Oliver Cromwell. I can well imagine the people of Drogheda gladly preferring that the decision as to their fate depend on the common counsel of almost any commission, provided it included one or two people responsive to Natural Law, to fundamental decencies, and to the general teaching of the Church, rather than that it depend on the sovereign, majestic, righteous but totally mistaken individual conscience of Oliver Cromwell—or, for that matter, any other individual, high or low.

Individual conscience is not always on the side of freedom, nor of life, nor of God, nor of man; *modern conscience* can mean moral solipsism, the arrogance and arbitrariness of which can be more horrendous, because more inaccessible to protest, than almost any despotism and certainly than any duly constituted authority which must function under written law—civil or canon.

Further, reflection on the deterioration of the sense of Christian community and the effect of this on both conscience and authority makes welcome the assurance of Westow—an assurance that all who live in these exciting years of the Council deeply feel—that we are on the threshold of a new era of human and of Church history. In this era the concepts of both conscience and authority will be revitalized and reconciled anew within the Church, where alone they can achieve that synthesis which enables both to serve the person, the image of God in creation. This fresh vision, both of human history and of the Church, is characterized by an awareness of the human person as being not exclusively communal nor exclusively individual, but both, being responsible simultaneously for himself and for his society and who must, therefore, have the full resources of enlightened conscience and responsible authority to guide him. In such a vision, personal morality is not centered on self, nor on society, but on both at once within, again, that *Christus Totus* of which Augustine spoke and of which the Church is at once the means, the instrument, and the *Other Self* in history.

Within the Church, freshly appreciated and newly loved, those who hold authority will be more sensitive to the nature of their offices and to what must be their spirit. In this new mood men may welcome more perceptively that *formation* of the enlightened conscience the need for which is, by all odds, our supreme need as we move from the fragmented age of individualism into a more organic society, consistent with and, please God, better serving the human person.

Accordingly, a chapter must consider the role of the Church in the formation of conscience. This need is made the greater by recent developments in Protestant theology, not without side effects in the thinking of some Catholics. It reveals itself, of course, in connection with moral judgments generally, but given the preoccupations of our generation, it has become publicized chiefly in connection with moral assessments of contraception, abortion, divorce, and euthanasia.

As we have seen, the traditional Protestant concepts of personal conscience were linked at least to the objective word of Scripture, however privately interpreted, or to norms of Natural Law, seen as God's Law almost as Scripture was God's Word and therefore as a control on conscience. But in the particular case of contraception Father de Lestapis sees a revolutionary change in the Protestant understanding of the nature of conscience.

Father de Lestapis put it this way: "The believer as he faces his God is the only judge in conscience, not only of the intentions which lead him to desire to limit births, but also of the validity of the means he employs for the purpose."

The moral philosophers who put forth this *law of liberty* wish to defend some binding force for moral laws; but, as Father Gerald Kelly points out, in principle they cannot admit an absolute binding force covering every concrete case because they think this would conflict with the liberty of God and also with the liberty of the Christian as the child of God. Hence, while admitting that the moral laws are good *general* guides to what is right, some influential Protestant theologians defend as the ultimate standard of moral conduct what they call the *law of liberty* or the *law of love* in the New Testament. This law of love is superior to all other laws and may contradict them. The individual knows this law as it applies to him in the concrete situations of everyday life, not through any verbal formula, but rather through a sort of divine inspiration received within his own soul. In other words, in the depths of the soul there is an immediate contact with God—an intuition of love, as they call it—and this is the ultimate guide for individuals in their moral choices. This direct word of *permissive love* from God Himself is what the voice of conscience appears to have become in this recent school of Protestant ethic; it has had traces of effect or perhaps parallel in the thinking of certain Catholics.

It is on this *law of liberty* concept of conscience that Pope Pius XII commented in a searching and significant radio broadcast made on *Family* Day, March 24, 1952, when he talked on conscience and education. Although delivered directly to Italy, the talk was a commentary on the most urgent aspect of the general problem of conscience in the present revolutionary transition from an age of individualism to an age of new, potentially good, potentially unfortunate, communal emphasis. It is the problem of the formation of the just and objectively justified conscience.

For Pope Pius XII conscience is

> that which is deepest and most intrinsic in man, . . . the inner-most and most secret nucleus in man. It is there that he takes refuge with his spiritual faculties in absolute solitude: alone with himself, or, rather, alone with God—Whose voice sounds in conscience—and with himself. There it is that he decides for good or evil; there it is that he chooses between the way of victory and that of defeat. . . . Hence conscience, to express it with an image as old as it is fitting, is a sanctuary on the threshold of which all must halt, even, in the case of a child, his father and mother. . . .[30]

How, then, can one talk of the education of conscience? We cannot do otherwise, of course, in the light of the Incarnation and claims of the Word of God in Christ and the consequent Christian obligation in matters of faith and morals to accept the will and the commandments of Christ and to conform one's life to them, i.e., each single act, inner or exterior, which the free human will chooses and decides upon. But what is the spiritual faculty, if not conscience, that in each particular case gives guidance to the will so that it may determine its actions in conformity with the divine will? *Conscience, the Pope argued, must be the clear reflection of human actions' divine pattern.*

> *Therefore, expressions such as the judgment of the Christian conscience, or, to judge according to the Christian conscience, mean this: that the pattern of the ultimate and personal decision for a moral action must be taken from the word and will of Christ. In fact, He is the way, the truth, and the life, not only for all men collectively, but for each single one; the mature man, the child, and the youth.*[31]

And so the formation of the Christian conscience consists, above all, in illuminating the mind with respect to Christ's will, law, and way; guiding it also, so far as this can be done

316

from outside, freely and constantly to execute the divine will. *This is the highest present task of moral education, and moral education presupposes authority; it is the first contact between conscience and authority, that of the parent, of the teacher, above all, of those who teach divine law—and of all these within the Church.* Nor is anything more consistent with the traditional Christian concept of conscience. For conscience, as Father Bernard Häring reminds us, since it is not an oracle which draws truth from its own obscure depths, by its very nature seeks illumination and guidance.

> God, the ultimate norm, the truth to which every conscience must conform, . . . always instructs conscience in accordance with its nature: the natural conscience through the order of nature, the conscience endowed with the supernatural grace of faith through supernatural revelation. Just as it is not alien to natural conscience to draw from the natural revelation expressed in creation and to learn from the natural communities which correspond to it, so it is also *according to nature* for the believing conscience elevated by grace and steeped in humility to harken to the word of revelation communicated to us in the Church. . . .
>
> Only one with a totally perverted concept of the real nature and function of conscience could repudiate the infallible *magisterium* of the Church in the name of conscience. Only a conscience which itself enjoys creative plenitude of infallibility in its own native right could *a priori* reject as contradictory every intervention of objective authority.[32]

Nor are Catholics yet alone in their sense of urgency concerning the role that authority, and especially the teaching Church, must play in the formation of the enlightened conscience. The Anglican scholar whom we have already cited, Professor Pierce, quoting a traditional Protestant source, argues appositely:

> Dreadful consequences are derivable to society . . . [from the use of] . . . a plausible word wrested from its proper sense. It has been imagined that provided men follow the directions of

their own *consciences* they are justified in whatever mode of conduct they may adopt, which (as the term *conscience* is now too generally understood) is . . . in other words to say that because men are persuaded a thing is right therefore it cannot be wrong. . . .

When men therefore *talk of liberty* of conscience they would do well to consider whether it is not, as the phrase is now understood, rather a liberty of their own making than any portion of that liberty with which Christ has made them free.[33]

For this reason, Pierce sees the Church as having five main duties, plus the resources for performing them, in connection with that training of personal *choice and conscience* which Pius XII found the urgent need of our civilization. He sees the Church as bound to make herself *the best possible environment* for the formation of conscience, a role of the Church that is no longer served when the concept of the Church evaporates from the notion of Christian community to that of an ecclesiastical center visited from time to time for ritualistic observances, conceived as strictly private duties. He speaks of the spiritual manner in which to do this the Church must influence the secular environment in which her members live, since this, too, shapes conscience; he describes the teaching responsibility on specific moral questions which the Church has, beyond her general witness to the truth, and how she must set before her members, and anyone else who will listen, the relevant facts on these specific issues, beginning with the great truths of revelation and the doctrines necessary to salvation, but including also the wisdom of her own experience, which is the sum of that of her countless members plus the corporate insight that comes from her immemorial dialogue with the cultural, political, and religious systems of all humanity. Above all—and here the Anglican scholar echoes Pope Pius—she must proclaim not only the teachings of Christ, but His life-giving Person as the pattern to be emulated, making the influence of everything Christ said and did and was penetrate the deepest depths of human intellectual, appetitive, instinctive, and emotional life where conscience stirs. Mindful that conscience can, while still claiming the name of conscience, be lulled, anesthetized, even deadened, the Church has the duty to seek the development in all her children of a moral sensitivity so acute that conscience would not merely react negatively to deviation from Christian perfection, but would impel positively toward personal perfection, social reform and the building of the Kingdom of God.[34]

Greater appreciation of this latter office of the Church in the formation of conscience would offset the temptation to pretend that the claims of authority to obedience have so stifled the initiative and freedom of devout consciences as to diminish the effectiveness of the gospel and the Church. But Father Daniélou proclaims the authentically heroic understanding of true obedience when he writes:

> Christianity would have had greater influence on social institutions if we had always had the courage to show that obedience to God, as an absolute duty, affects man's whole temporal, political, professional and family life. If *Christians have not been more revolutionary, it is not because they lacked freedom but because they have not been sufficiently obedient. . . . This is problem number one and it involves fully relating conscience to authority, above all, the authority of God. How?*[35]

The answer to Father Daniélou's "*How?*" is largely found in the study and experience behind Cardinal Newman's final judgment on the part of the Church in the formation of a Christian conscience. Newman was excruciatingly aware of the need for objective criteria for evaluating the dictates of conscience, and no small part of his life was a search for such criteria in what pertained to the basic moral act, the act of faith. He could not find such criteria in unaided nature alone, particularly given the fallen state of man, which was, of all dogmas, the one clearest to Newman. Neither could he consider Scripture itself an adequate objective means to the formation of conscience nor norm for judging its dictates; in Luther's protestation that his conscience was *captive to the Word of God* Newman would find the cry of a sorry captive, indeed, so long as the Word of God meant merely the letter of Scripture alone; also, Newman could find no adequate guide nor objective norm for conscience in Tradition alone nor in the teachings of the Fathers, and it is the point of his life that he could not find the rule of conscience in a national church. The Universal Catholic Church, he decided, endowed with infallibility and teaching through divinely appointed channels, must be the spiritual country in which authority brings supernatural doctrine to the direction of that conscience which is the herald of the Natural Law; the Catholic Church alone provides adequate objective criteria for the evaluation of those dictates of the sincere conscience which the upright man is bound to follow.

It would take a book by itself to discuss all that Newman contributes to the concepts of conscience and authority and the relations between the two. Brother F. James Kaiser, presently a professor at La Salle College in Philadelphia, has written just such a book, with special reference to the relationship of these to Newman's personal faith.[36]

Mr. Garry Wills, in a forthcoming book entitled *Politics and Catholic Freedom*, is indebted to Newman for many premises of his own argument on the role of conscience in the complex political area of urgent contemporary interest which his book explores. My hypothetical book will devote a chapter to Newman because no modern writer, probably no Catholic writer at any time, has shed such clear light on conscience and authority nor brought such tested practical qualifications to this doctrinal discussion. Moreover, in Newman's day there had long been rife the religious and political disorders resulting from polarization of moral theory around individual conscience, almost in a vacuum of moral solipsism. But by the same token, Newman's generation was beginning to feel the stirrings of the renewed universal aspiration and new social movements, theological and political, of which our generation is witnessing the developments in Christendom and in the world community.

To these John Henry Newman was sensitive, particularly in what pertains to their relationship to personal conscience, to authority, and to the deepest theological nature of the Church. On these points alone, a good case can be made for Bishop Robert J. Dwyer's description of Newman as the *absent Council Father* of Vatican Council II. Bishop Dwyer, noting that Newman has been cited in the Council more frequently than any other authority, not excepting Saint Thomas, finds his influence everywhere pervasive, especially in problems associated with the development of Christian doctrine. He declares that Newman's spirit must inevitably be present in the Council's final decisions; one prays this will be particularly true on questions of conscience and authority.[37]

My chapter on Newman will have to point out that the English scholar, although the eager and unmistakable champion of conscience, was no partisan of *modern conscience* nor of moral liberalism. Like C. A. Pierce among recent Protestants and Bishop De Smedt in the Catholic Council, Newman must include in his defense of the rights of conscience a repudiation of its caricatures and counterfeits. He exposes the scientific and literary efforts to be rid of conscience entirely, the

> resolute warfare . . . against that spiritual, invisible influence which is too subtle for science and too profound for literature. . . . As in Roman times and in the Middle Ages, its supremacy was assailed by the arm of physical force, so now the intellect is put in operation to sap the foundations of a power which the sword could not destroy. We are told that conscience is but a twist in primitive and untutored man; that its dictate is an imagination; that the very notion of guiltiness, which that dictate enforces, is simply irrational, for how can there possibly be freedom of will, how can there be consequent responsibility, in that infinite

eternal network of cause and effect in which we helplessly lie? And what retribution have we to fear when we have had no real choice to do good or evil?[38]

Then he sketches the present *notion of conscience in the popular mind*. The sketch is still lifelike after a century:

There, no more than in the intellectual world, does *conscience* retain the old, true, Catholic meaning of the word. There too the idea, the presence, of a moral governor is far away from the use of it, frequent and emphatic as that use of it is. When men advocate the rights of conscience, they in no sense mean the rights of the Creator, nor the duty to Him, in thought and deed, of the creature; but the right of thinking, speaking, writing and acting according to their judgment or their humour, without any thought of God at all. They do not even pretend to go by any moral rule, but they demand what they think is an Englishman's prerogative, for each to be his own master in all things, and to profess what he pleases, asking no one's leave, and accounting priest or preacher, speaker or writer, unutterably impertinent, who dares to say a word against his going to perdition, if he likes it, in his own way. Conscience has rights because it has duties; but in this age, with a large portion of the public, it is the very right and freedom of conscience to dispense with conscience, to ignore a Lawgiver and Judge, to be independent of unseen obligations. It becomes a license to take up any or no religion, to take up this or that and let it go again, to go to Church, to go to chapel, to boast of being above all religions and to be an impartial critic of each of them. Conscience is a stern monitor, but in this century it has been superseded by a counterfeit which the eighteen centuries prior to it never heard of, and could not have mistaken for it if they had. *It is the right of self-will.*[39]

But for Newman himself, beginning in his earliest Anglican days, conscience was a cognitive and affective act of profoundly theological overtones, God-centered, God-sanctioned, sensitive and responsible to God above all else. It involved the faculties by which man discovers God and pleases God.

322

From Newman's Anglican sermons, Brother Kaiser draws a total picture of the great preacher's view of the positive role of enlightened conscience in leading man to the point where authority, especially that of revelation, can work on a conscience illumined by grace to bring one to the highest religious knowledge and security.

This view goes far beyond the mere *accusing conscience* concept. He who faithfully follows the promptings of his conscience, his sense of right and wrong, Newman insists, will arrive at objective religious truth disposed to accept it and live by it. Brother Kaiser summarizes from Newman's Oxford preaching five propositions setting forth this matter so vital to Newman. They are: (1) conscience consists in a habitual orientation of the whole man to God; (2) conscience develops in man a profound awareness of the presence of God; (3) conscience implies that a man desires to serve God with a perfect heart; (4) this orientation to God and perfect service will be manifested by consistency in conduct; (5) finally, conscience imposes the duty of habitual obedience.[40]

It is here in Newman's argument that conscience, properly understood, enters the orbit of authority, not less properly understood—indeed cries out for its guiding help. It is here, too, that we become keenly aware of why the English Cardinal of the Vatican Council I period would second the arguments of those in Vatican Council II who argue that nothing will better serve the case for the *doctrinal authority* of supernatural Catholicism than a clear, unequivocal defense of the case for the *moral authority* of natural conscience. How promptly would Newman have perceived the implications, in terms of the future of the Faith, as well as the premises of justice and decency, behind that proposition in Pope John's *Pacem in Terris* which the captious seem disposed to debate as if it were somehow rash or offensive to pious ears: "Every human being has the right to honor God according to the dictates of an upright conscience. . . ."[41]

One of Cardinal Newman's deepest convictions and dearest consolations was that his own life story ("I have not sinned against the light!") proved how habitual obedience to such an upright (even erroneous) conscience eventually leads to objective truth; that those who act according to the light of conscience are increasingly rewarded with greater light. He saw evidence of this everywhere in sacred history, but his reflections on the case of Saint Paul are particularly revealing in view of his own conscientious attacks on Catholicism during his Anglican days. Newman considered that Paul differed from other enemies of Christ in that he kept a clear conscience and habitually obeyed according to his knowledge: " . . . missing the great truth that Jesus was the Christ, he persecuted the Christians; but though his conscience was ill-informed, and that by his own fault, yet he obeyed it such as it was."[42] Hence Paul's progress from error to faith, his conversion from hate to love.

In connection with the relation of authority to conscience, the case of Saul-turned-Paul was also instructive to Newman:

> God speaks to us in two ways, in our heart and in His Word. The latter and greater of these informants Saint Paul knew little of; the former he could not but know in his measure (for it was within him), and he obeyed it. That inward voice was but feeble, mixed up and obscured with human feelings and human traditions; so that what his conscience told him to do, was but partially true and in part wrong. Yet still, believing it to speak God's will, he deferred to it, acting as he would afterwards when he was not disobedient to the heavenly vision which informed him Jesus was the Christ.[43]

Again, then, conscience and authority not merely admit of reconciliation; they demand each other.

> The general sense of right and wrong, which is the first element in religion, is so delicate, so fitful, so easily puzzled, obscured, perverted, so subtle in its argumentative methods, so impressed by education, so biassed by pride and passion, so unsteady in its flight . . . this sense is at once the highest of all teachers, yet the

least luminous; and the Church, the pope, the hierarchy are in the divine purpose the supply of an urgent demand.[44]

But however *obscured* and *unsteady* conscience may be, it is still, says Newman, "a messenger from Him Who, both in nature and in grace, speaks to us behind a veil, and teaches and rules us by His representatives. [It] is the aboriginal Vicar of Christ. . . ."[45] Hence authority depends on conscience not only for the holy exercise of its claims; it depends on conscience for the very acceptance of these. The authority, that of the pope included, which would be unmindful of conscience or hold it in contempt would be suicidal, destructive of itself; but the conscience, even otherwise enlightened, which would not recognize its need of authority, above all the teaching authority in the Church, would be similarly destructive of its own purposes.

Newman's greatest apologetic task ultimately became to reconcile the natural *aboriginal Vicar of Christ* which is conscience with the supernaturally established Vicar of Christ in the Church. So far as infallible teaching is concerned, this presented no difficulty; but in specific decisions in the practical order, including those of a political nature posited by Gladstone in his reactions to the decrees of the First Vatican Council, Newman concedes that there are extreme cases in which conscience may come into collision with the word of a pope, but he has little difficulty establishing from Catholic philosophical, theological, conciliar and, indeed, papal arguments that in such a case conscience is to be followed in spite of that (papal) word.

Newman's detailed analysis of this problem of possible practical conflict between conscience and authority is the content of his historic *Letter to the Duke of Norfolk*; it is a classic contribution to the all-time literature on the questions, and it remains required reading for any with lingering misgivings about the direct doctrinal point defined in Vatican Council I or the indirect political corollaries implied by Gladstone. (I once had a first edition of Newman's *Letter to the Duke of Norfolk*, but I loaned it to a young Congressman from Massachusetts who thought he should study up on this controversy in case he ever campaigned for the presidency.)[46]

Newman's quip, for such it was, about the order of the toasts he could drink to conscience and to the pope takes its force from the fact that neither he nor Gladstone was concerned, at this juncture, with papal infallibility or with Church teaching at all. They were talking about the moral freedom of a Catholic to serve his country according to his conscience. This freedom of conscience, Newman maintains, can never be in conflict with the infallibility of the pope, because conscience is not a judgment upon any speculative truth or abstract doctrine, but bears immediately on conduct, something to be done or not done, *here and now*, and in which, by hypothesis, the pope might give a specific order or seek to impose a practical decision which an individual conscience found unacceptable. Newman's conclusion that a positive and clear dictate of a man's conscience regarding some act to be performed or omitted must be obeyed rather than an opposing precept of a superior is no less orthodox than that of Saint Thomas Aquinas in the same matter. It must necessarily follow from the Catholic concept of conscience, as Newman mischievously quotes against the British Prime Minister, defended by the Fourth Lateran Council and by the celebrated Spanish Carmelites of Salamanca.

Just as Newman's interior life prepared him to speak with grateful insight of the role of conscience, so his career in the Church prepared him to speak realistically as well as reverently of authority, its divine role and its human, sometimes galling, limitations. No one has preached more eloquently than he that *men, not angels, are the ministers of the gospel*, and few have had more acute personal experiences to add feeling to their preaching. But his view of the Church, as also his view of history and the Providence of God, enabled him to see occasional evil, including discomfort of spirit, as indispensable in the hammering out of the truth and the achievement of good. That view the cardinal set forth in a superb description of the Catholic interplay of conscience and authority:

> Catholic Christendom is no simple exhibition of religious absolutism, but presents a continuous picture of authority and private judgment alternately advancing and retreating as the ebb and flow of the tide;—it is a vast assemblage of human beings with wilful intellects and wild passions, brought together into one by the beauty and the majesty of a superhuman Power,—into what may be called a large reformatory or training-school, not as if into a hospital or into a prison, not in order to be sent to bed, not to be buried alive, but (if I may change my metaphor) brought together as if into some moral factory, for the melting, refining, and moulding, by an incessant, noisy process, of the raw material of human nature, so excellent, so dangerous, so capable of divine purpose.[47]

A book of reflections on conscience and authority must perforce include a chapter on the saint under whose patronage we meet. Your perceptive president, writing last month in *Sign*, describes the sentimental, political, and psychological pressures all but irresistibly at work on Thomas More to persuade him to take the oath so lightly taken by his lesser (which means almost all) contemporaries. Mr. Herr then writes:

> Thomas More sat with his conscience for fifteen lonely months in the Tower of London, . . . isolated from the other prisoners, forbidden his beloved books, deprived finally of even pen and paper. But neither his conscience nor his writing had lagged. He scrawled last messages to his family with charcoal (". . . that we may merrily meet in heaven") and went to his death proclaiming that he died "the King's good servant, but God's first".[48]

It is, indeed, a lonely picture, as is that of the martyr to conscience always and everywhere. But a devout humanist like More understood better than any other that the very nature of the informed Christian conscience is that it never leaves one spiritually isolated nor intellectually alone. For the invisible wall of Christian conscience closes compactly around its possessor a host of rare spirits that no prison wall can close out, *the choir invisible of those immortal dead who live again in minds made better by their presence*. John Lancaster Spalding described the companions of Father Delp in his Nazi prison, of Father Perrin in the concentration camp, and the spiritual company of the physically isolated Thomas More when he wrote, "If I am left alone, yet God and all the heroic dead are with me still."

Nor is the man of conscience without joy. To no man more than Thomas More could à Kempis' words apply: "Have a good conscience and thou shalt ever have gladness. A good conscience may bear right many things and rejoices among adversities."[49]

For your patron illustrates (as R. W. Chambers' biography and Robert Bolt's play unforgettably demonstrate) precisely the basic issues in any conflict between conscience and authority.[50] Conscience in the most exemplary Catholic sense was the core of More's character; it was the heart of his sanctity, of his tragedy, and of the eternal triumph of this urbane humanist of resolute, informed conscience.

But if my book gives a chapter to your patron, as the witness unto death of the things we have been considering—conscience, authority, and both within the Church—it must give another to a not less shining example of these. I refer, of course, to Saint Joan of Arc, whose memory for reasons historical, theological, and perhaps sentimental, I must cherish precisely because I am a bishop—that is, one bound by conscience, charged with authority, and tied by great love to the Church.[51] Jean Guitton, the first of the lay auditors admitted to Vatican Council II, has promised a book precisely on these aspects of the haunting case of Saint Joan.[52] No case in twenty centuries presents so dramatically nor in such brutal completeness the most extreme anguish of the conflict between conscience and authority. No others ever caught in this conflict, certainly not Galileo and most certainly not any usually cited as "modern Galileos", hold a candle light of moral splendor to the solar brilliance with which Saint Joan illumines the Catholic concept of martyrdom for conscience' sake.

Joan's testimony at Rouen is perlucid evidence of the clarity of Joan's conscience and the correctness of its relation to duly constituted authority, and all this within the Church, whose true nature she perceived with a lucidity amazing in view not merely of her lack of formal education but of the superficial understanding of this mystery in even her most sophisticated contemporaries, her judges included.

It is precisely for this reason that Jacques Maritain, in a moving recent essay, describes Jean Brehal's brief in Joan's behalf as the most important theological document in her rehabilitation trial. Brehal underscored that, for Joan, when an order clearly comes from God, no human superior can place an obstacle in its way; her understanding of this was strictly in the pattern of Saint Thomas, and no badgering of judges or baiting of cross-examiners could shake her from her repeated affirmations of this premise of her entire position. She said she submitted gladly to all constituted authority in the Church, to the pope, to other prelates, God being first served; she said that in all her words and all her deeds she gladly sought to follow the Church, even, as she understood it, the Church Militant, just so it commanded nothing impossible, explaining that by this she meant only that it would be impossible to deny what God had commanded. "What God commands [her very phrasing is almost that of Saint Thomas] I shall not desist from doing for any man alive, nor for any thing there is." In this, Brehal argues, there is not a shadow of fault; such words are morality itself.

Maritain then drives home the point. It is impossible that the Universal Church, infallibly guided by the Holy Spirit (as is no single prelate nor any particular sub-grouping of prelates), or that the pope acting as Chief Shepherd and Teacher of the Universal Church should ever impose a commandment contrary to that of God.

What, then, is the word *Church* doing in the adversative position to the word *conscience* in which Joan was so brutally crushed? Jean Brehal, within the lifetime of Joan's mother and those who watched Joan die, gives the answer:

Among all the equivocations [in the questions put to her], one of them is particularly tricky and it recurs constantly [in the trial]. They kept repeating that she should submit all her statements and her deeds to the judgment of the Church. So far as this might mean the Universal Church (the Church itself) and the Sovereign Pontiff, Joan never failed to declare her readiness to submit; but in their way of understanding it, (to her judges and accusers) *the Church was themselves; sed ad eorum intellectum de seipsis hoc intendebant.* . . .[53]

In brief, her judges did not think of themselves as merely the human wielders of authority; they thought of themselves as the authority, as the Church itself. There, comments Maritain, in all its depth, is the drama that involved Saint Joan. It is clear that the judges of Rouen and the learned doctors of the University of Paris lacked an integral, living theology of what authority is in the Church—and, as a result, of what lies on the consciences of those who hold authority in the Church.

Joan, untutored, caught the point of the nature of the Church by an instinct of faith and a grace of the Holy Spirit, and she clung to it in spite of every threat they made or trap they set. So she pinpointed with peasant directness the human wielder of authority responsible for her tragedy: "Bishop, I die through you!" It is a poignant accusation that must haunt all in authority forever; but it is without hate and so precise as to be without a trace of anticlericalism.[54] Moreover, Joan knew that there was a sense in which she, too, was the Church, and when she appealed to the Holy Father and to a Church Council she discerned, dimly I think, the Council called by Pope John. With the passing centuries we are appreciating with new depth that pristine Christian understanding of the Church that Joan sensed, *the Church of the Incarnate Word*, described in the very title of Monsignor Charles Journet's book (so necessary for our times, too, as Maritain notes), to the implications of which for conscience and authority alike the present Council and the studies surrounding it will doubtless bring luminous moral, ascetical, and dogmatic insights.

And so his close attention to the debates within the Council hall on the concept of the Church should greatly help Jean Guitton to write the book which he promises to justify his claim that ours is *the age of Joan*. He means by this, I suppose, that ours is an age of great deference—must we not even say, in all honesty, of sometimes mistaken deference?—to individual conscience; it is an age, alternately, of excessive expressions and excessive rejections of authority; above all, it is an age looking for terms in which it can express a dawning new love for the Church, a love such, as I think, as the twenty Christian centuries to date have not yet seen and precisely because it is sensed that in the Church and in the Church alone are reconciled human conscience made divine and divine authority made humane.

Saint Joan has so much to teach us about the claims of conscience, the pitfalls of authority, and why the Church, one with Christ, is supremely to be loved, no matter what. Joan reminds us that neither conscience nor authority amounts to anything, in final terms, except as means to an end greater than either or both, and that end is *neither the freedom* that conscience claims *nor the order* that authority imposes, but it is the sanctity to which conscience must bind us and authority must serve. Joan reminds us that the Church is on the side of conscience and canonizes those who follow it; the Church is on the side of authority and commands those who exercise it; but the Church is, above all, the kingdom of *sanctity*; and to *sanctity* everything, conscience and authority and all else, is utterly subordinate.

Those who realize this have found their way to the very heart of the Catholic Faith; everything else is at the periphery. That is why Bernanos, writing of the clash between the conscience of Joan and the authority of her judges, loses little time on analysis or rehearsal of the evil of the clash, but devotes his whole time, as Joan would wish, to the lesson of the good that hallows the otherwise-harrowing business. *Ours is the Church of the saints.* Who, reading of Joan, fails to see this and to crave to be at one with her? Is there one who would really wish to spend his life, like some of her judges, pondering the problem of evil rather than dashing forward with her, the saint? To be a saint, what bishop would not give his ring, his mitre, and his crosier? What cardinal would not give his purple; what pope his white robe, his chamberlains, his Swiss Guard, and all his temporal power? The whole vast machinery of wisdom, experience, discipline, power, and majesty is of itself nothing unless it is animated by love and productive of sanctity.

From the pope down to the little altar boy draining the wine left over in the cruets, everyone knows this. We may respect the Commissariat Service, the Provost Marshal, the staff officers and the cartographers, but our hearts are with those who get killed. *Ours is the Church of the saints.*

Joan has other things to teach us; and these, too, Jean Guitton promises to develop in his book. He suggests that Joan is not only the saint of conscience, but she is specifically the saint of *conscience impelling one to vocation*, a vocation within the Church, even though often involving tension with the institutional side of the Church and therefore, perhaps, with authority.

This makes ours *the age of Joan* in yet another dimension, since in our age the very sense of *vocation* has grown tenuous and vague, almost in proportion as conscience, for all the talk about its freedom and its sovereignty, has become more and more divorced from the voice of God. A whole literature is growing up around this subject, thank God, and its emphasis is happily on the relationship of *vocation* to *personal liberty* and of *both* to *enlightened conscience*.

Bernard Shaw links Saint Joan to all this in one of the most perceptive sections of the preface to his provocative play. For Shaw, Joan exemplifies the conflict between genius and discipline, by which he means the conflict between *vocation* and *institution* as one aspect of the conflict between conscience and authority. Jean Guitton's preface to Maurice Bellet's *Vocation et Liberté* leads me to hope that his promised book on Saint Joan will make Shaw's point profitable to our generation in the life of the Church, in political society, in science, and in the service of every aspect of truly humane culture.

And so my final chapter shall provide reflections on vocation, including the vocation of an organization like the Thomas More Association, and the vocation of publications like *The Critic*. I think it possible that from time to time in this quarter century of its so proud and so useful existence *The Critic* and its association may have had momentary occasion to run afoul of authority, near or far, greater or less. It is just possible that claims of conscience have sometimes been involved in such collisions; so, I think it likely, have been claims of authority.

In short-range terms, these have no doubt brought with them frustrations and vexation of spirit; in longer view, they must necessarily have served the values it is the vocation of the association to promote. The pursuit of vocation, whether clerical or lay, always presupposes dictates of conscience and sooner or later brings one into collision with one or another form of authority. Sometimes it is the authority of God, impelling one to the vocation of the needed but unattractive work that one fears or resists. Sometimes it is the authority of parents, resisting a vocation to priesthood, to marriage, or to one of those harebrained ventures which so frequently turn

333

out to the good name of the family and the glory of God. Increasingly in our day it is the authority of the State, seeking to regulate our vocations, sometimes through work authoritatively imposed (as in compulsory military service) and sometimes through the impersonal requirements of the Planned Society, rightist, leftist, or secular democratic. This may easily prove the greatest source of collision in an age of technocracy.

See how pertinent to the concept of *vocation*, which is, in turn, so pertinent to the vitality of human culture as well as of the Church, is this question of conscience and authority. See how important it is that conscience and authority be harmoniously related, but that neither be annihilated.

In fact, not only must each be strong, but the synchronizing of both must still leave a tension between them. In the dynamic society, and the Church must always be such, there is a *tension* as well as a *harmony* between the liberty that, unchecked, could degenerate into chaos and the control that, unchecked, could freeze into despotism. Hence in the Church, where the basic relations are in order and both forces are strong, we shall not regret the occasional painful stresses and perhaps embarrassing strains which reveal that the tension between individual conscience and collective authority is at work. Quite the contrary: we shall rejoice in the evidence this gives of organic vitality, recognizing not only that the tension remains even after the two forces are harmoniously reconciled but that tension is essential to the harmony itself.

This truth has its parallel everywhere. It is symbolized in the *basic dualism* that Curt Sachs finds at work in the world of art where the to-and-fro of shaping trends of perfection depends on two ideals alternately acting as magnetic poles. Sometimes this polarity and tension in art is set forth in metaphor from physics; then it is termed *static–dynamic*. Sometimes the antonyms are described as the Greeks expressed them, in terms of ethos and pathos. There is a tension underlying the harmonies of music, where the order of rules is imposed on the spontaneity

334

of sound. Biology reveals the *balance of nature*; a certain tension is everywhere in art and life, or there is no harmony and no health.

So for organic vigor, whether in the person or in society a certain tension is as inevitable and necessary as we saw authority itself and the impulse of conscience to be. It is in fostering and forming both, in the guidance it gives to conscience and in the controls it imposes on authority, with the harmony arising from their mutual interplay, that the Holy Catholic Church, which this association passionately loves and proudly serves, gives glory to God, makes its greatest contribution to civilization, and inspires vocations, temporal and eternal, pursued in freedom, illumined by faith, by the likes of Dan Herr, by each of you and, for that matter, by the likes of me.

XXVII

A Closed Retreat: Why Me?

Father Walsh's observations about the difficulties that are following from the liturgical renewal in the reformed Church brought to my mind a true story that I witnessed in Rome this fall, and typical of the shifting times in which we live. I do not know how many of you have had occasion to hear the lectures on the liturgy of the celebrated English Jesuit, Father Clifford Howell, but for a great many years Father Clifford Howell has been going about the world telling us how to say Mass facing the people and all the other things; and so you can imagine my pleasure as an unreconstructed rebel when I overheard the following conversation just outside Saint Peter's one morning this fall. An American priest walked up to a Jesuit from Farm Street in London, where Father Cliff Howell lives when he's home, and he said, "How's Father Clifford Howell?" and the British Jesuit said, "Oh, Cliff, oh, he's fine. He'll be getting back. He's down in Australia for the winter." He said, "He's been saying Mass facing the people, Mass facing Mecca, and Mass facing Bethlehem, and now all winter he's saying Mass upside down."

The date of the Regional Retreat Conference in Houston has been changed a couple of times because of the Council. The postponements of one sort or another have been very hard, no doubt, and so we are the more grateful for the persevering patience and great skill that has resulted in the extraordinary success of this weekend's Regional Conference.[1] If it be true that the Regional Conference has suffered from delay brought about by the Council, it is also true, as has been clear at the

This address was delivered at the Shamrock-Hilton Hotel, Houston, Texas, on April 4, 1964.

Retreat Director's Workshop today, that it has gained from the new emphasis and new points of view, from some of the new directives of which the Council is the center and perhaps the source. Certainly, the Retreat Movement has gained from this meeting in Houston, and so I wish to say a most special word of very sincere appreciation to Bishop Morkovsky for the patronage he has given, the encouragement he has given, the apostolic interest that he has taken in the retreat program and his eagerness to see us all present here in Houston for this weekend. We are deeply grateful to you, Bishop.

Somewhere in America tonight there is a kid, probably dozens of them, who will walk on the face of the moon. In all probability there is a couple (they probably haven't met yet) who will keep a date, not by the light of the moon, but on the far side of the moon. In fact I would think it was in the realm of possibility that travel in that area of space, so very close, will be constant before the youngest of your children has reached his fiftieth year.

There are people who walk on earth today who will travel into the depth of space. They will see, in instruments which they themselves will control, depths of the universe and surfaces of planets. That fact will greatly influence the politics, the economics, certainly the science, possibly the literature of your generation. Although in fact, long before the scientists were at work on the formulae by which this will be accomplished, poets and writers had it all projected. Journeys to the moon and into the depths of space—I think these are among the oldest themes of the literature of the Western world, written long before the scientists even began to give you a thought. The scientists are always a thousand or two thousand years behind the poetry—always.

Three years ago I attended a meeting of the Catholic Renascence Society, a kind of literary group, and we spent an entire session talking about the literature of the ancient world that was concerned with journeys to the moon and beyond, about the ancient civilization that centered around the hostility and the prospect of interstellar turbulence. These things were written two thousand five hundred years ago. We find these ideas among the poets and philosophers, along with the scientists, heavy fellows at best, gradually catching up with their thinking. How are people certain to be influenced by all this? Very greatly indeed. Our endeavors, and therefore economics and kindred secondary superficial things of that sort, are bound to be profoundly influenced. But these stellar revolutions and evolutions, relevant to technological science, will influence very much less and only indirectly the person, personality, the basic needs of person and the basic aspirations of person.

When that couple of whom I spoke, who haven't even met yet, have their date on the far side of the moon or on an orbit around the far side of the moon, no matter what their machinery or mechanism or mediate scientific formulae, the original reason for setting the date will be the reasons that have existed as far back as poetry runs, as far back as human nature runs. The things they'll say will be roughly the same beginning with "Do you suppose your mother's watching for us to get back?" or things of that sort.

These evasive things of human nature, of personality, of person, remain unchanged. I've often thought how actually the beginnings of the orbits into nearer space, the very tentative little trips that have been made one hundred, one hundred ten, one hundred thirty, one hundred fifty, one hundred fifty-five miles out into space hardly beat walking a yard or two from the back door. However, I wonder what people will say when they get farther into space and look down at the world, our world down below, from the moon. I think they will say the same sort of things that we said when we were young as our fathers and mothers used to take us on a Sunday afternoon to the highest hill near our town in the Blue Hills about six miles outside Boston; and what we used to say was "Can you see our house through there?" And that's what they've said before. When people first began to travel by air, that's what they said. When they make their first trip now, that's what they say. I was in the airport in Boston last year, and I was thrilled to death when a dear little old lady got off the plane. She had made her first trip in a jet, and what do you suppose she said to her waiting children and grandchildren? She said, "I could see our house." And what do you suppose was the thought uppermost in her mind as she went whizzing through space at twenty-two thousand or thirty thousand feet with about thirty million bucks worth of mechanism keeping her up there? Her thought was, "I wonder if the children will be at the airport." These are the thoughts that men had when they returned from war a thousand years before Christ. "Will our children be there? And will they be well? Will our wives be faithful?" These are the things that will trouble people as they come back from space—millions and millions of miles. When they land, they will say the things that they said when they got off the plane, off the train. All of us feel deeply touched by the remarks that the men make when they come back from space They say the same things. They usually burst into tears in their wives' arms, don't they? And it's sent all over the world instantaneously to show you, as a matter of fact, that though the formulae are terrific, and the mechanisms are fascinating, the men, thank God, are the same. And nothing is more touching and more dramatic and more reassuring in all these gala telecasts we get on the occasions of first orbits of one kind and another, nothing is more touching than pictures of their children watching television screens in their homes someplace in Ohio, or Texas, or Florida, or wherever. To me it is still vastly more impressive than that momentary thrill of seeing the thing go off the launching pad. Once you're sure that it isn't going to crash, you say, "Well, that's that." Foolish old thing that costs twenty million bucks, and there it goes. Then you watch it whiz, and when you've seen one whiz you've seen them all. If it whizzes a mile, it whizzes a thousand. And if it whizzes a thousand, it might as *well* go to the moon. And if the moon, maybe Mercury for all I know. And then the camera comes back and focuses on a woman and a couple of kids and perhaps his mother and his school teacher (she's usually there too), and his local minister. I was pleased as punch when that black astronaut was scheduled to go up and there was a big picture of his kid sister, a nun, and I thought to myself, "You're fairly sound." The whole thing adds up to a certain amount of sense. Still pretty expensive, but nonetheless it's sense. It's close to the things that I understand, take for granted, that never change. It's close still to the person. This is true of every single one of these advances that we think of as fantastic. I take great delight in one of these stories that came out of World War II. The story of a lad from Fortis Creek, North Carolina. A young soldier pulled into the war by the strange destiny of things wrote to his mother and said, "Dear Mom, I have now been in the service for three years. I've traveled by boat and jeep and airplane. I've been in London and I've seen the changing of the guard at Buckingham Palace and I saw the Queen ride by to open Parliament. I've been to Paris and I've seen the Arch of Triumph and I walked along the Champs Elysées. I've been in Rome and I saw Saint Peter's and the Forum and the Pope himself. I've been in Jerusalem and I stood in the place where Christ was born and I wish I were back in Fortis Creek, North Carolina, *where I was born.*" So it is. It all comes back to the ancient ultimate reality of person, personality, of our personal groups and our personal associations and all the things that make up our lives. At least, that is what we *hope*. But even as we hope it we know that these are still some built-in aspects of a civilization that can be so perfectly planned. Orbits planned so minutely that we can tell days and weeks and months ahead within, not a split second, but on the nose at what point to turn on the camera to get a picture of Venus eventually, or Mars, Jupiter, or whatnot as the contraption goes by. Civilization so planned that we can feed into Univac electronic computers, mechanical brains, information that can mathematically and by formulae figure out problems that it would have taken a human centuries to figure out by even the most rapid calculations possible to human procedures. In such a civilization the word *plan*, *plan*, *plan* looms larger and larger. Planned economy, planned parenthood, planned love, planned death, planned everything. In such a civilization there are built-in threats to these ancient values that still linger and make somehow bearable the suspense of the orbiting. Great masses of people in such an age, I suppose in any age, are bound to be conditioned by the dominant aspects of their culture; and those aspects of our culture, as we were reviewing last night in our meeting with the priests, are pretty mechanistic, pretty planned, pretty much a matter of formulae. We see this in education, in the decline of schools, of studies of the classics, of poetry, philosophy, and now the right to assert not merely the preeminence, but also exclusion of other studies in favor of the so-called exact sciences, harbinger sciences, electronic technology, and so forth. All these are bound to have their effect preponderantly, superficially, but nonetheless somewhat conceivably, and intangibly, not on the constituent elements of personality, perhaps, but on the habits of people and the outlook of people. Such an age is bound to carry with it effects on personal initiative and personal freedom. We spoke of watching the children as they in turn watch the television screen to see their fathers in orbit about the world, and that's rather pitiful when you state it that way. But there's another side to it, and that's the manner in which electronics are able now to invade the most hidden intimacies of our lives.

Three nights ago, I watched some television show where Vance Packard, the writer, was talking with some people about the manner in which electronics have now for all practical purposes made privacy all but impossible—the manner in which information can now be gathered, for good reasons or bad, by private eyes or public authority. We can remember just a few years ago when there was enormous popular resentment all over the land about the mere suggestion that there would be wiretapping done in order to listen to the conversations of people. Oh, there were a few nuts who said, "Well, they should wiretap the communists" and wiretap the people who disagreed with them, and that sort of thing, but it never crossed their minds that if you put in one wiretapping, that was reason to put in wiretapping everywhere, any place. But a wiretap now would be as crude and simple as Ben Franklin's kite. Kid stuff. Now the electronic devices are so compact, Vance Packard reminded us the other night on the program, that a simple little pocket cigarette lighter is no smaller, no larger than the instrument needed to follow a conversation within three hundred yards of any apartment house built of any material anywhere in the world. Whether it be in the name of fascism or communism or democracy or whatever, what difference does it make what name a political system bears when those who govern and those who hold power in the regime have access to conversations as intimate as those that can be penetrated by contemporary electronic devices? I'll give you a shocker. It was all in the papers and people took it completely in stride. Already they are so conditioned by this stuff that this is taken in stride. It ran for a day or so, made the morning editions, a short story in the evening paper. I saw no editorial comment on it anywhere in the world. But reflect on it for a moment in terms of what it does to the person, to civilization, culture, spiritual values.

Last week in Canada, in either Ontario or British Columbia, I've forgotten now which it was, there was a district attorney, or Queen's Prosecutor, who had been unable to convict a man of a crime that he was reasonably certain the fellow had committed. He couldn't get the evidence, and therefore by all the rules of civilization, as civilization used to see things when personal rights and personal dignity, spiritual aspects of

342

personality were sacrosanct, the fellow should have been let go. But the prosecuting attorney concealed in the cell an infinitesimally minute electronic device which picked up his confession to the priest. On the basis of that he was convicted, and it was reported as would have been reported the collision of two bicycles down at the corner, or the fact that a horse had run away from L.B.J.'s ranch, or something like that. Reflect on it for a moment, and then on the effect on civilization of efficiency so great and so cold, so impersonal, so devoid of values. Now in all manner of colleges, in schools and universities, they'll tell you quite frankly, "We don't indulge in value judgments. We're merely concerned with formulae and processes of contraception and euthanasia. It's effective, isn't it? Solves the problem, doesn't it? What's your complaint?" Well, I'd simply like to say that for several thousand years, influenced by the Bible and by poetry, by romance, by philosophy, by love, by faith, by theology many people have thought that there's more to value judgments; and while they're entitled to entertain those ideas privately, there's not a preoccupation about it.

Our civilization, with this mechanized, cold, formula-like efficiency, does not indulge in value judgments. And things are significant and viable, as the expression is, to the extent that they can be reduced to mathematical considerations which are by definition impersonal. Personality is up against a serious threat in a civilization of this kind because, you see, standardization of this kind seeps into the soul and doesn't stay on the level of formulae alone, contraptions alone, techniques alone— contraceptions here, electronics there, gadgets here. It seeps into the soul until you say I can't imagine why anyone ever thought there was any reason for hesitancy or for value judgments. I thought value judgments were so protective, so purely personal. And so out they go. So you know the stress of person to person in our civilization and the tremendous significance in our daily lives of numbers, numbers.

Once upon a time all convicts had a number, and they

used to wear the numbers hanging around their necks in the pictures you see in the post office. Now the mere innocent child is not in the world two weeks before he or she has picked up a number. There's a particular significance to the name by which a Christian is baptized—very important, as a matter of fact. The name in terms of our civilization or in the family is important because it makes you think of Grandma or Grandpa after whom the children are named, but in our civilization names couldn't be less important. My kid sister had a surprise baby.[2] We don't believe in planned parenthood. She had a surprise baby on her forty-sixth birthday, and as always in our family, which still retains large elements of caprice and Christian faith, we had a great deal of argument, about what we would name the baby. We have fixed policies in regard to the naming of babies. We allow no in-laws to express any suggestions. We name our sister's and sister-in-law's babies and tell them what names their babies have when they are strong enough to take it. Therefore we picked out very carefully the name of this little surprise because she was totally un-expected and therefore, in a Christian civilization, the more beloved. A couple of days after the baptism when all the little gifts she had received had been lugged around to the local bank, my sister called me up and she said, "Brace your feet." I said, "No, not so soon!" And she said, "No, that isn't what I mean." She said, "Joan Lorraine now has a social security number." She's exactly nineteen days old, and she's listed in Bob Kennedy's office down in Washington because in order to deposit the 129 bucks she had picked up from innocent relatives, she had to get on the record. The man had to give her a number for income tax purposes, and that number is duly on file at the place in West Virginia where they have a machine which makes value judgments about all the people who are in that classification and lets them know whether they'll still be free on the first of September, or whether they will be in the clink. All these things are handled by this magnificent big

344

machine. Our little girl had a card, proudly filing through that machine. Out of this tremendous mechanism come church numbers and school numbers. I know that this is the largest city in the largest state in the entire cosmos, but nonetheless I don't know whether it's large enough yet, so that you have to have in your school system, as they have in some school systems that I know, both Catholic and public, numbers for the children.

Beginning in kindergarten a boy picks up a number, and it dogs him all the way through like a convict number until finally he is out of high school, and when his little machine card is ready to go to Notre Dame, it's slipped in the machine there which chooses the students who will be allowed to go to Notre Dame, except that there is a little hole in the side to put in the recommendations for the quarterbacks and the tackles. The applications are presented by a file which will be handled by a most detached group—no human mind, hand, or heart. At the end of the machine there are three piles, and when they showed them to me I had to take aspirin for the rest of the day. There were three piles. One was a list of those whom the machine had found not worthy and had rejected. Another was a list of those whom the machine considered good enough to go to an American Catholic college. What a machine knows about that, I have no idea, but nonetheless, there it is. And a third you might call the standbys. They were the ones the machine didn't think good enough to put in the accepted group but didn't throw out, and they'll wait to see how they make out with the other machines in other colleges before they make the final decision—and it goes through *no human head*. By a delightful accident, the day that these foolish applications were processed at Notre Dame—the day I was there—was the day that postage rates went up from four cents to five cents, and human beings had to lick one cent stamps all afternoon. I was so pleased I could hardly speak, because they had just told me that once upon a time it took twenty-eight people three weeks to do all this, and now the machine does it in twenty minutes. It took them all day to put on one-cent stamps. I could see they were putting them on upside down. I knew they were going to be thrown out by the machine at the post office, but I didn't have the heart to tell them. At least I thought they became a little too automatic. As I remember when we were going to college, we met the dean. You had a chance to talk to him. He looked at you and he could tell, not much, but enough to decide whether or not you were worth taking a chance on, thank God!

Have you tried to make a telephone call lately? Do you know your own number? I don't know mine. I found myself in Chicago a short while ago, and I discovered that I had left all my money back home. All my money—that's just a figure of speech. I discovered that I had left the money I had, on the dresser back home. I didn't have a dime to my name. I tried to make a collect call back to the house in Pittsburgh to see whether or not someone would mail me a check or call up the hotel and say I'm solvent, and I couldn't remember my number. It's become so complicated. There's a number for Pennsylvania, and there's a number for our section of Pennsylvania. Once upon a time it was easy. There were pretty little names like Forest 2314, Sycamore 3951. I can remember that because it was a touch of poetry, but who could ever remember 412-967-8359?[3] Then carry all those around, the whole bunch of them all at once? It's easy if you come from a big family, but you see this is for the planned parenthood that have only a few people to think about. In the next generation they won't have any uncles and aunts. They'll all have been planned out. And then the next generation, only God knows what. No numbers at all! Well, in any case, this is part of it, and it's good. It hardly ever breaks down, but when it does it's magnificent.

How many of you have read the beautiful story covered by the Associated Press three years ago about the young bride in Holyoke, Massachusetts, who finally came to grips with the whole idea of machine-automated civilization and gave them a little run for their money for forty-eight hours?

I went in to my dreadful precooked breakfast one morning three years ago, and sat down to my TV breakfast, opened the paper and it said on page one that a girl in Holyoke, Massachusetts (a town I know very well), had gone the day before into the First National Bank of Holyoke (a bank I know very well, a typical Yankee bank). Even back in the days when they had human beings working there, it was a frozen place. Now that everything is done by automatic check writers and by computers, it's more frozen than ever. She went in and asked for a check for $14.17 to send to her husband to whom she had been married only seven months and who had been sent by some computer count in the Pentagon up to the Aleutian Islands. Out of the Pentagon they needed a hundred fellows or so to send up to the Aleutian Islands, so they threw into this machine the specifications of what they needed—so high, so fat, so tall, so interesting—and her husband's card was filed by this machine down at the Pentagon. So she went into the bank and asked for a check for $14.17 to pay for something that he had bought in the Aleutian Islands.

The check was filled out by the automatic check writer and was zoomed at her through one of those windows that they zoom at you through—you know, so you can't rob them; you can't do anything, for that matter. You can't even congratulate them. You can't admonish them, can't kiss them. There's nothing you can do. You just stand there and the thing shoots at you. Who would ever think of opening an envelope stamped hermetically sealed? I mean an enormous machine makes no mistakes, so she just put the envelope in her bag and she went home.

When she reached the modest little house that she had, the telephone bell was ringing frantically. She answered it, and the voice told her that it was the president of the bank. Now when the president of a Yankee bank calls you up on the phone, then

347

there has been some national disaster. Economy is totally wiped out. So she said, "What do you want?" He said, "Would you kindly come immediately back to the bank?" She said, "Why?" "Well," he said, "a horrible mistake has been made." She reasoned, not inaccurately, that any mistake that he thought horrible must have been a mistake in her favor, so she opened the envelope and found that their modern machinery had issued a check to her husband in the amount of one million, four hundred seventy thousand bucks. She was naturally pleased. This was the largest check she had ever held in her hand, and she knew that her husband would be pleased. And she thought that it might bring a ray of sunshine into the lives of his companions on the Aleutian Islands. So she hung up immediately. In no time, there was a police car at the front door. And that's where the Associated Press dispatch came in.

And so I went to the telephone, wishing to get out of the routine of the chancery work for the morning, and I called up a wild Irish lawyer in Boston, a friend of mine, Tom Maloney, and I said, "Tom, did you see the morning paper?" "I did," said he, "I thought of you right away." I said, "It's the most beautiful thing I have ever read in my life." I said, "It's more beautiful than *Thanatopsis*." I said, "What are you going to do about it?" He said, "I'm going to Holyoke right now, and I'm going to take her case. I'm taking it for nothing." He said, "For civilization, I'm fighting this case."

To make a long story short, they made the Yankee banker crawl. It was wonderful! She made him call a meeting of all the fossils on his Board of Directors, and they all sat there and she made them promise to God that they wouldn't fire the poor underpaid kid who had set up the little machine, and they said they wouldn't if she would give them back their check, because she was holding over their heads a beautiful thing, and this was it.

It's a great story for any one of you who has ever received, and every one of you beginning with Bishop Morkovsky has,

348

a letter from the bank telling you that you're overdrawn and you'd better run right down and pay up or else. The lawyer informed the president of the bank that if he got the least bit fresh, he would make it mighty hard for him. As for the girl, she got the check back from the bank, with a big *cancelled* sign on it, and it hangs proudly now in its frame just inside the front door of her home.

A year ago, a Hungarian refugee named Horvath wrote an appalling book, a novel, called *The Age of the Fish*. It was a novel that related the experiences of a man (himself) who took a teaching assignment in a tremendous high school in a metropolis where the spirit of *no value judgments* had frozen in. There had been all manner of little sex perversions breaking out in the school, little crimes of one sort or another, that indicated the absence of any value judgments among these children who were being prepared for examinations. And suddenly a horrible murder took place among the children, and the teacher brought together those who were suspected of having done it. As he looked at the open eyes of the corpse and then at the eyes of the living boys around him, it struck him the eyes were all alike. One was chemically dead and the others were chemically alive, but the eyes were equally lifeless—no value, no moral reaction, no personal emotion, no touch of any spiritual kind. It suddenly occurred to him that he was living in the age of the fish. He was getting what the children called the fisheye. So impersonal. No values. No sins. It happened. "Say not", as the line at the end of *John Brown's Body*, by Stephen Vincent Benét puts it, "Say not this is good. This is bad. Just say, this is."[4] This happened. No values. No personality.

If, then, our machinery, our techniques, our formulae, our mathematics—all the things that can put us on the moon—are going to be so controlled, so sweet and so soft, so good in their human, not to say, divine context, that those who walk on the face of the moon will still be human and conform with human anxieties and human anticipations and human loves, then other things than science are needed. Among those other things there must be poetry and music and art. Nothing at the World's Fair will be more important than the Pietà, to remind us of the skill of human art by which Divine Love even in death was memorialized forever. Nothing in the electronic exhibits will have a better effect in favor of personality and values than the mere presence of that five tons of white Carrara marble of the Virgin and her Son. There will have to be these, poetry, art, song, philosophy, love unplanned, unplanned love, still spontaneous, still human, still subject to the Providence of God and the caprice of the whims of human hearts— all these and faith and theology. Retreat houses are where you think on these things. So, as to the question that has been the theme of your gatherings this weekend, *A Closed Retreat: Why Me?*—well, the answer is simple. In the civilization in which you live you will need the things of which the retreat is the channel, or never mind the salvation of your soul. You won't be able to remain sane in human terms unless there be love; unless there be freedom; unless there be the movement of the Spirit breathing where it will and not subject to the formulae of a cold civilization.

Facts, Truths, and the Christian Journalist

The vocation of Christian intellectuals was set forth centuries ago by one of the earliest of them. He was a bishop and a poet. Writing to another bishop, being sent into a then relatively savage country as a herald of the word of God, Paulinus of Nola described the part of the world where his young friend would teach as *wordless*, *mute*. But he said it would yet resound with echoes of the truth that is Christ Himself as a result of what the barbarians would learn from the scholarly apostle: ". . . muta in orbis regione per te / barbari discunt resonare Christum / corde Romano placidamque casti / vivere pacem . . ."[1]

Here is the vocation of the Christian intellectual: "In this mute region of the world, the barbarians through your schooling learn to make Christ's name resound from Roman hearts, and to live in purity and tranquil peace."[2]

Paulinus' poem was addressed to a bishop, but it was to the bishop as a teacher of the truth, an intellectual bearing witness to the truth that is Christ. It applies as well to all Christian intellectuals, for these all share, according to their several gifts, offices, ministries, and sometimes charismata in the general teaching mission of the Church, which is that of Christ—to bear witness to the truth and to set up, as in chain reactions, the resounding echoes of the truth of Christ all over the otherwise wordless, savage world.

Since the key phrase of Paulinus applies to every bishop, it applies somehow to me, and I have chosen it as a motto to provide a certain pattern in the midst of frenzy: *"Resonare Christum."*[3] It applies not less to you, for the Christian journalist must be an intellectual and share the vocation and

This address was delivered at Pittsburgh, Pennsylvania, on May 27, 1964, on the occasion of the Catholic Press Association convention.

responsibility of those in the Church who bring Christ's accent and power to a religiously wordless world.

It may be objected that there is scant parallel between the uncouth world of Paulinus and Dacius and that of our twentieth century. True, the admitted religious illiteracy of our culture places it, alas, *"muta in orbis regione"*—religiously and theologically wordless and mute.[4] But surely the high level of our technology, the scientific *breakthroughs* of our civilization warrant at least for its builders and rulers some better name than that given by Paulinus—*"barbari"*.[5]

Jacques Maritain is but one of those who are not so sanguine about the measure and the quality of the civilization which you must teach to echo the accent of Christ. He senses a certain savagery at work in the very developments and directions of a civilization which he indicts as not merely negatively illiterate about the things of God, but positively determined to make its citizens forget God.

Maritain's description of that civilization in *Art and Scholasticism* grows daily more pertinent and is one that matches the *"muta regio"* which so desperately needed Paulinus' Christian scholar:

> Founded on the two unnatural principles of the fecundity of money and the finality of the useful, multiplying needs and servitude without the possibility of there ever being a limit, destroying the leisure of the soul, withdrawing the material factible from the control which proportioned it to the ends of the human being, and imposing on man the panting of the machine and the accelerated movement of matter, the system of nothing but the earth is imprinting on human activity a truly inhuman mode and a diabolical direction, for the final end of all this frenzy is to prevent man from resembling God, *"Dum nil perenne cogitat, seseque culpis illigat!"* Consequently he must, if he is to be logical, treat as useless, and therefore as rejected, all that by any grounds bears the mark of the spirit.[6]

We can easily underestimate the danger to the human spirit that threatens our civilization. It involves a kind of barbarism, but a barbarism we may be slow to recognize as such because we are ourselves enamored of its conveniences and efficiencies. It is a barbarism with fascinatingly complex toys, machinery and weapons—toys, machinery, and weapons so elaborate technically that one might falsely suppose them to demonstrate a high level of culture among those who produce them. We easily fail to appreciate the extent to which our civilization tends to depersonalize and therefore to dehumanize, thus reducing to barbarism those who become dependent upon it to the point of enslavement. There is a steady weakening of the faculties of intellect and will upon the robustness of which depends any culture illumined by the truth that feeds the mind and the love that inflames the heart.

Here is where our civilization calls out, however mutely, to your vocation as Christian intellectuals: *"Resonare Christum"*— to proclaim Christ, to trumpet the truth.[7] But here, too, we encounter a current confusion in the concept of your specific vocation as Christian journalists. It is a confusion that shows up in other intellectual vocations, too; but many things written at the moment and some things said suggest that it may especially diminish, if not destroy, the needed contribution of religious journalism to the ransoming of the times and the accomplishment of its own unique and highest purpose. I refer to the confusion between *the facts* and *the truth*, between our dependence on you for the facts and our much greater dependence on you for the truth.

It is a part of your business to find out *the facts* and to give us these; but it is the very heart of your vocation to be the servants of the truth. We Christians believe that Truth is one of the revealed names of God. In this we are not alone; to the Muslim, Truth is also one of the names of Allah. But we Christians go further; we have a cult of the Truth Incarnate in the Eternal Word of God made Man.

Unhappily, not all men of our times share this faith in the infinite majesty and absolute worth of Truth. People who covet power hold truth in low esteem, whether they be

Hegelians, who despise the very word, or pragmatists who, like Pilate, cynically question whether it corresponds to any worthwhile reality. (I note parenthetically that the *power people* relish facts; information, for them, is power, and they tend more and more to confine the concept of truth to accurate and reliable facts.)

But because we Christians do believe in the reality and supreme worth of Truth (and therefore give capital letters to the names of its derivatives, like Law, and Right, and Justice, and Morality), we greatly esteem the intellectual, the man who ponders Truth and, in the midst of the relativism of pragmatic life, in the confusions of empirical facts, bears witness to the transcendence of Truth.

So, though we are grateful to you for the facts you turn up and transmit, none the less in a civilization that is *fact-happy* and indifferent to truth, we depend on you to defend the human character of society by serving the truth that is a cement to all its values, indeed is its soul, as against the mere *facts* that can so fragment it as to turn human society into an insect world— in Marrou's vivid phrase—an antheap civilization, a city of termites.

Permit me to dwell for a minute on this distinction between *the facts* and *the truth*, because it involves some reflections that some of your colleagues wrote on some aspects of the Council.

Under a journalistic barrage of mere facts, especially in the recounting of a council on theology and ideas generally, one recalls Sidney Smith's protest: "Don't tell me of facts, I never believe facts; you know Canning said nothing was so fallacious as facts, except figures."

I submit for your reflection that in addition to the obvious distinction between truth and untruth, or between truth and error, there is also a less obvious but nonetheless sharp distinction between *the facts* and *the truth*, certainly between the fragmentary facts that may suffice for random reporting and the integral truth that is and must be the great concern of responsible journalism. There can be a great accumulation of facts—undeniable facts, brutal facts, intriguing facts—and still the truth may be lacking. A reporter—or, for that matter, a phothonotary apostolic—can ferret out an impressive, a bewildering mass or mess of mere facts and lose the truth in the midst of them, much as a clever cross-examiner can bury the truth in a court case under a bombardment of blasting facts.

If our journalists are to serve the truth as Christian intellectuals are called to do, they must protect us against the effects of the various fallacies of facts. They must sift for us the incomplete facts, the unassimilated facts, or the facts that are just plain irrelevant to the truth at issue in a given question. Above all, they must be quick to expose the fallacy of equivocation that confuses fact and truth; then those who are called to explore, discover, proclaim, and serve the truth will not settle for sniffing out and peddling a fact or two.

The difference between the facts and the truth, in the sense pertinent to the values we are considering, may be driven home in sundry ways. The facts are cold, dead; the truth is alive, warm. The truth must include the facts; but no single fact includes the truth; nor, indeed, do all the facts necessarily add up to the truth. Facts can be the trees, truth the woods, in the wisdom that warns against those who cannot see the woods for the trees. The truth shall make you free; no like promise is attached to the facts. The facts can be fed into computing machines; truth eludes the mechanical brains and motivates the free lives of persons. The facts come by the dozens and can be bought by the gross; the truth is beyond measure and infinite in its value.

This distinction between the mere facts and the total truth is everywhere valid and always worth noting. It is particularly pertinent at the moment in discussions of the Church. Henri-Irenée Marrou, in his essay on the current responsibilities of the intellectual, tells of a friend who came to him long-faced and heavy of heart over some unhappy *fact*, indeed, scandalous fact that he had stumbled on in connection with the Church. Marrou pointed out that, whatever the facts and however many, they did not constitute the truth about the Church, nor was the crisis that confronted the Church because of the embarrassing fact a crisis for the truth.

The Church, said Marrou, has been faced with crises ever since the Tuesday after the first Pentecost. He chose Tuesday, he said, on the rough guess that Monday, the day after the outpouring of the Holy Sprrit, probably found the first Christians still so overwhelmed by the Spirit that they were unselfishly and unqualifiedly cooperating with God's grace. But, he pointed out, you need not read farther than Chapter Five of the Acts of the Apostles before you have Ananias and Sapphira on your hands. Nor does their story differ a whit from the origins of most of the dismaying *facts* which are often urged to discredit the truth of the Church; it is typically a story of cash and of the kind of power to which cash is the key. These are facts; they are unpleasant facts. There are other facts, happier facts. But neither the one kind nor the other constitutes the transcendent Truth to which the intellectuals bear their witness.

Note well that the author of the Acts of the Apostles prints the facts; he prints the embarrassing facts about Ananias and Sapphira, just as he prints the happy facts about the moral courage of Peter and the other apostles when they were hailed before the council and the high priest. He prints the bold words of the pope (when Peter and the other apostles answered and said we ought to obey God rather than men) and the historical decision in favor of the hierarchy handed down by the Supreme Council, with good quotes from Gamaliel, speaking for the majority. He reports the facts, but he does so in balanced fashion, so that he, the intellectual documenting and commenting upon the Acts of the Apostles, also "ceased not to teach and preach Jesus Christ".[8]

Indeed, this fifth chapter of the Acts of the Apostles, with its unpleasant facts, inspiring facts, and transcendent truth served by both, is a compact model of the balanced writing (as well as clarity and exact detail) that one should expect of the Christian journalist.

But the right and duty to print the facts rest on the premise that the truth must be served; it therefore sometimes falls out that the servant of the truth finds himself bound to file or even forget what are indubitably *facts*, but facts which do not convey the truth involved or which even obscure it. More often, the service of the truth merely requires that the *facts* be supplemented so that they satisfy the often uncritical demand for facts, facts, facts—but also, and above all, satisfy the passionate human quest for the need of the truth.

It is, then, on intellectuals, as on artists, that the Church must depend if in our fact-happy, gadget-ridden age we are to accomplish the task set by Paulinus of Nola. Only thus can we make possible the survival of the human by the echoing of the Divine Christ above the din of material power or in the cold silence of the smooth, deadly efficiency of the automated mechanisms, some of which used to be men. This is why one found so hopeful and so thrilling in its significance the recent appeal of Pope Paul to artists, above all to the creative artists with new, fresh ways to say things likely to echo throughout a civilization as unresponsive to the true artist as it is to the authentic intellectual.

Reading the Pope's intensely passionate call for help to the artists, one thought of Maritain's description of the twin fate of the intellectual and the artist in a materialistic civilization, yet of how the artist, if he blends his ministry with that represented by the Pope, gives humanity its chance.

Persecuted like the wise man and almost like the saint, the artist will perhaps recognize his brethren at last and find his vocation once again; for in a way he is not of this world, being, from the moment he begins working for beauty, on the road which leads upright souls to God and makes invisible things

357

clear to them by visible ones. However few they may then be who will disdain to gratify the beast and turn with the wind, in them, for the simple reason that they will be exercising a disinterested activity, the human race will live.

So shall be the part of the intellectual; so, therefore, that of the devout journalist. Indeed, your part is the more urgent and fundamental, since you nourish the truth which must evoke love and give beauty its pattern. This, presumably, is what Remo Branca means by his insistence in *L'Osservatore Romano* that the *fourth estate* of the journalist must come to the rescue of the *mechanized man* lest he become a calculating robot, filled with statistics and facts, instead of a Total Man, keenly interested in everyone and everything, sensitive to truly human experience, that of children and that of every category of adults, so that he is imitating the ecumenical and universal Christ.

You meet the defy that Charles Malik gave to modern technocratic barbarism when he addressed the "great powers" at the United Nations:

Material force by itself, no matter how overwhelming, is interesting and important only insofar as it may prove a means to bringing about a condition in which spiritual and intellectual values can begin to operate again; otherwise, it is of no significance. Sooner or later, when you have finished your bombing, your armament production, and all your marshaling of physical forces, there must be penetration of minds by minds and spirits by spirits. This means that the future belongs not to those who have the most trains or the most machinery, but to those who have the most ideas. It means that over and above your stockpiles you must have a cultural and spiritual message so profound, so true, so universal that it will satisfy the souls of men everywhere and make them forgive you your rich supplies and your privileged resources.

The question, therefore, which confronts us, is not who has this bomb or the other, but who can develop a true person who will sum up in his character such qualities of understanding and humility, of truth, of humor, of moral stature, of strength and resourcefulness of mind, of pregnant ideas, of universal sympathy, of capacity for friendship and love that he will be admired and respected even by those who might otherwise have every reason to hate him.

This describes the kind of Christian intellectual that is typified by Frédéric Ozanam and his apostolic friends, lay professors, writers, and journalists. And this is why I pray that he may be the inspiration, the *uncanonized patron*, of the growing number of apostolic laymen who are so fortunately echoing Christ and the truth in contemporary publishing and journalism. It is why I urge you to interest yourselves and your readers in the cause of Frédéric Ozanam; his beatification would give your episcopal patron, Saint Francis de Sales, an exemplary and effective lay collaborator in setting that mood of openness to truth, genial charity, intellectual integrity, and capacity for friendship with all men of good will which, together with uncompromising commitment to the Faith, should characterize the Catholic press.

XXIX

The Religious Needs of Patients in Institutions Caring for the Chronically Ill or the Aging

I am deeply grateful for the privilege of striking the keynote of today's deliberations. I particularly welcome the opportunity to do so under the circumstances of place and auspices that bring us together. These give me an opportunity to visit again at John J. Kane Hospital, a county program of which we are all understandably and pardonably proud. They also give me an opportunity to say (and in this I am confident that I speak for all the clergy) a warm, sincere word of thanks and of grateful admiration to the leadership responsible for the hospital on the county level and on every echelon of the institution's administration.

I welcome the opportunity, too, to say a most especial word of appreciation to the representative of Mr. Arlen Adams for the leadership that the State Department of Welfare is giving on this, as on so many levels of thought and action concerning the problems confronting us in social service. Within the month I experienced this initiative and leadership on the part of the State Department in certain problems associated with underprivileged areas and potential delinquency zones. Today, at the other end of the calendar of life, we find at the John J. Kane meeting the same direct interest and desire of Mr. Adams' department to provide leadership.

Most important of all, today's meeting gives us clergy an opportunity to pledge the resources at our disposition and such help as we can bring to the work of John J. Kane Hospital and to other public institutions of the community, the

This address was delivered at the John J. Kane Hospital, Pittsburgh, Pennsylvania, on August 5, 1964.

responsibility for the religious care of which we are privileged to share. I emphasize this point because I am aware that our discussions today extend to all institutions, private included, which are concerned with the care of the aged, the chronically sick, and the senescent. I am, of course, constantly conscious of the special place in the American tradition and the American community of what we might call an American witness before the world, namely, our private institutions, and particularly those under religious auspices. These constitute a witness to freedom as well as a witness to individual and private group responsibility. They are a witness to many values which, as religious and as Americans, we hold very dear. But I am particularly eager, in these opening remarks, to speak of our responsibility precisely as religious not to our own institutions nor to similar private institutions, the importance of which we well know, but specifically to *public institutions* for the care of the aging and the sick.

The duty of the churches and the religious communities to public institutions is manifold. I mention only those which are most obvious and which will undoubtedly be the object of development at today's meetings, and I mention these because I take it to be my responsibility to suggest in summary fashion the general lines of thought along which the discussion of the day will develop.

At the moment one of the greatest responsibilities that the religious communities have toward public institutions is to encourage the growth within them of that volunteer spirit which is and should be the soul and genius of our private institutions. The place of volunteer service in contemporary private hospitals has become indispensable. As a mere matter of budgeting, it would be completely impossible to provide private institutions of any kind, certainly hospitals in our day, except for the extraordinary part played by volunteer services. Public institutions are sometimes at a disadvantage in this matter of volunteer service and of the special spirit that volunteers bring into the work of a hospital. There is always the danger that tax-supported or public institutions may all take on the mood that characterizes so often the most familiar, most established, most uniform of these: the post office. A drearier building than the post office in the average community would be difficult to imagine, unless it would be a railroad station of the nationally owned railroads of Europe. The drabness of the average post office strikes pretty much the mood of those institutions which are left to function in a vacuum void of love and of loyalties warmer than those which surround the collection of taxes. As a result of their being looked upon as the parts of a tax program, things which it is the business of the State to handle, they are apt to be of no great concern to the volunteer energies and interests of the community.

The place of the volunteer and of the volunteer spirit in the institutions for the aging and the chronically sick, however, takes on its importance and its part in the total programming, not from any mere budgeting considerations, but from the indispensable spirit that the volunteer, if only by reason of her cheerful smock and general attitude, brings to the institutions. And so I take it to be among the prime responsibilities in our civilization and our way of life for church groups to identify themselves with the recruiting, encouragement, and recognition of volunteer service in public institutions for the care of the aging.

In this connection, I particularly underscore the responsibility of the Church to encourage *young people* to enter the volunteer service of such public institutions in the communities where they live. The reasons for this are many. Some of them are merely psychological. Young people are attractive and they are important for that reason alone in the corridors and the labyrinths of any institution, but especially those filled with the tired, because aged. It is important, however, also for the young people themselves. It will help to teach them a philosophy badly needed as an antidote to many of the attitudes and many of the philosophies they inevitably pick up from other aspects and contacts in our particular moment of civilization. The plain fact is that ours is not a civilization that is particularly concerned with or interested in the aged or with any persons, in fact, who are *inefficient*. The emphasis in our civilization is heavily and increasingly on *efficiency*. Ours is an automated civilization, a technological and more and more a technocratic civilization; it is a civilization for the fit. We who live in what are presumably the representative and typical democracies like to attribute contempt for the inefficient and unfit to Nazi regimes and similarly impersonal totalitarian regimes; but such contempt is increasingly the mood of our own culture.

It would be a grave spiritual and cultural error to be unmindful of this ominous trend and of the necessity to counteract that cult of cold efficiency that is the inevitable byproduct of intensive technology, automation, and scientism generally in the minds, hearts, and outlooks of our young people. Nothing is more likely to accomplish this desired educative role than their encouragement and training to work as volunteers in programs which bring them in constant contact with persons who can no longer be *effective* members of the highly efficient, technological, automated civilization of the know-how of which our young people are made so proud by almost every other aspect of their education.

The manner in which this characteristic of our civilization has taken its toll in our culture is reflected in the very architecture of our communities. We all remember communities, in whatever part of the United States, where the mere architecture of the houses indicated an interest in children, beginning with *having* them, and, not less, an interest in the aged and in retaining them proudly and affectionately at home. Those who have read *The Late George Appley* recall how impatient George was with Aunt Harriet and lamented that she cluttered up the scene unduly long; but nonetheless, one of the family homes included a room for Harriet, eccentric though she was. We live in a civilization of picture windows, even when the picture window looks out only on the picture window of the house five feet away; in an age of Cape Cod cottages a thousand miles from Cape Cod; in an age of *efficiency* apartments and the planning of houses so that there is no place either for those who have the presumption to be born nor for those who have the insufferable folly to remain alive unduly long. In the case of these latter, the result is that many institutions originally built for mental cases are now custodial-care places for people who reveal often no clinical mental condition, save perhaps those evidences of senility which once resulted in a stronger bond in the family unit, but have become the objects of that impatience that wants no part of inefficiency, no part of the nonfunctioning, the worn out or useless.

The very architecture of contemporary homes, I repeat, demonstrates the extent to which our culture resists and rejects the exhausted, above all the *unfit*. Those of us clergy in whose programs there are included visits to mental hospitals know perfectly well the tremendous proportion of people in these who have no request to make of us except that we ask their sons, daughters, and daughters-in-law and sons-in-law occasionally to visit them. In such institutions I have spent hours simply making lists of addresses and telephone numbers of prosperous, strong sons and daughters, sometimes living within a radius of five or ten miles, who never spend time with those who have once been their own, who gave them, in fact, the breath of their own so-healthy, efficient and now so-well-planned lives. The architecture of our efficient civilization is, of course, but the outward sign of inward values or defects of values which result in a cult of efficiency and a general contempt for the dependent.

In any instance, the institutions are full, as you and I well know, and one of the best possible contributions we can make to their needed service and to correcting the cultural factor in

364

young people which often leads to the excessive burden on their service is the encouragement of volunteer service by young people, above all, service by the young to those tempted to think of themselves as not wanted simply because they are no longer attractive or *competent*.

A second great responsibility of the churches to public institutions lies in the careful selection of their chaplaincy personnel. The choice of such personnel should be made not only in the light of the spiritual and doctrinal orthodoxy of those whom we choose but also, and above all, in the light of their capacity to work with others of other traditions and to blend generously with the legitimate requirements of others on the level of staff, on the level of those served, and on the level of their brethren in other religious traditions.

It seems to me that we have a third and great responsibility with respect to public institutions. I refer to the encouragement of warm acceptance by our respective communities of public institutions as serving precisely a religious spirit and doing precisely a religious work acceptable and praiseworthy as such even to our churches. No one is more aware than the average Catholic bishop in America of the American tradition of separation of Church and State. We are reminded of it almost every day by kind neighbors seemingly unaware that there is no need to remind us since we deeply feel that we have played our part in the development of the tradition. But in this tradition of the separation of Church and State there is the danger that we may all tend to write off as merely *secular* the work that is done in state or public institutions, that we may all neglect to remind ourselves and to teach our people the precisely religious and spiritual inspiration of certain work done in even the most firmly and constitutionally *separate* state institutions and programs.

There is sometimes a certain misgiving on this point with respect to public education, for example, but it is a misgiving sometimes even more widely and sharply felt with respect to public institutions for the aged and the chronically sick. Perhaps it would be wise to face the origins and the roots of certain of the cultural reasons for much of the religious resistance to, interest in and even use of public institutions. By such a candid look at the historical background of such attitudes, we can recognize the extent to which it has been remedied if not entirely eliminated in our day. Some of this feeling on the part of the devout is a carryover from a past when certain attitudes reflected in some who were responsible in another day for the care of public institutions (poor houses and the like) were probably not the most pleasant people in the world and certainly not the most open-minded, openhearted, or open-handed. But in this, as in all things, there has been a great change, and the consequent responsibility is now clear for us in every religious tradition to be much more positive and cooperative in recognizing the welcome and truly spiritual content of many public institutional programs.

Part of the resistance which one encounters among devout people of every religious group, resistance even to the idea of being taken care of in public institutions, is a symbol of the sort of thing I have in mind when I speak of our obligation to teach more positive attitudes to such institutions precisely as involving religious values even when formally public or civic in their auspices. I would assume that fairly commonly among Jewish people and probably among certain, perhaps all, the Protestant groups, as certainly frequently among Catholics, there exists such resistance, even when there is clear necessity for placement of loved ones in the care of state, county, municipal or other public institutions. I well know some of the historic reasons for the fears underlying such resistance, but the present attitude is often a bit of a scandal to me because I fear that I see in it the result of our over-preaching or falsely preaching of the responsibility religious people have to their own institutions. But honest analysis also finds a hangover from experiences of other days and from attitudes encountered by specific religious groups, perhaps, in their contact with public institutions as they were then staffed. Sometimes, too, there is that false emphasis on the nature of the distinction between Church and State to which we have already alluded, the emphasis on the gulf between the zone of the secular and the zone of the religious, with a resultant false dichotomy between the values of both. One even detects sometimes the establishment of a positive adversity between those things which are under the auspices of the State, which are publicly run, and those things which are under the auspices of the Church or privately run and which are therefore thought of as much closer to the family and to the private structure of our personal lives.

I have been the more ill at ease about this attitude when I encounter it in my own people with a resistance to having their people taken care of in public institutions as if this were less than consistent with due religious piety, because, together with my brothers and sisters, I gladly placed my own beloved parent in the care of a public institution. My own Dad could not possibly have been better taken care of, during the long and tortured months of his chronic sickness, in any institution of my own Church more affectionately or efficiently than he was in the Lemuel Shattuck Hospital of Boston, similar to John J. Kane in Allegheny County; and it was, in fact, the hospital which we could afford.

I say all this to underscore the responsibility we have to teach that the religious nature of the work done in public institutions and the spiritual aspect of the contribution made by those on the level of the public Commissioners, all through the various levels of staff, are precisely analogous, in their constituent elements, to those made in Church institutions by the staffs from the bishop down to the personnel, however religious or explicitly and by vocation especially dedicated.

We have special reason for gratitude to the Allegheny County Commissioners, the present ones and their predecessors, and to the Commonwealth of Pennsylvania, for the manner in which it has been made possible for us who are clergy enthusiastically to commend public institutions, notably that in which we find ourselves today, because of the proper place they have given chaplaincy service, both from the angle of American constitutional tradition and from the aspect of a humane understanding of the total nature of personality. The importance of this cannot possibly be overemphasized.

Finally, it is sometimes said that the measure of the decency of a civilization is the place it gives to the child. Such is, in fact, the best single measure, by and large, of the humanity of civilizations from the days of Sparta down to our own day. But not to be underestimated is the index to the work of a civilization provided by the manner in which its aged are taken care of, and this for the reasons which have already been suggested in our reflections on homes which have no places for children or for the aged, but only for the efficient, the well-functioning who can take complete care of their self-centered selves.

So in their way, too, the institutions provided by the public authority provide an important index to the true humanity of the civilization of which this public authority is at once the servant, the guardian, and in no small degree the architect. This is especially true of the institutions and/or programs for children and those for the care of the aged. The reason is simple: the quality of such institutions reflects the extent of a civilization's practical witness to its ideological acceptance of the spiritual elements basic to human personality. Let us be perfectly frank about it: unless there is such emphasis on every level of a civilization, then, as a matter of brutal truth, the logical alternative is, in fact, the scientism of the Nazi, the coldly secularist position of the Nazi in face of the needs of the unfit, the aged, the unuseful, all of whom are to be eliminated by the means most likely to leave undisturbed the lives of the fit, of those who can function to their own satisfaction and to the service of the efficient society. If the norm of a society is economic stability only; if the norm of a society is the efficiency of its functioning only; if it is basically scientific, basically technological, basically eugenic, then there is no ultimately cogent basis for the special care of the aged, none for the care of the exceptional child, if, indeed, for the conception, bringing to birth, and education of children beyond the economic, technological, coldly efficient *needs* of the State.

As a matter of ruthless logic, it is difficult to see what ultimately is the case against euthanasia for the aged or against the exposure of infants, either in the ancient pattern of exposure to wild animals or in a more modern Nazi pattern of exposure to the mercies of conscienceless, spiritually stunted medical scientists. Therefore our programs for the care of the aged sick reflect with accuracy and cogency the total humanity of the civilization which produces them and within which they function. The conference today is a wholesome recognition on the part of those responsible for the care of the aged in our Commonwealth that here, at least, the basis for the respect of the person is not his efficiency, nor his economic capacity, nor his physical strength nor mental capacity. It is, therefore, no merely technological, economic, or eugenic consideration, but is rather the recognition of his spiritual personality, which personality requires spiritual direction and the sensitive care of those who have been brought together for today's discussion.

One prays that our part, the part of clergy, in the work of our public institutions will be played with total loyalty and with a generous reciprocal recognition of the roles of Church and State (and the representatives of both) in the care not only of our aged citizens but of all our people. Thank you very much.

XXX

Intervention on Religious Liberty

I have asked special permission to speak because I fear that our question has been discussed thus far with excessive pragmatism. The report itself speaks too sparingly and cautiously, perhaps, of the connection between religious liberty and that common good which would put the discussion on the level of principle.

All sides agree that the question of religious liberty and its exercise ultimately touches the question of the common good. Therefore, the analysis and defense of religious liberty ought to take into account the nature and protection of that common good which, in a way, constitutes the very *res publica* and thus must be promoted by the directors of the State.

There are those who strongly assert that the defense of religious liberty, even for those who set forth errors contrary to Catholic truth, disrupts or damages the common good, which indeed can scarcely be denied at times. On the contrary, there are those who affirm, from another angle, that paradoxical though it be, the denial of recognition to religious liberty in its own way and often to a far worse degree harms the common good because the common good by its very nature positively demands and presumes as an integral and essential element such liberty and its recognition by the civil power. It is on this point that I have a few things I would like to say.

The common good involves a certain order of things and qualities; certainly it includes peaceful relations among citizens. But the concept of the common good should never be compared to that kind of impassive order or forced conformism which would be pleasing, perhaps, to the totalitarian or police

This intervention was delivered, in Latin, at Saint Peter Basilica, Rome, on September 28, 1964, during the third session of the Second Vatican Council.

State, but which would in no way befit a truly human society of persons created in the image of God and responsible finally to God—to God "who has made of one all mankind, causing them to dwell together on the whole face of the earth . . . that they should seek God, if haply they may grope after him and find him."[1]

Now in these words of Saint Paul there is suggested a hint of the necessity of religious liberty among those elements of the common good shared by all the human race, dwelling over the whole face of the earth, called to seek God and dimly grope after Him and perhaps find Him, . . . even though at times such liberty gives rise to the danger of controversies and contentions as a result of the very seeking after God.

A common good worthy of persons always presupposes a moral, intellectual, and spiritual element as essential and fundamental. Obedience and conformity to the moral law, divine and positive, ought to be always present in the common good and among other virtues. But such obedience, if it is to nourish a true common good, must be a virtue, the *virtue* of persons acting with knowledge and consent and, consequently, acting *freely* in a spirit of justice.

The common good is not just a certain physical or mathematical accumulation of material goods which citizens share. Certainly, it includes civil services, public highways, firefighting equipment, police protection, and other such things, lest turmoil break out among the populace. But all these things do not constitute the common good. Nor is it a mere treasury of acquired goods, technical machines, artifacts, and objects such as are preserved in museums but which are nothing more than booty or spoils, such as might unite thieves, rather than a common good, if they are not *ethically* acquired and cherished. *For the common good is always something living, ethical, spiritual, intellectual, and therefore fully humane.*

The Christian philosopher Jacques Maritain has written to our point: that the common good is something *ethically* good.

And in this common good is included as an essential element the greatest development possible *hic et nunc* of human persons, of those persons who make up the united multitude and thus constitute a people bound together by ties not only of force but of justice.[2]

Hence it seems to follow that the common good of mankind, to the extent that it is ethical and moral, demands and presumes religious faith, true and whole, strong, fruitful and, therefore, a reasonable assent to truth freely accepted and freely professed. But also, and equally as a matter of justice, it follows that the common good demands the necessity of liberty from external coercion in the matter of religion, if the common good is not to lose its very soul which is virtue and especially the virtue of justice.

A certain non-Catholic professor once said to me, "You can well say that the idea of religious liberty should justify itself pragmatically to Catholics in the light of the way it seems to have worked out in regions where the Church is obviously flourishing under a system of just such liberty." But this pragmatic argument is less than satisfactory because it is really not worthy of the subject. It is far better to recognize, with all Christian simplicity, that the idea of religious liberty corresponds to the *truth*, to the truth not only about the nature of the person but also about the nature of the common good itself.

Therefore those who seek the common good in its full and true sense—and according to authentic Catholic teaching with the philosophical and theological principles of which our *practice* ought to conform and not *vice versa*—those who defend such a common good will wish to strengthen, foster, and extend as far as possible all truly human liberties, especially religious liberty—that is, the liberty to learn, to meditate, and to worship the Supreme Good, God, the source and author of all goods. Such religious liberty can be worked out even in a state favoring some particular religion for historical reasons—

as it does in England, where a Protestant church (the so-called Established Church) traditionally enjoys special privileges, but now (at least) all, except the king and queen (unless I am mistaken), have full religious liberty. The case of Ireland is also pertinent, for there the Catholic Church is held in special esteem by the full religious liberty. As a matter of fact—and it should be acknowledged openly—religious liberty is often more complete in other countries than it is in America; this is certainly the case in England with regard to school rights, and it also is in Holland.

There can be no doubt that Catholics—and especially the pastors of souls—will pray and work tirelessly to the end that all men will use their liberty to advance to the full and perfect knowledge of the one true God and Him whom God sent, Jesus Christ. We will be witnesses to Him to the very ends of the earth, witnesses by word and by deed. We will debate, we will implore, we will rebuke in all patience and in the light of true doctrine, so that error may have no *place*, whether or not it has any *right*; but we shall do this always recognizing the rights of any who are in error. *We* will fulfill our right and duty with the help of the grace of Christ, in the light of the gospel, by the power of the Holy Spirit and armed with the spiritual might of the Church, neither fearing nor exploiting the constraining power of the kingdom of this world. Whatever may be said of times past and of political cultures once, perhaps, more consistent with the work of the gospel but now obsolete, it is now, in the present order, necessary that Christians ask of the civil power only that it respect in justice our right to fulfill the commands of Christ; that it assist in justice our efforts to play our rightful and necessary part in furthering the common good through our work in behalf of education and peace; and that it leave inviolate, as a matter of justice, the religious liberty of all those for whom the message of the Gospels and the grace of Christ are destined, namely, *all men*.

God, who gave us the duty, right, and liberty to preach,

gave those to whom we preach the duty, right, and liberty of hearing and believing as a means to that religious perfection which the civil power can neither give nor take away and which, therefore, it should scrupulously respect, especially as regards its liberty.

We, the successors of the apostles, men of God, bishops of the Catholic Church—we ought to be foremost and fearless leaders among the heralds of liberty, because historically we are the heirs of liberty in matters religious acquired in almost every case and in almost every nation only through the blood and tears of our fathers. Thus we know from the experience of our own history how dear and how fruitful liberty is. Much more, supernaturally we are heirs of an even greater liberty, the liberty by which Christ has made us free by His own free obedience—a free obedience which we will freely imitate, always in the hope and with the purpose of freely persuading our neighbors and brothers to a similar free obedience—a liberty that is saving because it is obedient, an obedience that saves because it is free.

XXXI

Family Life in a Changing Society

The phrasing of my subject sounds so placid that an initial word of warning strikes me as urgently in order.

No one should underestimate the titanic scale, the feverish tempo, and the far-reaching effects of the revolutions under way on every level of the thought, life, and action of a world in upheaval which the wording of our topic describes in the deceptively quiet phrase: *a changing society*.

The accelerated rhythm of change is obvious at the moment, even to the most imperceptive. But to sensitive Christians, to prophetic spirits among us, it has long been clear how staggering are the changes that our age is destined to experience.

A great archbishop in my own country, writing at the dawn of the century more than sixty years ago, had this to say:

> We are advancing towards one of those great epochs of history in which mighty changes will be wrought. The world is in throes; a new age is to be born. . . . The traditions of the past are vanishing; new social forms and new political institutions are arising; astounding discoveries are being made of the secrets and the powers of nature; unwanted forces are at work in every sphere over which man's control reaches. There is a revolution in the ideas and the feelings of men. *All things which may be changed will be changed, and nothing will be tomorrow as it was yesterday, save that which emanates directly from God, or which the Eternal Power decrees to be permanent.*

I remind you that Archbishop Ireland thus described our revolutionary *changing society* years before most of us gathered here were even born, let alone bewitched, bothered, and

---

This address was delivered at Bombay, India, on December 5, 1964, during the Eucharistic Congress.

bewildered by the way in which *all things which may be changed are being changed, so that nothing will be tomorrow as it was yesterday, save that which emanates directly from God, or which the Eternal Power decrees to be permanent.*

Among the realities which Christian witness, if not, indeed, human experience itself, sees as rooted in that very nature of things the laws of which emanate directly from God must be numbered the family. The family is a social unit which antedates, historically and logically, all other societies and which all other societies exist to serve; it is the image of that supernatural society, the family of God Himself, which we know and love as the Church. The laws and the life of the family, its very reason for being, derive from its purpose as the servant of personality; all the ethic which governs the family, as also the ethic which rules the claims of the family on other societies, flows from its function to protect and nurture persons— the persons of those who seek their perfection in the nuptial love that brings the family into being and the persons of those born of that love and for the procreation and perfection of whom the Eternal Power has decreed the existence and the nature of the family.

It is for this reason that when the family society is unable to attain its purposes unaided, it has the right to turn to those other societies whose reason for being is the protection and service of the family, even as that of the family is the protection and service of the person. And so, in the first instance, the civil society has among its highest purposes and functions the help of the family; in the order of nature it must not compete with the normal family, nor is it conceivable that it could use its authority to undermine, least of all to pervert, the authority and the life of the family.

Should organized society, which came into being largely to supplement and strengthen the family in its divinely appointed service of personality, prove finally inadequate to its task or (what is worse) seek positively to act contrary to its purposes and to those of the family, then such a society would have lost its reason for being. It would then become the holy right and imperative duty of persons, whose well-being depends on the well-being of the family, to alter or abolish the forms of their civil society.

The social forms, in the nature of things, admit of change; they often demand revolutionary change. The claims of personality, and of the family as the first school of personality, should be the *last* to be changed or challenged; those of the civil society should be the *first*, especially when there is question of conflict between the claims of society and the rights and purposes of the family. The latter are always more nearly a part of that which emanates directly from God; the forms and programs of organized society are numbered among those things which may be changed and will be changed so that, if need be, nothing of them will be tomorrow as it was yesterday. The family is first; all other societies, the organized State included, are subordinate; *it is not the other way around*.

When there is question of whether to cut down the rights of the person and the life of the family to fit the demands of the State or to alter, if need be totally, the pattern of society to fit the needs of the family and the person, there is no doubt as to where the revolution should be aimed.

And yet, despite its priority in nature and in right, family life, too, is inevitably powerfully affected by the revolutions of each age. The family is *threatened* by some; it is *strengthened* by others of the influences let loose by the present revolutions in traditions, in social forms and political institutions, in the astounding discoveries being made of the secrets and the powers of nature, and, above all, in the ideas and the feelings of men.

Hence we do well on this historic occasion, which finds the attention of Catholics and of their like-minded neighbors focused on Bombay, to take an inventory of the forces at work *against* family life and those at work *in favor of* that life in a time

377

of revolutionary changes good and bad, some fraught with anxiety, but even more great with fair promise.

Our inventory must be brief; it makes no claim to completeness. It is offered as points for meditation by those who understand how close is family life to the unchanging decrees of Eternal Power. It may serve as a basis of discussion and action for those determined to play a Christian's part in the changing of all that may and will be changed as a result of revolutions that swirl around the family and the person.

Among the forces presently working *against* the family must be noted some arising from specific political, sociological, and cultural concepts powerfully operative around and among us.

The totalitarian state, the tendency toward which is all but universal in modern civil societies of every form, involves essential concepts hostile to the autonomy of the family and to the laws of its life; frequently these concepts are systematically expressed in policies and programs which, on the basis of a totalitarian reading of the equivocal formula *salus populi suprema lex*, sometimes unintentionally but usually effectively debilitate family life, even pervert it or seek deliberately to annihilate it. Rightist, Leftist or otherwise Statist, those dominated (even unconsciously) by totalitarian concepts tend to judge the worth of the family by how it serves the *necessities* of the State.

A Eucharistic Congress, warmed by awareness of spiritual values and of the need that first things be kept first, is a good place to put ourselves on guard against those who, with whatever noble but distracting preoccupations, speak to us of *the necessities of society* in any manner unmindful of the due order between the State and the family, between the prior protection of family life and the consequent service of the valid *necessities of society*.

Many and grave are the forces working *against* the family as a result of concepts of marriage and of the family which in fact undermine the stability of family life. Some disintegrate its unity, as do regimes of easy divorce, lightly permitted or

378

cynically facilitated. Some obscure or impede its purposes, as do regimes of contraceptive orientation with respect to the social purposes of family life or regimes of impersonal legalistic orientation, indifferent to those purposes of family life which make the family a community of love. Some defraud the family of the positive, strengthening help that it should receive from the political, economic, and religious world; such is the damage done to family life by regimes with concepts of economic *laissez-faire*, political individualism, technocratic scientism, moral neutralism, or that pseudo-religious, mystical flight from realities and responsibilities which leaves the family defenseless in the face of brutal injustices and cold inequities. All these concepts, each in its different way, contribute to the degradation of the family which finally leaves personality bereft of the reverence due life, life which makes even nature majestic because it mirrors God; life which makes the animal kingdom somehow mysteriously awesome because it is alive with powers evocative of those of God; life, which makes each man somehow divine because he is God's most perfect image in creation—the link, indeed, between God and all that God has made.

Jesus told us that we must fear not so much those who kill the body but cannot kill the soul, but rather the one who is able to destroy both body and soul.[1] This tells us that spiritual evil, moral evil, is always more to be feared than physical evils, however sordid and serious. But in fact, of course, Jesus made it clear time and again in His teaching and in His example, above all in the healing of the evils of bodies and in the forgiveness of the spiritual evil of sin, that the enemies of the body and the enemy of the soul, superficially distinct, are ultimately a single enemy. Body and soul constitute a psycho-physical unity; the person is neither angelic nor animal, neither body nor soul. It is sin in society (social injustice, arrogant indifference to the evils that others suffer) that begets the social evils that degrade and waste creation.

379

And so disease, degrading involuntary poverty, and like evils which cause men to rot and the world to grow vile are never unrelated to sin, to the spiritual death and moral chaos in the soul which cause men to despair and which mock heaven. The relationship is mutual; it results in a vicious circle of ever-greater sin of the soul and ever-greater affliction of the body. The decay of the body and the disorder of the world dispose to sin and resist grace; but even more profoundly and fatally, resistance to grace, the surrender to sin, and above all its rationalization, lead to disintegration on every level and to the decay of even the material man.

That is why the warning of Jesus that we should rather fear those who can kill the soul involves no exclusive disjunction between the evils that rot the body and the evil of the soul that is sin; His warning drives home the built-in ultimate order of cause and effect in setting up the initial circle of evil and the consequent priority, at least in intention, which must govern the Christian's approach to the breaking of that circle. False rationalizations which cloud the mind; evil concepts which corrupt the heart—these must be the more feared because they bring with them that death of the soul which *initiates* the decay that spreads, by foul contagion, to the body and to the world, setting up the recurring reactions of a re-infection and further debilitation which hasten final and total catastrophe, individual and social, in body and soul, in time and eternity of the *person*.

Wherefore the peculiar power to destroy family life of those concepts which strike at the soul of the family, at the divine life that must add its energies to the natural life of the family society, at the divine grace that must add its gifts of enduring beauty to the love that gives being to the family. And hence the fatal effect of those concepts of marriage which exclude or deny its special sanctity, its sacramental character; or of those concepts which deny the exclusiveness of the love in marriage or which cheapen this by *trial marriage* or premarital counterfeits of marriage's unique privileges and sacred rights; thus, in a word, every denial of the eternal dimension of the vocation of

380

the family to serve as a school of *sanctity* as well as a source of *life* and a community of *love*.

The general forces working *against* the family throughout the world take particular forms in each nation, sometimes in different regions of each nation. In parts of India, as everywhere in the world in one degree or another, degrading poverty and consequent social chaos sometimes make all talk of *family life* sound absurdly monstrous, while for millions the phrases of family morality become hollow rhetoric. As in other ways for other parts of the world, so for India, radically changing traditions undermine the one-time patriarchal structure that so long made the family, for millions of persons, the protector of the economic, social, and religious stability of the individual. Migration patterns within the nation; the rise of city life and industrialization; the invasion by occidental cultural influences (through music, cinema, and other art forms)—all these must be included among the factors frequently operating *against* the stability of family life, with varying degrees of effect. Each nation could list like evidences of changing patterns, changing spirit, changing values, great and small.

But in India, too, as in other parts of the world, though there be forces *against*, at least as many forces, probably even more, are at work in *behalf of* family life. Some of these positive forces, constructive, healthy, and powerful, grow precisely out of the revolutionary developments in our times, the flourishing of new traditions, new social forms and new political institutions, the astounding discoveries being made of the secrets and the powers of nature, the hitherto unsuspected forces at work in every sphere over which man's control reaches. It is never true that revolutions in the ideas and the feelings of men are necessarily regrettable, necessarily unfortunate, necessarily destructive of family life or of any other human value. Some of the present revolutionary trends are certain to prove big with blessings for the human person, for family life, for society, for the Kingdom of heaven.

The new preoccupation with the family in contemporary

thought, discussion, controversy of almost every kind is itself ultimately a force on the side of the family and working for its increased stability. Some of this preoccupation is touched even with heresy and with errors which are the more frightening because of the fundamental issues and values involved. Some of the things said are not without scandal, and some of the solutions suggested are not without sin. All this must be faced with intellectual clarity, spiritual optimism, resoluteness of character, total charity.

But no small part of the present discussion and the pre-occupations behind it is honest, conscientious, and loyal to the divine values and human integrities at the heart of family life. It must, therefore, be seen as ultimately beneficial, a refreshing force on the side of the family as a source of life, even life more abundant, of love more faithful, of sanctity more conducive to the peace, perfection, and personal growth which are the fruits of God's grace.

On the level of nature there remain powerful forces on the side of family life. The very nature of things to the recognition of which men of sound reason and enlightened faith must sooner or later return, the laws of nature and of nature's God—all remain unchanged and unchanging in the midst of the storms. They wait ready to reveal themselves, still there and sturdy, when the storms of moral crises and debates pass, even as the rocks and the boundaries of the sea are found the same and unshaken in their ancient places once the turbulence of the flood and the disorders of the hurricane have passed. History and human experience continually confirm, in lessons sometimes sad, sometimes gentle, sometimes tragic, the wisdom of those verses of the Book of Genesis which speak of the personal and social reasons why God brought into being that community of love that projects man, for whom it is not good to be alone, and that human source of life by which our world, the boundaries of which we can no longer measure, is peopled in order that it may be subdued to man's service and

God's glory.[2] Nature and her constituent laws remain on the side of family life; reason could ultimately demonstrate this, even if faith were smothered in silence.

That is why we always have more reasons for confident optimism than we have for moral defeatism as we face the future. There are forces loose in the world which are anti-life, anti-love, anti-child; but it is still a world of expanding programs of social security, maternity aid, child guidance, parent and child education, housing action, social justice, and family welfare under the auspices of municipalities, provinces, national and international governmental agencies, as well as of continuing private initiative and philanthropic action. Not all defective social efforts, even of states or organizations with unfortunate political theories, will prove finally *against* the family, its life and its love; indeed, as so often in the past, so the future may find that good effects have survived when faulty theories and sinful policies have inevitably gone their way into oblivion. It will again fall out in the future, as has often happened in the past, that *unintended good*, thanks to the resilience and direction of nature herself, may prove the only lasting result of objectively evil policies and mistaken motivation.

Nature herself has picked up from the creative power of God something of His power to bring good out of evil and to make things turn out for her purposes once those who sought to defraud her or to bend her to their unenlightened purposes have finally played out their hand and dropped from the game.

Meanwhile, the supernatural forces on the side of family life increase daily both in number and in power. An aroused Church, ever more conscientious of itself as the family of God and the source of God's grace for families singly and for all the family of mankind, is proving to be rich in resources to aid the development of family idealism, the solution of family tensions, the promotion of family life. Christian family movements in some parts of the world, movements the very names of which reveal their passion for life and its fostering within purified family patterns (*Nouvelle Vie*, *Cana l'Anneau d'Or*), a harvest of publications on family liturgical life, on nuptial spirituality, the special sanctity and sublime dignity of marriage and of the family—all these reveal the Church at work on the side of family life.

The doctrinal treasures of the Faith are being searched to discover new stories for the enrichment of the Church's moral and ascetical contribution to the hallowing of family life. Saint Paul's doctrine of the fecund, ecstatic union between Christ and His Church as the exemplar of the life-giving, sanctifying union of love between spouses has long provided the premise of a vital theology of the family. The concept and the quality of the life of every family is given new dimensions, meaning, and worth by meditation on the manner in which the Adorable Trinity makes even the Unique and One God somehow an image of the family; the Holy Family of Nazareth has become once again the inspiration of families seeking their share in the holiness that this Family made possible; the Church herself, our Holy Mother the Church, is daily better understood as a warm, united family surrounding with its consolation and its strength each of our families; the phrase *the Holy Father* has taken on new meaning, greatly increased by the events in Bombay this week and the personal presence of the Holy Father in the midst of the Indian members of his worldwide spiritual family. These phrases of the Catholic Faith are sacramental in their power to hallow, to fortify, to illumine family life on every level.

But the circumstances of our meeting make it particularly appropriate that we emphasize the particular relationship to family life of the Holy Eucharist, the sacramental channel of God's own life into our lives on every level. The Eucharist is uniquely related to questions of family life.

Marriage is a union between two persons, a union in love out of which comes life. It results in a community that the

Church has always expressed in terms of certain goods: *bonum fidei, bonum sacramenti, bonum prolis*. A community is as compact as is its sharing of the goods by which it is constituted. But what community can possibly be more intimate and compactly *one* than the community of those who have in common their very flesh and blood? Yet such are the spouses in every true marriage. The words which so describe this community of marriage—a singleness of flesh and blood—are not phrases out of philosophy books or books of law. They are words straight out of Sacred Scripture, the Old Testament and the New, and therefore words of theology, these words that speak of two people in one flesh, of one who shall be flesh of the other's flesh, bone of the other's bone.[3]

These words, descriptive of every valid marriage, impel the mind immediately to other words of Scripture that also speak to us of flesh and blood, this time the flesh and blood that God took to Himself in the human nature of Jesus Christ. It is the flesh and blood that Christ shares with us in the life-giving Sacrament of Love that our Bombay Congress praises and proclaims. The Blessed Sacrament, the Holy Eucharist, thus becomes for Christians foremost among the forces on the side of the family both as a community of love and as a source of the life more abundant.

Of old it was said that in marriage two would become one flesh, the one bone of the other's bone, flesh of the other's flesh; marriage then became a unity such that no man could imagine another more intimate. But God could devise a greater intimacy, and the greater intimacy that Christ made possible for all Christians brings to those who are one flesh in marriage an immeasurable intensification of community literally expressed in terms of flesh and blood: He who eats my flesh and drinks my blood has life everlasting. . . . He who eats my flesh and drinks my blood abides in me and I in him. . . . He also shall live because of me.[4]

And so the Eucharistic Congress is a providential reminder

of the most powerful of all the forces that the Church places in the service of married love and family life. The spouses who are nourished by the Holy Sacrament find their human flesh and blood, already close-knit in the unity of their marriage, now reinforced in unity, quickened in life, and wonderfully lifted up to new heights of love by flesh and blood that belongs to God Himself and yet becomes so interwoven with flesh of their flesh, so saturates their blood, that even as they love one another, they understand, in terms of their marriage, its pure passion and its creative power, what God meant when He promised Ezechiel:

> I will give you a new heart and put a new spirit within you: I will take away the stony heart out of your flesh and will give you a heart of flesh. And I will put my spirit in the midst of you: And I will cause you to walk in my Commandments and to keep my judgments. . . . And you shall dwell in the land which I gave to your fathers and your people shall be my people and I will be your God. . . . And I will save you from all your uncleannesses. . . . So shall the waste cities be full of flocks of men; and they shall know that I am the Lord.[5]

Thus in faith and divine love does the Eucharist become the living center of the Church's part in restoring and energizing family life. Thus, too, the devout family becomes, in new hope and human love, the living source of the regeneration of the world unto a life that is not sick and a love that is not ashamed, life worthy of man, love blessed of God!

XXXII

Conciliar Rome

The sorely missed Bishop Griffiths tossed at me a couple of months before he died a popular magazine article rich with *inside stories* of Vatican Council II.[1] Several of its best yarns involved persons and events to which we had been close for almost four years of the Conciliar experience. "Tell me," he demanded wearily, "what Council have *we* been attending?" Obviously, it was not the one described in the magazine.

Bishop Griffiths and I had a hunch that the author of the "all about the Council" article did not know what Council we were attending. But we, too, would have been mistaken if we had supposed, at any given moment, that we could be certain in our evaluation of what was taking place even before our very eyes. For, like peace in President Kennedy's oft-quoted phrase, the Council is a *process*. It is an unfolding—kaleidoscopic in its changes of impressions. It is fixed, I have no doubt, in its divinely appointed direction, but fluid in its bewildering shifts.

Some matters, however, are already clear even in the present stage of the Council. The process has been long. It has involved thousands of miles of travel, hundreds of hours of work, countless units of emotional fatigue, intellectual effort, spiritual tension, and fervent prayer. Not a bit of any of these does one regret. Quite the contrary.

One's reactions in present retrospect and reasonable anticipation are those of unqualified gratitude to the grace of God for this indisputably major religious event of our century. Gratitude, too, to Pope John for his openness to the breathing of the Spirit that moves where it will; gratitude to Pope Paul

This article was written for and published in *America* on March 27, 1965.

for his sturdy perseverance in ways that must be mysterious even to him—particularly, perhaps, to him, given his intellectual sensitiveness and his high sense of responsibility. Gratitude to the known, but not less to the anonymous heroes—the conscious ones, the unconscious ones, the confident ones and the frightened ones, for there *are* frightened heroes—caught up in the conciliar experience.

Glancing back over Council diary notes, I see clearly that some things will certainly call for developed analysis in that sweet by-and-by *after the Council*, when its major events and principal effects admit of documentation in balanced fashion. Genuine theologians will number among these a force that, inevitably and understandably, does not show in the newsreels, the press photos, or the day-to-day coverage of the Council. This is, of course, the role of the Holy Spirit in the progress of the Kingdom of heaven—which "cometh not with observation".

Some of the best jokes in the Council have been about the presence (or, on occasion, the alleged momentary absence) of the Holy Spirit. During one of the crises of the third session, the story ran through the stalls that Pope John, apprehensive in heaven about the fate of his Council, importuned the Holy Spirit for a firsthand account of what was taking place in Session Three. He was said to have received the answer, "Don't ask me! I didn't even get to the first two!"

But the Holy Spirit *was* present at the first two, as at the third—sometimes almost palpably so. It is always dangerous (it is sometimes bad theology) to talk glibly of *experiencing* the presence of the Holy Spirit; it is impossible, however, to be unaware of the operation of the Spirit in frequent moments of the Council. Sometimes the presence of the invisible and inaudible Spirit is enormously more certain (and happy) than the all-too-obvious presence of personalities photographed with routine ease and heard with painful clarity. There must be few close to the Council who have not felt this presence of the Holy Spirit. Jean Guitton, first of the lay observers, describes it with Gallic grace; but even those with no gift to articulate their deepest spiritual sensations were time and again grateful for awareness of the Holy Spirit in the Council.

An old conciliar commonplace speaks of the stages of the history of every ecumenical council in terms of the phase of man, the phase of Satan, and finally, the phase of the Holy Spirit. The reality is never that neat; the stages of Vatican II have certainly not been thus neatly successive.

For a while, one might have spoken in rough but handy fashion of the phase of the *periti*, the phase of the bishops, and then, perhaps, the phase of the Holy Spirit. There were some reasons to see the first session as a Council of *periti* and to argue that only with the second session did the Council move from the gallery of the *periti* to the floor where the bishops sat. This was undoubtedly as it should have been in the working out of the dynamics of the Council.

True enough, the first session heard the reading by many bishops of *position papers* obviously prepared by *periti*. But the end of the third session found very few Council Fathers still standing up to read, with varying degrees of insight, the opinions of their *periti*, complete (as in the case of one who left the copy of his intervention on the coffee bar one morning) with accent marks on the tougher Latin words and phonetic breakdown of two fairly recondite name references from among the Fathers of the Church!

On the human side, even the key role of the *periti* in the early phases was all to the good. It brought to the Council floor the fruits of years of scholarship and special study—though these sometimes showed up in the midst of special pleading. But even on the divine side, which ultimately alone matters, the Holy Spirit was present in all these phases from the beginning. He could not possibly have been absent from the years of meditation, research, and ferment among theologians that preceded the call of the Council and filtered through the carefully prepared and casually read interventions. The Holy

Spirit was definitely present in the magisterial exercise of their governing, teaching, and other priestly offices by which the popes without exception who followed Vatican Council I prepared for Vatican Council II. Pope John XXIII has borne personal witness to the impulse of the Holy Spirit in response to which he called the Council. It takes no great subtlety of mind or gift of faith to perceive the operation of the Holy Spirit in many of the circumstances of persons, places, things, and events that eventually added up to the opening and the progress of the Council. Some of us sensed the Holy Spirit at work in the delegate-observers' box and often thought that we detected His influence (once therapeutic) among the reporters and commentators.

In all the stages and aspects of the Council, the awareness of whose shadow we have been walking in is the dominant conciliar experience; it is more easily sensed and intimately felt than any tensions, joys, apprehensions, or details of heat or cold, physical fatigue or intellectual stimulation.

At this writing, the Council is that of the bishops. Reflection on the conciliar experience brings back many impressions under this heading. It is still insisted by some writers, somewhat petulantly on occasion, that the Council Fathers fall into two camps, the one *conservative* and the other *progressive*. It is even suggested that any who deny or even qualify this alignment do so because they have a *thing* on the subject and are, for some subliminal reason, annoyed or terrified by the distinction.

I confess that I do have a *thing* on the subject, and my *thing* becomes more deeply *thinged* in me as the Council process unfolds and I find the alleged *conservatives* and the alleged *progressives* figuratively crossing the aisle in a fashion that mixes them up as much as they are mingled in the aisles when they pour in and out of the morning sessions. My experience has been not so much one of *conservatives* and *progressives* (though the distinction is doubtless valid even though the validity is of secondary relevance); it is rather an experience of Council Fathers and *periti* of both camps, some of whom are *open-minded* and some *close-minded*.

Other attitudes show up also in both camps in about the same degree and frequency; for example, the disposition to take advantage of any card that may turn up in order to win a trick. For this reason, one is unable to understand the distinction between *good guys* and *bad guys* found in so many Council stereotypes in the early coverage of the event; one was perpetually astonished by the number of *good guys* who acted like *bad guys* when something close to their hearts and their understanding of the needs of the Church was at issue.

When it becomes possible to analyze one's conciliar experiences with final judgments, certain points can be set down more satisfactorily than is presently possible. For example, one will then know the precise moment when he became aware that the distinction between the *Christian world* and the *missionary world* is now largely illusory, filled with snares and delusions. The conciliar experience has taught that the whole Church is a missionary Church; that all the world, from Trastevere to Tibet, is missionary country; that only the mission *problems*, *challenges*, and *graces* constitute any real differences as you move from venerable, well-organized dioceses to the most recent and inchoate vicariates apostolic.

Other testimonies from the conciliar experience will underscore the distinction between mere *facts*, however many or however interesting, and the total *truth*, however elusive or tenuous. At the 1964 Catholic Press Convention, I felt bound to dwell on this difference between the bewitchery of *facts* and the service of *truth*; it is a theme we will recall whenever we revert to certain Council chapters. Fascinating, too, will be the case histories illustrating how differences in age, career backgrounds, nationality, and like secondary considerations fade before the forces of a spiritual and intellectual kind, which bring together those temperamentally alike, so that some of

391

the eldest turn out to be more akin to the most youthful than to their own contemporaries, and vice versa.

The future scholar will verify how often in the conciliar experience it turned out that the most recent and *exciting* of supposedly revolutionary *breakthroughs* are best expressed in quotations from the most ancient Church Fathers or in phrases of writers centuries dead. Time and again, documents like the anonymous *Epistle to Diognetus* provided the most effective phrases to express the *astounding* discoveries of the riders of the *nouvelle vogue*, at least when the riders were on secure water skis and the *vogue* was sufficiently related to the movements of the Holy Spirit to win the approving votes of the Council Fathers.

Other elements of the Council experience are beyond number. How does one express them in one thousand five hundred words? When Council Fathers turned historians attempt to express them in one hundred and fifty thousand words, a minor irony will come home to roost. They will find themselves confronted with the problem that caused so many little tensions between high-minded prelates and hard-working reporters trying to tell the Council story to readers of the secular press.[2]

One example illustrates what I mean. Lou Cassels was among the most conscientious of the newsmen covering the Council. One afternoon it was my fell destiny to be assigned to help out at the American bishops' press conference. Lou put up his hand to ask clarification of the doctrine of the collegiality of the apostles and their successors, which had been discussed in the morning Council session. I tried to provide a brief summary of the scriptural exegesis, the theological interpretations, the historical complications, and the canonical developments, not to mention the heretical aberrations, on this knotty point throughout nineteen centuries of fierce speculation and activity surrounding it. When I finished—alas, a little vaingloriously— my twenty-minute attempt at a synthesis of the thoughts and actions of the centuries, Lou looked desperate and said: "How the heck do you compress all that into a five-hundred-word cable that must be in New York by five o'clock this afternoon?"

Well, *how do you*? How will *we*—even for more patient readers and within a more leisurely deadline? And so how can anyone compress a tasting of the work of eternity into a casual discussion of his space-time experience of the Council? He can't. He can only tell whom he saw and some of what he heard. The great result transcends experience; "the kingdom of heaven cometh not with observation."[3]

XXXIII

Seed Ideas–Reflections at
Easter after the Council

In what direction, even if we do not yet see it clearly, must we judge the Church to be moving in these predestined times? Whither are the prevailing winds of the Spirit blowing? What, in a word, is the authentic *thrust* of the Second Vatican Council?

A general normative answer to the third question, which sums up the first two questions, seems warranted by no little evidence. That *thrust* underwent superficial changes during the course of the Council itself, though its more profound orientation, appointed by Divine Providence itself, was probably secure and certain from the beginning, could one but know the counsel of God.

In the first session, the perspective of the Council was, in no small degree, toward the past. The clear intent was to encourage *dialogue*—the awkward current word for decent Christian conversation—among the divided traditions of Christendom in the present; but the look was to the past. There was much talk about the tragic divisions of the sixteenth and seventeenth centuries; people speculated on what would have been the reactions of the sixteenth century and the period of the Protestant revolutions to the sheer goodness of Pope John XXIII and the ecumenical spirit of Vatican Council II. What would Luther and his German princes have done had there been granted vernacular liturgies then as there are such granted now? Would the sad divisions in Christendom have taken place as they did? The Lutheran bishop of Berlin, Dr. Dibelius, and the American Cardinal Cushing both thought not, but the point is academic

This lecture was delivered in Pittsburgh, Pennsylvania, on April 14, 1966.

and the discussion was and is largely nostalgic, wistful, and romantic; moreover, it leaves out too much history and plain theological substance to be taken permanently seriously.

Nonetheless this was, in marked degree, the mood of the first session and no small part of the second session. It was symbolized by the excitement over the presence of so many and such sincere non-Catholic delegate-observers; by the ecumenical preoccupations with which the first Council documents reported on the floor were—properly enough—read, debated, and, on occasion, rejected; by the central importance attached to the opinions of the Secretariat for Christian Unity; by the personal—and deserved—preeminence of Cardinal Augustin Bea, S.J.; and by the response among all Christians to the pilgrimage of Pope Paul VI to those shrines of the Holy Land equally and universally cherished in Orthodox tradition, Protestant hymnody, and Catholic Faith.[1]

But with the third session—really, already within the second—the perspective broadened immeasurably. It remained essentially Christian ecumenical; it could not do otherwise. It still fostered and depended upon present dialogue and reform; these, too, remained of the essence. But new dimensions were demanded and new frontiers were opened up with the establishment of the Secretariat for Non-Christians, with the heightened appreciation of the long-range spiritual possibilities—as opposed to the short-range polemical exigencies—of the dialogue between Christians and Jews, as well as with the other *people of the Book* and between the great world of Oriental religions and of all who seek Jesus Christ in any way or believe in God at all. This new thrust of the Council gathered incalculable momentum in, at, and after Pope Paul's dramatic visit to Bombay.[2]

Yet even this does not suggest the final—and, I believe, permanent—thrust of the Council as this was to become, in the fourth session, as clear as God's hidden plans can possibly be clear in the midst of man's work and man's confusions.

That further perspective of the Council took less notice of the sixteenth and seventeenth—or even the nineteenth and twentieth—centuries; it looked forward rather to the twenty-first or perhaps even later centuries to a world in the making, out of elements conceived and brought to being outside what either Catholics or Protestants know as either Christendom or the Church. It was less concerned with what Luther, Calvin, or Knox or others on either side of divided Christendom's arguments might think, but with opening up dialogue in the name of the unique and undivided translucent Christ with a generation for whom these names out of Christian history are already meaningless and seem destined to become even more so. The thrust is now toward a force, that of secular or atheistic humanism, which is presently intent on rejecting the whole script of the drama we were reading when the Council opened, its entire plot, all its *dramatis personae* and even its very Author Himself as irrelevant, unimportant, without existential meaning.

In a culture which has calmly heard the news that *God is dead*—has, in fact, read His obituary in the style of the *New York Times*, complete with the usual unctuous professions of bereavement from the White House—there is not likely long to be interest in Luther's hypothetical stance vis-à-vis Vatican II nor, indeed, much speculation about how Leo X might react to new murmurings from the non-monastic monks of the north and northwest.

The Council thus is now fully focused on the future and on dialogue with the present and coming world of unbelief, dogmatic or practical. The evidences of this are in the new importance of the Secretariat for Non-Believers—as central to the work at the end of the Council as was that of the Secretariat for Christian Unity at the beginning; the content of the *Pastoral Constitution on the Church in the Modern World*—the last document to be worked in the Council—the significant polemic that it aroused within the Council, plus its invitation to a new dialogue of the future; the spirit and emphasis of the *messages to the world* proclaimed in the ceremonies of adjournment; and the *secular* pilgrimage of Pope Paul to the assembly of the United Nations, the Charter of which is still silent about God but eloquent with certain of the *validities*—basically Natural Law truths but always with close connection to the lessons of the gospel—which must be the object of the *dialogue* of the indefinite future.[3] It is this dialogue toward which the Council was pointed at its ending and which Pope Paul valiantly inaugurated at the United Nations by everything he said about peace and war, the sanctity of life, the irrationality of contraception in a truly loving and generous world, and the claims of the *Unknown God* upon a world eager for unity and disposed to study all ideas, values, and means essential to such unity.[4]

And so one sees the Council not at all in terms of *aggiornamento* merely understood as revising received values and ideas, least of all junking them, for the purpose of any merely present dialogue, however attractive or even urgent. But one sees it in terms of a setting of our house in order, balancing our own books, and discovering what friends and colleagues we may have kept or acquired for a future dialogue with a world presently indeed hostile, but which must also be encompassed by the Christian creed and code, beginning with basic friendship. In this connection, I am reminded that the dictionary sense of *aggiornamento* may include just such overtones of meaning as balancing one's books, not excluding the idea of deferred action pending such inventory of resources.

Moreover, against the background of this perspective of the Council one chooses a little more carefully the figures of speech, taken from the seasons of the year, by which one tries to express the function and the direction of the Council in God's plan for His people.

Some, I suspect, saw the Council as a season of harvest, an autumn after the long generation of hard polemic and divided struggle, a kind of coming together of the scattered workers to bring their different grapes to the wine-harvest—*vendemmia*, *vendage*—of the Lord.

One cannot see it so. Neither does one see the Council period as a golden summer of religion's history, glorious in its spiritual vitality, its religious action, its exploits for and in the Lord. Sober realism forbids such a reading either of the Church in our day or of the times which engulf us.

Pope John XXIII often used figures of speech that dealt with spring. He was quoted by Norman Cousins and others as speaking of "opening the windows" as one does in spring and, especially, of seeking for the Church and her truth the verdant, pristine beauty that things have in spring. Perhaps this is closer to the mark, but it is not quite exact.

Peasants have immemorially sought to anticipate the spring, to prepare for its beauty and even hasten it by planting grain that can mature—in the scriptural sense, even die, to come to life again—under the killing snows of the long winter. Pope John's Italian peasants speak proverbially of *il pane sotto la neve*, of how under the wintry snow there is life-giving bread so long as the seeds are maturing in preparation for the eventual spring.

One suspects that Pope John called the Council to provide just such a providential planting of certain *seed-ideas* against the severe winter of unbelief of scientism, atheistic humanism, and moral scepticism which lies between us and the next springtime for both faith and humane hopes, the spring that will add divine life and beauty to the valid human ideas and values which survive—may perhaps be strengthened by—a winter that he, in common with Newman and Soloviev, saw fatally approaching.

Pope John thought of spring all the time; he talked of it readily and willingly. But he had served long years in three diplomatic centers, two in the East and one in the West, where the advance chill of the winter of unbelief—whether from jaded indifference, Marxist atheism, or existentialist negations—

would have been felt deeply by so sensitive a spirit as his.[5] Fortunately, his temperament and spirituality were formed in a part of the world and among a people who, with indomitable optimism, know how to plant before the winter the grain that survives the frosts and gives the spring at once its first beauty and its enduring life.

And if Pope John's prophetic preparation for the coming winter by so confident a fall planting was providential for the Church—and, by the same token, for civilization itself—so must we see as dispositions of God's gracious purpose the capacity of Pope Paul for disciplined, patient, and intelligent direction of God's people through the severe initial period of the maturing of the Council's *seed-ideas*.

For it is only by such *seed-ideas*, planted for maturing in the dialogue persevering through a winter of unbelief which is destined to end in an eventual Second Spring, that the major actions and themes emerging from the Council experience take on something like the proportions due the human good-will engendered in the Council and the divine presence of the Holy Spirit. Thus understood, certain Council *seed-ideas*, whatever their present tentative and unformed shape, have manifest future potential for life and action in the coming spring. I suggest these as typical and as perhaps the most promising:

1. The emphasis on the Church as the people of God—the new Israel, regenerating the world through a mystery.

2. The concept of collegiality in its theological and, so to say, non-political dimensions.

3. The Catholic concept of the priesthood of the laity.

4. The pastoral and teaching functions of the liturgy—it is this emphasis that is new and probably explains the universal support of reform, even the vernacular, by the Council Fathers; most else was in *Mediator Dei*.[6]

5. The emphasis on the person in an impersonal automated culture.

399

6. The communitarian nature of personality.

7. The Church as a universal sacrament of salvation.

8. The divine roots and measure of human life and love—a point of utter urgency for the survival of either and both in an age of test-tube and UNIVAC approaches to both life and love.

9. The recognition of a new humanism.

10. The condemnation of total war.

11. The suggestion of a world commission on justice and development.

12. The pattern of the Trinity for the unity of the Church.

13. The relation of the Eucharist and Peter to ecumenism.

14. The Church and the churches.

15. The missionary corollaries of collegiality, plus the *common good* of all the churches.

16. The mission of the laity in the temporal order and the validity of the goodness, truth, and beauty served there.

17. The truth and holiness in non-Christian religions.

18. The real relation of the crucifixion to Jew and Christian.

19. The de facto premise and nature of religious liberty, with the consequent demands on personal moral responsibility toward community and toward God of those who claim it so passionately.

That these these *seed-ideas* finally found acceptance so unanimous in the Council argues more than the human ingenuity of bishops and their *periti*. And so I conclude: the Spirit of God breathed where It willed in the Council. No person was more present, more active, more relevant in the Council's progress than the Third Person of the Most Blessed Trinity. That Divine Person was hard at work achieving His ancient task: vivifying and unifying the Church for a long, hard winter and renewing the face of the earth for a predestined Spring.

Blessed be the Holy Spirit!

XXXIV

Franciscan Joy

It is (I hope) a happy omen for the next chapter in the history of the Sisters of Saint Francis (and perhaps a symbol of God's own rejoicing in their centenary jubilee) that we are favored with so resplendent a noon day after so unpromising a dawn.

Those who were able to watch, as I hope all the sisters were, the splash-down of the astronauts in the ocean this morning will have observed that the historic event was surrounded by a considerable mist; nonetheless, the joy on board the *Wasp* and the enthusiasm in the voices of all those interpreting the event to us were indicative of how unimportant was the mist, how fragile the clouds, and how substantial the accomplishment. So, too, on the centennial of the presence of the Franciscan Sisters among us, all the mist and even occasional seasons of stormy weather which are inevitable in the history of a great religious community must be seen in retrospect as unsubstantial as contrasted with the solid accomplishment in, with, through, and for the Lord of our so-dedicated Franciscan sisters.

Newspaper feature stories in these recent days, plus, I am certain, conversations among the religious and their friends, have reviewed the high points of the hundred years of history and the graces of those years for which we return thanks this morning. I shall not do so. It is much more important on an occasion of this kind that, taking our theme from a phrase of this morning's Epistle, we center our thoughts on the *new creature* that is continually reborn in the history of a religious community, particularly in times of jubilee.

This sermon was preached at the Saint Francis Convent-Motherhouse, Millvale, Pennsylvania, on June 6, 1966.

Any moment of this kind involves a taking leave of some aspects of the work, of some adventures of the history; but it involves also a welcome opening to new developments and new directions on the level of the apostolate and its works, together with a renewal of those who do the work and, above all, of the spirit of those who do the work, the spirit by which the community is made a community, united, vital, holy. And so a jubilee occasion, particularly one so significant as a hundred-year anniversary, is chiefly occasion for the renewal of the traditional spirit and for the acquisition of fresh elements, perhaps, conducive to any needed new spirit.

If we were to single out a new element or a refreshed and renewed spirit especially needed in the Church at the moment, in the work of the Church and in the hearts, the minds, and all the being of those who do the work of the Church on whatever level in our day, there is one, I suggest, that we have a particular right to expect, indeed to demand, of Franciscans. That desperately needed spirit (and I choose the word *desperately* to indicate not only the nature of the general need, but also the mood of the speaker on occasion) is the spirit associated invariably with Saint Francis. It is a quality of the saint heralded not only by the sentimental or the romantic, but also by the most sober and coldly analytical of the students of his spirituality. That value, that desperately needed quality; is the spirit of *joy*: joy in the work, joy in being alive to do the work, joy in having the ability to do it, joy in honestly recognizing one's lack of ability when it is absent; joy in the existence of God before we even begin to consider the myriad and multiplying motives for further joy in all His attributes, His mercy, His providence, His goodness, and, on occasion, His justice.

If there is a virtue, I repeat, that is *desperately* needed in the life and the work of the Church today, that virtue is *joy*. In one of the most bleak developments of modern times, Christians have suddenly become a people seemingly without humor. By a singularly unhappy chance, Catholics in particular have lost (please God only momentarily) the gift of laughter. We are now a sarcastic people, a stridently indignant people speaking in glib phrases with a certain acid cleverness; but we are a people without humor. How this dreadful fate befell us, I have no idea; it is one thing, I hope, that cannot be blamed on the Second Vatican Council! It would be an irony beyond acceptance if a period of Church history inaugurated by the radiant Pope John left us a people without joy!

Less than a generation ago, sometimes in great poverty, in second-class citizenship and in the midst of other limitations, we Catholics were universally accredited with being the light-hearted Christians; now we appear to have become the grim ones, marked by an air of deadly earnestness and an appalling absence of the light touch; joy seems never more lacking than when we are discussing the Church, the Lord, and Christian life and work.

The present almost pathological lack of joy shows up in every vocation and in every area of life. There already exist among us people who rejoice as little in the coming of children as once used to do only our neo-pagans. Among descendants of people who spoke, only yesterday, of the coming of a baby as a *blessed event* (a *lieto*), maternity is no longer thought joyful. A Catholic woman recently wrote a novel in which she spent endless pages debunking all the scriptural, liturgical, and traditional poetic phrases that used to speak of the joys of maternity. She specifically finds fault with the idea that a wife should be as a *fruitful vine*. She finds this colorful, happy phrase, filled with life and joy, too much for our dismal overcrowded days. She is particularly indignant at the use of the hallowed phrase *the joyful mother of children*. Her clear message is that there are no joyful mothers except those who have a calculated one or two problem-less children and are, therefore, joyful in the accuracy of their calculations, but in nothing else.

What is true on the level of the once-joyful vocation of

403

family founding, the vocation made joyful by everything we used to mean by human love and the creative spirit, I regret to say is true on the level of other vocations in the life of the Church. Not long ago a secular magazine featured (with a sick joy all its own) the joyless reflections of a priest miserable in that celibacy which, in more hardy spirits, can be the very condition of joys beyond limit, joy in the Lord and in the unrestricted loving service of all God's children. At about the same time a priest with a woebegone look on his face made the observation that drove home to me the degree of our present dreariness. We have always been taught that when there is the danger that, for his sins, a priest might be named a bishop, he should have the attitude of *nolo episcopari—I would rather not!*— but this man said, "There can't be much fun in the job of being a bishop these days; it must be a dismal job." I am not sure there was ever much *fun* in the sense he may have meant, but there was great joy, I assure you.

In the priesthood you meet many earnest little men these days determined to blueprint us into some species of a joyless City of God, a bleak castle in which everything will be on a schedule of their devising, meeting sober standards they have set up and grimly conforming with all manner of a priori concepts of dull excellence and performance, but totally devoid of joy. As you read in the newspapers of the widely publicized crisis in seminary life, you think a little wistfully of the days when speakers used to say after addressing audiences of seminarians, "What a joy to talk to an audience like this!" The laughter was always clean and the responses spontaneous; the whole mood of the meeting was characterized not by the simplicity of the booby, but by the simplicity of the seraph. The close attention was the result of clear heads, clean hearts, and lives uncomplicated by anything that destroys Christian joy. They were not *uncomplicated* lives, believe me; they were complicated by all manner of questions: How am I going to pay my tuition? Am I going to qualify? Will I get out of this place eventually so that I can get to work?

Nor were spirits indifferent in those days to the woes of the wider world than that of one's own seminary enclosure; memory is clear, eloquent and cogent on that point. But even in the midst of personal frustrations and social concerns, hearts were joyful, heads were serene, thoughts were lucid, the will was steadfast, and emotions, though deep and passionate, were under the dominance of mind and will. The mood was closer to the mood of Saint Francis, whose life was singularly complicated—not at all as simple as sentimental legends make it out to have been—singularly complicated from every direction; but his thoughts were clear and his will was steadfast, and he had that simplicity that is called seraphic because Saint Francis was permeated in mind, heart, and total being with joy, a joy that found the whole universe not the object of mathematical calculations alone but a source of lyrical reactions; everything in it, death included, became as a brother or a beloved sister.

This mood of Christian joy, I regret to say, is momentarily under a certain trauma or paralysis—an eclipse of some kind; it cannot possibly come back too soon for the sanity of civilization and the salvation of the Church. And if there is one group more than another who have it as their special vocation to bring back the spirit of joy, to bring back laughter, to relax our tensions in the face of the titanic problems which have people standing militantly at attention, or grimly pushing their placards in everyone's face, declining to discuss things, unable to laugh, incapable of being patient even with God, that group is surely those who bear, in whatever relationship to him, the name of Saint Francis, as priests, as sisters, as tertiaries.[1]

I repeat, that joy cannot possibly be reborn too soon. The joy of Saint Francis is the joy of the Church. It is the joy that is echoed in the liturgy, but, alas, I must say, not always present in its performance. It lingers in the phrases of even the worst translations, but it is certainly not in the faces of the grim people who so often gather to perform the liturgy as it *should* be performed! How often these, like most *reformers*, are without laughter, without love, without caprice, without anything except dull determination; their absence of joy, their paralyzing grimness, is not at all concealed by the melancholy lines of many of the so-called *folk* Masses. These are about as grim as can be borne. Some youngsters who by every circumstance of age, nature, and grace should have been rhapsodic greeted me in the cathedral within the month with a dirge palmed off on them by a depressed religious; every stanza ended with a plaintive plea: "When will we ever know; when will we ever know?" I was tempted to tell them that, in fact, they have known, if they've been reading the Scriptures, for these last two thousand years! They have been spirit-charged witnesses since the first Pentecost. If any part of the Christian claim has any measure of validity, then they have known for a long, long time. Moreover, they have known not only unto their own edification and perfection, but unto what should be their joy and the joy of the world.

Such joy of the Church, as in the Franciscan tradition, is not at all inconsistent with full recognition of the suffering or privation that are the tragic aspects of the human condition. It does not render the devout insensible to these or unwilling to do one's part in remedying them, but it does preserve them from the absurd air of personal offense which the reformers invariably bring to their reaction to evil in the universe or to inadequacy in its inhabitants. Surely you have noted this curious blend of humorlessness and perverse arrogance in so many of our young protesters against the modern world and all things in it: *Who allowed this? Who failed to prevent it?* Who in the previous generation allowed this situation that so inconveniences *me*? Scandalizes *me*? Who allowed it, so that he can be the object of our prompt retributive justice.

But the joy that the Church sings, the joy that Saint Francis found, was the joy of Jesus crucified. "Not mine to glory but in the Cross of Jesus Christ." That Cross, far from being the denial of the joy that must be restored to the Church, is essential to its very existence. It is the symbol of its presence and is the source, not only of its exaltation, but, be it said with great care and no mere poetry, the source of its laughter. And I think that Christ laughed when they took Him with staves the night before He died. Thus did Theodore Maynard sum up the place of the Passion and the Cross in the mood of the poets who wrote for us a generation ago—in the days when laughter, the laughter of Chesterton, the laughter of Belloc, the laughter of scores of others greater and less, rang through our halls. Then we were truculent toward our neighbors, but now we are truculent toward the members of our own household, toward those who gave us life, truth, and almost all we possess. Our present absence of joy—joy in creation, joy in being, joy in knowledge, joy in love, joy in beauty, and above all, joy in that which sanctifies and ennobles and immortalizes these, joy in that Cross of Jesus Christ that was impressed on the body of Saint Francis on the heights of Mount La Verna— lies beneath our truculence. God grant us grace to grow in joy!

So we return thanks for all the joys of the hundred years, and for all the suffering and the pain; and if it be the price of restoring Franciscan joy, we will welcome back the pain, welcome back the poverty, and welcome back anything and everything that yields the spiritual joy so strangely absent in our times, so cherished by a part of the memories of the past, so essential to the future work of this community and the progress of the work of Christ.

XXXV

Colonel de Corbiac 1872–1965

Good evening.

Somewhere I once read some lines descriptive of the difference between birth and death, in terms of our reaction to them, who experience them, and the reactions of our friends, of those who love us. The lines which I read ran something like this. When we are born, we cry, but those who love us rejoice. When we die, those who love us weep, but we rejoice. Certainly the devout understand this because we understand that with death we enter into life everlasting—the life of the world to come. And such an entrance into undying life is necessarily the beginning of joy for those certainly who die in the friendship of God and with a claim to eternal happiness.

I read these lines tonight because during the last twenty-four hours I received word from France of the death of a friend, a very remarkable man about whom I'd like to talk during our visit together this evening, first of all because it is pleasant to talk about one's friends, particularly when they die, but also because there are certain things about this particular man which make him of interest to those who might hear about him by the conversation and the praise of his friends, as I'd like to talk about him with praise this evening.[1]

The man who died was an old man, and therefore there should not have been too much weeping over his death among those who love him. He was ninety-three when he died. He led a very full life, a life characterized by very great patriotism, by very great devotion to his family and satisfaction in his family. They had all lived to bring very real joy to his heart

This address was delivered over Radio Station KDKA, in Pittsburgh, Pennsylvania, on August 7, 1965.

during the long years that he lived. His life was characterized too by a very real, very manly, very remarkable personal piety. And it's about some aspects of this that I should like to speak.

We hear a good deal these days about the place of the laity in the life of the Church. We hear talk about the emerging layman. We talk about the concept of the priesthood of the laity. We say how wonderful it is that these things are recognized in and encouraged by the Second Vatican Council. And we take intense satisfaction from the reflection of how many of these concepts we Christians, Catholics, Protestants, and Orthodox share. And all that we say is very true, and all of it is ground for great joy. But sometimes the emphasis that we place on the relative recentness of the discovery of these truths is a little misleading and a little false.

The man to whom I refer, the Colonel de Corbiac, who died this weekend, is one of the examples I remember from thirty years ago of a layman who though an Army officer in his day, a gentleman farmer in his day, the father of a large family, the mayor of a little town, a hundred and one things in the kingdom of this world, was nonetheless an example of the priesthood of the laity, what we mean by the lay apostle, who accomplished more, I honestly do believe, in the way of leading others to salvation, to perfection, than probably most priests can ever do no matter how zealous they may be or how hard they work.

I'd like to give you a little example of the manner in which he did this work as a lay priest representative of Christ back in the years of World War II. When World War II broke out, the Colonel was too old to go away with the Army. The young men of the little village where he lived had to go away. And so he volunteered to take on the office of mayor of the town. That really meant in that particular town that he became responsible for the few public records, for the granting of a few routine licenses, but chiefly for organizing the men, women, and children of the town each fall for the harvesting of the grapes and the gathering of the things needed for the pressing of the wine which was done under the direction of the mayor of the little town. In other words he was mayor so that the life of the town could go on during the war, so that the grapes would be harvested and pressed, and the people wouldn't starve. However, while he was mayor the collapse of France came. And in order to be mayor of the town, he of course had to become what was later denounced as a collaborator with the Vichy regime. And so this completely un-Fascist man suddenly found himself denounced as a Fascist, with the result that when the Maquis took over in that part of France he was thrown into a concentration camp as a collaborator with Pétain and the Vichy regime, which indeed he was for the reasons that I have indicated, and he was sentenced to be shot.

The first night that he found himself in the concentration camp he was in a room about forty feet long, fifty feet wide, which I visited after the War. The walls were lined with bunks that went from the floor to the ceiling. There were about a hundred and sixty men gathered in the room and destined to share that room as their sleeping place every night until they would either be shot or released. At lights out the Colonel stepped out into the middle of the floor and asked how many of those in the bunks around him would join him in the recitation of the Rosary for the deliverance of France and for the intentions of their loved ones back home. He was bombarded in the darkness by the shoes of the men or most of the men in the bunks which lined the walls, and he was called all manner of obscene names, greeted with catcalls and boos. When these subsided and the shoes all landed safely on the floor, the Colonel nonetheless began the recitation of the Rosary, and before each decade of the beads he gave a little meditation. For four or five nights this continued and was greeted with the same hostility, but gradually the scoffing group became either tired or bored or realized the futility of their scoff, and it all subsided. Some, I later learned from a school teacher in the town when I went back there following the war, began to join in the prayers, listened very carefully to these meditations which he preached, a different set of them every single night. The school teacher who had for a long time been away from the sacraments and the practice of the Faith told me that he began to listen after a couple of weeks, not at all because he was interested in the meditations but because the meditations were the only decent French that he heard all day. In the work camp and in the work brigades he heard nothing but obscenity, complaining, whining, recrimination, criticism, but he began to wait for those fifteen, twenty minutes or half hour every night after the lights went out, in which the Colonel spoke of the things of God, of the saints of France, of the Blessed Mother, of the life of the spirit, the gospel, things of eternity, and then led with each passing week an increasingly large number in the recitation of prayers for France and for their folks at home.

Before the sentence of execution could be carried out, the fortunes of war shifted, and after ten months the prison camp was opened and the men got out. When they left, two-thirds of those who on their first night had booed and hissed him and thrown shoes at him gathered together with the Colonel and took a common oath that on the anniversary of their release each year they would meet for a luncheon and after luncheon together they would go for a walk through the streets of a different city or town. And on their walk they would recite the beads together. And at the end of each decade they would pause, and the Colonel would give one of his little meditations, preach one of his little sermons. It turned out that the men in that barracks during those months less than a year had, I shall not say, returned to the sacraments or in any full sense to the life of the Church, but they had returned to something of the sense of prayer that they had as children and something of the respect that they had for divine things when they were very young.

And when I visited there five years after the war ended, they had had their fifth such walk, on the principle that if France could build a concentration camp in which they would relearn the art of prayer and the consolations of the devout life, then France would have to be very patient with them, if they walked publicly through its streets reciting the prayers they had learned again while in prison, and meditating on the things of God which they had forgotten before they went to prison but which this one man had recalled to them. And the school teacher who spoke of the beauty of the French that he heard each night in the meditations and of the soothing influence that the Colonel's example and words had had on him began after a month or so of listening to these meditations to write them down in the dark in a copybook. He gave the copybook to me because he knew of the affection that I had for the old man, and I have it still. And every now and again I open it and I read some of the meditations that he delivered in the prison camp, and there I find in the thoughts that he expressed in the midst of hatred, in the midst of all the conflicts and tensions of a wartime concentration camp for condemned men—I find there a dignity and a majestic spiritual calm, a sense of the presence of God and of the Communion of the Saints that sometimes you do not even find in cloisters, and almost never find in our relative comfort and relative ease.

There is an old Latin phrase, *inter arma caritas*—"in the midst of the conflict of arms, charity"; it's used to describe things like the Red Cross and other movements which bring human sympathy and divine mercy into the war-torn battlefields and bombed-out towns, devastated areas. The Colonel was an example of charity, of faith, of hope, of the very spirit of God Himself in the midst of all the frustration, all the belligerence, all the resentments, and all the hatred of a concentration camp. A very remarkable man, and I ask your prayers for him.

He was not unique. There is some very wonderful literature coming out of all the concentration camps of World War II reminding us of how many were those priests and laymen,

Lutheran pastors, ministers, rabbis, Jews, all manner of people, who demonstrated in the midst of the concentration camps and the horror of the war a sublime primacy of the spiritual over the political, the military, and the economic which is a rebuke to us in times of peace when we forget these things, and which is a suggestion sometimes to me of the reasons why within the Providence of God these disasters may befall us, as they apparently shall for the indefinite future, in order to break up the human calm in which we forget the sources of our divine dignity—and give us an opportunity in the midst of the horror of war to have such examples of the source of our true peace as the example given by the wonderful old man the news of whose death came to me this weekend.

God bless you!

XXXVI

Discovering One Another
In Facing Great Issues

Permit me to plunge immediately into the heart of my topic and, indeed, to push forward promptly to its conclusion. My conclusion serves, I hope, as the premise of the topic to which Dr. Martin Luther King will address himself: *Beyond Discovery—Love*.

The connection between my topic (discovering one another while sharing with one another the work of social reform that needs to be done) and the topic of Dr. King, *Beyond Discovery—Love*, is intimate and inescapable. Alas, it is not always obvious, particularly in a civilization more aware of groups—nationality groups, cultural groups, class groups, political groups, other groups beyond counting—than it is of *persons*.

You can only love a *person*. We can only love *persons*. It is one of the tragedies of our times that we not merely have forgotten this but have actually come to talk as if the contrary were true. For example, we talk about love for *humanity*. This is a logical and psychological absurdity. Humanity has no face to admire or to reject. Humanity has no address: you cannot send it a Christmas card, a threatening letter, a valentine, or a bill. *Humanity has no existence* save as an abstraction, a concept, or a figment of the imagination.

Love for humanity is an illusion, and many who profess most loudly their love for all humanity frequently turn out to be frauds; they usually qualify for the rebuke that G. K. Chesterton gave to muddle-headed people who love the human race but despise the man next door.

This address was delivered at the International Convention of Christian Churches, Disciples of Christ, in Dallas, Texas, on September 25, 1966.

What is true about love for humanity goes with only slightly reduced truth for any other groupings of the human race. You may love a *white* person; you cannot literally and effectively love Caucasians. You may love a *person* from Texas or any number of specific *persons* from Texas; I do not know how you would go about loving Texans as such save by some vague, diffuse, and ultimately ineffectual disposition merely to wish them all well whoever, wherever, and whatever they may be. You cannot love Negroes, or Jews, or Catholics, or Democrats, or bricklayers, or intellectuals, or deep-sea divers as such, save, perhaps, in the very broad sense that, for special reasons and in certain circumstances, you find the company of these particularly congenial or you agree with these more than with most or are at home with these more than you are with Republicans, pearl fishers, Eskimos, Connecticut Yankees, Amish people, or Daughters of the Eastern Star, precisely as such. *We can only love persons.*

Now it is precisely *persons*, emancipated from or otherwise lifted out of their various groupings, that we discover when we work together in community, particularly in facing up to the great social issues of war and peace, poverty, civil rights, and social justice. It is precisely *personality* that becomes the object of our gratitude, our admiration, our affection, our confidence, or, on occasion, our reserve, when our mutual responsibilities demand our common effort in behalf of the common good and the realization of our shared human hopes.

At first, when we rally for the work or initially enter upon it, we may be more aware of our respective classifications— classifications of shades of color, perhaps the superficial differences which add up to variations in class, cultural, partisan, or even age-group differences among us. But as the work goes forward these differences tend to fade; *personalities* emerge, and we found ourselves face to face with that which, in each of us singly and in all of us together, stamps us as *persons: that image of God in which each person is created.*

415

That is why shared work, involvement in the common problems of the human community (local, national, or international) is the best means and instrument for building ecumenism on the religious front, for creating mutuality and a sense of community on the civic front, for forging friendships and producing the climate of love in neighborhoods, within nations, or all over this mass of cosmic dust on which we children of Adam ride together through space from the hand of God at work in creation to the hand of God lifted in judgment.

It is in the common task required to avert a common danger or to achieve a common good that we first and best discover one another for what we are: *persons*, the persons whom alone it is possible for the normal heart and the sane mind of another *person* to love.

We might as well be perfectly honest on this point. For example, I, who grew up in a community with many Unitarians, have never met a Unitarian with whom I could agree on theology or who made Unitarianism as a system or the Unitarian Fellowship as a movement attractive to me. However, neither have I met a Unitarian whom I disliked. Quite the contrary; engagement in work for peace and in facing problems of social justice has brought it to pass that many of the friends whom I most love are Unitarians. Some of these have rather intense reservations about Catholicism and have proved capable of saying some exceedingly critical things of Catholics; but I personally have been the beneficiary of all the kindness, cooperation, generosity, sympathy, and confident sharing which constitute their love as *persons* for me as a *person*.

The point is obvious, and it is the best possible starting point for this evening's discussion. It is only *persons* who can love; it is only *persons* whom we love. It is in the discovery of the *person* within the classification or behind the label of the group-kind that we can best come to the love which is the soul of the good society and the condition of our salvation, here or hereafter.

For many years on occasions like these, I have been recalling two experiences which have intensified in my own moral consciousness this awareness of the person as the subject of rights and responsibilities, as the object of love and respect, as the unit and the living center of any truly humane civilization.

Back in 1936 I visited Munich to use a great public library there in connection with a doctoral dissertation I was writing. It was at the height of the collective brutality that was German Nazism; however, one might have thought to be beyond the reach of the crude exclusions, the discriminations, and the injustices of Nazism within the hallowed halls of the library in so sophisticated a city as Munich.

Although I filled out the call slips for the books that I needed, I never, in fact, saw the books. On the table in the reading hall where I sat down to await their delivery there were two signs which awakened memories in my mind and stirred emotions in my heart such that I left the great hall before the books could have been located by the stack boy. The signs said: *No Jew may sit here.*

I must confess to you that the memories awakened were not of Jewish history, nor of the Jewish religion, nor of the Jewish race, whatever the word *race* may mean. My emotions did not center on any abstract Jewishness nor organized Zionism nor, in another direction, any impersonal anti-Semitism. *My memories were of specific Jewish persons*—the Jewish boys who had been my classmates at the Boston Latin School, many of them brighter than I and perhaps far more eager to use such books as those in the Munich library. My memories were of the specific *persons*, boys and girls, men and women, whom I had known from my boyhood in the part of Boston where I grew up and where, whatever we thought of some aspects of Jewish history or whatever they thought of some chapters of Christian history, we were *neighbors*, genuinely loving one another in

417

shared interests and together caught up in all the crises appropriate to our respective ages and work in the community of which we were each and all parts.

That day in Munich I thought of persons whom I loved, *persons* whose exclusion from the common table of a common heritage to which they and theirs had, in fact, mightily contributed, so outraged me as a *person* that I did not care to enjoy the benefits which they would be denied.

You will say that this traumatic experience may well be commonplace in places like Munich and in times like those of the Nazis. You may even be tempted to say that you would not be surprised if you heard of like things in Milan in, let us say, the days of the Fascists or in Madrid in moments of certain Spanish excesses. You and I, as Americans, seem disposed almost to expect such things in *Munich*, or *Milan*, or *Madrid* or other places closer to what we would like to think of as *medieval* or, in any case, non-American.

Then what about my second, similar traumatic experience? It did not involve Munich and Jews. It involved Memphis, Tennessee, U.S.A., twentieth century. My experience of Memphis was not direct, but again it involved a library and was therefore traumatic for me because I, as a *person*, have all my life loved libraries and have been greatly influenced by them.

It was after I returned from studies in Europe, including the Munich experience, that I read Richard Wright's book *Black Boy*. Some of the book said little or nothing to me; but the chapter describing this bright young man's effort to borrow books from the public library of Memphis drove home to me the tragedy of a *person* disqualified by the hatred of other *persons* from sharing in benefits which should have nothing to do with his membership in a group. Young Wright, as a Negro American citizen living in the American city of Memphis, could not borrow a book—however eager he be to read—from the Memphis Public Library. Let me read you a page that tells of the *indignity done his person* because, by an accident of birth, he was born with a color somehow and somewhat different from the prevailing color among the trustees of the Memphis library.

There remained only one man whose attitude did not fit into an anti-Negro category, for I had heard the white men refer to him as a "Pope lover". He was an Irish Catholic and was hated by the white Southerners. I knew that he read books, because I had got him volumes from the Library several times. Since he, too, was an object of hatred, I felt that he might refuse me but would hardly betray me. I hesitated, weighing and balancing the imponderable realities.

One morning I paused before the Catholic fellow's desk.

"I want to ask you a favor." I whispered to him.

"What is it?"

"I want to read. I can't get books from the library. I wonder if you'd let me use your card?"

He looked at me suspiciously.

"My card is full most of the time," he said.

"I see", I said and waited, posing my question silently.

"You're not trying to get me into trouble, are you, boy?" he asked, staring at me.

"Oh, no, sir."

"What book do you want?"

"A book by H. L. Mencken."

"Which one?"

"I don't know. Has he written more than one?"

"He has written several."

"I didn't know that."

"What makes you want to read Mencken?"

"Oh, I just saw his name in the newspaper", I said.

"It's good of you to want to read", he said. "But you ought to read the right things."

I said nothing. Would he want to supervise my reading?

"Let me think," he said. "I'll figure out something."

I turned from him and he called me back. He stared at me quizzically.

419

"Richard, don't mention this to the other white men", he said.

"I understand", I said. "I won't say a word."

A few days later he called me to him.

"I've got a card in my wife's name", he said. "Here's mine."

"Thank you, sir."

"Do you think you can manage it?"

"I'll manage fine", I said.

"If they suspect you, you'll get in trouble", he said.

"I'll write the same kind of notes to the library that you wrote when you sent me for books", I told him. "I'll sign your name."

He laughed.

"Go ahead. Let me see what you get", he said.

That afternoon I addressed myself to forging a note.

Now, what were the names of books written by H. L. Mencken? I did not know any of them. I finally wrote what I thought would be a foolproof note: Dear Madam: Will you please let this nigger boy—I used the word "nigger" to make the librarian feel that I could not possibly be the author of the note—have some books by H. L. Mencken? I forged the white man's name.

I entered the library as I had always done when on errands for whites, but I felt that I would somehow slip up and betray myself. I doffed my hat, stood a respectful distance from the desk, looked as unbookish as possible, and waited for the white patrons to be taken care of. When the desk was clear of people, I still waited. The white librarian looked at me.

"What do you want, boy?"

As though I did not possess the power of speech I stepped forward and simply handed her the forged note, not parting my lips.

"What books by Mencken does he want?" she asked.

"I don't know, ma'am", I said, avoiding her eyes.

"Who gave you this card?"

"Mr. Falk", I said.

"Where is he?"

"He's at work, at the M—— Optical Company", I said. "I've been in here for him before."

420

"I remember", the woman said. "But he never wrote notes like this."

Oh, God, she's suspicious. Perhaps she would let me have the books? If she had turned her back at that moment, I would have ducked out the door and never gone back. Then I thought of a bold idea.

"You can call him up, ma'am", I said, my heart pounding.

"You're not using these books, are you?" she asked pointedly.

"Oh, no, ma'am. I can't read."

"I don't know what he wants by Mencken," she said under her breath.

I knew now that I had won; she was thinking of other things and the race question had gone out of her mind. She went to the shelves. Once or twice she looked over her shoulder at me, as though she was still doubtful. Finally she came forward with two books in her hand.

"I'm sending him two books", she said. "But tell Mr. Falk to come in next time, or send me the names of the books he wants. I don't know what he wants to read."[1]

We are all conscious, or are becoming so, of the affront to the *person* in places where the sale or rental of houses prescinds from personal rights and qualities and is linked to considerations of color or creed or nationality. We are becoming more sensitive to the fundamental evil, not merely economic but all-embracingly social and moral, when *persons* are debarred from employment opportunities to which they have a right as *persons* simply because of their backgrounds of a religious, national, or color kind. For personal reasons, the insult to personality, the degradation of the person, at the heart of exclusion from public libraries, traumatizes me quite as much as do these other, perhaps more hurtful, exclusions. However, they are *all* interrelated, *all* symbols of one another, all evil, and they have in common contempt for *persons* just as the *good* social life consists in love and respect for the person.

I submit that we must find our release from these evils in whatever opens up to us the dimension of *personality*, whatever reveals to us *the person* within, above, beyond the group, whatever the group to which the *person* belongs.

That is why I echo to you, urgently and emphatically, the plea of a Negro school teacher (Phyllis Wiggins, writing in *Report* of July 1966) to all who wish well of the civil rights movement: *don't talk about the Negro*, whatever your attitude or your gratitude to qualities that he has in common with the group that is Negro; to do so is to drown the person in the race, whatever race may be; to do so is to annihilate a person in a faceless crowd; to do so is to forget entirely the human conscience and the living intellect of a man as a person. It is not Negroes, any more than it is Protestants, or Republicans, or workers, or Irish that we are called to respect, with whom we are privileged to work, whom we are eager to discover and to love; *it is persons*.

There is great wisdom in Phyllis Wiggins' cry that she does not primarily belong to an anonymous crowd; there is fundamental social and philosophical truth in her assertion that she wishes to be seen, accepted, loved, or even criticized adversely as a *person*, not as the member of a group.

You will not misunderstand her plea nor the point that I am trying to make tonight. It is no plea for *individualism*; quite the contrary. It is a plea for the human, which means for the *social*; the *person* has dimensions which are both individual and social; a community of mere individuals is not a community at all; a community of *persons* excludes no *person*.

Mine is no plea for anarchy, for the dissolving of group loyalties and preferential group friendships. For religious reasons, I would be the last to ask for an amorphous melting or attrition of our attachments to our group religious traditions when these are dictated by conscience and required by truth. I am all together too proud of my own regional, religious, nationality, and family ties to repudiate them, to wish them diluted or to talk about their equal acceptance by me in the general marketplace of traditions, values, and the other things

422

men cherish. My plea has nothing to do with these things. It is simply that I be accepted as a *person* by all others who are conscious of their *person*, whatever the groups to which they are loyal and the incidental companies of persons to which they belong. My plea is for the rediscovery of the *person*, and my argument is that it is by *persons* that love is communicated and to *persons* that love (and all the other virtues, beginning with justice) must be directed.

Pope John has been a luminous example in our generation of what I mean. I suppose that the countless Protestants who came to love him still remembered that he was, in fact, the *pope*, just as snobbish Catholics never forget he was a peasant and proud of his peasant family. I'm almost certain that most people know that the pope is a *Catholic*, more often than not an Italian, frequently a member of the older generation, always a priest, and therefore the potential object of the group passions bound up with clericalism or anticlericalism. *But everyone thought of Pope John and loved Pope John as a person.*

Let us not pretend that this love affair between a Roman pope and a whole generation of other humans is something without precedent or parallel in our communities or neighborhoods. Each of us can think of like warm experiences in the places from which we come and within which we work. But such experiences are always in terms of *persons* known and loved by *persons*. More often than not, such *persons* are discovered in each community or neighborhood at times of community crises or experiences—in seasons of great joy or great trial, on occasions of great tragedy or triumph, in the midst of the laughter that rejoices all a community: *Suddenly everyone burst out singing!* or at the height of the heartbreak by which people discover that we are a *community*, divided religiously, culturally, tribally, but united by *persons*, *persons* each of whom possesses in himself and perceives in his neighbor that image of God which constitutes *the person*.

XXXVII

David L. Lawrence, 1899–1966

The custom of the Holy Catholic Church does not encourage eulogies at the requiems of our faithful departed. Perhaps the reason is bound up with the futility of praising the blessed dead; when one already stands before the awesome judgment seat of God, it does seem vain and empty for him to be praised or censured by lips not less mortal than his own. Perhaps the reason derives from a deep democracy in the Church, a recognition that ranks and offices fade among the people of God, particularly when, at the equal and impartial call of death, we join the great majority.

Perhaps, too, our Catholic custom is set by the fact that our people, most especially men of the spiritual simplicity and authentic religious instincts of the late Governor Lawrence, do not expect the Church to praise them; they ask of the Church only that it help them prepare for that which supremely, that which alone, matters: the judgment of God.

I shall not attempt a eulogy of the faithful lover of this hallowed shrine, the truly greatest mayor of this city, a distinguished governor of our Commonwealth, a humanitarian in national public office—and all the while an affectionate spouse, loving father, and generous friend.[1] I intend only a brief comment to console his bereaved wife, his children, his associates, and the community that was so proud of him following his career with such intimate admiration, enthusiasm, and joy.

David Lawrence's earthly story ends where it began—here at the Point of his beloved native city of Pittsburgh.

This eulogy was preached at the Church of Saint Mary of Mercy, Pittsburgh, Pennsylvania, on November 25, 1966.

This circumstance of his requiem confirms what so many characteristics of his personality and career made clear; namely, that he was the type of the wise who soar but never roam, true to the kindred points of heaven and home.

Thus loyal to the end, loyal to the twin pieties of patriotism and religion, he chose to be brought back precisely to this part of Pittsburgh to take leave of his friends and precisely to this church to receive the final blessing of his Church.

On the civic side, it is as if he wished his new friends from afar, the ever-widening circle of friends with whom his busy years and genial spirit surrounded him, to see here in this Golden Triangle, at first hand and on the very spot, so to say, the signs and symbols of the wondrous transformation that love for his boyhood neighborhood had inspired him to help so mightily to bring to pass.

On the religious side it is as if he wished to remind his first and oldest friends, his family, and others formed by his example, perhaps even to remind God Himself that however far political fortunes brought him, however awesome the influence he wielded or the posts to which he attained, he never outgrew his initial loyalties, never forswore his baptismal vows, never lost the love for the simplicities of this church of Our Lady at the Point, the center of his first and lifelong devotion.

Human life, however poor or stunted or underprivileged, David Lawrence saw as the basic good, as that gift of God most to be cherished, to be reverenced, and to be served. All life he saw as holy and rich with promise.

One of our local papers, editorializing recently on the dignity of life, quoted with apparent agreement the opinion of the pagan philosopher Seneca that mere living is not a good, but (only) living well.

David Lawrence has so much reverenced a love for life. His love for life and reverence for it in every person, whatever the condition of the person, his color or plight, her background or

425

handicap, was infinitely more profound, more humane, I dare to say it, more divine. The meanest life, the least promising, the life most fraught with difficulties and beset with problems, called out to a greater reverence, a more generous service, a more respectful love in David Lawrence.

This explains the passionate drive of his life as a civil servant, a legislator, and an executive entrusted with the common good of millions, many of whom merely lived and could not even hope to live better, let alone well, unless there are men like David Lawrence with a sense of the dignity of life more profound than Seneca's and a burning desire to serve life, a desire more ardent and unselfish than that of any mere philosopher.

David Lawrence demonstrated his value-judgment on life by the fight for social morality that he waged from his first efforts at slum-clearance to the last post he held as a battler for fair housing and a foe of discrimination against or disparagement of any being endowed with the divine gift of human life.

I was privileged to discover this quality of David Lawrence on one of the first of the many occasions when I enjoyed his company at Rosalia Hospital, the Pittsburgh shelter for unwed mothers and their babies that he, following the example of his devout mother, loved so much to visit and to befriend. We wandered together into the nursery there one evening; there was no one in sight but one sister, no one he could hope to impress. The manner in which David Lawrence reacted to these babies, the attention he gave them, the relaxed and gentle laughter with which he elicited their responses and identified with them—all these told me, then and forever, that here was a *man*, a *good man*, a *great man*. One knew that he had great jobs, great posts of trust, a great reputation, but one also knows that there are more great jobs, and indeed more great reputations, than there are great men. David Lawrence would have been a great man whatever his post, whatever superficial public opinion might have ever decided about him.

During his remarkable career in public office he proved that he had a rare sense of what are the real assets of a good community—what it needs in the way of highways, financial resources, buildings, all the machinery of life in the political or economic community. But David Lawrence saw *people* as our greatest asset—all *people*, everywhere, but, above all, *people* whom the routine judgments of the world tend to downgrade or drop out of consideration: minorities, for example. Significant was his special affection for his Jewish and Negro neighbors. Characteristic was the manly piety, totally non-political in its nature, of his special friendship for priests and for nuns.

This latter quality of the man made him for long years the object of prayers beyond counting at this altar and in this very church. When his pastor and friend Monsignor Lawless died a few years ago, I spoke of the unique tie between these two great men.[2] I spoke of the scrupulous care with which the priest kept free from the politics which were the very stuff of his friend's daily life. But Monsignor Lawless, I suggested, stood on these altar steps somewhat as Moses stood on the mountain top with arms uplifted while the secular chieftain of his flock fought for God's people on the battlefield below. So long as the arms of Moses were uplifted in prayer, the battle went forward—and so long as the prayers were needed, the arms were never relaxed.

Faith encourages the belief that the prayers of those who love us go on even when death intervenes. We might, therefore, conclude that Monsignor Lawless, now that the champion he so revered is finally dead, may cease his intercession. More likely, however, the two heroic souls who loved this little church and all the world around it shall henceforth together plead for God's blessing on Pittsburgh, on life and life ever more abundant in our land, and on *people*—wherever people stand in need of the help of God's grace in the forms in which David Lawrence brought that grace to them.

XXXVIII

The Church Is Always Young

"For see, the winter is past, the rains are over and gone. The flowers appear on the earth. The season of glad songs has come. . . ."[1]

It is fitting that the consecration of a new bishop to help hasten the renewal of the Church in Peru should take place here in Boston.

The new chapter of an ancient people's religious history which is now underway in Peru follows upon a long postlude to an earlier chapter of that history best told by a Boston scholar, William Hickling Prescott. Few American writers have demonstrated greater qualities of intellect or character than this proper Bostonian who was blinded by a luncheon bun, thrown at him by another student in the Harvard College dining room; none has ever told the story of the displacement of an older order by a new as did Prescott in his *Conquest of Peru*.

In the opening of the present new chapter in the religious history of Peru, few in the entire Church, none in the Church in this hemisphere, can have played a part comparable to that of the charismatic Cardinal Archbishop of Boston, Richard James Cushing, whose name is already a legend wherever the Faith is preached in Peru and one of whose name saints is the patron of a major missionary force in the renewal of Latin America, including Peru—the Society of Saint James, brought into being and directed by the Cardinal of Boston.

It is appropriate that the bishop consecrated to coordinate

This sermon was preached at the Holy Cross Cathedral, Boston, Massachusetts, on May 25, 1967, on the occasion of the episcopal ordination of the Most Reverend James C. Burke, O.P., Prelate of Chimbote, Peru.

the works of the Church in the Peruvian city of Chimbote should be a Dominican. Most of the people there are Indians descended from the ancient Inca tribes to whom the Spanish explorers brought military and political conquest, but to whom the Spanish religious orders, particularly the Dominicans, brought the name of Christ and the preaching, both to the Spaniard and to the Indian, of those moral principles which, in fact, guaranteed the survival of the Indians as *persons*, if not as a nation of their own, and spared them the fate of the Indian elsewhere in the Americas, notably here.

At a time when it is fashionable to revive less favorable memories of the political and social impact of religious leaders, it is well to recall the moral and cultural influence of the Catholic clergy in colonial Latin America. Prescott describes it in the *Conquest of Peru* with justice and grace when he writes:

> The Fathers of Saint Dominic, the Brethren of the Order of Mercy, and other missionaries, now busied themselves in the good work of conversion. We have seen that Pizarro was required by the crown to bring out a certain number of these holy men in his own vessels; and every succeeding vessel brought an additional reinforcement of ecclesiastics. They were not all like the Bishop of Cuzco, with hearts so seared by fanaticism as to be closed against sympathy with the unfortunate natives. They were, many of them, men of singular humility, who followed in the track of the conqueror to scatter the seeds of spiritual truth and, with disinterested zeal, devoted themselves to the propagation of the gospel. Thus did their pious labors prove them the true soldiers of the Cross, and show that the object so ostentatiously avowed of carrying its banner among the heathen nations was not an empty vaunt.
>
> The effort to Christianize the heathen is an honorable characteristic of the Spanish conquests. The Puritan, with equal religious zeal, did comparatively little for the conversion of the Indian, content, as it would seem, with having secured to himself the inestimable privilege of worshiping God in his own way. Other adventurers who have occupied the New World

have often had too little regard for religion themselves to be very solicitous about spreading it among the savages. But the Spanish missionary, from first to last, has shown a keen interest in the spiritual welfare of the natives. Under his auspices, churches on a magnificent scale have been erected, schools for elementary instruction founded, and every rational means taken to spread the knowledge of religious truth, while he has carried his solitary mission into remote and almost inaccessible regions, or gathered his Indian disciples into communities, like the good Las Casas in Cumana, or the Jesuits in California and Paraguay. At all times the courageous ecclesiastic has been ready to lift his voice against the cruelty of the conqueror and the no less wasting cupidity of the colonist; and when his remonstrances, as was too often the case, have proved unavailing, he has still followed to bind up the brokenhearted, to teach the poor Indian resignation under his lot, and light up his dark intellect with the revelation of a holier and happier existence. In reviewing the blood-stained records of Spanish colonial history, it is but fair, and at the same time cheering, to reflect that the same nation which sent forth the hardhearted conqueror from its bosom, sent forth the missionary to do the work of beneficence and spread the light of Christian civilization over the farthest regions of the New World.[2]

It is frequently amazing how alive, even in the midst of pathetic deprivation of all things else, are the memories of the consolations of the Faith which survive among the Indians of Peru since those early days of the Spanish missionaries and through all the neglected and decadent generations since. These memories account for the ready affection with which the people of Chimbote greet any priest and the passion with which Indian mothers plead with any bishop to confirm their children; it is among people long since disposed to love him because of their ancestral memories of the Friars that Bishop Burke is privileged to bring back the sacraments, the truth, the very life of Christ.

It is a commonplace to say that a priest or prelate called to serve in Peru, as is Bishop Burke, is faced with grave problems; that his work is made bewildering, is even bedeviled by the stupidities, mistakes, and sins of the past and complicated by the inadequacies and ineptness of the present. All this is, of course, true; the evils which underlie the problems of the Church in Peru or in the rest of Latin America might well dismay the prelate called by the Holy Spirit to help restore God's order and vindicate God's honor there. But if it is, as it is, a worry to do God's work in Peru, it is not less so to attempt this work in France—or America—or Poland—or Palestine— or Rome.

Moreover, Bishop Burke, and every apostle who works in Peru, has many and wonderful things going for him. First of all there are the *people*, above all the *poor*, the descendants of the Incas and the Spaniards. These people are many and, as we have said, still touched by memories, confused memories overlain with obscurities but capable of requickening, above all in a people who love their children and wish for them all the blessings and even more than those of their sires.

Then there are new legions of generous collaborators, many represented here in this cathedral as we watch the first and most fervent of them perform the consecration of Bishop Burke. These collaborators include priests and sisters, religious brothers and laymen of self-sacrificing zeal beyond my power to describe, though I know them well and love them for the luster they give to the names of the dioceses from which they come, including my own. Bishop Burke's collaborators include the lay members of the parish committees and like apostolates—educational, medical, and social—which increase with each passing year in Chimbote; all, clergy and laity, have the unfailing aid and encouragement of the truly Apostolic Nuncio of the Holy Father in Peru, Archbishop Carbone.

High among the factors on the side of Bishop Burke and his associates in the work of the Church is the fact that to them belongs the future. That future is sometimes frightening;

many of us believe that it includes Peru's part in a worldwide wintry season of unbelief, of denial of faith, decline in love, and grim threats to life itself. Will that winter be long, or short? No man can tell—but since it is part of the story of the Church, it must inevitably end in a new spring. As Cardinal Newman has forever reminded us, the history of the Church is a history of recurring springs and of second comings to life again; in God's plan for His Church nothing ever dies; from each sad remnant of decay new forms of life invariably arise.

And so the greatest thing going for the work in Latin America is the nature of the Church herself. Almost twenty years ago, Archbishop Cushing, preaching at the consecration of two young missionary bishops at Techny, Illinois, said things which I now echo because they are more manifestly certain at the moment than they may have been when the Cardinal then described the relationship of the Church to the seemingly fatal crises of our times.

Cardinal Cushing said at Techny: The Church is not old. The Church is not weak. The Church is not finished. And so it is all the other way: the Church is young as each new bishop consecrated, each new priest ordained, each new marriage blessed, each new baby baptized, each new religious vow pronounced makes her ever younger and stronger. The Church has an unlimited work yet to do; almost beyond number are those to whom she is sent and who constitute at once her challenge and an element of her strength.

And so the Christian perspective always forbids the defeatism of any description of the Church in terms of old age, of weariness, of spent forces, or of decline. The perspective of the Christian, of one who meditates the Gospels and especially the parables of Christ, focuses his attention not on the brief past and transitory present, but on the ever-expanding future, bewildering, no doubt, but bewildering because of its infinite possibilities for growth and demands for achievement, rather than because of any inevitable problems or momentary grounds for passing fears.

The true perspective of Christianity never permits the devout to suppose that the last page has been turned or the last word recorded, that the book is about to be closed; it teaches rather that even *now*, after two thousand years, we have scarcely grasped the first page of the gospel; the whole book still lies before us to be translated into living history and implemented in ardent faith and loving deed. The prophecies are far from fulfilled; the gospel is only at its beginning. The end of the world is not at hand, and the harvest is still far distant. The Kingdom of Christ is still in its infancy on earth; it has many crises of growth to undergo, including those of adolescence and of first maturity, before there can be talk of even the beginnings of problems of age. To change the figure, the seed has scarcely been sown, and there must be long weeks of weeding, of watering, of husbanding the harvest that is to come before we can talk of the measure or the problems of the harvest.

The gospel is but at its beginning. The Kingdom of God is scarcely founded. The two thousand brief years of Christian history, the few centuries of Christian history in Latin America, are but the prelude to tens of thousands of years yet to be, years of preparation, of planning, of progress, and of perfection in comparison with which, if things be seen in their proper perspective, the few generations since the apostles were first sent forth to preach are but a watch in the night, a mere *moment* of occasional fleet visions of the consolations which are yet to be and of occasional passing fears lest these consolations be lost.

And so Christianity is not old, but young. The Church is not at the harvest; it is still at the planting. Catholicism is not ancient and dispirited, nor is its history behind us in old civilizations and effete nations; it is before us in new chapters yet to be written in the history of new nations yet to be born or of old nations destined to be reborn—some, like Peru, already in process of rebirth.

Bishop Burke and the priests and religious taking up with

him the work in Peru are not *heirs* to a diminished and dying heritage. They are *founders* of a tradition destined, under God, to flourish and to spread, forefathers of a new generation that is coming to birth. They are not descendants of a jaded, spent lineage; they are ancestors of spiritual generations yet to be. The eternally youthful Church does not consecrate her bishops to be merely *witnesses* to the past, least of all *historians* of the past, but to be the heralds of her future, *witnesses* to a kingdom that is to come. She does not see in them only the guardians of her accumulated treasury of Faith, though they must be such guardians; she hails them as the prophets of the centuries of faith which are yet to be hers, heralds and prophets because apostles, members of the apostolic college dispersed to the ends of the earth to work until the end of time through the power of Christ, in unity with Christ, in the truth and vitality of the Risen Christ.

All of which means that those at work, like Bishop Burke, in the reborn Church of ancient lands have on their side all the power of that Spirit which renews the face of the earth, which recreates out of ashes and makes dry bones to live again. The winds of that Spirit are sweeping the world. They are bending and breaking before them all that is not deeply rooted in the permanent plan of God, all that is not securely and unshakably part of the panorama of the Church's life and action. The dried out, lifeless trees, however monumental and venerable, however seemingly sturdy when seen in the tranquil sunlight, are being tumbled before that powerful wind; but so, too, are the giddy, inconstant saplings with only shallow roots and green immaturity. The old timber is devastated, while the weak and wavering sprouts are speedily dislodged, to be then blown about by every wind of doctrine.

The Church recognizes this wind for what it is—the wind of the Spirit that first she heard as a great noise filling the place where her disciples were gathered after the Lord had ascended into heaven. She welcomes it as the divine source of refreshment and renewal to all things that deserve to live, as the force that lays low and scatters whatever is marked for death. She revels in that Spirit, rejoicing in all the new generosity, the new visions, new dreams, new hopes, new charity, new faith that the Spirit produces in her, ever ancient, ever new, the Spouse of Christ, one of whose sons is today consecrated to bring these gifts to the rebirth, in new beauty, of the ancient spiritual heritage of Peru—when finally the winter is past, the rains are over and gone, the flowers appear on the earth again, and among God's people returns the season of glad songs.

XXXIX

The Year of Faith

Our Holy Father, Pope Paul, has called for a full year of meditation on the Faith. It is to begin on the Feast of Saints Peter and Paul, June 29.

This focus on faith has not come a bit too soon; its importance cannot possibly be exaggerated.

Sometimes it is said that the crisis of the moment is one of faith. This may ultimately turn out to be true; many of us think that mankind is headed for a winter of unbelief, of denial of the Christian Faith and rejection of the law of Christ, a winter that Cardinal Newman and Vladimir Soloviev, among many, foretold and the preparation for which prompted (one thinks) the canny Pope John to call the Ecumenical Council.

But the present religious turbulence may not yet be so profound as a crisis in faith, however much it may touch on corollaries of the Faith or even threaten it. There is probably a crisis in hope, especially, perhaps, in areas of personal and social life where moral idealism increasingly calls for heroism in the face of the compromises, personal and social, demanded of the Christian. Certainly there is a crisis in theology—but theology is not the Faith, and all the *theologies* combined do not add up to the Faith.

It is quite possible to be adept in theological speculation and yet be quite devoid of faith. We have had widely publicized evidence recently that men could write, with scholarly competence and persuasive erudition, theological commentaries on the Faith while themselves unable to make or persevere in the personal act of faith which is the heart of the matter. Few

This official statement, written on June 22, 1967, was addressed to the clergy, religious and laity of the Diocese of Pittsburgh, Pennsylvania.

men could expound with greater lucidity or poetic grace the Christian theology of the Trinity, the Incarnation, and certain concepts of Mariology than could a gifted Spanish-American philosopher of whom I thought constantly while reading of certain defectors from the Faith; this philosopher wrote with seductive beauty of theological concepts dear to us believers, but he had no faith (or said he had none), any more than Bulfinch believed the *theologies* of the ancient world that he analyzed so competently in *the Age of Fable*.

Conversely, as millions have understood with Louis Pasteur, it is possible (even common, though not ideal) to have the faith that justified and saves while one is totally innocent of theology in any academic or technical sense.

The first point to be kept clear in the present religious and spiritual crisis is that there is a sharp distinction between the Faith and the *theologies*, between belief and theological speculation. The distinction is as real and as wide between Jesus Christ, the source and object of Christian faith, and any theologian, even one whose opinions, insights, or speculations may have won for him a school of admirers, a group of partisans, or a reading public. Theologians and their schools of thought are the objects of interest, criticism, often admiration or gratitude for the lines of thought that they open up; Jesus Christ, and the Church as His appointed Voice, can alone be the object of faith.

Much of the present crisis in religion is perhaps due to confusions arising from failure to keep clear these distinctions between the *theologies* and the Faith. The exciting years of the Council experience, years ultimately rich in spiritual profit even as the Council itself, can only be seen as providential; they have stimulated minds and dizzied some imaginations with the theoretical speculations, reasonings, wit, wisdom, subtlety, and occasional aberrations—*omnis homo mendax*—of scores of theologians who suddenly became popular lecturers, authors of bestsellers, or TV personalities. We have heard,

437

with varied reactions and profit, the widely different voices of the theologians, not to mention theologizers; their role in the thought-life of the Church and in the culture of the general community is great, at times fortunately colossal, usually positive, occasionally confusing, and sometimes potentially calamitous.

Theologians are men; the thoughts of men are many and divided. Theological theories set forth aspects, elements, corollaries of the Faith. They provide reasonings about the Faith. But theologians are not sources of faith, nor are their speculations the object of faith.

Jesus Christ is God. The thought of God is one and unites; God's revelations are the object of faith. His Church authoritatively sets forth God's revelation. The Church is not a forum or a school of theologians and theologies, though she is greatly helped by these in the total work of explaining the Faith that she is called to do. The Church is the channel through which God's revelation reaches men, including theologians, so that believers may enjoy the privilege of reflecting on the content of revelation, as do theologians, but may also, and above all else, *live* in the light of revelation—as must all the faithful, including the theologians. Only what the Church teaches authoritatively as the mind and the will of Christ Jesus is the object of faith; all the theologies, even those which most she welcomes as helpful to understanding the Faith or blesses as most consistent with the content of Faith, are secondary and peripheral, related to the Faith, perhaps, but not to be confused with it.

The crisis disturbing so many in our generation derives from the fact that such a confusion has taken place. Suddenly caught up in the intricacies and the fascinations of theologies, people have supposed the Faith to be at issue in the speculations that they have found so heady. And so it is well to recall, as should be obvious, that Father Baum or Monsignor Bandas, Father Häring or Father Connell, Hans Küng or Cardinal Brown, Fathers Congar or de Lubac, either of or both the

Rahners, Charles Davis, the Council press panels (including Bishop Bekkers or even me), Teilhard, Scotus, Bonaventure, Aquinas (not to mention Bonhoeffer, Cox, Altizer and Who Not?) may be scholars but they are also fallible men; some are professional theologians of measurable competence and degrees of insight, perhaps (as we have discreetly suggested) degrees also of faith. In any case, they are the objects of such attention, gratitude, and agreement as the critical, intelligent listener or reader may deem them to deserve. It is entirely different, as any one of these would, please God, be the first to confess, with Jesus Christ and the authentic teaching voice of His Church. Christ and what God teaches through the channels of revelation committed to the care and judgment of the Magisterium in the Church are the objects of our faith.

The various theologies may be freely examined, freely espoused, some freely rejected; not so with the Faith as such. Here, as Pope Paul has recently pointed out, freedom takes on other formalities so far as the Christian is concerned. Although we are free (psychologically, though not equally so morally) to accept the Faith of Jesus Christ or not, we are not free in the formulation of the content of the Faith; we are not free to pick and choose among the articles of Faith, as we would be to choose critically among the contentions of the theologians. The Faith involves a total, unqualified commitment to God in His Christ, echoed authentically through His Church; the Faith is an integral response, *the one Faith* willed by Christ and transmitted by the apostles. It may be weak; it may be faltering; it may be (often is) excruciating in its obscurity ("I believe, O Lord, help Thou my unbelief!"),[1] but it is a total commitment that the Christian can give to no man, to no theological opinion and, therefore, to no theologian.

Any crisis in the Church arising from confusions among theologians and rival commitments to theological parties or personalities is no new thing. Saint Paul was confronted in the Church at Corinth with a situation which seems precisely parallel to the confusions which so challenge Pope Paul and all others who cherish the Faith as the foundation of Christian hope and the fountainhead of divine charity. Pope Paul, pleading for a Year of Faith, might easily substitute contemporary names for those which Saint Paul used in his letter to the Corinthians when partisan theologies and conflicting personalities threatened the unity of the Faith among his people: "I appeal to you, brethren, by the name of Our Lord Jesus Christ, that all of you agree and that there be no dissensions among you, but that you be united in the same mind and the same judgment. For it has been reported to me by Chloe's people that there is quarreling among you, my brethren. What I mean is that each one of you says, 'I belong to Paul', or 'I belong to Apollos', or 'I belong to Cephas', or 'I belong to Christ'. Is Christ divided? Was Paul crucified for you? Or were you baptized in the name of Paul?"[2]

Clearly this is an old story—and a new one. Theological debate, lively and fruitful, is indispensable to religious progress and to renewal of Christian life, thought, and values; but the loving service of the Faith and unqualified adherence to the univocal teaching of the Church concerning the undivided Christ, Who alone was crucified for us and to Whom alone we were committed by faith at baptism—these are the basic, the essential, the enduring needs, demands, joys of the Christian creed and code.

That is why we who dearly love freedom cherish faith even more passionately. That is why we who rejoice in the renewal of theological studies in and around the Council, welcome even more the Year of Faith by which Pope Paul hopes to make secure the good coming out of the Council and fortify that authentic teaching of the Church without which theological discussions and speculations become unsubstantial and fanciful, like to the fragile writings of so many romanticists and aesthetes who speak nostalgically but unprofitably of the beauty of a Faith that they no longer believe as true or live as good and essential to salvation.

In the Diocese of Pittsburgh plans for the observance of the Year of Faith are already underway. *The Pittsburgh Catholic* will carry news of programs sponsored by organizations in various areas of the diocese. The School Department, the CCD, the Holy Name Society, and the Council of Catholic Women have filed with me broad indications of projects by which they intend to implement the educative and spiritual objectives of this special season of renewal of faith. We beg God's blessing on those responsible for the detailed development of these programs.

Consistent with our determination to make the local deaneries more effective communities of religious life and action, we ask the deans of the diocese to initiate, together with the clergy and laity of their deaneries, such liturgical and other observances as will help accomplish the purposes of the Year of Faith. Individual parishes and families, each in its own way *the Church in miniature*, should plan appropriate ways and means of promoting within their communities of spiritual life and of supernatural love that unity and vitality in faith which make them the healthy cells of the total body of the Church.

Permit me to suggest one simple practice that might powerfully and yet simply accomplish the hopes of the Year of Faith. At all parish meetings, when the opening prayer is said, or at family meals, when the household unites in asking God's blessing, it would be well if for a whole year any other prayer usually said or grace recited were preceded by the devout recitation, aloud and in unison, of the Apostles' Creed. Each of us should simply and personally begin the day with the thoughtful repetition of that same Creed and take frequent daily occasion during the day to repeat the simple Act of Faith that we learned among the prayers of childhood. *No subsequent growth in theological interest of sophistication has brought us beyond these—the Creed and the Act of Faith—so far as the Faith itself is concerned.*

Our theological reading, ecumenical conversations, and spiritual lives will be the more profitable, to ourselves and to others, according as we mature in the stability of faith that comes from devout appreciation of these prayers.

Once these are in their proper places—the Faith pure in our hearts and the Creed clear in our heads—then all else becomes a source of intellectual profit, spiritual joy, and religious renewal. Once Christ, His Vicar, His apostles, His Church have their due place in our loyalty and love, then we can revel in the intellectual excitement of the theologies and join with sympathy, gratitude, and profit in the speculations of the theologians.

May the Year of Faith thus become a prelude to renewed delight in all the things of God, now and forever!

XL

Project Equality

Representatives of most religious traditions in the Greater Pittsburgh area have been meeting for a number of months to work out their common responsibilities to the problem of the employment opportunities of members of minority groups.

We see social progress, the building of the good society, as resting on four cornerstones which, while involving economic, sociological, and political elements, are ultimately moral and therefore our direct concern.

These four cornerstones are: first, the right to education in accordance with one's ability and interest; second, the right of access to decent housing under the formula called open housing; third, the right to participate in the benefits of community health and welfare programs; fourth, the right to voice and vote in the affairs of civil society.

Basic to all these, as Labor Day reminds us, is the right of equal opportunity to secure employment proportionate to one's skills, needs, and ambitions. We have therefore addressed ourselves to this question in the first of our interfaith efforts to bear a common witness in the realm of community morality and social justice.

Prominent among programs proposed to implement equal employment opportunity is one called Project Equality. The purpose of Project Equality is to work toward the elimination of employment discrimination, even unconscious, in organized religion and in the firms which receive the patronage of churches, synagogues, and their institutions. It asks the voluntary acceptance by religious agencies of certain requirements

This official statement, written in January 1968, was addressed to the clergy, religious and laity of the Diocese of Pittsburgh, Pennsylvania.

443

which parallel those imposed by law upon Federal agencies and an increasing number of state and municipal communities. It thus adds a dimension of morality and conscience beyond mere legal obligation; for this reason it has been endorsed and implemented by religious groups separately or in ecumenical cooperation.

We have studied this program in its principles and to some degree in its performance elsewhere. We do not pretend that we find it a cure-all for the social problems of minority groups; we cannot claim that it is all, or even most, of what is needed to save or strengthen the civil rights of minority group workers. It is, however, one positive approach to a fundamental aspect of the grave problem of social justice which weighs on the conscience of us all. In the determination to leave nothing untried which can mobilize the forces of conscience behind the effort to promote social justice, we have decided to impose upon ourselves and to sponsor the Project Equality program on an interfaith basis. We have already invited the national office to come to Pittsburgh to establish their program among us.

We wish to be candid about the initial reservations we all felt in its regard. Each of us in his own religious tradition and all of us together have historic reasons for avoiding economic boycotts or organized discrimination, even in the name of religious or moral motives. We shall not use Project Equality as an economic boycott but as an instrument of self-discipline and of community education.

Our motivation in testing Project Equality as a weapon in the present fight for social justice is entirely positive. It is the motivation which, in other periods of our history, prompted seekers after justice to fight the use of child labor, slave labor, or similar morally unacceptable policies in the production of goods which may otherwise have met marketing standards. Once it became a moral imperative in the struggle for social justice to buy from those who did not exploit child labor or use

444

slave labor. Now it is an imperative to give preferential patronage and the support of our organized purchasing power to those who deliberately and conscientiously promote equal opportunity of employment of all who are objectively qualified applicants.

As representatives of religious communities, we shall not seek to police the commitments in conscience which we ask of suppliers to our institutions and organized purchasing programs. Obligations in conscience do not admit of policing, and no one of our groups is prepared to set up policing or coactive agencies. Our task is the education and guidance of conscience, not check-up on conduct.

Therefore, we are uniting to underwrite and to establish a Project Equality office which will be identified with none of our religious organizations nor with all of us combined as an interfaith group. Our respective religious headquarters will be the first voluntarily to submit our policies and procedures to the scrutiny of Project Equality. We will be the first to make the pledges in conscience which we shall ask of others. We are confident on the basis of the performance of Project Equality elsewhere that it can do its work of promoting social justice without recourse to procedures offensive to conscience or destructive of good will. On the basis of this confidence we have united in the decision to give Project Equality every opportunity to prove itself in the Greater Pittsburgh area.

We feel it particularly appropriate, once we have pledged ourselves, to appeal, precisely on Labor Day, to the enlightened conscience of organized labor for full and generous compliance with the Project Equality requirements. These will be set up among us in the fiscal year 1968. Many, probably all, of our religious groups have long since bound themselves to help promote social justice by the support of organized labor and by restricting our major construction contracts to contractors or companies using organized labor. Our Project Equality commitment in behalf of minority groups is in this same

445

tradition; it is, in fact, a necessary consequence of our commitment to social justice for workers. It is one further step toward realization of those ideals, personal and social, to which organized labor appealed in the days of the struggle for its rights and which still motivate labor today.

We are confident that we shall not take this step alone but that organized labor will take it together with us; some groups have already taken steps similar to it. It is important that religion and labor be supported by the management, the industrial and the political leadership of the community in this and like projects to give moral reinforcement to decent community desires; an encouraging number of our major industrial enterprises have already demonstrated their eagerness and ability to provide not only support for example in forward-looking social programming.

May 1968 be a year which finds religion, labor, industry, and government in our corner of America united in the insistence that no discrimination inconsistent with human dignity and civil rights will stand in the way of any man or woman or of any minority group that seeks the opportunity for that employment essential to all the other rights and advantages bound up with personal fulfillment and social justice.

XLI

A Prayer for President Posvar
And the University of Pittsburgh

May the faith of those who dreamed this university remain
constant and operative among us! May it give foundation and
substance to new hopes, new loves, new achievement! As God
was with our fathers, so may He be with us!

May every hope kindled here today burn brightly and come
to its full flame!

May all the loves blended here—love of learning, love of
life, love of liberty, love of one another, divine charity itself—
help bring it to pass that all those privileged to enjoy under the
auspices of this university the banquet of the good, the true,
and the beautiful will be inspired to play their parts in building
a world where every man, no matter what his race, religion,
nationality, or family background, can live a fully human life,
freed from servitude imposed upon him by ignorance, by
other men, or by natural forces over which he has not sufficient
control; a world where freedom is not an empty word, and
where the poor man Lazarus can sit at the same table with the
privileged!

Over the contribution of the University of Pittsburgh to all
this may Wesley Posvar preside with grace, dignity, humility,
laughter, and music, as well as effectiveness, as he leads us
labore ad astra—through hard work to (literally in our times)
the stars! *Ad multos gloriosoque annos!*[1]

This prayer was delivered at the Carnegie Music Hall, Pittsburgh, Pennsylvania, on March 17, 1968, at the ceremonial installation of Wesley W.
Posvar as President of the University of Pittsburgh.

XLII

The Use Christ Made of Public Dinners

Some of us are obliged by the duties of our state in life to spend long hours at banquet tables. Usually, in all honor, circumstances of occasion or persons make the time pleasant and worthwhile. But sometimes one has a twinge of conscience. Could not such time be put to better use? Above all, should not a bishop or a priest, indeed every Christian, decide that public banquets, testimonial dinners, even *Communion breakfasts*, all such social gatherings at table involve a certain vanity and a waste of time if nothing else.

At a Serra banquet in Genoa, Cardinal Siri made a remark in conversation which has helped solve this problem of conscience, for me at least. And this remark has gone far toward eliminating lingering impatience with dinner programs except, of course, for the righteous wrath that every rational man must feel toward toastmasters who never come to the speaker and speakers who never come to the point.

I had said to the Cardinal something that scores of sympathetic souls have said to me at dinners: "I suppose that the necessity of constant dinner appearances wearies you and that there are a dozen things you could better be doing this evening."

Cardinal Siri's answer carried an undoubtedly unintended rebuke and opened up a refreshing line of thought. "Reflect", said he, "on all the things that Christ accomplished at dinners."

The suggested reflection has proved rewarding. I pass it along for prayerful thought by all who resent even the thought

This address was delivered at the YMCA, Pittsburgh, Pennsylvania, on March 29, 1968, on the occasion of the one hundred and fourteenth anniversary meeting.

of banquets, whether because they are not invited at all or because they think that they are invited too often.

Jesus began His public life and His personal apostolate at a wedding feast; He climaxed His redemptive life at a banquet that was the prelude to His atoning death. His Resurrection brought Him back not only to the company of His followers, but to their tables for dinner. All the times between, He frequently used gatherings for eating as the occasions of his principal lessons and examples. In fact, Saint Luke reports His critics as finding fault with the frequency and the (to them) indiscriminate nature of His *wining and dining*:

> "To what then shall I liken the men of this generation? And what are they like? They are like children sitting in the market place, calling to one another and saying, 'We have piped to you, and you have not danced; we have sung dirges, and you have not wept.' For John the Baptist came neither eating bread nor drinking wine, and you say, 'He has a devil.' The Son of Man came eating and drinking, and you say, 'behold a man who is a glutton, and a wine-drinker, a friend of publicans and sinners!' "[1]

The first occasion that finds Christ using human feasting for His divine purposes has long been a scandal to the Puritan and the prohibitionist. Most Catholics, on the other hand, have delighted to find Christ's Mother prominent among those present on the happy occasion which Saint John describes in the second chapter of his Gospel:

> And the third day, there was a marriage in Cana of Galilee: and the mother of Jesus was there. And Jesus also was invited, and His disciples, to the marriage. And the wine failing, the mother saith to Him: "They have no wine." And Jesus saith to her: "Woman, what is that to Me and to thee? My hour is not yet come." His mother saith to the waiters: "Whatsoever He shall say to you, do ye." Now there were set there six water pots of stone, according to the manner of the purifying of the Jews, containing two or three measures apiece. Jesus saith to them: "Fill the water pots with water." And they filled them up to the

brim. And Jesus saith to them: "Draw out now, and carry to the chief steward of the feast." And they carried it. And when the chief steward had tasted the water made wine, and knew not whence it was, but the waiters knew who had drawn the water, the chief steward calleth the bridegroom, and saith to him: "Every man at first setteth forth good wine, and when men have well drunk, then that which is worse. But thou hast kept the good wine until now." This beginning of miracles did Jesus in Cana of Galilee; and manifested His glory, and His disciples believed in Him.[2]

Jesus seized upon the marriage feast of Cana to teach many lessons. Some of them are obvious; others more subtle. For one thing, His mere presence attested to the sanctity of marriage and to the soundness of the joyful festivity by which human instinct surrounds the marriage rites. For another, He clearly inculcated the essential goodness and beauty of at least two things that experience finds easily perverted and that ill-considered moral philosophy often holds suspect: *human love* and the *use of wine*.

Spiritual writers find other lessons in Christ's action at Cana. Some see in the circumstances of this feasting a clue to the place of Mary in the prayer life of the faithful and in the intercession by which the Church presents to God our needs. All perceive the power and glory of God at work in Christ: this lesson, the evangelist expressly notes, His disciples carried away from Cana.

One saint draws from his meditation on the Lord's presence at the marriage feast a conclusion which serves as a premise for Christian humanism. He points out that Christ's demand that water be provided before He would bless the feast with wine must have been purposeful. That purpose was mystical, bound up with a teaching that Christ wished to impart. No one who has ever drunk both water and wine can suppose that there was any connection between the water that the steward brought and the wine that Christ made it possible for the host to serve;

the best of water is no *head start*, so to say, toward a supply of wine!

Why, then, did Jesus order that water be brought forth before He gave them the wine they asked? Perhaps, Saint Bernard hints, it was to teach us that we must bring our highest human gifts before God will transform them into the supernatural perfection that is His will for us. God does not waste His grace on nonentities; but if we bring the water of our best natural being to the work of our perfection, then He will freely and bountifully transform this into the wine of divine worth. The divine life within us is a transubstantiation by God's favor and power of the natural goodness, truth, and beauty we leave open to the transforming power of Christ. Nature is water and *relatively* worthless; grace is wine and supremely to be desired. In proportion as we offer the water of our natural best selves, Christ gives us the wine of supernatural worth.

At all events, after Cana Christ was invited always and everywhere to feasts. Saint Luke tells that

> Levi made him a great feast in his own house; and there was a great company of publicans, and of others, that were at table with them. But the Pharisees and scribes murmured, saying to Christ's disciples: "Why do you eat and drink with the publicans and sinners?" And Jesus answering, said to them: "They that are whole need not the physician; but they that are sick. I came not to call the just, but sinners to penance."[3]

At one such dinner Jesus took occasion pointedly to teach unforgettable lessons concerning how and by whom salvation is achieved. Saint Luke tells the story in his seventh chapter:

> And one of the Pharisees desired him to eat with Him. And He went into the house of the Pharisee, and sat down to meat. And behold a woman that was in the city, a sinner, when she knew that He sat at meat in the Pharisee's house, brought an alabaster box of ointment; and standing behind at His feet, she began to

451

wash His feet with tears, and wiped them with the hairs of her head, and kissed his feet, and anointed them with the ointment. And the Pharisee, who had invited Him, seeing it, spoke within himself, saying: "This man, if he were a prophet, would know surely who and what manner of woman this is that toucheth him, that she is a sinner." And Jesus answering, said to him: "Simon, I have somewhat to say to thee." But he said: "Master, say it." "A certain creditor had two debtors, the one owed five hundred pence, and the other fifty. And whereas they had not wherewith to pay, he forgave them both. Which therefore of the two loveth him most?" Simon answering, said: "I suppose that he to whom he forgave most." And he said to him: "Thou hast judged rightly." And turning to the woman, he said unto Simon: "Dost thou see this woman? I entered into thy house, thou gavest Me no water for My feet, but she with tears hath washed My feet, and with her hairs hath wiped them. Thou gavest Me no kiss; but she, since she came in, hath not ceased to kiss My feet. Wherefore I say to thee: Many sins are forgiven her, because she hath loved much. But to whom less is forgiven, he loveth less." And He said to her: "Thy sins are forgiven thee." And they that sat at meat with him began to say within themselves: "Who is this that forgiveth sins also?" And He said to the woman: "Thy faith hath made thee safe, go in peace."[4]

At another dinner the reactions of his supercilious host gave the Lord His topic for a moral instruction; the very dishes and utensils gave Him the figures of speech of the instruction. Again, it is Saint Luke who, in his eleventh chapter, relates the incident:

And as he was speaking, a certain Pharisee prayed Him, that He would dine with him. And He going in, sat down to eat. And the Pharisee began to say, thinking within himself, why He was not washed before dinner. And the Lord said to him: "Now, you Pharisees make clean the outside of the cup and of the platter; but your inside is full of rapine and iniquity. Ye fools, did not he that made that which is without, make also that which is within? But yet that which is within, give as alms; and behold, all things are clean unto you. But woe to you, Pharisees, because you tithe mint and rue and every herb; and pass over judgment, and the charity of God. Now these things you ought to have done, and not have left the other undone."[5]

Saint Luke's fourteenth chapter finds Christ at another public dinner. There, appealing in His parables and conversation to the manners and familiar customs observed at dinners, he taught many and momentous lessons.

And it came to pass, when Jesus went into the house of one of the chiefs of the Pharisees, on the sabbath day, to eat bread, that they watched Him. And behold, there was a certain man before Him that had the dropsy. And Jesus answering, spoke to the lawyers and Pharisees, saying: "Is it lawful to heal on the sabbath day?" But they held their peace. But He taking him healed him and sent him away. And answering them, He said: "Which of you shall have an ass or an ox fall into a pit, and will not immediately draw him out, on the sabbath day?" And they could not answer Him to these things. And He spoke a parable also to them that were invited, marking how they chose the first seats at the table, saying to them: "When thou art invited to a wedding, sit not down in the first place, lest perhaps one more honourable than thou be invited by him: And he that invited thee and him, come and say to thee: Give this man place; and then thou begin with shame to take the lowest place. But when thou art invited, go, sit down in the lowest place; that when he who invited thee cometh, he may say to thee: Friend, go up higher. Then shalt thou have glory before them that sit at table with thee. Because every one that exalteth himself, shall be humbled; and he that humbleth himself shall be exalted." And He said to him also that had invited Him: "When thou makest a dinner or a supper, call not thy friends, nor thy brethren, nor thy kinsmen, nor thy neighbours who are rich; lest perhaps they also invite thee again, and a recompense be made to thee. But when thou makest a feast, call the poor, the maimed, the lame and the blind; And thou shalt be blessed, because they have not wherewith to make thee recompense: for recompense shall be made thee at the

453

resurrection of the just." When one of them that sat at table with Him, had heard these things, he said to Him: "Blessed is he that shall eat bread in the Kingdom of God." But He said to him: "A certain man made a great supper and invited many. And he sent his servant at the hour of supper to say to them that were invited, that they should come, for now all things are ready. And they began all at once to make excuse. The first said to him: 'I have bought a farm, and I must needs go out and see it: I pray thee, hold me excused.' And another said: 'I have bought five yoke of oxen, and I go to try them: I pray thee, hold me excused.' And another said: 'I have married a wife and therefore I cannot come.' And the servant returning, told these things to his lord. Then the master of the house, being angry, said to his servant: 'Go out quickly into the streets and lanes of the city, and bring in hither the poor, and the feeble, and the blind, and the lame.' And the servant said: 'Lord, it is done as thou hast commanded, and yet there is room.' And the Lord said to the servant: 'Go out into the highways and hedges, and compel them to come in, that my house may be filled. But I say unto you, that none of those men that were invited, shall taste of my supper.' "[6]

The sixth chapter of Saint John's Gospel foreshadows on the level of action and doctrine His eucharistic banquet, the table that will be the meeting place between Christ and all His brethren until the end of time. It is this chapter that records Jesus' promise of the Bread of Life, a bread from heaven which would be so much more wondrous in the manner of its coming to us and in its power to sustain us than was the bread from heaven that God gave the Jews in the desert. In this same context Saint John reports how many who originally wished to follow Jesus were scandalized by His teaching concerning the eucharistic banquet, much as the Pharisees had been scandalized by His banqueting of every kind.

It was appropriate that Christ should have prepared His disciples for the doctrine of the Blessed Sacrament by a manifestation of His divine power at another type of meal, a meal that was what we would probably call a picnic and that involved a miracle.

The miracle of the multiplication of the loaves and fishes is told by all the evangelists, but I prefer the account of Saint John because he thought to include the gracious detail that it was a young boy present who provided the loaves of bread and the fishes out of which Christ fed the multitude. The Vulgate text describes the boy simply as *puer*; a Protestant version speaks of him as "a lad". I like to think of the consternation that the boy's boldness in offering his meager store of food for so large a crowd must have caused the bystanders. Andrew, in reporting the lad's offer to Christ, said simply, "There is a boy here that hath five barley loaves and two fishes", but he hastened to add, as if to disassociate himself from the folly of the boy, "but what are these among so many?"[7]

If the young fellow's mother was with him when he decided to make his paltry loaves and poor fishes available for the feeding of the five thousand, she undoubtedly shushed him and told him not to act like his father's people! But Jesus did not dismiss him, as did Andrew, nor despise his gift, as the others doubtless did. The Gospel suggests the gentle courtesy with which Christ gave thanks and then, supplementing the human generosity of the young boy with the divine power of the Son of God, distributed the loaves to those who had assembled to hear him "in number about five thousand. . . . In like manner also the fishes, as much as they would."[8]

Saint John's account is worth reading as a reminder of how Jesus welcomed the circumstances of a meal as the setting in which to teach so many of His principal lessons:

After this Jesus went away to the other side of the sea of Galilee, which is that of Tiberias. And there followed Him a great crowd, because they witnessed the signs He worked on those who were sick. Jesus therefore went up to the mountain, and sat there with His disciples. Now the Passover, the feast of the Jews, was near. When, therefore, Jesus had lifted up His eyes and seen that a very great crowd had come to Him, He said to Philip, "Whence shall we buy bread that these may eat?" But He said this to try him, for He Himself knew what He would do.

Philip answered him, "Two hundred denarii worth of bread is not enough for them, that each one may receive a little." One of His disciples, Andrew, the brother of Simon Peter, said to Him, "There is a young boy here who has five barley loaves and two fishes; but what are these among so many?" Jesus then said, "Make the people recline." Now there was much grass in the place. The men therefore reclined, in number about five thousand. Jesus then took the loaves, and when He had given thanks, distributed them to those reclining; and likewise the fishes, as much as they wished. But when they were filled, He said to His disciples, "Gather the fragments of the five barley loaves left over by those who had eaten." When the people, therefore, had seen the sign which Jesus had worked, they said, "This is indeed the Prophet Who is to come into the world." So when Jesus perceived that they would come to take Him by force and make Him king, He fled again to the mountain, Himself alone.[9]

When the time came for the establishment of the eucharistic banquet by which Christ would Himself become the food of our souls, the institution of the Sacrament and instruction in its divine dignity were linked to a human banquet traditional among the Jews. Saint Paul would later recall this fraternal gathering at table which on the night before he died Jesus made the occasion of the establishment of a heavenly meal in the eating of which we would win supernatural life in a fraternity more profound and more lasting than any that this world knows.

Saint John describes the Last Supper; so do Saint Matthew and Saint Mark. Saint Luke's account includes details the very phrasing of which hints at the readiness with which Jesus spoke of dinners and of the places where He and His friends gathered for them:

And he sent Peter and John, saying: "Go, and prepare for us the pasch that we may eat." But they said: "Where wilt thou that we prepare?" And He said to them: "Behold, as you go into the city, there shall meet you a man carrying a pitcher of water:

follow him into the house where he entereth in. And you shall say to the master of the house: 'The Master saith to thee: Where is the guest chamber, where I may eat the pasch with My disciples?' And he will show you a large dining room, furnished; and there prepare." And they going, found as He said to them, and made ready the pasch. And when the hour was come, He sat down, and the twelve apostles with Him. And He said to them: "With desire I have desired to eat this pasch with you, before I suffer. For I say to you, that from this time I will not eat it, till it be fulfilled in the Kingdom of God." And having taken the chalice, He gave thanks, and said: "Take, and divide it among you: For I say to you, that I will not drink of the fruit of the vine, till the Kingdom of God come." And taking bread, He gave thanks, and broke; and gave to them, saying: "This is My body, which is given for you. Do this for a commemoration of Me." In like manner the chalice also, after He had supped, saying: "This is the chalice, the new testament in My blood, which shall be shed for you."[10]

The words "when they were at table and eating" pinpoint many of the discourses and deeds of Jesus during all the years of His public life. After His return from the dead it was by His presence at table that He demonstrated the reality of His physical Resurrection; it was probably in some characteristic gesture, belovedly remembered from the days when He broke bread with them, that two of His disciples, in fearful pursuit from Jerusalem to Emmaus, recognized the Risen Lord.

In the beautiful account Saint Luke gives of the conversation between Christ and the disciples on the road to Emmaus, we note that what He said and did in their twilight conversation did not, so to say, register with the disillusioned disciples until, significantly enough, they found themselves at table with Him. The narrative is familiar:

And the one of them, whose name was Cleophas, answering, said to Him: "Art thou only a stranger in Jerusalem, and hast not known the things that have been done there in these days?" To whom he said: "What things?" And they said: "Concerning Jesus of Nazareth, who was a prophet, mighty in work and word before God and all the people; and how our chief priests and princes delivered him to be condemned to death, and crucified him. But we hoped that it was He that should have redeemed Israel: and now besides all this, today is the third day since these things were done. Yea, and certain women also of our company affrighted us, who before it was light, were at the sepulchre, and not finding His body, came, saying that they had also seen a vision of angels, who say that he is alive. And some of our people went to the sepulchre, and found it so as the women had said, but Him they found not." Then He said to them: "O foolish and slow of heart to believe in all things which the prophets have spoken. Ought not Christ to have suffered these things, and so to enter into His glory?" And beginning at Moses and all the prophets, He expounded to them in all the scriptures, the things that were concerning Him. And they drew nigh to the town, whither they were going: and He made as though he would go farther. But they constrained Him, saying: "Stay with us, because it is towards evening, and the day is now far spent." And He went in with them. And it came to pass, whilst He was at table with them, He took bread, and blessed, and broke, and gave to them. And their eyes were opened, and they knew Him: and He vanished out of their sight.[11]

Saint John relates another of the visits that Jesus made to His disciples after the Resurrection. The manner in which Jesus dispelled their fears and demonstrated His true identity again involves the phrases and the formalities of a dinner:

Jesus saith to them: "Come, and dine." And none of them who were at meat, durst ask Him: "Who art Thou?", knowing that it was the Lord. And Jesus cometh and taketh bread, and giveth them, and fish in like manner. This is now the third time that Jesus was manifested to His disciples, after He was risen from the dead.[12]

It was, then, at table, sometimes as host, sometimes as guest, that Christ confirmed the reality of His Resurrection. It

458

was following a dinner that he conferred on Peter the primacy over the universal Christian flock that He had promised by the lake shore months before. Perhaps the fact that they had just been at table is the explanation of the figure of speech by which this time Christ indicated the regal responsibilities and the pastoral relationship that Peter would have to the lambs and the sheep of His fold. Saint John reports these:

> When therefore they had dined, Jesus saith to Simon Peter: "Simon, son of John, lovest thou Me more than these?" He saith to Him: "Yea, Lord, Thou knowest that I love Thee." He saith to him: "Feed my lambs." He saith to him again: "Simon, son of John, lovest thou Me?" He saith to Him: "Yea, Lord, thou knowest that I love Thee." He saith to him: "Feed my lambs." He saith to him the third time: "Simon, son of John, lovest thou Me?" Peter was grieved, because He had said to him the third time: "Lovest thou Me?" And he said to him: "Lord, Thou knowest all things: Thou knowest that I love thee." He said to him: "Feed my sheep."[13]

Immediately after this mighty grant of power to Peter, Christ said a curious thing to the new prince of the apostles. It has been variously interpreted, and no one is quite sure what He meant. He observed that when Peter was young he had girded himself and had gone wherever he wished, but that when he would be older, another would gird him and lead him about without reference to his own wish. Some writers think this was a prophetic reference to the manner of Peter's death.

Perhaps so. But perhaps, too, the Lord was describing the way in which all those who are called to lead others are also led by them, being called upon by men to do all manner of things in order that they may accomplish the work which God has called them to do. Among the things that God's agents must do, whether they wish it or not, may well be numbered the making of speeches at public dinners and attending banquets! This, too, is part of the doing of the work of the Lord, and we have the example of the Lord Himself as to how public banquets can be turned to the advantage of the Kingdom.

And so, when Christian prelates, priests, and people are tempted to weary of the round of social events to which they are invited and incidentally upon which the work of the Church so often depends, perhaps it will help if they remember that *Jesus, also, was invited . . . and that while they were at table, He spoke to them* the truths by which we are saved!

XLIII

Martin Luther King, Jr., 1929–1968

We meet in the first days of Holy Week. Martin Luther King has made Holy Week 1968 forever memorable. He has driven home indelibly one of the principal points of Holy Week and of Easter.

I would wish my brief reflection in tribute to him, made at the gracious invitation of his wife and co-workers, to stress a theological aspect of his life and death.[1] Martin Luther King was many things to many people, but in the midst of his absorbing commitments and multiple activities he was always the Christian preacher, an ardent listener to the Word of God and eager to be a doer of that Word.

The son of a devout family, he was nurtured and lived by the piety inspired by a scriptural theology, the traditional hymns and themes of which, woven into the ceremonies at his church this morning, must have deeply moved the millions privileged to be present through television and radio. Everything sung at the service in the church, every line of Scripture read, every word of meditation uttered dramatized, I hope, to millions the profound appropriateness of the fact that we are gathered precisely in Holy Week to ponder the life, death, and significance of Dr. Martin Luther King.

Speaking as if in prophecy of his own death, Martin Luther King once said: "The only way we can really achieve freedom is somehow to conquer the fear of death. . . . Deep down in our non-violent creed is the conviction that there are some things so dear, some things so precious, some things so eternally true that they are worth dying for. . . ."

This tribute was prepared for the Obsequies of Martin Luther King, Jr., held at the Campus of Morehouse College, Atlanta, Georgia, on April 9, 1968.

Dr. King has now become the latest of those heroes of our race—our *one race*, the single family of God, "Who hath made of one, all mankind, to dwell upon the whole face of the earth . . . that they should seek God . . ."[2] who, aware of the transcendent value of life, have nonetheless been prepared to forfeit it, the better to bear witness to God's truth. Such heroes help make somehow glorious the history of our sinful humanity; they give depth to our faith, grounds to our hope, direction to our love.

Such heroes of human history derive their special dignity from the way in which their lives and deaths are caught up in the *mystery of iniquity* and yet also in the mystery of the redemption made possible by the Passion, death, and Resurrection of Christ which are the themes of our meditations during Holy Week.

The Holy Week mysteries recall the use that the Incarnate Son of God made of His liberty, the love by which He laid down His life for the world, the peaceful victories which He alone could bring into unruly nature and the tormented human heart; they recall also the gift of the Life by which we are redeemed.

Speaking in Rome on Palm Sunday, Pope Paul did not hesitate to link to these mysteries the life and death of Martin Luther King. The Holy Father put all the tragedy of these recent days, the seeming victory of the mystery of iniquity over the hopes and efforts of Dr. King, in the theological perspective of the Holy Week mysteries and the manner in which the brethren of Christ are called upon to participate in the tragedy and *therefore* the victory of His redemptive striving, suffering, death, and vindication.

The death of Christ is unique at once in its tragedy, its sanctity, and its worth; it is beyond all comparisons and parallels, even as is Christ Himself. But brutal events in human history from the beginning, iniquities of which the murder in Memphis is a frightening, close-to-home example, are illumined by the tragedy of Calvary and even shed light on its mystery.

Except for the Passion, death, and Easter Resurrection of Jesus—except, in a word, for the *gospel* which Martin Luther King so passionately loved and so earnestly sought to live—a murder like that of last week and events like those which we have experienced in these recent days are simply hellish, insane chaos. But seen, however dimly, in the light of the Cross and of Easter, they became part of a mystery, a mystery which involves the further mystery of iniquity (as did the crucifixion) but also the *mystery of God's mercy*, the way in which God's grace is more powerful than our capacity for evil. They thus become part of our redemption, the restoration of sanity to the City of Man, and the attainment of salvation in the City of God.

Martin Luther King well knew that only of Christ could the high priest say: "It is better for one man to die for the people than for the whole nation to be destroyed . . . and not for the nation only, but to gather together in unity the scattered children of God."[3] Only of Christ could all this be said. But by the power of Christ all others who die for the people help bring together the divided family of the Lord. Because of the crucified Christ, by the grace of the Risen Christ, in the light of the life of Christ, we understand how everyone who dies for freedom, for love, for peace, and, above all, for life plays a part in building, here below and hereafter, the kingdom that Christ made possible.

That kingdom the Scripture describes in a vision of the Beloved Disciple, words of which were consistently on the lips of Dr. King, and the reality of which he preeminently helped to make possible. Saint John's vision of the New Jerusalem is that of a kingdom not built with hands, the kingdom of a world to come which men like Dr. King hunger after and one day attain. However, that kingdom is prefigured and somehow begun even here on earth when God's will is done on earth as it is in heaven; when, therefore, the world is renewed in justice and in equity, in faith, in hope, and in charity.

And so John's vision of the New Jerusalem is at once a prophecy of what shall be forever in heaven and a proclamation of the dream that possessed the mind and sustained the heart of Dr. King:

> Then I saw a new heaven and a new earth. The old heaven, the old earth had vanished. . . . And I, John, saw in my vision that holy city which is the new Jerusalem, being sent down by God from heaven, all clothed in readiness, like a bride who has adorned herself to meet her husband. I heard, too, a voice which cried aloud from the throne, Here is God's tabernacle pitched among men; He will dwell with them, and they will be His own people, and He will be among them, their own God. He will wipe away every tear from their eyes, and there will be no more death, or mourning, or cries of distress, no more sorrow; those old things have passed away. And He who sat on the throne said, Behold, I make all things new. (These words I was bidden write down, words most sure and true.) And He said to me, it is over. I am Alpha, I am Omega, the beginning of all things and their end; those who are thirsty shall drink—it is my free gift—out of the spring whose water is life. Who wins the victory? He shall have his share in this; I will be his God, and he shall be My son. . . . And He carried me off in a trance to a great mountain, high up, and there showed me the holy city Jerusalem, as it came down, sent by God, from heaven, clothed in God's glory. . . . The nations will live and move in its radiance; the kings of the earth will bring it their tribute of praise and honor. All day the gates will never be shut (there will be no night there), as the nations flock into it with their honor and their praise. . . .[4]

May Saint John's vision be the consolation of the family and friends of Dr. King. May it give strength to all who work for a City of Man consistent with human dignity, divine promise, and the relationship of man's city to the City of God, the New

Jerusalem. May these words of Scripture provide the common bond uniting our national community, indeed all the nations of men!

Blessed are they who strive to build God's kingdom on earth, the promise and the beginning of what shall be in heaven! Such was the work of Martin Luther King. God grant him eternal joy—as his soul goes marching on!

XLIV

Robert F. Kennedy, 1925–1968

This is no time for further statements. Wednesday's wild incident piles up the evidence that we have already become a nation frenzied by wild slogans, irresponsible talk, and fear-packed phrases which lead to the mad violence and brutal divisions which are now our daily humiliation.

For several years now those of us who lived and studied in Europe in the early 1930s have been haunted by the memory of the tensions, the partisan hatreds, the labyrinth of undergrounds, and the general paranoia which deeply divided and then completely paralyzed great nations. Some of us think we see like things happening here; twice this year we have been reminded by events at home of the burning of the Reichstag in Berlin in 1933. That thought has imposed upon us the effort to be balanced and sane in what we say even about the evils which have made our society, our world, so sick.

The latest violence to shock the nation and mankind confirms more than ever the need for Christian restraint, for disciplined speech, for maximum forbearance, for avoiding the violent word or deed which estranges the evildoer beyond recall, and for speaking only the word that seeks to reconcile.

This is a time for the spirit of Gamaliel, of Saint Francis de Sales, of Pope John, of those who well know the reality of evil and fight it at every turn, but refuse to be overcome or disoriented by it.

Such men do not give in to evil; in patience and in truth they resist it and conquer it. But they call it by its right name. That name is sin. Sin reveals itself in the spirit of division. Sin is charged with suspicion, intemperance, loud talk. Sin is stamped

This official statement, written on June 7, 1968, was addressed to the clergy, religious and laity of the Diocese of Pittsburgh, Pennsylvania.

all over the present national crisis. But this is no time for loud-mouthed denunciation, even of sin, if by such denunciation we play into the hands of the opportunists and ambitious, the revolutionaries or the reactionaries, political and even religious, who, also in the spirit of violence, exploit the crises which sin produces in order to have their own way.

In the face of political moral paralysis, surrounded by the violent, screaming mob, Jesus, the Scriptures tell us, kept silent. Pilate issued a statement. So did Herod. The crowd yelled all the slogans that the instigators of their frenzy taught them. Jesus kept silent.

The silence of Jesus was not because He had no plan, purpose, or feeling for the human condition. It was precisely because He had a plan of peace, a purpose of unity, and a compassion so profound that He did not utter the angry, defensive word which would further divide or express merely his personal hurt. It is a time for similar creative disciplined silence on the part of all who seek to do the work and perpetuate the spirit of Jesus. That work is the work of reconciliation. Reconciliation at the moment calls for a responsible guard on our tongues, a careful control of our emotions, a season of silence, not in flight from either thought or action but in order to produce ideas and deeds somehow matching the desperate need in which we stand and the titanic task of total moral renewal which calls out to every resource left to us in the midst of our chaos or still available to us from the mercy of God.

As one listened to the whirlwind of words which followed on the airways the news of the tragedy in Los Angeles—the crescendo of confused talk, building up all over the land, which has become so characteristic of us in times of crisis and is itself so great a part of our problem—one thought again of the mood of pre-Hitler Germany as violence was preparing to take over there. One thought also, by total contrast, of the majestic silence of Jesus when His ministry of reconciliation was beginning its witness and work.

In the face of violence unleashed and evil in possession, Jesus kept silent; strangely but significantly, He made no comment. There was a time when He spoke, passionately and prophetically, but that was when the violence was not yet in unholy riot and the evil not yet triumphant. Our present moment is one in which the inflammatory word and the violent deed, the word so easy to utter in anger and the reaction that is almost compulsive when we are frustrated, can only multiply the evil and make all but impossible the work of reconciliation. This is a time to be guided by the Old Testament proverb: "A man who can control his tongue has knowledge, a man of discernment keeps his temper cool" (Prov 17:27).

This year has become, urgently, a time for the soft answer that turns away wrath, for the persevering work that seeks no acclaim but produces peace, for the prayerful meditation that prefers self-examination and self-renewal to the denunciation of others, even of those who do evil. It is no time for recrimination. It is a time for utter sobriety, for honest self-searching and quiet self-sacrificing, for the silent labor that binds up wounds, not inflicts new ones; that builds with what we have and what we hope that God will give us, not destroys further the ties of trust. It is no time for blasting, counterblasting, and further alienation even of sinners, certainly not of those who, however blindly, seek, as Christians must, sanity and salvation.

The need is for that ministry of reconciliation which is the heart of Christ's priesthood. All who have a share in that priesthood, on whatever level, under whatever aspect, are called as rarely before to play their part in Christ's ministry of reconciliation.

Priests of our diocese met at Saint Paul's Seminary as the storm of emotion swept the nation Wednesday. They had gathered in the spirit of priestly unity symbolized by the concelebrated Mass of their Silver and Golden Jubilarians. Their prayers immediately became for Senator Kennedy and his loved ones stricken by the particular form that the universal

468

spirit of violence and antagonism produced for them this week. Their prayers were for all victims of violence, callous indifference, and irresponsibility everywhere, close to home, abroad in our land, throughout the world. But their prayers were, above all, for peace, not the peace of the cemetery, inert and sterile, but of living community where people resist the divisive influence of sin and work together in loving, mutual confidence.

Grace is God's response to our sin; our sin resists that grace.

Confidence and love are graces of God, and so the priests gathered at Saint Paul's prayed, as must all of us always and everywhere, for openness to God's grace. That grace is the force behind and the fruit of the ministry of reconciliation, the ministry which Senator Kennedy, as he spoke his last words minutes before he was wounded by his assailant, seemed to recognize as the supreme need of our nation.

God give us priests, laity, neighbors disposed in this penitential spirit to work together in the patient, undiscouraged ministry of reconciliation by which we in the Church, the nation, in all the human family, can alone be brought, through our suffering and God's grace, to unity in peace.

XLV

Billy Graham in Pittsburgh

Billy Graham is preaching an evangelistic crusade in the Pittsburgh area between August 30 and September 8. The crusade is under the auspices of a local Executive Committee representing most of the Protestant denominations of our community.

Representatives of the Executive Committee have courteously informed me concerning the hopes, objectives, and guidelines of the evangelistic program they are planning. They have done so by personal visit and by letter. They could not have been more neighborly or considerate.

For reasons of faith and conscience the Catholic Diocese cannot cosponsor Dr. Graham's evangelistic crusade. I expressed these reasons to the Executive Committee of the crusade, and they immediately declared their sympathetic acceptance of our Catholic position. Men of unqualified commitment to their fundamental understanding of the gospel, the associates of Dr. Graham recognize the requirements and limits imposed by conscientious faith on others.

The spokesmen for Dr. Graham's crusade made it clear that they did not ask participation of the Catholic diocese, but the pledge of our good will and prayers. Mount Mercy College, I am happy to learn, has shown its good will by making available parking space for the crusade meeting at nearby Pitt Stadium. I am confident that all our priests and people will be eager to offer like cooperation when facilities of ours would contribute to the convenience of those attending the crusade.

It is easy to respond generously to a request for prayers so generously made. It is good that so many of our Protestant churches are cooperating in a program emphasizing the basic

This official statement, written on September 8, 1968, was addressed to the clergy, religious, and laity of the Diocese of Pittsburgh, Pennsylvania.

truths of Christian Faith which Dr. Graham drives home in his evangelism. Even those who do not share other elements of the crusade theology will rejoice that a powerful voice will be lifted up in Pittsburgh to proclaim anew the Divinity of our Lord and Savior Jesus Christ, the terrible reality of sin, the power of God's grace, the choice which every person must make between God and whatever excludes God's love, the manner in which God must ultimately punish evil and vindicate good, the Providence of God, and the moral responsibility of men.

I look forward to meeting Dr. Graham while he is in Pittsburgh and have invited him and his associates to dinner while he is here—so that we can talk of the things of God. Meanwhile, I ask the clergy, religious, and laity of the Catholic diocese to pray that the Spirit, breathing where it will, may find a generous response in the minds and hearts of those to whom Dr. Graham and his team will preach the Word of God.

The Executive Committee assures me that the Pittsburgh Crusade will scrupulously avoid proselytizing. In the pastoral follow-up involving persons who make commitments which are a part of the evangelistic crusade, counselors will refer such persons to clergy of the religious tradition in which these persons have been baptized and from the practice of which they may have lapsed. In response to the assurance that the commitment cards of persons declaring themselves of Catholic background or interest will be referred to us for pastoral follow-up, I have nominated four specific priests to receive such cards for subsequent interviews with persons seeking strengthening in their faith or for referral to local parishes, according to the requests of the persons involved. I point out, gratefully, that this arrangement is made at the suggestion of the local Executive Committee themselves. I see in it a pledge, once again, of the regard for conscience and the sense of Christian fraternity which prompted the sponsors of Billy Graham's Pittsburgh Crusade to ask the prayerful good wishes I gladly promise in the name of the Catholic community.

XLVI

The Catholic Parish

When a child is born we already begin to think on the joyful, sorrowful, and glorious mysteries of the life opening before him. So when a new church is dedicated as is Saint Mary's tonight, we promptly begin to live over in advance the memories which will cluster around its hallowed walls as the years go by—we look ahead to reflect upon the force for good which will radiate from this new church into the life of this diocese and of this civil community! How great a debt will be owed this altar and this pulpit for public honesty and civic loyalty learned here, for family discipline and personal sanctity fostered here and preached, for faith and hope and charity born here, nurtured, and brought to maturity. How many personal memories, wonderful medleys of experience human and divine, will one by one take their concrete form from the material features of this church! Holy memories they will be, of moments we eventually most yearn to recapture, of Communions worthily received, of graces almost sensibly perceived; thousands of men and women will recall all these in terms of this church and of its sanctuaries. Tender memories there will be, for those whose marriages will be sanctified here and their children christened; secret memories of hope reborn and joy recaptured will hallow forever the confessionals of this church for some; sweet memories and sad, confided to no man, will always bring to certain of you the vision of these shrines, hushed by the whispered hopes and fears and holy confidences of the sons and daughters of this parish; bitter memories, even, though eventually made almost palatable by

This sermon was delivered at the Church of Saint Mary, Corvallis, Oregon, on November 10, 1968, on the occasion of its dedication.

a sacred Savior given them at this altar, for those whose beloved dead will be brought here for the last prayers of this parish and the last blessing of its priests. Memories of holiness, memories of happiness, memories of Christ—these will accumulate in this sacred place as the years go by. Such is the peace of a parish church.

Christ Himself might be considered the founder of parish life. "Wherever two or three are gathered in My name, there am I in the midst of them"—so spoke Jesus Christ.[1] Now, every parish is essentially a group of souls gathered in the name of Jesus, gathered about a tabernacle in the care of a priest, a tabernacle in which Jesus dwells under the sacramental species of the Eucharist. The parish is the normal point of contact between Jesus Christ and His faithful. Parish life is the ordinary means by which we become citizens of and active in the Kingdom of Christ on earth, the Church. The parish, with its pastor and priests, its altar, its confessional, its pulpit, its schools, its good works, its sinners and saints, is a microcosm; it is the whole Church in miniature, and through it Christ does for a limited community what He founded the universal Church to do for all the world. Through it, a group of the faithful, in a corner of the world, do for Christ what all the transcendent Church, in heaven, in Purgatory, and on earth does for Him throughout creation. Christ is adored in the parish liturgy; Christ is preached in the parish pulpit; Christ is praised by the parish choirs; Christ is meditated in the parish convent; Christ is imitated, reproduced, in all the mysteries of His life, by the hidden lives of unknown parish saints, by the public zeal of parish workers, by the sufferings of the parish sick.

The parish priest, custodian of the keys of the parish tabernacle, is, in miniature, Peter himself, custodian, as Vicar of Christ, of the keys of heaven. That is why there is no need for a man ever to leave his parish, in life or in death, in order to receive from the Church everything needed in order to bring

473

him from earth to heaven. When a child is brought to the parish church to be baptized, his parish priest does not inquire what he seeks of the *parish* or of its priest, but rather "What dost thou ask of the Church of God?", as if the parish priest were prepared to give in his local church whatever of faith and of life everlasting the child might expect to receive from the total Church, everywhere. Only in material terms—in point of territory and the mere measurements of area and population— is there a distinction between the parish and the Church. Only materially is the parish a portion of the Church. Spiritually, the parish *is* the Church, the whole Church. Just as the entire Christ is present in any consecrated particle of the Eucharist, so the Church is present and at work in any canonically erected parish, however fragmentary. There is a sense, familiar to every Catholic, in which the Church is Christ; there is also a sense in which the parish is the Church, the whole Church, the Church in miniature.

The history of the parish in the life of the Church suggests how this is true. The parish has come to be a definite territory, with a church under the direction of a priest, to which the faithful of a particular area belong; but the parish is a late development in the Church. In the very beginnings of the apostolic Church there was, of course, but one flock, gathered timorously about the apostles at Jerusalem. Scattered by the winds of Pentecost, however, the apostles left Jerusalem to catholicize the Church, to render Jesus Christ and His redemption universal. Wherever they went they founded new Cenacles, patterned on that at Jerusalem, new tabernacles, multiplying the presence of Christ throughout the world. Because these apostles were bishops, the first territorial divisions made in the Church were dioceses. They were founded and ruled by those who, together with Saint Peter, had received at once the priesthood and the episcopate. Peter, bound forever to Christ, was the bond which united among themselves these several and scattered sees of the single Church, *The Church*. Between

the faithful and the Church there was but one intermediary—
the bishop. Peter was jealous of his flock, committed to him
by Christ's double charge, and he did not wish the distance
between him and them to become too great. He wished his
voice to reach the furthermost boundaries of the believing
world, echoed by the bishops, but without other overtones or
the accents of other voices. And so the primitive dioceses had
each but one church, the cathedral; each one baptistry, one
altar, one pulpit. The diocese was then a parish, and the bishop
was its parish priest.

But the flock grew great; as Christ had foretold, the grain of
mustard seed grew and multiplied, reproducing itself a thousand-
fold. Into the towns and villages the news of redemption
spread like wildfire, and everywhere men gathered to thank
God for it and to ensure the perpetual presence of its channels
in their midst. Then the bishops became obliged to delegate to
auxiliaries some part, at least, of the mandate they had received
from Peter, as Peter from Christ and Christ from the Father.
And so priests, hitherto co-celebrants at Mass around the altar
of the bishop, assistants around his throne, received from the
bishops, while remaining still subject to them, power to offer
Mass at local altars, to bless and forgive and preach and baptize
in local churches. These priests received a portion of territory
with a group of faithful, and on the territory thus assigned
them they built a church which was to be an image of the
cathedral, as the cathedral had been an image of the original
Cenacle, as the Cenacle had been an image of heaven. Thus
was the parish born.

Four elements, then, blend in the notion of a parish; *territory*,
people, *priest*, and *church*. Of these *territory* is first because in it
all the other elements, physical and spiritual, nonhuman and
human, have their roots. Out of its territory, its mere earth,
comes the water which cancels, through the sacrament of
baptism, the sin inherited by the children of the parish, and
puts to flight, when blessed in sacramentals, the spirits hostile

to the parish life. Out of its land, in symbol at least, comes the wheat which, made into bread, gives place to the Body of Christ in the Eucharist; out of the land come the wine, the olives, the oils which sanctify in the sacramental life of the parish, which strengthen and save its members. Out of its land come the flowers which make glad its altars, the materials with which its church is constructed and adorned. Thus mere land, mere matter, comes to share in the ends and the purposes of the parish, the ends of the Church, the purposes of God.

The second element is the *people*: the *souls* of the parish, as the ancient idiom of the faithful calls them, the parishioners. In the life of the church *parishioners* and *brethren* are interchangeable terms. The prayer at the parish altar or in parish devotions *pro fratribus nostris absentibus*—for our absent brethren—means a prayer for our absent parishioners, and it is on the parish as a family of brethren that the priest calls down the blessing of God when, in the liturgy, he prays: *"Respice, quesumus, Domine, super hanc familiam"*—Look down, we beg Thee, Almighty God, on this Thy family. The domestic spirit of the parish is never more manifest than on Sunday, the day reserved to God, and of all days the most typically parochial. On that feast and in the liturgy of the parish Mass the people carry on, as it were, a family conversation with their priest, following his every movement at the family table, the parish altar, with their reverent gaze; answering "so be it . . . amen", to all the supplications he makes in their name; answering *"et cum spiritu tuo"*—and with your Spirit—to all his paternal good wishes; striking their breasts in humility of spirit with him whenever he does so in their name; bowing their heads together with him whenever he names their elder Brother, Jesus their Savior; and suddenly growing silent as he pauses in the Mass to recall the names of their living and their dead.

The *parish priest* is the third element in the notion of the parish, for of his family he is the father. If the voices with which our children speak echo the accents of their earthly fathers, the thoughts their voices learn to speak echo the teachings of the spiritual fathers who are their priests. At every stage of their lives they seek him out, and he them. With the dawn of reason and the possibility of revolt from God, he is present to guide them Godward and to nourish them with God Himself. In the crises of adolescence he prepares them for the strengthening and the confirmation in the Faith which the bishop comes to his parish to bring. On the threshold of maturity he fosters in them their vocations, and whatever these may be he has paternal part in them, whether it be as official witness to their weddings, or as their responsible director toward the priesthood of other consecrated lives. And while his people in their fields or shops, at home or abroad, wage their unrelenting battle of life, their parish priest, like Moses on the hill of Raphidim, lifts his arms unceasingly in prayer for them. More powerful is he than Moses as he intercedes for them, for Moses held in his hands the symbol of God's power, but our priest holds in his hands the God of power Himself.

Last of the elements in the notion of the parish is the *parish church* itself. If the parish is a family of which the parish priest is the father, the parish church is its house, its hearth and home. All the little rites and observances of a domestic life take place within its walls, with God Himself made at home, so to speak, within it. All of the houses in which Jesus Christ dwelt during His life on earth, all of the homes made holy by His presence, have their little history renewed in the liturgical life of the parish year. Bethlehem, Nazareth, Cana, Bethany, the Cenacle, Emmaus—all these dwelling places where God found hospitality when He visited our earth are reconstructed one by one to house Him mystically in the parish church. And mystically, once more, for their little time each year, there gathers about the same Divine Guest the ancient family of the faithful, numbering like shepherds to those of Bethlehem, like Wise Men to those from the East, like apostles to those of Galilee, new Marthas and other Marys, Lazarus again and Zacchaeus—and all the others whose homes were ever houses for the Lord Jesus find their counterpart within the walls of the house of God that is the parish church. With all the ancient needs, the timeless tears, the unceasing petitions, the same gratitude, the same joy, the same faith, the Catholic people find in the parish church their home, the house of God among men.

Oh, my parish church! Not even death can separate me from thy love. The liturgy offered within thy walls will always include me in its supplications. If anything on this devastated earth will make me dream of heaven, it will be what I shall see and hear and feel in the moments when I visited thee. If the paradise in which I believe will one day confirm for me the faith by which I have believed, I shall owe it to the things which are done to me and taught me under thy roof. Small wonder, then, that I love thee, O my parish church! For the life I first learn to live in thee is the undying life that I will live in heaven, if I be faithful to thee. The gate of heaven is the door to thy temple; the key to heaven is the key of thy tabernacle; the joy of heaven is the possession forever of that God whom first we find on earth at home within thy holy walls.[2]

XLVII

Human Life in Our Day

During this past week the bishops of the United States met in Washington for their annual conference together. They put out a collective pastoral at the end of the conference, in fact in the last few minutes of the conference when many of the bishops from more distant parts of the country had already left to go home to take care of their weekend responsibilities.[1]

The collective pastoral of the hierarchy has already been reported in the communications media—sometimes with curious obscurities and seeming conflicts. The obscurities and conflicts rise out of the instantaneous reporting out of context inevitably—since you can't quote a fifty-three page document during a station break or even in a news summary at the end of the day.

I hope that all our people will read the entire statement and read it with great care. I particularly hope that they will read it, not in order to justify some position or to find out the bishops' position only on any one subject on which any one of us may be "hung up", as the expression is, but in order to grasp something of the total theme of the Collective Pastoral. Most of the communications media—television, radio, and press—would leave you with the impression that the bishops discussed contraception and birth control all week. This is not at all the case. These are very grave problems—personal, familial, community in their dimension. But they are problems which have to be seen in their proper subordinate place in the total structure of the problem of contemporary life, contemporary culture, contemporary anguish. Some of the people in the

This address was delivered over KDKA Radio, Pittsburgh, Pennsylvania, on November 17, 1968.

world are more worried about war than they are about contraception. Some people are more worried about poverty than they are about birth regulation. Some people are worried about housing—where to find a place to place their weary heads—than they are about the details—extremely important both for time and eternity but in the total picture details—or morality on any one point.

And so it is hoped that people will read and, indeed, accept what the bishops have had to say on the subject of artificial contraception—it's essentially, of course, what the Holy Father said—because for the bishops, as for Catholics in general, the ordinary teaching authority of the pope is normative on the interpretation of Divine Law.

But it is hoped even more that readers will begin more and more to agree with Father Bernard Häring, who, during the past week, asked for an end of opposition to the Holy Father's encyclical and the beginning of a positive study of what the Pope had to say. In that positive study we believe that the commentary of the bishops who explicitly declared themselves to be teaching in collegial solidarity with the Pope will be helpful. But we hope even more, I repeat, that an effort will be made to read the *entire* Pastoral and to weight carefully what it has to say before one begins to react to it in specifics or isolated details or any point taken out of context.

The document was a very ambitious one. Its wide scope was made necessary by the wish of the bishops themselves. Last summer a letter was sent to all the bishops in the United States with a consultative ballot. That ballot asked the bishops to indicate whether or not they wished to include in their Collective Pastoral the discussion of some of the most controversial and debated questions of the moment, contraception among them, the encyclical *Humanae Vitae* among them, but the whole wide range of anxious social questions at the moment. The reply to the ballot was astonishing. It was sent out at a time when, I think, most people think the bishops are away in the mountains or at the beach; though there are a few of us among the bishops who haven't seen a mountain or a beach—for vacation purposes—in a long, long time. I think other people think that bishops never answer their mail, and, alas, some people have good reason to think it because some bishops have mail so piled up on so many subjects that they're very slow in answering even though they try eventually to do so. But in any case, two hundred and nineteen bishops answered within a very few days. Of these, one hundred ninety-four said that they wanted the Pastoral Letter to discuss the problem of contraception and abortion. Nineteen said they thought it would be better not to do so. One hundred sixty-one said they liked the encyclical [*Humanae Vitae*] and the Council's teaching on these matters to be recalled again. Seventeen thought it would be better not to do so. One hundred twenty-one said they would like a comment of some kind on the war in Vietnam, not necessarily for it, not necessarily against it, but to put it in something like perspective for the thinking of ourselves and our community. Sixty-four said they'd rather not. To the question of whether there should be discussion of selective conscientious objection, one hundred forty-one said yes, there should and that explicitly one way or another. Fifty-one said it wasn't ours to discuss at this moment. And other questions in connection with conscience and the morality of specific wars—one hundred forty-three said they wanted these discussed in their Pastoral, and forty-four said to wait. I find this a very impressive response. And it certainly indicates no desire on the part of the Catholic bishops of the United States to duck their responsibility to bear witness—whatever the content of the witness may be—on the questions which are agitating the whole community, their own people specifically, and the hearts of the priests and the bishops who are responsible for the guidelines to preaching and teaching to the people of God.

The result of the questionnaire and of over forty written letters—some of them at great length—from members of the hierarchy is a Collective Pastoral which is divided into two parts. One part is concerned with the Christian Family and its problems, and the other part is concerned with the Family of Nations and its problems. The two are held together by the theme of love for life, the defense of life, the promotion of life, the primacy of life, the analogy to God Himself that is present in human life.

The first chapter, the one on the Christian Family, discusses the family as a force for life, and in this connection it discusses responsible parenthood. It discusses the encyclical of Pope Paul VI and its content. It discusses the problem of conscience in connection with moral doctrine and how the teaching of the Church is always an essential factor in forming one's conscience.[2] It discusses some of the negative reactions to the encyclical and why these took place and what's to be done about them. And the special responsibility of theologians, particularly professional theologians, responsibly, prudently, honestly, but with regard to all the values involved to help clarify difficulties and set forth the truth. But it puts all this into wider context, as I indicated before: all the contemporary social problems of the family; and naturally we see a key to the resolution of these problems, or at least to the control of their more oppressive elements in the development of a refreshed, contemporary, family theology or family spirituality.

We have the feeling that sometimes we talk too much about moral theology or about doctrinal theology and too little about spiritual theology. So we make a plea on that point. We speak of the need for the education of children in human sexuality in a manner proportionate to their age but, none-theless, in a manner also proportionate to the development in them of healthy and holy attitudes. We speak of the problems of the changing family, particularly here in America, and the relationship to the problems of the family of needed social legislation—wage reforms, family allowances. We speak of the special problems of different types of families—large families to which the Church always pays its tribute because to these it is historically so indebted. We set forth the Catholic position on the question of abortion and the threat of changes in abortion legislation which, in our opinion, would constitute a very grave source of concern for all who love life.

The second chapter, on the Family of Nations, calls for an entirely new attitude toward war, the relationship of the message of the gospel to the development of such an attitude, the concept of peace as not merely the cessation of hostilities but, also, and more particularly, what Pope Paul called it before the United Nations when he said, "The modern word for peace is development."[3] He spoke of the need for arms control, the endorsement of reciprocal and collective disarmament and partial test-ban treaties, nonproliferation treaties. We quote the Council and the popes on the question of the arms race. And we make their position our own even in the case of our own country. Naturally, we ask for prayers for peace and stress the importance of these if a climate for peace is ever to be realized. We speak of the special responsibility of intellectuals and the contribution they can make to the development of a climate for peace and for building the necessary structures for an organized world order of justice to which charity will give an organic soul. We speak of our own admittedly limited efforts in this direction and those of our own country, and we make a strong plea for maximum foreign-aid programs dictated by unselfishness and by a concern for that development of peoples which Pope Paul insists is the essence of peace. And here, too, we speak of the role of conscience in connection with selective service and war. And through all this there runs, I repeat, an emphasis on passion for life and the primacy of life.

We end up quoting Moses, who was speaking for God when he said, "I call heaven and earth to witness against you this day, but I have set before you life and death; therefore, choose life that you and your descendants may live."[4] The Catholic bishops have pleaded with their people and our community to put themselves always on the side of life.

God bless you!

The Formal Call of the Synod

I take the occasion of this ceremonial observance of the one hundred and twenty-fifth anniversary of the Diocese of Pittsburgh to issue, for the record, our formal call of a diocesan Synod which, after its preparatory stages in 1969, is, please God, to conclude its business in 1970.

We choose this time for the calling of the Synod for many reasons. Its principal purpose is the systematic application to diocesan life, on every level, of the teachings of Vatican Council II. There has been time for study of these and a measure of experimentation where such was necessary; it is time now to get down to cases. Moreover, the whole Church is in the midst of the revision of its Code of Canon Law; at the same time the National Conference of our hierarchy is in the process of reconstructing its structures and procedures. Our own diocese has behind it two, approaching three, years of experience of its diocesan Pastoral Council. All this makes the Synod timely.

In fact, preliminary work of the Synod has been underway for some months. Its first general preparatory session will be held in this cathedral, the nearby Synod Hall and, if need be, the Cathedral High School auditorium on Sunday, February 9, at which time, according to a program to be sent out by Father Leo Vanyo, Executive Secretary of the Synod, we shall have, simultaneously and all together, the taking of their pledge of office by all the elected members of the Parish Committees, these elections being scheduled for the first Sunday in February.

This address was delivered at Saint Paul Cathedral, Pittsburgh, Pennsylvania, on December 8, 1968.

The General Coordinating Board of the Synod, under the honorary chairmanship of the senior Auxiliary Bishop, Bishop Leonard, and with executive implementation by Father Vanyo, has been at work these many months. The Coordinating Board is unique among the executive bodies of synods to date in that its leadership is made up of representatives of not only the clergy and religious but of the men and women of the laity. Under the auspices of these, the preparatory commissions to work out the agenda of the eventual Synod have been named; they will be announced this week. These commissions are made up of sixteen members each, plus an honorary chairman, two priest secretaries and selected nonvoting consultants appointed officially to serve as research people and to provide expert counsel to the working commissions of priests, laity, and religious. Additional such consultants may be named by me, as the work progresses, on an ecumenical basis.

The commissions are assigned to the preparation of materials for Synod action in the following areas of concern: worship or liturgy, the spiritual life of the diocese, the life and work of the clergy, the apostolic action and spiritual life of the laity, the witness and work of religious among us, the general question of Christian education, the participation of the Church in community affairs, the use of communications for the work of the Church and the service of souls, the ecumenical relations of our diocese, the pastoral government of the diocese, the deaneries, and the parishes, and the future planning of our financing, our stewardship over property, and our diocesan planning or development. There are other obvious concerns of the postconciliar Church which will find their due place on the agenda of the Synod but for which separate commissions have not yet, at least, been recommended; I mention only youth work (a major worry at all times), the apostolate of conversions here at home and of missionary action abroad. Others will think of other questions not less urgent.

In order to provide the climate of prayer essential to work so basic to the salvation of souls, so intimately bound up with the good of the Church, there has been established a special ad hoc committee to provide a year-round program of prayer during both years of the work of the Synod. This life-giving, sustaining *climate of prayer*, surrounding and energizing the deliberations at the Synod, will be the result of plans to be developed by a committee of diocesan and regular clergy, contemplative and active religious, laity young and old; the programs will reach the hospitalized, the aged, school children, the cloistered, the imprisoned—everyone who has a prayer to offer for the success of the Synod.

A brief, formal word is in order on the nature of a Synod. A Synod is a consultative body called into session by the bishop of a diocese. It is the diocese, the Church in miniature, at work with its local bishop in the self-study, the planning of the self-renewal, essential to the refreshing and, where need be, re-direction of its work.

In the case of the present Synod, it is an organized, thought-through application to our diocese, in this place, at this time, of the teachings and the spirit of the Second Vatican Council. Nothing is more structured than is a Synod. Nothing calls for more careful organization. Nothing should be given more thought, especially the thinking in the heart which, the Scriptures imply, saves the land from desolation.

Traditionally Synods have been limited to the clergy. Ours will not be. It will include, always within the canonically organized structure of the parish, the deanery and the diocese, laity, religious, and clergy. Our Catholic instinct would wish us to hear the responsible thoughts, recommendations, and sentiments of all who have anything they think worth saying, and that the Synod finds worth hearing, on the proper business and concerns of a diocesan Synod. That same Catholic instinct, however, suggests that we not be drawn afield from the broad but fixed path of the Synod's agenda.

Within these structures, maximum freedom of discussion

not only prevails but is always in order, indeed, devoutly desired. The bishop of this diocese will act without fear or favor in confirming, modifying, or rejecting whatever proposals come through the structures of the Synod. He will do so with the better grace and the more responsibly because he will expect all who work within the Synod to speak similarly without fear or favor. It will be assumed that they, as he tries to do, speak with great love for the Church, with a holy regard for due process and a decent respect for the gifts of others.

A brief description of a Synod, as extant Church law conceives it, is provided by Fathers Bouscaren and Ellis. According to them, the diocesan Synod is a consultative body which, according to the law, is supposed to be called by the bishop every ten years to consider measures for the welfare of the clergy and the people of the diocese. (I note in passing that this Synod will begin its preparatory work in the tenth year that it has been my privilege to serve as bishop here in Pittsburgh.) It is convened and presided over by the bishop. It is held in the cathedral church. Those who must be called and must attend the Synod are the vicars-general, the diocesan consultors, the rector of the seminary, the rural deans, a deputy from each collegiate church, the pastors of the city where the Synod is held, at least one superior from every clerical and religious institute in the diocese, and at least one pastor from each deanery. In addition to these, the bishop may invite others also to the Synod with the same consultative voice unless the invitation provides otherwise. In our Synod all the clergy of the diocese, religious and secular, are invited to take part by the invitation issued in today's *call*. So are the laity duly elected from the parish committees, and the laity and religious appointed by the bishop on recommendation of the synodal executives. The agenda of our Synod will be prepared by the mixed working commissions already described and which have been appointed so that they can begin, effective immediately, their study of our existing legislation or customs on

487

the points pertinent to their respective commissions and can weigh against the existing legislation or customs the eventual recommendations they will receive from the deanery discussions, study groups, and the deanery commissions parallel to those at work on the diocesan level.

What is the purpose of this historic Synod? It is, as I have already indicated, to apply to our diocese the teachings and spirit of the Second Vatican Council, not the one without the other, nor either without reference to the other, but both together, *literally* in the case of the teaching, *fully* in the case of the spirit. It is to do for the diocese what the Council sought to do for the Church, the Church universal. Our purpose in calling the Synod, then, is that of Pope John in calling the Ecumenical Council and which Pope Paul has summed up in these words:

> To reawaken, reform, rejuvenate the Church; to enlighten her conscience, to strengthen her forces, to purify her defects; to strengthen her structures, to widen her frontiers, to recompose her unity; to prepare her for new defenses and new contacts with the world; to place her in renewed contact with her own sources and at the same time to hasten her fruitful journey toward the eschatological goal of her final open and glorious meeting with Christ her Lord.[1]

What results may we expect? Among the many specific realizations of the broad purposes to which I have appealed there are certain concrete results especially to be desired of our Synod. I name the following: first, the organization of our own presbyterium, the structurally, organically united body of all the clergy, compactly united with the bishop in all things, with all the committees and commissions needed to provide for the well-being of the clergy but, and especially, the service of the people of God who constitute our diocese both by their visible membership in it or by their presence in the corner of the world where we are commissioned to teach and to bring the influence of Christ; second, the reform of our Diocesan Pastoral Council so that it may, to the fullest measure, be consistent with the letter and spirit of Vatican Council II, bringing together clergy, religious, and laity in a collaborative effort, again with the bishop, to discover and accomplish God's will for and Christ's work in our diocese; third, the fuller and more wholesome entrance into the active life of the diocese of all orders in the Church, the clergy through the organized presbyterium, the laity and religious in what the Council declares to be their part in the active work of the redemption as well as the enjoyment of the fruits of the redemption, all this in union with one another and with the bishop. Since in the Holy Catholic Church there has never been, there is not now, there never will be the presence and proper action of the Church except when all, though each responds to his grace and exercises his charism (*does his thing*), are at one with the bishop in the unity which Pope Paul describes as the organic pastoral action of a total ecclesial community, for such is a diocese.

A fourth concrete result of our Synod should be to render more effective the presence of the laity in the life of the diocese: this would be the updated implementation and fuller realization of the purposes of our parish committees, not as lay committees, not as clerical committees, but as parish committees, perhaps councils, but in any instance representative boards in the form that seems best suited to our diocese, to its needs in this moment of history, and to the letter and spirit of the Vatican Council.

Further, and greatly to be desired, is the decentralization of responsibility and, in this sense, authority within the diocese by the strengthening of the deaneries along the lines, but beyond the limits toward which we have been working since the *New Year's Letter to the Clergy*, in 1966.[2] This is essential if the principle of subsidiarity is to become a creative force for the intensification of the life of the Church and the increase of its service to the local communities in a diocese like ours. Our *subdivisions*—they must never be divisions among us—even these, cannot be on ethnic, age group, vocations with the Church, or occupational lines, even among the clergy, certainly not in the community of faith, love, and service that is a local Church, the Diocese of Pittsburgh.

Our concept of the diocese, in the Synod as always, will be that of the *Church in miniature*, and therefore our effort will be to reproduce, through the Synod, in the diocese what the Second Vatican Council attempted in the universal Church. After all, the most exact description of the Church is that of a diocese, and the best description of a diocese is that description of the Church which Saint Ignatius of Antioch gave and which was a theme of the *Dogmatic Constitution on the Church* in the Second Vatican Council. The Church is a community, Saint Ignatius said. It is a community of Christ, gathered around the bishop, who, as the representative of Christ, celebrates the Eucharist, guarantees the unity of the local Church, and exercises and ensures its catholicity by his union with the other bishops.

To make good this concept in all our practices, in our laws and regulations, our teaching, our liturgy, our very spirit, the final practical effect of the Synod should be our spiritual renewal, the quickening of the Faith among us, without which all the rest is no more than theological nit-picking, mere canonical machinery, the logistics of a pointless army moving nowhere.

In all this work of the Synod during 1969 and 1970 we shall have certain norms. These norms will not be verified in catch-phrases like *conservative* or *progressive* or *moderate* or *liberal*—words which, as presently bandied about, have little or no meaning in the long-range life of the Church. In the Catholic Church, words are not canonized; persons are. What we shall be looking for in the Synod, counting on God to provide among the persons identified with the Synod, will be these qualities: first, openness of mind and of heart to the inspirations of the Spirit, a quality that can be present in *conservatives* who guard with love or in *liberals* who seek with love; second, commitment to the Church as the living personal presence of Christ in history but also, quite frankly, as an institution, the institution provided by Jesus to achieve his purposes in so organized and structured a world as ours is; third, an authentically Catholic spirit characterized, therefore, by *stability*, an attachment to all that is valid out of the past, and yet *sensitivity*, awareness of the needs of change wherever change is God's will, whether or not it is man's desire.

In brief, then, the norms governing the procedures and decisions of our Synod will be: (1) the sound traditions of this century-and-a-quarter-old diocese; (2) the needs of the diocese in the present moment and for the measurable future; (3) both of these studied against the documents of the Second Vatican Council.

In evaluating our traditions and interpreting our needs we are not walking in darkness. The Spirit walks with us and has given us, through the Vatican Council, a body of teachings which can and must serve as our guide and our stimulus to renewal and development. The constitutions, decrees, and declarations of Vatican Council II will be our compass. They provide the indispensable combination of a coherent and sound tradition and a continuous guide for our movement toward a Christianity ever more alive and authentic, toward a Church in its every part always her essential, ancient self and at the same time always young and ever new.

And so everything discussed at the Synod, certainly everything voted in the Synod, and most certainly everything finally promulgated in the Synod, must be checked against chapter and verse of the documents of the Second Vatican Council. These and their authentic interpretations and guidelines, as provided by the Holy See and by the consensus of the American hierarchy, will be our basic constitutional documents, so to say, our Magna Carta. At this stage in the updating of a typical American diocese, there is no point in attempting to anticipate any hypothetical Vatican Council III or any illusory coming great Church. We must deal with the Church as it is against the sure standard of the documents we have. In any direction lies the arbitrariness that leads to chaos, and of that we shall not be guilty. Our purpose to apply Vatican Council II is an objective more than ambitious enough; this is our clear mandate and our compelling necessity.

In token of all this, I am giving into the care of Father Vanyo's office a gift of the Holy Father to each of us who took part in the Council. It is the official text, without glosses or commentary or questionings, of all that the Council actually decreed, declared, or taught; it will serve, in the sense I have indicated and within the usual norms, as the universal norm against which to check our local efforts.

We shall not wish our eventual synodal guidelines or legislation—it is still an open question what proportion of either will be profitable—to be doctrinaire or to reflect an inbred reading of the Council's mind and will. And so we shall be willing to learn from the experiences of other churches than that of Pittsburgh or those of America; as in the past, so in the present and for the future, we must learn from peoples elsewhere or in other times. The American Church, and the Diocese of Pittsburgh is in every aspect an example of the American Church, has learned through the experiences of every church. Our daily lives reflect the manner in which we have profited by these experiences.

Works like the Saint Vincent de Paul, the Propagation of the Faith Society, some of our patterns of religious life or piety, are all reminders of our debt to the experience of the Church in France. The Legion of Mary, temperance movements, many of our devotions, the Newman Clubs—these reflect our indebtedness to the experience of the Church in Ireland, in England, in the British Isles in general. The patterns of our schools, many of our religious orders, our bent for Christian social action bespeak our indebtedness to the experience of the Church in Germany. No small part of our religious culture, our customs, the memories of our saints we owe to the Church in Poland, Lithuania, Croatia, Slovakia, Italy, and elsewhere. We are already learning much, and we have vastly more to learn from the new churches of Africa and Asia as well as the older churches of the lands from which our ancestors came.

We remain open to the experiences of the various Catholic traditions everywhere in the world so long as their fruits conform with our local genius and our needs. The other Christian churches, the believing world, that of the *peoples of the Book* especially, human history and all human experiences have their contributions to make to our correction, our guidance, our profit. But in what pertains to the Faith we are a Church completely in communion with Rome. No experience in any land will at any time come between us and our complete identity in communion of faith and order with Rome. We understand and accept what Saint Patrick said to the Irish—what the founding fathers of the churches everywhere said one way or another to their peoples in the time of their beginnings: "You are Christians. Be also Romans!"

Profiting, then, from whatever experience anywhere, near or far, may be conducive to our intellectual, pastoral, or sociological growth and consistent with our Roman communion in faith; profiting from the memory of the lessons taught by the experiences of our own peoples here in this already-venerable corner of the world; profiting from an honest reading of the signs of the times and, again, from the letter and the spirit of the Second Vatican Council, we shall seek in this diocesan Synod to strengthen for the present task and the future opportunity this holy Church of Pittsburgh. We cannot imagine a better way to observe its one hundred and twenty-fifth anniversary, to meet our debt in gratitude to it, or to help it meet its responsibilities to the universal Church and the community around it.

493

XLIX

Statement upon Being Named a Cardinal

This news is bewildering. As of this minute, I am not sure what it means, except that a lot of people had better do a lot of praying.

As a priest I can already do everything that I could possibly do as a cardinal in the way of that which chiefly matters, like the sacramental service of souls and the preaching of the glory of God.

As a bishop I can do special works for peace, for the defense of the Faith, for social justice, for the intellectual life, for the reconciliation of God's people.

I hope that as a cardinal I can help even more, certainly not less!

Knowing Pope Paul on the basis of all things he says and does, I am sure that he intends his cardinals do more, not less. He will always get a ready response from me.

A cardinal has special ties with the Holy Roman Church. But no scarlet cords could possibly tie me more closely to Rome and to the Church Universal over which the Bishop of Rome holds the "presidency of charity" than do all the loves I have shared all my life with the parents, family, brother-priests, devout sisters, lay associates, and friends whom God has given me so generously.[1]

Many of the dearest among these friends and co-workers are not in full communion with Rome, but as much as any they have shared the intellectual and spiritual pieties which have made me glad, through the years of my priesthood, *to echo Christ with a Roman heart*. One of my most cherished Protestant

This statement was delivered at The Bishop's House, Pittsburgh, Pennsylvania, on March 28, 1969.

teachers introduced me to the Latin poem from which I took my motto as a bishop: *"Resonare Christum corde Romano."*[2]

I particularly hope that the people in the area served by the Diocese of Pittsburgh—all of them without exception, my own people and our neighbors of every color, ethnic culture, and creed who have been so generous, so good to me—are grateful that the Holy Father thought of this corner of the world when he was choosing members of his College of Cardinals.

Pittsburgh deserves the salute implicit in this news. Our diocese is the Church in miniature; our six counties are America in small scale. Every culture is here; every nationality; every ethnic group; every kind and condition of Adam's breed, of God's children, of Christ's brethren. And the plain fact is that, despite occasional family tensions, we all love one another. Moreover, we all know it!

Now we must pray for one another, all of us in the whole community, with greater love and more than ever. Ten years have taught me the strength that comes from the prayers of Pittsburgh priests, Pittsburgh sisters, Pittsburgh lay people—Catholic, Protestant, Jewish, and kindly sceptics all included.[3]

L

The Resurrection: Fact or Myth?

All over the world and almost every day people are revealing one or another "hang-up" about the Faith.

Some of these difficulties pertain to precepts of the Christian moral code. Others touch on dogmas of the Christian Creed, including its sources in the authoritative witness of the Church and in the claims of Christ Himself. All the points challenged, whether doctrinal or moral, involve "hard sayings" among the teachings of Christ in His Church, like the "hard sayings" concerning the presence of Christ in the Eucharist which prompted some of his earliest followers to exclaim: "This is more than we can stomach! Why listen to such words?" And they walked no more with Him, the Gospel declares.[1]

Easter is a time to think of "hard sayings" which many of Christ's present-day disciples find *hard to stomach*, intolerable burdens on human reason, impossible of acceptance. The Paschal mystery is one of these.

From the first days of reflection on the mystery of Christ's coming among us, men have found the central event of that mystery, His Resurrection, a stumbling block, and have attempted to *talk it away*. Saint Matthew's Gospel records one of the first such efforts. Faced with the fact of an empty tomb, the enemies of Christ contrived this explanation: "Say that His disciples came by night and stole the body while we were asleep."[2]

Side by side with ready and literal acceptance of the Resurrection through all the centuries since the first Easter stand attempts to explain or to explain away the Scripture story. The

This Pastoral Letter, issued during Holy Week 1969, was addressed to the clergy, religious, and laity of the Diocese of Pittsburgh, Pennsylvania.

approaches vary. They range from radical views like those of Ernest Renan and David Friedrich Strauss, which reduce the Resurrection to the result of subjective visions in the minds of emotionally exhausted disciples, to the milder current discussions concerning the nature of a *historical event* when faith or feeling are involved.

We are told, for example, that the Resurrection of Jesus is a *myth* in a somewhat special sense of the word. It is argued that the story of the raising of Jesus reflects influences of Oriental mythologies about many ancient divinities. It is related of these that they had suffered the human fate of death but had triumphantly risen again from the dead.

What do we mean when we say that Christ has risen, literally and historically, from the dead? For one thing, such a claim runs counter to human experience. Perhaps the Gospel accounts should be seen as symbolic. Perhaps, as some assert, His followers, as a community of charity and good deeds, in carrying on Christ's work with lively love inspired by Him, renew the life by which He went about doing good and thus become a Risen Christ. Might we not say, with such scholars as Rudolf Bultmann, that the Resurrection is an expression of man's conviction that the origin and the purpose of the world in which he lives are to be sought not within it but beyond it, without getting bogged down in speculations about a body brought back to physical life? For many, even among *practicing* Christians, this seems sufficient since it enables them to get on with the work (which, they point out, matters most) rather than worry about details of dogma, even on a doctrine which gives the work its point, its sustaining power, and its sure direction.

Perhaps the Resurrection of Christ is more an expression of the force of His personality, His spiritual influence which transcends all barriers, even death itself, and which does not depend, it is suggested, on physical or bodily presence. Even after Calvary, could not His captivating and luminous personality live on in Christ's followers through their ardent faith in Him and in His mission? Why not just as well say that this is His Resurrection and that He is, therefore, still with us? Had He not said that wherever two or three would be gathered in His name, there He would be in their midst?

Perhaps some *cosmic Christ* of eventual human perfection is meant when we speak of the Easter event, rather than the physical person of Jesus of Nazareth. After all, Christ did accomplish the mission of setting men on their way to a higher social consciousness and a more sublime understanding and eventual perfection of human nature. Need we constantly rely so on the figure of the Son of Mary resurrected in the flesh? Perhaps the account of the Resurrection of the Galilean as a historical event is only for the *crowd*, for their consolation and strengthening, while the *enlightened* may understand its meaning from a higher viewpoint proportionate to their greater intellectual sophistication and spiritual sensitivity. And so why need we insist that Christ has literally risen from the dead?

Saint Paul took to writing against these views—ever with us, never new—in his earliest letters to the Corinthians. He was clearly appalled by the prospects for the faith and the very lives of Christians if full awareness and acceptance of the historical fact of the physical Resurrection of Jesus were to be forfeited or even diminished. "He has appeared to Cephas, and afterwards to the twelve. Then He appeared to over five hundred of our brothers at once, most of whom are still alive, though some have died. Then He appeared to James and afterwards to all the apostles."[3]

Saint Paul clearly understood that the Person to Whom the Church prays and in Whom Christians believe is Christ the Lord, enthroned in great power and majesty, but Paul well knew that his Lord is the same Jesus of Nazareth Who was crucified and now is risen in a manner that not merely compels faith but convinces eyewitnesses.

The other early followers of Jesus proclaimed Him Lord even as do we. It is precisely because of the Resurrection that they did so, as it is because of the Resurrection that we do so. We cannot make a distinction between the Lord Who is God and Jesus Who is Man. The Faith of the apostles, as ours does, says that Jesus the Carpenter is Christ the Risen Lord. He is gone into the kingdom of death and emerged again the same Person, not a phantasm, not a being so transformed but that He is still identical with the Jew Whose accents Magdalen knew, still recognized by gestures familiar to His friends, as, for example, in the breaking of bread. He is God's Son with new clarity, but still Mary's flesh.

Saint John, who had multiple titles to trustworthiness in identifying the Master, recounts the glory of the Risen Lord in the grand apocalyptical "I am the beginning and the end, the first and the last, the alpha and the omega".[4] But it is no *mythical* personality to whom he refers, no ideal *cosmic Christ* yet to be. The eyes of the Risen Lord are those that looked at him so many times, the feet are those that had walked many miles with him in Palestine, the voice is that same voice he had heard and loved so often. This is Jesus. It is the Jesus of the Last Supper close to Whom he had eaten, the Jesus of Calvary Whose agonies he had witnessed and Whose provisions for His Mother's care he would implement. And this Jesus is the Lord. The Jesus of history and the Christ of faith are one. And that is what our Faith proclaims. *He is risen as He said!*

True, John had heard (even as had the others) the pledge of His mystical presence, even to the end of time, among those who would gather in His name. But he had also heard the promises of the renewed physical presence of His Master, restored from death after three days, and it is this promise that John proclaims as fulfilled at Easter.

Our Faith illumines us not with *how* this all came to be, but only with the *what* and the *why* of the events of the first Easter. We are required, if we be Christians in any full sense, to believe that Christ is risen even as He said He would be. We are told this as a fact and asked to hold it in faith. For only faith can make sense out of this Easter event. There is no possibility nor point in God's plan of knowing how this Israelite of Galilee could rise, conquering death. No science, no intellectual insight, can yield the Faith to which the witnesses of that fact lay claim when they testify: Christ is risen.

I have seen the Lord! Mary Magdalen, in the garden of the empty tomb, saw the Lord and so testified to the apostles and to the early Church; through them she testifies to all subsequent Christians. Those five words, the original good news, contain the essential message of Christianity. For the believer, the testimony handed down from generation to generation gives rise to faith sufficient for each also to say Christ is risen. Jesus rose, and therefore men believe in Him, strive to do His Will, and seek to identify with Him by faith in His teaching and imitation of His deeds. So has it been since the garden of Easter, since Emmaus, since the Cenacle, since Pentecost— and all because of things seen, heard, touched, known.

Jean Guitton, in his book *Jesus: The Eternal Dilemma*, sums up this point of fact and logic. The first articles of Faith, the first hymns to Christ in a just-beginning liturgy, the words of Saint Paul and the other writers in the New Testament Epistles, the deeds of the apostles as recorded in the Book of the Acts, the observations of the Roman magistrates—these all assure us of the fact that the first followers worshiped Jesus, adored Him, and that, in these often-divided communities comprised of Jews and pagans, there was no argument at all on this point. It was Jesus Who was risen.

It is frequently pointed out that the New Testament biblical writers were not trying to write documented scientific history or systematic biography. It is said that their writings were, in an honest sense, *propaganda*, enthusiastic proclamations. All this is true enough, but we must not be misled by such descriptions. Enthusiasm is not its own source. This propaganda was the work of conscientious men supremely concerned with serving and spreading *truth*; their enthusiasm was not in a vacuum or directed toward an abstraction. It was a response to a *fact* involving a *person*.

The *fact* was precisely the Resurrection; the *person* was Jesus Christ, Whose risen life they proclaimed with the same fervor and conviction as they proclaimed His death. It was not an abstraction that died on the Cross. Nor was it a ghost that rose from the dead. The witnesses to both events were the same. This *fact* is set forth thus by Saint Paul: "First and foremost, I handed on to you the facts which have been imparted to me: that Christ died for our sins, in accordance with the Scriptures; that He was buried; that He was raised to life on the third day, according to the Scriptures."[5] A special solemnity was attached to the truth of this fact by Paul: "If there be no resurrection, then Christ was not raised; and if Christ was not raised, then our gospel is null and void, and so is your faith."[6] Nothing could be more candid, more clear, more cogent.

For us the Resurrection is, then, not simply one among many articles of Faith; it is the heart of the matter, the beginning of the Christian experience, the cornerstone of the Christian Creed, the central premise of Christian liturgical cult. We believe it on the witness of others, as men do all things that they believe. But for those chosen in God's Providence to be the witnesses whom we believe, the Resurrection was an objective experience. They not only believed; they *saw* the Lord. Their testimony was to a fact and to a fact that gives origin, purpose, and substance to everything we mean by Christianity.

The scriptural texts are without ambiguity. The object of their testimony does not rest on the vague affirmation that Christ is alive, somehow, somewhere, but directly and concretely on the physical reality of a resurrected body, the body of a Person they well know and recognize.

Cardinal Daniélou, facing up to the question of whether we

have here a *myth* or a reality in his recent work *La Résurrection*, flatly states the issue: the word *resurrection* does not have two senses. Either it signifies that the body of Christ lay no longer in the tomb, but was alive by the power of God and, therefore, able to be unmistakably identified as He always had been by the witnesses—or it signifies nothing. It is at this point that the precision of the witnesses takes on great seriousness. They invoke the words of the Risen Christ Himself to express and confirm their certainty: "See My hands and My feet. Touch Me and see; no ghost has flesh and bones as you can see that I have. Place your fingers here, see My hands; reach your hand here and put it into My side; be not unbelieving but believe."[7]

The apostles and their disciples are the witnesses of the Risen Lord, not because they first believed, but because they *saw* Him and therefore believed. It is on account of their testimony, transmitted to us by the living Church, that we believe. In the same sense that the apostles are the witnesses to all that Jesus said and did in Judea and Jerusalem, they are the witnesses to the Resurrection and its results.

It is this view of the testimony of the disciples concerning the Risen Christ that sustains us when some question the historicity of the accounts of the Resurrection. Despite the enthusiasm of the evangelists and their intense commitments, the narrative of the Resurrection still remains history. The loving faith of the authors of the Gospels does not annul the historical value of the events they felt obliged to proclaim. The fact that they related these events with joyful fervor should confirm rather than call into question the reality of what they saw. The confrontation with the Risen Christ is the fact that the Gospels are intent on relating; the testimony to the Resurrection had this fact as its point of departure.

Concerning the reliability of the Gospels as historical documents, recent studies have, if anything, confirmed their basic historicity. Common to them all is the one tradition, in various forms, that Jesus proclaimed the Kingdom of God, was crucified, died, was buried, and rose again on the third day.

If asked what happened on Easter morning, the convert Paul, the ardent John, the doubting Thomas, the discouraged pilgrims to Emmaus, the faithful women, the temperamental Peter, all the diverse company of the infant Church would have replied not in terms of the mystery of *how* but in terms merely of *what* they knew as facts: we saw an empty tomb; we saw the Risen Lord; we talked with Him, walked with Him, planned with Him—and we now bear witness to all this for all mankind.

For the *why* of the Resurrection we must turn to the meditative passages, the theology, so to say, of Scripture, as distinct from the passages recording events. Christ is risen, and in the mystery of His person lies the answer to what the Resurrection means for those who believe in Him.

Saint Paul explains to the Corinthians and Romans that Christ's Resurrection is a pledge of our own life to come in an immortality as personal as that of Christ and in an eventual resurrection as real. It is through the Resurrection of Christ that the human body finds its place in God's great plan for redemption and in the Catholic tradition of Christian humanism. "If the Spirit of Him who raised Jesus from the dead dwells within you, then the God Who raised Jesus Christ from the dead will also give new life to your mortal bodies through His indwelling Spirit."[8]

This is the Christian premise for the rejection of all Manichaeanism, Jansenism, Puritanism, or like heresies which see the body as irredeemably evil, mere dirt, or otherwise debased—heresies the names and historic forms of which we do well continually to recall if we are not forever to repeat their errors and endure their evils. It is also the foundation of the Christian humanism which accepts all God's gifts, above all life, as good and disposes us to exercise purposeful and fruitful dominion over them.

The Resurrection is also our release from fear. It was in anticipation of this victory that Christ bade His followers to fear not, since He had overcome the world. Above all, the believer in the Resurrection is freed from fear of death. Nor is his fearlessness the forlorn courage of the Stoic; it is warm with the promise of the traditional Preface of the Mass for the Dead:

In the same Christ the hope of a blessed resurrection has dawned for us, bringing all who are under the certain, sad sentence of death the consoling promise of future immortality. For those who have been faithful, life is not ended but merely changed, and when this earthly abode dissolves, an eternal dwelling place awaits them in heaven.[9]

This hope has its firm foundation on the fact that Christ is risen. The Father Who raised up Jesus pledges in and through Jesus His life-giving power to the bodies of all who die, as did Jesus, obedient to His will. It is the work of His Spirit to prepare us for the day when the Resurrection will accomplish in each of us, if we be faithful, all that God did for our Elder Brother and Lord.

This will be finally and universally achieved at the Lord's return in final judgment. But in the meantime the Spirit of life works within the soul of each of us:

We are citizens of heaven and from heaven we expect our deliverer to come, the Lord Jesus Christ. He will transfigure the body belonging to our humble state, and give it a form like that of His own resplendent body, by the very power which enables Him to make all things subject to Himself.[10]

By His death He would be glorified, said Jesus, and through Him, we also. "The hour has come for the Son of Man to be glorified. In truth, I tell you, a grain of wheat remains a solitary grain unless it falls into the ground and dies, but if it dies it becomes a rich harvest."[11] It is for this reason that Jesus' death is a glorification; His life is given up, offered in sacrifice through His death, in order that it may have a permanent, redeeming effect. He sought to win by His death a new life for all men, and the first fruit of that new life in His own Resurrection.

Through His Resurrection Christ releases in history and to all men the Spirit of God. This Spirit, the Spirit of Truth and of Love, gives life to all men who accept Him.

"The words that I have spoken to you are spirit and life."[12] The Resurrection is the act by which that life-giving Spirit is let loose in the world. So we are not only confronted in the Resurrection of Christ with a pledge of a life to come, but we are given clues as to the manner of our share in the life of God's life-giving Spirit. But all these hints of the *why* of the Resurrection depend on the *fact* that Jesus is risen.

When we say "I believe in Jesus Christ Who rose again from the dead . . . and in the resurrection of the body and the life of the world to come" we are only repeating what the author of the Apocalypse meant years earlier: "Jesus is the living one . . . I died and behold I live forevermore."[13]

Paul Claudel, writing on the resurrection of the body, speaks of how, by His Resurrection, Jesus makes the continuity of this life and the life of the world to come clear to our mortal eyes: human life, he says, will continue. Our Savior's assurance is formal: "There where I am, you also will be." Our life after death will thus be His life. In the world beyond we shall not be exiled; there will be no radical change. We shall pass from the world of effects to the world of cause. Instead of seeing reality in terms of its effects, we shall see it—in God—in terms of cause.

There are other implications in the *why* of the Resurrection, especially for an age that speaks so frequently of *meaning* and *value*, of *personal worth* and *human dignity*. With the Resurrection of Christ, the whole perspective of life is changed. Man can now look at a world and a humanity great with meaning not only in itself as the result of its divine creation but also in its re-creation by a redemption and renewal not less divine; the Christian can see all creation, above all its human stewards, against the horizon of the ultimate realities of a life to come as well as against those of its own space-time validities.

With what our elders in the Faith used to call the *perspective of eternity*, we can approach each day, its vexations, its joys, its threatening problems, and its fleeting consolations. We have here no lasting city; but whatever our worth, our dignity, our value, it is immeasurably increased when we see it in the light of a life to come that knows no end. What an irony it would be if human life, so rich with promise, so limitless in its hopes, so determined to survive in the face of whatever outrage or affliction, were confined within the tragic dimensions of a body that begins to die at birth.

Gabriel Marcel once spoke with great force to this point. The world today, he said, can be endured only if one's spirit is riveted on this hope in the Resurrection. For us Christians living today, something especially influences us to believe in the resurrection of the body; it is, for example, what we know the body endured in the concentration camps. One feels that human flesh has undergone such intolerable outrage that it must receive some kind of reparation in glory. I believe life today is unendurable if one's spirit is not rooted in the hope of our creed. If this hope were shared by a greater number, perhaps a respect for the flesh and for the body, so terribly lacking in our time, would be restored.

Marcel's reflection suggests new (and intensely relevant) points for contemporary meditation on the fuller theological content and social message of Saint Paul's insistence that those who suffer with Christ, not only in spirit but even in their bodies, are destined to share the glory of His Resurrection: "For I reckon that the sufferings of this time are not worthy to be compared with the glory to come, that shall be revealed in us."[14] "Always bearing about in our body the mortification of Jesus, that the life also of Jesus may be made manifest in our bodies. . . ."[15]

To a world permeated by relativism, the Resurrection, set forth as a historical fact, stands for a complex of values based on absolutes. To an age beset with fear, doubt, and rumors of worse things yet to come, the Resurrection heralds a joyous triumph over death, a victory over time, but also the reality of justice and a judgment to come. It is an anchor of steady mooring in a world buffeted by the waves of relativism, lack of vision, even despair.

Those in suffering, in frustration, in abandon, the Resurrection consoles with the hope by which Job in the Old Testament was sustained. "This I know, that my Avenger lives and he, the Last, will take his stand on earth. After my awakening, he will set me close to him and from my flesh I shall look on God."[16]

Ours is a generation frequently close to tears, often short on joy. Its mood is that of the melancholy disciples described by Saint Luke in what I, at least, have always found one of the most touching and persuasive of all the passages in Scripture. They were crushed by the crucifixion and burial of Jesus. They are described as sad, men who used to hope but no longer do. Their hope was restored when Jesus Himself joined them on their journey and they returned to Jerusalem saying, "The Lord is risen indeed, and hath appeared to Simon."[17]

In a day and to a culture similarly diminished in hope and tempted to forfeit faith itself, the Church, remembering the Resurrection, sings its Easter refrain: *"This is the day that the Lord has made; let us rejoice and be glad in it."* And we, with joy restored and faith reborn, echo Saint Paul: *"Rejoice, again I say it, rejoice!"* For Christ indeed is risen and has obtained for us new life.

Let us live, beginning now and here below, the Paschal life with joy. Faith always expresses itself in joy. Joy is the evidence of lively faith at work in a person or a community, even as melancholy is the sign of faith compromised or troubled.

May the faith that gives substance to our joy be faith precisely in the Risen Christ and in the Church that remembers

His Resurrection! Such faith the Risen Jesus Himself described as being even more praiseworthy than the faith of the witnesses who beheld Him with eyes of flesh: "Because thou hast seen Me, Thomas, thou hast believed: Blessed are they that have not seen and have believed."[18]

Let us devote the renewed life that the Church transmits to us from the first Easter to the works of peace. Those works bring to pass a renewal by which we, the Church which is the Body of Christ, and all creation are continually refreshed in holiness and truth. They are the works of that peace so frequent on the lips of our Lord, a peace which He alone can give us, though the world cannot, because He has overcome the world.

LI

The Church and the Urban Crisis

Last year at our meeting in St. Louis we issued a statement on the so-called national race crisis.[1] This conference of bishops then placed upon the Social Development Department a mandate to respond by word and deed to the report of the National Advisory Commission on Civil Disorders. It is time for an interim accounting to this body.

Accepting the basic position of that report—that racism has permeated our population and our institutions—we renounced the masochistic satisfactions of breast-beating and recrimination of self or of others. We committed "our full energies to the task of eradicating the effects of racism on American society".[2]

Specifically, we declared that we would endeavor to build bridges of justice, compassion, and understanding by entering into full dialogue on matters of substantial interest with members of minority groups.[3]

Within the Catholic community we pledged to strive toward:

a. total eradication of any elements of discrimination in our . . . institutions.

b. to use our resources responsibly and generously in view of the urgent needs of the poor.[4]

In the general community we accepted, over and above our internal Catholic responsibilities, a need for openness to ecumenical planning and a united religious front as the mode of action most likely to be effected. Here we promised co-ordinated efforts to raise substantial funds needed for the implementation of local programs, and continuing interfaith

This paper was delivered at Washington, D.C., on April 16, 1969, during the General Meeting of the National Conference of Catholic Bishops.

efforts to push for enactment of critically needed legislation in the fields of employment, housing, health, and welfare.[5]

A year has passed. Whatever we may or may not have done during that year, we *know* more. For one thing, we know more about the problems; for another, we know more about our potential and more about our limitations.

At a press conference at the St. Louis meeting, I was asked how far the Church was prepared to go. I did have enough sense to say that whatever we or anyone else did, the job would require the rest of the century to get it done. A little flippantly, I said we would have "to go for broke". I have since discovered that some of us are already broke—and deep in debt as a result of commitments already made, many of which, indirectly at least, face up to the problem. Typical of these commitments were and are the schools and centers built in once-flourishing parishes and now still maintained in the inner city where the Church has remained at work with new peoples.

But now we can look back over a year of effort. In reviewing our commitments of last April, it seems clear that in some areas real and measurable progress has been made. In others we are still at the starting line. In all areas, the need far outdistances our efforts and the employment of our resources to date. The plain fact is that the need exceeds our resources, actual and potential. But we agreed in St. Louis that this fact, while it might explain failure to solve the problem, would not excuse failure to act.

As an aid in implementing the goals we outlined for ourselves we set up within the Social Development Department the National Task Force on Urban Problems. This task force has been in operation for a little over eight months. Although its staff is not large, it is already representative of the color and interest groups involved in the problem, and it is beginning its role of coordinating Catholic offices and organizations in developing programs aimed at the twin problems of poverty and racist attitudes. The task force, working with diocesan and other Church structures, is sparking cooperative programs in the critical areas of education, housing, employment, health, and welfare.

Most of our programming is of necessity organized along diocesan lines, close to the problem and to the widely diverse forms that it takes in a nation so vast as ours. Therefore, any fruits of our efforts will be seen at the local level. Perhaps the best results of the National Task Force have been to promote diocesan task forces, suggest programs for them, and stimulate local action, the lines and results of which have been shared through the national office with the increasing numbers of local forces.

The National Task Force has conducted eighteen regional conferences, and to date 126 diocesan task force directors have been appointed and are heading programs that are in various stages of development, some substantial.

Most of our programs have been unified in the task force concept for less than six months, and hard data are not yet available from throughout the country. Nevertheless we do have enough information to see in outline at least both the strengths and weaknesses of this approach.

These diocesan programs are as varied as the dioceses themselves and are not easily described or summarized in a report such as this. But some indication of their efforts can be seen from a survey last month of fifty-four dioceses.

Forty out of the fifty-four had programs underway in the field of housing, either under direct Catholic auspices or as part of an interfaith effort. The survey indicated 4,000 units constructed, with another 3,400 in planning or under construction. These figures are *admittedly* small in view of the number of units desperately needed today. On the other hand, impressive are the reports of housing in Cleveland, Baton Rouge, Superior, Nashville, and others from among those who have thus far reported. They do, however, indicate a new direction in the Church and a new area of social involvement. I might add that a new approach is being developed right here in Texas. I was just informed that the ten dioceses of the Texas Catholic Conference are setting up a unified state program.

Educational efforts are showing the best progress. Project Community is underway or planned for early implementation in virtually every metropolitan diocese. This program develops positive Christian attitudes in matters of intergroup relations and poverty and seeks to train leaders in supportive roles in community involvement.

Project Equality—for which we are indebted to the National Catholic Conference for Interracial Justice—is now an ecumenical program in many places and is widespread—so widespread in fact that fears are felt that it is revealing signs of being spread so thin that it is becoming unable to recruit sufficient competent personnel. It took my own diocese several months to find a qualified man. Some dioceses have had even greater problems.

The Catholic Church authorities alone have, in fact, taxed to the testing point the resources of this project by their growing espousal of it. Nevertheless Project Equality typifies the moral and pragmatic possibilities of using our resources responsibly in the service of the needs of the victims, conscious or unconscious, of prejudice in employment practices. Some archdioceses and dioceses have set up alternative programs equally effective, e.g., Philadelphia and Washington.

Let me mention briefly the Diocese of Pittsburgh, only on the principle that its bishop would be sorely embarrassed if under his hat as chairman of your department he appealed for national programs and under his mitre as ordinary of his own See, planned nothing. We have Project Equality, Project Commitment, Interfaith Housing, Neighbors in Need Tithing, intensive school programs in underprivileged areas.

I am fully aware that many of you have established comparable and more ambitious programs, direct and indirect—as in Washington, Chicago, Detroit, Rochester. The survey made in preparation for this meeting reveals that on the point of housing programs alone, forty out of fifty-four dioceses reporting on their task forces are already at work on one or another form of housing provision; twenty-seven of these are also committed to one or another form of organized fair employment programs in the communities which they serve. It is not yet possible to fix a money figure on these which would be firm and significant.

Despite these excellent beginnings, despite our organizational efforts to date, there is scant cause for complacency in comparing our pledges to our performance.

Our statement of last year followed by just a few weeks the publication of the report of the National Advisory Committee on Civil Disorders, with its dire prediction of a nation divided. This year our meeting follows on the heels of the Kerner Commission's latest publication entitled *One Year Later*, in which it assesses the nation's response, or rather the lack of a response, to the original report. Our own failure to respond in proportion to the magnitude of the problem reflects that national stance.

One result can be measured, namely, that our relative immobility in the fact of crisis points out more clearly than ever the seriousness of our problem. The dangers that beset us as a nation—the crisis of our cities—is far greater than even the Kerner Commission realized.

As we look around our nation in the spring of 1969, it is obvious that it is a nation filled with tensions. Despite the unparalleled prosperity reflected by the gross national prcduct we see serious unemployment among minorities. A three percent national average still swells to a frightening thirty percent for ghetto teenagers. Lacking jobs and educational opportunities, those who lack hope and are therefore open to the temptations which beset the frustrated are thronging the streets of our inner-city areas by day. By night they are filled with the fears that afflict the alienated and those who move among them.

The oft-quoted statement that a black infant will get less

education, be more frequently unemployed or underemployed, more frequently ill, and die earlier than a white infant is still painfully accurate, although the figures are moving somewhat closer together. What is true of the black child applies to the child of other minority backgrounds, especially those admitting of classification under one or another color.

If this situation does not change drastically we may well be headed, despite all the good will, toward two nations, one white, one black; or in terms of poverty, one affluent, without reference to color, one desperately poor, without reference to color. One thing we have had driven home to us during this year since St. Louis is the fact that the American race problem is from one point of view distinct from the poverty problem, and from another, infinitely complicated by it.

Poverty victimizes people of all ethnic groups. By governmental measurement of poverty (family income of $3,000–3,500), almost 70 percent of the poor were white. The poor, then, include such widely diverse racial groups as Appalachian Whites, the Negroes, Mexican-American, Puerto Ricans, and other Spanish-speaking minorities, American Indians, and migrant workers of various descents. Where race and poverty converge, of course, the victims are doubly burdened.

What I have reported to you this morning has been admittedly a matter of samplings, fragmentary, incomplete, but typical. Monsignor Welsh, not the least of Newark's contributions to the resolution of our worries, is distributing a summary of further effort. The Department of Social Development will in due course submit to you complete reports detailing finances involved and programs undertaken; others than I will have the privilege of providing these and coordinating the divisional and departmental activities behind them.

I wish to underscore that whatever has been done in this brief year has been the merest beginnings of programmed action in the direction of meeting the new demands on the American Church in the modern world. But they *are* beginnings; they provide several new directions, like co-operation with State poverty and health programs; some new formulae, like Project Equality and reverse tithing; a few new frontiers for the works of justice and mercy, like housing and specialized education enrichment projects. But withal we have, in fact, done little indeed in the face of the problem.

One word of warning may be in order, not to this body, perhaps, but to those who, because we are their servants, have the right to command your action and mine.

Our Social Development Department and our task forces fighting racist attitudes, poverty, and the compromises of the Christian ideal and the American dream, have special works to do for the universal and local Church. But the Church itself is not a competitor with or substitute for the health and welfare departments of the State.

The chief contribution that the Church has to make in the democratic community remains what it was in monarchical and feudal orders; now as then it must continue to be on levels of charity, justice, and equity distinct from those proper to and incumbent upon the organized civil society. That contribution includes the example of social justice and of unselfish charity. But the essential mission of the Church in this, as in all things else, consists in the prophetic appeal to the *conscience* of the king and of the citizenry; in the sparking of motivation for Christians to go the extra mile—the mile of charity that goes beyond the mile required by justice.

Such motivation and such effective appeals to conscience presuppose *faith*—not so much theology (a theology of poverty, or a theology of race, or a theology of society), but *faith*, a lively faith concerning where Christ is to be found, served, honored, and satisfied; a faith capable of moving mountains, giving substance to hope and direction to love. Nowhere is the distinction between theology and faith more pertinent.

That essential mission gives top priority to the works of

healing and of strengthening what Jesus did, supremely in that which pertains to the teaching of the Faith. This was the mark of His credibility: "Go tell John what you have seen and heard: the blind receive their sight, the lame walk, the lepers are cleansed, the deaf hear, the dead are raised up, *and the poor have the gospel preached to them. . . .*"[6]

Hence the need that as works to those inside, outside, and around the Church increase, we increase also and even more the evangelizing of the poor, the *preaching of the Faith* by the very ones who do the other works. Otherwise, the poor will become the prisoners of ghettos of the spirit more bleak and more deadly than the physical slums which have been recognized for the ugly, inhuman things they are. Man cannot live without food and shelter, but *"not by bread alone does man live, but by every word that proceeds from the mouth of God."*[7] These words are not the content of a theology lecture, nor of a sociological analysis so much as they are the words of a proclamation to be heard and lived in faith: the proclamation by which Peter linked Christ with the living God, and that by which Christ linked our chances for eternal life to the linking of Himself to the hungry, the thirsty, the imprisoned, the homeless, the naked, the sick.

Hence our satisfaction that the priests, religious, and laity at work in our task forces, operating above ground and in open collaboration with the organized and organic Church, not only do the works needed for renewal of society, but preach, teach, and live the Faith which makes the renewal of this world the means to attaining the life of the world to come.

Jesus, the gospel tells us, began to *do* and to *teach*—not the one alone, nor the other alone, but *both* at the same time.[8] Faith without works dies from apathy; works without faith suffocate the human spirit not less fatally—especially if they leave those whom we serve no one and nothing to believe in but our sinful selves and our, at the best, inadequate resources. Thank you for the chance to help!

LII

Doing and Teaching

The happy circumstance that finds us gathered under the patronage of Christ the Divine Teacher suggests reflection for a moment on the *works* of the Christian and the *faith* of the Christian in the contemporary world.[1]

The Scripture tells us that at a given moment Christ began to *do* and to *teach*, not the one alone, not the other alone, but both together.[2]

In the Church, Christ continues to *do* and to *teach*. In what spirit, then, does He now urge us to *do* the works of justice? What demands does He make on our fidelity to *His teaching*?

In the doing of its works, the Church in our day seems *open* or *forward-looking* in facing social problems. Yet in her teaching she seems cautious, or conservative, especially in matters of faith and morals. Such is the import of the Pastoral Constitution *Gaudium et Spes*; such certainly is the tenor of the Dogmatic Constitution *De Ecclesia*.

In like manner, our Holy Father, Pope Paul, like his predecessors from Leo XIII to Pope John XXIII, brings to social questions a prevailing *liberal* outlook, a clear openness to the future, the outlook of Pope John's *Mater et Magistra* and *Pacem in Terris* or his own *Populorum Progressio* and address to the United Nations. But also like his predecessors, the Pope speaks on doctrinal points with the fidelity of that witness to Tradition which is echoed in the Year of Faith Credo, the encyclicals *Mysterium Fidei* and *Humanae Vitae*, and in Pope Paul's repeated affirmations of the received Faith of our fathers.

The contrast recalls a parallel in Saint Paul, a parallel which

This sermon was preached at the Chiesa di Gesù Divino Maestro, Rome, on May 2, 1969, on the occasion of Wright's taking possession of his titular church.

may be instructive for the times. No one can fail to note the openness of Saint Paul to the wide and varied world of the Gentiles of his time, to their cultures and to the need for changes in the old order to meet the needs of the new. And yet Saint Paul was intransigent in his fidelity to the revelations made to the prophets and, above all, to the truths proclaimed in and through Christ Jesus.

The present-day seeming contradiction which occurs to me can be stated thus: in our moment of history, both the history of the Church and the history of mankind, a *liberal* social attitude and a *progressive spirit* are the need of the hour. But such openness requires, as an indispensable condition of its health and effectiveness, a jealous regard for doctrinal soundness, an attachment to the Faith that is unqualified save for human frailty. I offer the thesis that in a period of social turbulence, indeed of revolution, those who are committed to *openness* and needed change on the level of things human are doomed to be blown about by every wind of doctrine unless they have a commitment not less certain to fixed principles of faith and morality.

I am suggesting that it is not only possible but desirable, even necessary, for the prevailing mood of the Church in our day to be one of open, progressive positions on social questions, above all in what pertains to the freedom due the sons of God, but together with a profound fidelity to the established truth at the heart of religious faith, the faith by which we are, in fact, made free.

With a measure of oversimplification, perhaps, but I trust no injustice to the realities, my thesis is this: *Social openness is the need of the hour; theological caution is not less greatly the need. Doctrinal integrity is essential to the Faith, but it is not less essential to freedom. The Faith provides the absolutes against which the relatives of social change are necessarily judged by Christians; absolutes concerning God, the person, the honor of God and the dignity of the person, the value of life and the primacy of the spiritual as Christians must see these always and everywhere.*

Herein lies, one strongly feels, the saving formula for the resolution of the tragic ironies set forth by Bonhoeffer, that the demand for absolute liberty brings men to the depths of slavery. The master of the machine becomes its slave. The creature turns against its creator in a strange reenactment of the Fall. The liberation of man as an absolute ideal leads only to man's self-destruction.

At our stage in history the temptations of social conservatism could be perilous to the prospects for human freedom, while those of theological liberalism would be fatal to the substance and the future of divine faith and therefore to the very good of honest liberalism.

Religious faith, properly accepted and lived, provides the moral climate in which human freedoms have their best chance to survive. The Catholics of Poland proclaimed this to Catherine II of Russia: We love *liberty* and therefore we love *religion* even more; we are *free* because we love *religion*. We shall not deny our *religion* lest we straightway be deprived of our *liberty*.

Conversely, political and economic freedom should provide the social climate most favorable to responsible and vigorous religious faith.

Hence it turns out, by a curious but persuasive paradox, that social outlooks usually identified as *conservative*, certainly those which are *reactionary*, by tending to inhibit social growth and personal liberty, impede the common good, even as that good is preserved and fortified by the conservative instinct with respect to the Faith, an instinct which keeps one on guard against what Cardinal Newman identified as *liberalism* in religion.[3]

And so social progressivism and theological conservatism, far from being inconsistent, can be mutually supportive. They are logical allies in the face of the present crisis in the Church, the crisis of our culture, our political order, our very own civilization.

That is why those who love both faith and freedom are

always *doubly concerned* when the Faith appears to be in jeopardy or when the Church, the living presence of the teaching Christ in history, is in whatever peril.

Their preoccupation sometimes expresses itself in language that is anxious; it cannot do otherwise, given the gravity of the issues. But they do not, they cannot, lose heart. They know how much of human history, as well as Christian theology, Cardinal Newman summed up when he said:

> In truth the whole course of Christianity from the first, when we come to examine it, is but one series of troubles and disorders. Every century is like every other and to those who live in it seems worse than all times before it. The Church is ever ailing, and lingers on in weakness, "always bearing about in the body the dying of the Lord Jesus, that the life also of Jesus might be made manifest in her body". Religion seems ever expiring, schisms dominant, the light of Truth dim, its adherents scattered. The cause of Christ is ever in its last agony, as though it were but a question of time whether it fails finally this day or another. . . .[4]

The Christian answer to all this is, of course, confident hope and sustaining love, but these because of steadfast faith and yet more faith. "I believe, Lord, help thou my unbelief."[5] If Newman described the recurring condition of turmoil in which the Church always finds herself, he pointed out not less clearly the solution. He said:

> Doubt and difficulty seem our lot; the simple question is What is our duty under it? . . . Scripture is quite aware of those difficulties . . . it knows them all; it has provided against them by recognizing them. It says, "Believe".[6]

The problem of *Whom* we shall believe and its solution in Christ, the Divine Teacher, are both seen in the sixth chapter of Saint John's Gospel. Again Cardinal Newman is our guide to their understanding:

After our Lord had declared what all who heard seemed to feel to be a hard doctrine, some in surprise and offence left Him. Our Lord said to the Twelve most tenderly, "Will ye also go away?" Saint Peter promptly answered. No! But observe on what ground he put it: "Lord, to *whom* shall we go? . . ." If Christ were not to be trusted, there was nothing in the world to be trusted; and this was a conclusion repugnant both to his reason and to his heart. He had within him ideas of greatness and goodness, holiness and eternity—he had a love of them—he had an instinctive hope and longing after their possession. Nothing would convince him that this unknown good was a dream. Divine life, eternal life, was the object which his soul, as far as it had learned to realize and express its wishes, supremely longed for. In Christ he found what he wanted. . . . He might have misgivings at times; he might have permanent and in themselves insuperable objections; still in spite of such objections, in spite of the assaults of unbelief, on the whole he saw *that* in Christ which was positive, real and satisfying. He saw it nowhere else. "Thou", he says, "hast the words of eternal life, and we *have believed* and *have* known that Thou art the Christ, the Son of the Living God." As if he said, "We will stand by what we believed and knew the day before. A sudden gust of new doctrines, a sudden inroad of new perplexities, shall not unsettle us. We *have* believed, we *have* known, we cannot collect together all the evidence; but this is the abiding deep conviction of our minds. We feel that it is better, safer, truer, more pleasant, more blessed to cling to Thy feet, O merciful Saviour, than to leave Thee. Thou *canst not* deceive us: it is impossible. We will hope in Thee against hope, and believe in Thee against doubt, and obey Thee in spite of gloom."

Now what are the feelings I have described but love of Christ? Thus love is the parent of faith. . . . Love of God led Saint Peter to follow Christ, and love of Christ leads men now to love and follow the Church, as His representative and voice.[7]

In brief, then, Christ offers mankind that truth which makes us free. But we must be tenacious of the Faith through which there comes to us that truth which frees if we are to be, as the voice of the times invites us to be, the heirs to liberty and the builders, in responsible freedom, of a more sane and saving order.

In this, too, Newman may well have been prophetic when on the occasion of his coming to Rome ninety years ago to receive his cardinal's hat, he warned against what he called "the spirit of liberalism in religion".[8] He praised what is good and true in liberal theology generally, "for example, not to say more, the precepts of justice, truthfulness, sobriety, self-command, and benevolence."[9] But he saw this spirit when looked at from firm attachment to the Faith, as prompting a *great apostasy*, "one and the same everywhere [though] in detail, and in character, it varies in different countries."[10] He saw that spirit, already shaping up in his times, as ultimately inconsistent with the recognition of any religions whatever as *true*, all being matters of opinion, never of objective fact. Because of its mischief, "over-spreading as a snare, the whole earth",[11] Newman made his admittance to the Sacred College the occasion to protest that "never did Holy Church need champions [against this kind of 'liberalism in religion'] more sorely than now".[12]

One wonders what Newman would have said had he lived to see his name and his words invoked in defense of a religious spirit which he found so mischievous and which he repudiated in his own times so pointedly, so passionately, and, on occasion, with such personal suffering!

Newman's passion for the Church of the Fathers, for the primacy of the papacy, for the witness of hierarchy and laity alike to the Faith committed to the apostles, is preeminently needed if liberalism in the building of peace, the flourishing of the intellectual life, the recognition and service of the person, the progress of civil rights, is to have firm roots in truth from which to flourish and fixed unyielding standards to guarantee its freedom.

Newman lamented the theological trend of his times because he feared that it would be the ruin of many souls. But he added:

> I have no fear at all that it really can do . . . serious harm to the Word of God, to Holy Church, to our Almighty King, the Lion of the tribe of Judah, Faithful and True, or to His Vicar on earth. Christianity has been too often in what seemed deadly peril, that we should fear for it any new trial now. [To offset and survive these] . . . commonly the Church has nothing more to do than to go on in her own proper duties, in confidence and peace.[13]

What we have thus said about the majestic calm and Christian optimism which the ancient Faith inspires, together with the magnanimous, venturesome social action which the new hopes invite, is valid everywhere. Everywhere and always we must *do* with the boldness and generosity of Christ, and *teach* without compromise or confusion the Word of God still echoed across the ages and throughout the world by the voice of the Church, obedient to Him as is He to the mind and the will of His Father in God.

We must repeat these joyful, consoling truths in all seasons and all places. But it is especially appropriate to proclaim them on this occasion and here in Rome, where Christ's own Vicar gives the example of *doing* and *teaching*. It is easy to believe them here where the trophies of the apostles, the memories of the martyrs, all the symbols of the City not lightly called *Eternal*, declare the abiding strength of truly human aspirations and the immortal power of divine promises.

Let a paraphrase of the words of Saint Bernard inspire us here in Rome to deepened identity through the Church with the unchanging Christ Who ultimately changes everything. Surrounded by a company of single-hearted brethren, what have you to fear? What have you to fear at whose side angels stand and whom Christ leads into battle encouraging His friends with the words: "Fear not, I have overcome the world"?[14] If Christ is with us, who is against us? You can fight with confidence when you are sure of victory.

With Christ and for Christ, victory is certain. Not wounds, nor falls, nor bruises, nor—were it possible—can a thousand deaths rob us of victory, if only we do not forsake the fight. Only by desertion can we be defeated. Desertion from Christ the Divine Teacher, Christ the Example of our deeds.

Let us, then, recognize with Cardinal Newman that, in the order of Providence, our seeming dangers are often our greatest gains. In the words of the Protestant poet William Cowper:

> The clouds you so much dread
> Are big with mercy, and shall break
> In blessings on your head.

Abbreviations

AAS   *Acta Apostolicae Sedis* (Rome, 1909–).

ACW   *Ancient Christian Writers*: The Works of the Fathers in Translation, ed. J. Quasten and others (Westminster, Md.: Newman Bookshop, 1946–).

CCL   *Corpus Christianorum*, Series Latina.

CSEL   *Corpus Scriptorum Ecclesiasticorum Latinorum* (Vienna, 1866–).

PG   *Patrologia Graeca*, ed. J. P. Migne (Paris, 1857–66).

PL   *Patrologia Latina*, ed. J. P. Migne (Paris, 1844–64).

RC   *Resonare Christum*, Volume I: A Selection from the Sermons, Addresses, Interviews, and Papers of Cardinal John J. Wright. Prepared and edited by R. Stephen Almagno, O.F.M. (San Francisco: Ignatius Press, 1985).

Rule   *Francis and Clare*: The Complete Works. Translation and introduction by Regis J. Armstrong, O.F.M. Cap., and Ignatius C. Brady, O.F.M. (New York: Paulist Press, 1982).

Notes

Chapter One
Leadership in Serra and the Church

[1] Charles T. Carey was born in Omaha, Nebraska, in 1916. After graduating from Cornell University he worked for the Union Pacific Railroad from 1938 to 1951. He then embarked on a forty-year career in hotel management across the nation, which included stewardship at the Santa Barbara Biltmore, the Omaha Sheraton, the Sheraton-Ritz, Minneapolis, the St. Regis in New York City, and the old Penn-Sheraton—now the Westin William Penn Hotel—of Pittsburgh, Pennsylvania. In 1975, very much influenced by Wright, Carey began his studies in preparation for the priesthood in Rome, at the Beda, and was ordained in 1980. Death came to him—in the sixth year of his priesthood—on July 16, 1986, while he was preparing to offer Mass at St. Patrick Church, Miami Beach, Florida.

[2] In 1937, and again in 1938, Wright ministered in the village of Lembras par Bergerac, Dordogne, France. Concerning this period of Wright's life, Msgr. Edward G. Murray wrote in his introduction to Volume I (The Boston Years: 1939–1950) of *Resonare Christum*: "With the exception of a summer spent in Northern England, all other summers were spent in Corbiac, a village in the Dordogne. The Dordogne is famous throughout France for its truffles, but not for much else. Father Wright stayed at the home of Colonel de Corbiac, and made friendships which lasted until his death. I met the Colonel de Corbiac in London in 1948 with Bishop Wright. He was a man of profound traditional piety, and he spoke of the love that Father Wright had left behind him in France. In the Dordogne he perfected his French the better to converse and preach, and he pursued an avocation which had been with him since Latin School days—collecting memorabilia concerning Joan of Arc. Over the years his interest and his collection grew, until he was invited to give the panegyrique at Orleans, on the anniversary of the lifting of the siege" (*RC* I, 15).

[3] St. Augustine, *Confessions* (PL 32, 757): "Da mihi castitatem et continentiam, sed noli modo."

[4] St. Paulinus of Nola, *Carmen XVII* (CSEL 30, p. 93): ". . . per te barbari discunt resonare Christum corde Romano placidamque casti vivere pacem." P. G. Walsh, in his translation of *The Poems of St. Paulinus of Nola* (ACW 40, 112) renders the text as: "In this mute region of the world, the barbarians

through your schooling learn to make Christ's name resound from Roman hearts, and to live in purity and tranquil peace." Sometime during his student days, Wright came across this text, and it deeply impressed him. He included it in his thesis and, when ordained a bishop, selected it as his motto and included it in his coat of arms.

Cardinal Wright's personal coat of arms is composed of the shield and its charges, the motto beneath the shield, and the external trappings around the shield.

Arms: a cauldron in silver resting upon a fire, or rising from the fire, and an eagle of gold between two fleurs-de-lis. The Cardinal's arms are based upon those sometimes attributed to his patron saint, St. John the Evangelist, in allusion to the Roman tradition of St. John before the Latin Gate and the miraculous escape of the saint from the cauldron of boiling oil prepared for him under the Emperor Domitian.

The fleurs-de-lis are taken from the arms of the Archdiocese of Boston, where Wright was born and served as auxiliary bishop before being named to the See of Worcester and subsequently to the Diocese of Pittsburgh. These fleurs-de-lis also appear frequently on arms associated with the name Wright.

The Cardinal's motto: The words "Resonare Christum" are from the above-quoted passage in the writings of St. Paulinus of Nola: ". . . per te barbari discunt *resonare Christum* corde Romano placidamque casti vivere pacem." Wright's own translation of the text reads: "Through you the heathens of our world's unheeded parts / Have learned to *echo Christ* with Roman hearts / And live a life of chaste and stable peace."

The external ornaments are composed of the scarlet pontifical hat with its fifteen scarlet tassels on each side, arranged in five rows, with the episcopal gold cross indicating his Sacred Congregation. These are the presently accepted heraldic trappings of a prelate of the rank of Cardinal-Bishop. Before 1870 the pontifical hat was worn at solemn cavalcades held in conjunction with papal functions. The color of the pontifical hat and the number and color of the tassels are signs of the rank of the prelate. This custom is preserved in ecclesiastical heraldry.

The arms were designed in 1947 after Wright was named an auxiliary to the Archbishop of Boston and titular bishop to the See of Tegea. These arms were designed by Dom Wilfred Bayne, O.S.B., of the then Portsmouth Priory, now Portsmouth Abbey, in Portsmouth, Rhode Island.

The shield has a tint rose red. The cauldron is, as mentioned, silver, with the eagle and the fleurs-de-lis of gold.

This description and explanation of Wright's coat of arms is based—with my additions and corrections—on the text published on page 12 of the booklet entitled *The Pontifical Liturgy in Memory of John Cardinal Wright* (Pittsburgh, St. Paul Cathedral, August 20, 1979).

See John J. Wright, *National Patriotism in Papal Teaching* (Westminster, Md.: Newman Press, 1956), xii; also, *Classica et Iberica, a Festschrift in Honor of the Reverend Joseph M.-F. Marique, S.J.*, ed. P. T. Brannan, S.J. (Worcester, Mass.: Institute for Early Christian Iberian Studies, 1975), 417–25.

Chapter Two
The Bicentennial of
The Founding of Pittsburgh

[1] John J. Wright, *National Patriotism in Papal Teaching*, 67–69.
[2] Woodrow Wilson, *Selected Literary and Political Papers and Addresses* (New York: Grosset and Dunlap, 1926), 241.

Chapter Three
Khrushchev in Pittsburgh

This official statement was published in *The Pittsburgh Catholic* (September 10, 1959).
[1] Robert C. Alberts, *Pitt: The Story of the University of Pittsburgh, 1787–1987* (Pittsburgh: The University of Pittsburgh Press, 1986), 275.

Chapter Four
Exceptional Children

This address was published in *Second Annual Symposium. Saint Anthony's School for Exceptional Children* (Pittsburgh, Pa.: The Diocese of Pittsburgh, 1960), 13–18.
[1] *Second Annual Symposium. Saint Anthony's School for Exceptional Children*, 3–11.
[2] Robert F. Kennedy presented Wright with a $50,000 grant from the Lt. Joseph P. Kennedy, Jr., Memorial Foundation.
[3] Mt 25:40, 45.

Chapter Six
Haec Studia

In order fully to appreciate this text, it must be remembered—as Msgr. Edward G. Murray wrote in his introduction to Volume I (The Boston Years: 1939–1950) of *Resonare Christum*, that "John Wright was a loyal alumnus of the Latin School. Many times when he felt that some adverse influences were conspiring to bring down the School's high standards, he would do that which he best of all the alumni could do: he would write and talk until the danger was over. See, for example, the address *Haec Studia*—published in Volume II— which he delivered on April 25, 1960, at the Three Hundred Twenty-Fifth Anniversary Dinner of the Boston Latin School. Many years ago the custom was started of giving a Paul Revere bowl to the Latin School Man of the Year. No one was surprised, nor did anyone cavil, that the first recipient was Bishop Wright" (*RC* I, 13).

This is, too, the right place to add a word about Msgr. Murray. In Wright's notes for his autobiography, he singled out Murray as one of the great influences in his life. And, certainly, Murray—a friend of Mr. and Mrs. Wright, the Wright Family, and John Wright's professor, mentor, superior— was the Cardinal's closest confidant.

Msgr. Edward G. Murray was born in Boston's Bay Back in 1906 and died at the Regina Cleri Residence for Retired Priests, Boston, on July 8, 1986. He attended the Prince School, on Newbury Street, and the Boston Latin School, from which he graduated in 1921. The recipient of a four-year scholarship to Holy Cross College, Worcester, Massachusetts, Msgr. Murray obtained a B.A. degree *magna cum laude* in 1925. After a brief stay at the Harvard Law School he entered Saint John Seminary, Brighton, Massachusetts, and in 1927 was sent to the North American College, Rome. In 1930 he was ordained a priest and soon after obtained a doctorate in theology. Upon his return to the Archdiocese of Boston, Murray taught philosophy, psychology, and theology at St. John Seminary. In 1938, when he was thirty-three, Cardinal O'Connell appointed him as rector of the same seminary, a post he held until 1951. He then went on to be pastor of the Sacred Heart Church, Roslindale (1951), and from 1971 to 1974 he was pastor of St. Paul Church, Cambridge, with the added duty of serving as chaplain to the Harvard-Radcliffe Student Center. Msgr. Murray was a distinguished scholar, an urbane gentleman, an official of the Archdiocese of Boston, the Vicar for Ecumenical Affairs and, unofficially but in fact, the Archdiocese's ambassador to Boston's world of literature, music, and art. He was a trustee of the Boston Museum of Fine Arts and of the Boston Symphony Orchestra. He served as President of the Boston Public Library's Board of Trustees and in 1981, in honor of the Golden Jubilee of his ordination, Msgr. Murray had named in his behalf a permanent section of books and documents in the Boston Public Library—a gift supported by Boston's ecumenical leadership. Always the priest, Msgr. Murray will long be remembered for his ministry to seminarians, the poor, and especially with unwed mothers.

[1] "In 1835, however, a really permanent educational establishment was made in the city. In 1835 St. Paul's Parish, located at the present site of the Union Trust Building, on the corner of Grant Street and Fifth Avenue, opened a day school for boys and girls and an academy for young ladies. Fr. John O'Reilly, C.M., was pastor of the parish at the time, and he invited the Sisters of Charity from Emmitsburg, Maryland, to staff these two schools." Thomas J. Quigley, "The School System of the Diocese", *Catholic Pittsburgh's One Hundred Years* (Chicago: Loyola University Press, 1943), 128.

[2] Cicero, *Pro Archia*, VII, 16.

[3] Ibid.

[4] The *Boston Globe* (April 24, 1960): editorial page.

[5] Philip Marston, *A Teacher Speaks* (New York: D. McKay, 1960).

[6] On January 21, 1935, Andrew Oliver (Harvard 1922) and Peter Oliver (Harvard 1928) published a nine-page open letter to Dr. James B. Conant, president of Harvard, concerning Conant's recommendation that Latin be eliminated as a requirement for the B.A. degree.

[7] *Oliver to Conant*, 3–4.

[8] Ibid., 2–3.

[9] Marston, *A Teacher Speaks*.

[10] John McCormack, "The Boston Latin School's 325th Anniversary", in *The Congressional Record* (April 18, 1960): 8107. Speaker of the House McCormack and Wright enjoyed a long friendship; and it is supposed, as Msgr. Murray told me, that Wright was the author of McCormack's text.

[11] Cicero, *Pro Archia*.

[12] Ibid.

[13] Shakespeare, *Love's Labour's Lost*, Act IV, sc. ii.

[14] Virgil, *Aeneid*, I, 33.

Chapter Seven
Catholic Optimism

[1] Beginning in 1948, Wright was the Episcopal Moderator of the National Retreat Movement for the Laity. See C. Hennessy, S.J., *The Inner Circle: The Closed Retreat in the United States* (Chicago: Loyola University Press, 1965), v–vi, 156–57, 162–63, and 167–68.

On April 13, 1959, less than a month after becoming bishop of Pittsburgh,

Wright wrote to Mother Gertrude M. Coleman: "When may I hope—or even may I hope?—to have a Cenacle in Pittsburgh? I beg you to include us on your list of *futurabilia* and to let me gnow whether I may not begin to look about for at least eventual places suitable for the supremely important work of the Cenacle."

But, because of Cenacle foundations in Florida and Lima, Peru, in the early 1960s, Pittsburgh did not get its Cenacle until the summer of 1965.

A press release, issued by Msgr. Daniel H. Brennan on June 19, 1965, stated: "Bishop Wright at a business meeting of the Diocesan council of Catholic Women today announced the establishment here of a retreat house of the Religious of the Cenacle to be located on Fifth Avenue at Clyde Street in Oakland, on property formerly occupied by the Winchester-Thurston School.

"Bishop Wright's interest in the Order and its work has been both personal and official. During his days as a student priest in Rome he frequently offered Mass in the Catacomb of St. Priscilla, which is connected with the Cenacle Convent in Rome, and later gave weekend retreats at the Cenacle Convent in Brighton, Massachusetts. In 1953, as the first bishop of the Diocese of Worcester, Massachusetts, he introduced the Order into the new diocese at Lancaster, Massachusetts.

"Expressing his deep admiration for the Order in his prefatory note to the book *Women in the Cenacle*, Bishop Wright wrote: 'Any bishop whose heart burns with even a small part of St. Paul's solicitude for the Church would welcome in his diocese these spiritual coadjutors [the Cenacle Sisters] so like those devout women of apostolic days in Rome whose households were places of prayer and spiritual refreshment for the Christian laity.' "

Daniel H. Brennan, News Release (June 19, 1965) and letters of Wright to Coleman (April 13, 1959, June 1, 1959, March 10, 1960, May 16, 1960, July 20, 1960, June 18, 1965, and July 9, 1965).

[2] See John J. Wright, *Words in Pain* (San Francisco: Ignatius Press, 1986), 18–19; also Chapter XXXV, *Colonel de Corbiac*, and note 1 of Chapter XXXV, page 557 below.

Chapter Eight
Temples of the Living God

[1] The Diocese of Altoona, Pa., was established on May 27, 1901. On October 9, 1957, it was redesignated as the Diocese of Altoona-Johnstown. Its first bishop was Eugene Garvey. Ordained bishop on September 8, 1901, he served the diocese until his death on October 22, 1920.

[2] John T. McCort was bishop from 1920 to 1936.

[3] Richard T. Guilfoyle was bishop from 1936 to 1937.

[4] Howard J. Carroll was bishop from 1957 to 1960.

[5] J. Carroll McCormick was appointed bishop on June 25, 1960.

[6] Henry Wadsworth Longfellow, *Collected Poetical Works* (Boston: Houghton Mifflin, 1926), 292.

[7] *Pontificale Romanum*, "De Ecclesiae Dedicatione seu Consecratione".

[8] *Pontificale Romanum*, "De Consecratione Electi in Episcopum".

Chapter Nine
Ecclesiastical Art and Architecture

[1] Msgr. Charles O. Rice was born in New York City in 1908. Ordained for the Diocese of Pittsburgh in 1934, he has distinguished himself by his pioneering efforts on behalf of labor, peace, prisoners, racial justice, and court and prison reform. When Wright came to Pittsburgh he appointed Rice to the Diocesan Board of Consultors and restored him to the *Pittsburgh Catholic* to which Rice, due to actions from Wright's predecessor, Bishop (now Cardinal) John Dearden, had not been permitted to contribute since 1953. See William Serrin, "Priest Spans Five Decades of Church and Labor Alliance", *National Catholic Reporter* (September 3, 1982): 1 and 8.

In 1983, when the Diocese of Pittsburgh was awaiting the appointment of a new bishop, Rice—in an August 10 column in the *Pittsburgh Catholic*—remembered that "we mark the fourth anniversary of the death of a man whose appointment and arrival as our Bishop twenty-four years ago was a spectacular. John Cardinal Wright died August 10, 1979, ten years after he left us, and twenty years after he arrived with a bang.

"We had the usual welcomings: the Mass in the Cathedral, the dinner for the priests, etc., but the smash feature was a reception that took up most of a Sunday and attracted 25,000 (many not Catholics), all of whom he greeted personally.

"That was a total change from what we were used to; he continued to serve up that which we were not used to. We became an open diocese with the Bishop himself joining in the openness and a lot of fun. From the turn of the century we had been a solid, well-behaved diocese. We had a full complement of priests and nuns and institutions. We had been building schools and stuff since the end of World War II. We were correct and quiet and dull as blazes. Among the clergy one was to be prudent and low-keyed. That was more important than efficiency, actually. I had been keeping quiet for a while, but I did not like it.

"By the time of his appointment, although he was Ordinary in the small diocese of Worcester, Massachusetts, John Wright was famous and had stature as an intellectual and a spokesman for the Church and Catholic values. He was known as being open and liberal.

"This was a time of intellectual ferment in the Church. John XXIII had been elected Pope and was opening 'windows on the world'. In the same month that he appointed Wright our Ordinary he announced the convening of the Second Vatican Council.

"We all knew some change was coming in the Church. To be sure, we did not know what course it would take, nor did we foresee its negative elements. John Wright, liberal as he was, had premonitions, but he remained friendly to change and intellectual stirrings.

"From a closed diocese we changed to one that hosted every national Catholic convention you could think of. Historians, librarians, liturgists, philosophers, theologians, canonists, social activists. Those were heady days. I saw it from the inside because I, to my amazement, was named to the Diocesan Council. His was a tolerant rule; he accepted disagreement and would modify his plans if you could convince him.

"He was tolerant of everything but intolerance, and he would get furious at priests who were tyrannical or high-handed. He wanted you to give the other guy a hearing. The only two rumbles he and I had were when he suspected me of having refused to listen to someone whom I had pasted in a column. Once he was correct and I straightened it out. The other time he ended up mad at the other fellow, who proved to be the hardhead.

"Putting it in show business terms, everybody loved his act. Protestants and Jews, even those of no religion, as well as Catholics, appreciated him and wanted him to come to their celebrations; and he did. He simply tried to get to everything he was invited to, and he would not just hit and run; he sat through some awful stuff. A couple of times I was trapped at long, dull events along with him. No matter how dull the occasion, or unfunny the jokes, he acted as if he enjoyed it all.

"Being a bishop had its obligations, and he took them seriously. For this reason he was available. Actually, I doubt that he was bored by what would bore the rest of us, because he would elevate any occasion so much that others would enjoy it hugely, and that had to give him a lift.

"By any definition he was a great man.

"Some thought he had grown conservative, but no, he never wavered in his support for racial justice, for peace, for ecumenism, for labor unions and the working man, and for freedom and toleration in general." Charles O. Rice, "Remembering Cardinal Wright" the *Pittsburgh Catholic* (August 10, 1983): 6.

[2] The construction of the magnificent Cathedral of Chartres, one of the finest French Gothic buildings, was begun in the eleventh century. Chartres was dedicated in 1260.

³ Both the Immaculate Conception Convent and the John F. Kennedy School, of Washington, Pennsylvania, were designed by the Deeter Ritchey Sippel Architectural Firm of Pittsburgh.

Chapter Ten
Men to Match Their Mountains

¹ Ps 71:3. (Vulgate numbering is used for Biblical references.)

² Rev 22:3.

³ Urban J. Vehr was bishop from 1931 to 1967. Elevated to the archiepiscopal office in 1941, he resigned in 1967 and died in 1973. David M. Maloney was his auxiliary from 1961 to 1967.

⁴ David M. Maloney was ordained in 1936, appointed auxiliary to the archbishop of Denver, Colorado, in 1960, and transferred to the Diocese of Wichita, Kansas, in 1967. He served as bishop of Wichita until his resignation in 1982. Maloney—together with Daniel J. Honan, Alexander Miller Harvey, Carroll T. Dozier, and John A. Reddington—was Wright's Roman schoolmate and in the inner circle of his friends.

About Wright's student days in Rome and the friendships then formed, Fr. Robert F. McNamara—another of Wright's Roman schoolmates and a former professor of history at St. Bernard Seminary, Rochester, New York—has observed: ". . . from the start I was very much impressed by him. He had a quick and ever busy mind. His mental processes kept him so occupied that he was always irregular in his eating habits. Because of his brilliance he was held in very high respect by his contemporaries at the North American College. This is not to say that he was necessarily liked by all. Like all very brilliant men he would leave most of his companions way behind him in his intellectual interests and quickness of perception. It is sometimes very uncomfortable to be in the face of such brilliance of wit and of speech. More, it can be quite exhausting to slower thinkers and even rather incomprehensible to men of the administrative type—and there were several in his own class who looked upon him with little fondness. This was true, partly, because they could not understand him. Still there are always in groups like this certain people that click in their companionship with each other. There were two in particular that John Wright associated with and that were able to almost match him in his wit. One of these was Daniel J. Honan, of Portland, Maine, and the other was Alexander Miller Harvey, who had been converted to Catholicism at the age of 13 from the Campbellites and was from the Diocese of Kansas City, Kansas. It was one of the rarest treats of my whole experience to listen to John Wright, Daniel Honan, and Al Harvey engage in witty chit-chat. The wit sparkled. What the one said was quickly taken up by the other, given a new twist, and thrown back to the third" (Tape from McNamara to Almagno, December 29, 1982).

⁵ Ps 71:1–4.

⁶ Ps 71:12–15.

⁷ Ps 71:3.

⁸ Is 52:7.

⁹ Wright's reference to the mountain and hills in this sermon merits the following note from Msgr. Matthew P. Stapleton: "John was not an athlete in the regular sense of the word. But he did love to walk city streets. Back in 1942, when the seminary had a summer villa in New Hampshire, he and I and Rev. Msgr. J. Joseph Ryan (now retired) climbed Mt. Lafayette (not as high as the Alps, but a good-sized and steep mountain in New Hampshire). It was tough going, but Joe and I, who were somewhat experienced, were amazed and delighted at the determination on John's part to reach the summit, despite his puffing and straining, and the pain in his legs. We made the summit, stayed at the Appalachian Mt. Club Greenleaf Hut and after supper lapsed into that silent admiration of God's beauty as revealed in the mountains, characteristic of mountain climbers.

"In those days priests who wanted to celebrate Mass on mountains had to carry Mass kits, and John carried ours his share of the climb. The next morning, as dawn was breaking, we celebrated Mass on Lafayette—the first (the only?) time.

"We took snapshots that day, and in John's last days in Rome, when he really was, I believe, weakening fast, I sent him a copy, and what a beautiful letter I received from him—the last from *mountain-climbing John Cardinal Wright*" (Letter of Stapleton to Almagno, February 9, 1982).

Chapter Eleven
The Loving Obedience of Free Men

This sermon was published in *Social Thought* (series no. 4, 3, no. 61, 10), publication of the Social Action Department, Canadian Catholic Conference.

¹ Gen 3:5.

² Jn 8:32.

³ Phil 2:8–9.

⁴ John Lancaster Spalding, *Means and Ends of Education* (Chicago, 1897), 220.

Chapter Twelve
Monsignor Vincent J. Rieland 1898–1961

¹ Wright delivered this eulogy without a text. Msgr. Oliver D. Keefer remembers: "Shortly after Msgr. Rieland's funeral, I asked Bishop Wright when we were to get a copy. He was startled and told me that he had no text. Then two weeks later he called me aside to say that they had located a man from Beaver Falls who had taped the sermon and that he would send me some copies" (Letter of Keefer to Almagno, November 7, 1985).

Monsignor Rieland was born in Pittsburgh, Pa., on October 20, 1898, and died in Beaver Falls, Pa., on June 3, 1961. Ordained in 1925, he had only three assignments, in the Diocese of Pittsburgh, throughout his life: he was a curate at St. Raphael Parish for nineteen years, pastor at the Most Blessed Sacrament Parish, Natrona Heights, from 1944 to 1951 and pastor at St. Mary Parish, Beaver Falls, from 1951 until the time of his death.

² Bishop John Wright, *Words in Pain: Conferences on the Seven Last Words of Christ* (Notre Dame, Ind.: Fides, 1961). *Words in Pain* has been published as follows: *Words in Pain: Conferences on the Seven Last Words of Christ* (Notre Dame, Ind.: Fides, 1961), the French translation, *Paroles dans la Souffrance: Les Sept Paroles du Christ*, trans. Louis de Corbiac (Montreal and Paris: Fides, 1963), the Italian translation, *Parole nella Sofferenza: Le Sette Parole di Cristo in Croce*, trans. Massimo Giustetti (Fossano: Editrice Esperienze, 1972), a second English edition, *Words in Pain: Meditations on the Last Words of Jesus* (Notre Dame, Ind.: Ave Maria Press, 1978), and a third English edition, *Words in Pain*, prepared and edited by R. Stephen Almagno, O.F.M., illustrated by William Hart McNichols, S.J., with an introduction by the Most Reverend Alberto Bovone (San Francisco: Ignatius Press, 1986).

Chapter Thirteen
Catholicism: An Unknown Quantity

¹ William Sperry, *Religion in America* (New York: Macmillan, 1946). Some years before this address, Wright was very instrumental in having Harvard University invite Christopher Dawson as the first holder (from 1957 to 1962) of the Charles Chauncey Stillman Guest Professorship of Roman Catholic Studies. See C. Stillman, "Christopher Dawson: Recollections from America", in *The Chesterton Review* (Dawson Special Issue) 9, no. 2 (May, 1983): 143–48; and C. Scott, *A Historian and His World: A Life of Christopher Dawson, 1889–1970* (London: Sheed and Ward, 1984), 179–85, 193.

[2] William Sperry, *Religion in America*.

[3] Theodore Maynard, *The Story of American Catholicism* (New York: Macmillan, 1941).

[4] William Sperry, *Religion in America*.

[5] James A. Healy, son of Michael Morris Healy (an Irish-Georgian slave owner) and Eliza Smith (a slave) and one of three brothers, all of whom were priests, was born in Macon, Georgia, on April 6, 1830. Ordained in Paris on June 10, 1854, Healy was the first chancellor of the Boston diocese. From 1857 to 1900 he was bishop of Portland, Maine.

[6] On October 13, 1947, at the ninth annual C.I.O. convention, held that year in Boston, the then Archbishop Cushing said: "I have said this before, but it is important to repeat it here: in all the American hierarchy, resident in the United States, there is not known to me one bishop, archbishop, or cardinal whose father or mother was a college graduate. Every one of our bishops and archbishops is the son of a working man and a working man's wife" *The Pilot* (October 17, 1947), 1.

Concerning Cushing's text it is important to remember what Msgr. Edward G. Murray wrote in his introduction to Volume I (The Boston Years: 1939–1950) of *Resonare Christum*: "On April 21, 1944, Cardinal O'Connell died after a brief illness, at the age of eighty-four. The Consultors of the Archdiocese a few hours later selected Bishop Richard J. Cushing as administrator of the archdiocese, until a new archbishop should be chosen. The new administrator continued Father Wright in his post." Wright had been O'Connell's secretary "and invited him to live in the archbishop's house. Thus began a collaboration which was to last for many years—speeches delivered by Cushing, but with the bred inflections of Wright. One of these, *I Belong Here*, delivered before the National Convention of the Congress of Industrial Organizations, was reprinted by the labor union in more than a million copies" (*RC* 1, 18).

[7] William Sperry, *Religion in America*.

[8] Theodore Maynard, *The Catholic Church and the American Idea* (New York: Appleton Century Crofts, 1953), 13.

[9] "My teachers of that time were of the strictest Puritanical mold, with the coldest idea of duty as they saw it, without the slightest understanding of a child's mind and heart, and with a suspicion and distrust of everything Catholic. That coldness dried up every vestige of sympathy that ought to exist between teacher and child, so that school hours of the day were a perfect torture. We lived actually in an atmosphere of fear. We sensed the bitter antipathy, scarcely concealed, which nearly all these good women in charge of the schools felt toward those of us who had Catholic faith and Irish names. For any slight pretext we were severely punished. We were made to feel the slur against our faith and race, which hurt us to our very heart's core. As all the

teachers were of this same stamp, it was little wonder that from my fifth to my twelfth year school life meant nothing to me but a dreary drive, with a feeling of terror, lest, for any reason or no reason, the teacher might vent her ill feelings upon our defenseless person. At that time I was serving at the altar and I remember absenting myself so as to assist at the Mass on Good Friday. There were two or three other Catholic boys in my class who did the same. Immediately on the opening of the class on Saturday morning, the teacher, a rabid anti-Catholic, called our names and bade us arise in our places. With a voice which struck terror in our childish hearts, she angrily demanded an explanation of our absence the day before. I answered that I was absent to be present at Mass, for yesterday was Good Friday. With a sneer, she told the whole class that that was no reason whatever. 'Good Friday!' she said. 'I want you to know that all Fridays are good, and the boys who absented themselves may now come forward for punishment.' " William H. O'Connell, *Recollections of Seventy Years* (Boston, 1934), 5–6.

Chapter Fourteen
Perseverance in the Seminary:
Problems and Remedies

This address was published as follows: *Priestly Vocations in the World Today: Acts of the First International Congress for Priestly Vocations. Rome, 22–26 May 1962* (Vatican City: Sacred Congregation for Seminaries and Universities, 1963), 152–64; *The American Ecclesiastical Review* 147 (August 1962): 73–87; *National Catholic Educational Association Bulletin* 61 (August 1964): 103–12 and (excerpts in) *The Serran* (September–October 1967): 5–7.

On June 3, 1962—upon his return to Pittsburgh—Wright shared some insights concerning the International Congress during his KDKA radio program:

"I have been in Rome to attend the International Congress called by the Congregation of Seminaries to discuss the world problem of vocations. One of the remarkable aspects of this particular Congress was the way in which the laity of America took part in the discussion. It was a meeting of some six hundred delegates, presided over by Cardinal Pizzardo, the head of the Sacred Congregation, and the discussions ended with an audience with the Pope, who spoke to us on the theme we had been discussing all week. Several cardinals took part in it, as well as many archbishops and bishops, rectors of seminaries, prelates of every rank and many priests. Notable was the group of laymen, all from the United States and all members of the Serra Club. I mention this because it is an indication of the place that the Serra Club has achieved in the approach to the problem of vocations. It is also an indication of the respect and regard that the authorities on the highest level of the Church's policy-making have for those laymen who take an interest in the problem of vocations and who, as Serrans, are giving so much leadership to the American solution to the problem."

[1] 1 Cor 1:27.

[2] Paul Grieger, *Caractère et Vocation* (Monaco, 1958).

[3] Pope Pius XI, Encyclical *Ad Catholici Sacerdotii* (December 20, 1935). English translation: *The Catholic Priesthood* (Washington, D.C.: National Catholic Welfare Conference, 1936).

[4] Mt 18:3 and 1 Cor 14:20.

[5] Robert Hugh Benson, *The Friendship of Christ* (Chicago: Thomas More Press, 1984), 73–76.

[6] Paul Claudel, *Coronal* (New York: Pantheon, 1943), 238.

[7] Prov 26:13.

[8] *L'Esortazione Menti Nostrae e i Seminari* (Città del Vaticano, S. Congregazione dei Seminari, 1955), 271. Pope Pius XII, Apostolic Exhortation *Menti Nostrae* (September 23, 1950). English translation: *On the Development of Holiness in Priestly Life* (Washington, D.C.: National Catholic Welfare Conference, 1951), 38–39.

[9] Pope Pius XII, *Menti Nostrae*.

[10] Emmanuel Suhard, *Priests among Men* (Notre Dame, Ind.: Fides, 1960), 111. Wright was a great admirer of Cardinal Suhard (1874–1949). See Wright's "Introduction" to *The Church Today: The Collected Writings of Emmanuel Cardinal Suhard* (Chicago: Fides, 1953), xiii–xvii.

[11] Ibid.

[12] Mt 11:30.

Chapter Fifteen
Social Morality and the Christian Intellectual

This address was published as a monograph, *Social Morality and the Christian Intellectual* (Pittsburgh, Pa.: St. Joseph Protectory Printery, 1963), 24 pp.

[1] Col 2:3.

[2] *Missale Romanum*, "Credo".

[3] Frédéric A. Ozanam was born in Milan, Italy, on April 23, 1813, and died in Marseilles, France, on September 8, 1853. Founder of the Society of St. Vincent de Paul (1833), he was degreed in literature (1835) and law (1836). A professor at Lyons and the Sorbonne, Ozanam was an exemplar of lay

ministry in family, social, and intellectual life. His cause for beatification was introduced in 1923.

⁴ E. E. Hales, *Pio Nono, Creator of the Modern Papacy* (New York, Kenedy, 1954).

⁵ Kathleen O'Meara, *Frédéric Ozanam, Professor at the Sorbonne* (New York: The Catholic Publication Society, 1891), 44.

⁶ Ibid., 313–14.

⁷ Ibid.

⁸ Ibid., 343.

⁹ Ibid.

¹⁰ Ibid., 252.

¹¹ Ibid.

¹² Pope John XXIII, Encyclical *Mater et Magistra* (May 15, 1961). English edition (Washington, D.C.: National Catholic Welfare Conference, 1961), 67.

¹³ Kathleen O'Meara, *Frédéric Ozanam, Professor at the Sorbonne*, 65.

¹⁴ Ibid.

¹⁵ Ibid., 177.

¹⁶ Ibid., 65.

¹⁷ Ibid., 65–66.

¹⁸ Ibid., 336.

¹⁹ Ibid., 82.

²⁰ Ibid., 87.

²¹ Eccl 9:10.

²² Pope John XXIII, *Mater et Magistra*, 67.

Chapter Sixteen
The Place of the Laity in the Church

¹ Almost a year later, on October 17, 1963, Wright would address the Fathers of Vatican Council II on the historical and theological importance of the text—on the laity—then under study. From the Council floor, Wright said: " 'The faithful have been waiting for 400 years for a positive conciliar statement on the place, dignity, and vocation of the layman.' He found fault with the traditional notion of the laity as defined in Church law as being too negative; the layman was defined as neither a cleric nor a religious. Once the Council had declared the theological nature of the laity, Wright said, 'the juridical bones of the Church would come alive with theological flesh and blood.' " Ralph M. Wiltgen, S.V.D., *The Rhine Flows into the Tiber* (New York: Hawthorn Books, Inc., 1967), 111. See also Vincent Yzermans, *American*

Participation in the Second Vatican Council (New York: Sheed and Ward, 1967), 61–63.

² Mt 5:48.

Chapter Seventeen
The Place of Work in Religious Life

¹ Jn 10:10.   ³ Jn 3:16.
² Gen 3:5.   ⁴ Phil 2:6.

Chapter Eighteen
The Human Person in Religious Life

¹ Rafael Merry del Val was born in London, on October 10, 1865, and died in Rome on February 26, 1930. This saintly priest, diplomat, cardinal, papal Secretary of State (1903–1914) was a close friend of Cardinal William H. O'Connell (1859–1944). Wright often recalled that O'Connell kept a picture of Merry del Val in the dining room of the archbishop's residence and that del Val's face—which Wright looked at during every meal—was so striking that "it is impossible to find a hue of crimson so brilliant that it would tone down the luster in his eyes."

² 1 Cor 3:23.

Chapter Nineteen
Interview with Gereon Zimmermann

This interview was published in *Look* (October 23, 1962), 55–64.

Gereon Zimmermann, then *Look*'s Senior Editor, prefaced his interview with these words: "A Summons from Pope John XXIII has converted the soaring nave of St. Peter's Basilica in Rome into the scene of the first Ecumenical Council of Roman Catholic bishops since 1869. More than 2,500 will be in attendance, and they will come from dioceses remote as Moshi and familiar as Pittsburgh. For months, the Eternal City will be awash with the purple of the bishops' robes and rumors about the Ecumenical Council's proceedings, many of which will be conducted in secrecy.

"Pope Pius IX called the first Vatican Council, which opened on a rainy day relieved by ceremonial flashes of gunfire. The shots were portents of the spirited and often angry deliberations that arrived at the *Petrine Doctrine*—the infallibility of the Pope when solemnly pronouncing on matters of faith and morals. The decree was expected by most, and it was greeted with hails and wails alike. Today, it is a rock in the belief of 537,000,000 faithful.

"Bishop John Joseph Wright of Pittsburgh will be one of the prelates seated in the tiers of bleachers erected in the nave of St. Peter's. He served on the Council's theological preparatory commission. A native of Boston, he was consecrated a bishop at 37. He is a scholar whose friends embrace all faiths, and he exemplifies the ecumenical spirit that stirs within all mankind. This exclusive interview with Bishop Wright gives new insight into the historic religious event that begins on October 11."

[1] First named a member of the Council's preparatory commission, Wright—at the time of the Council—was elected by his colleagues to serve as a member of the Theological Commission. Two other Americans, Archbishop John Dearden of Detroit and Auxiliary Bishop James Griffiths of New York, were also chosen.

"The tireless work of the members of the Theological Commission can never be adequately recorded. Archbishop Dearden made at least ten trips to Rome to take part in at least two hundred meetings of the Commission. The meetings he attended averaged at least three hours, and thus at least six hundred hours were spent in this work, not to mention the countless hours of study and consultation that the Commission work also demanded. Bishop John Wright made 32 trips to Rome and took part in about 160 plenary and 80 subcommission meetings. . . . Bishop Wright was chairman of the schema's fourth chapter concerning the laity.

"Commenting on the work of the Commission, Bishop Wright said: 'In the Theological Commission the issue was repeatedly joined between the *open* approach to Council issues and a more *closed* approach. The most *crucial* work of the Commission was the winnowing of the wheat from the chaff in both approaches.' "

When asked what he thought to be the most satisfying work of the Commission, Bishop Wright said that his most satisfying experience on the Commission was "the opportunity to share the thinking of men from other *worlds* within the modern Church, from France and Belgium and especially from the Iron Curtain countries".

Finally, when asked what he felt might be the most lasting fruits of the Theological Commission's work, Wright declared: "I am convinced that the Church is faced, as is the world, with the long *winter* that must follow the rise of atheistic humanism and *technologism*. It is a chapter of history foretold by prophetic spirits: Newman and Soloviev, among many. During that *winter* the seed-ideas sifted chiefly in our Commission will *incubate* under the soil against the inevitable *second spring*." Vincent Yzermans, *American Participation in the Second Vatican Council* (New York: Sheed and Ward, 1967), 20–21.

Chapter Twenty
Vocation and Virtues of the Scientist

¹ These references are from Gen 1:28 and 1 Cor 3:23.

² Coventry Patmore, "Magna est Veritas" in *The New Oxford Book of English Verse* (New York: Oxford University Press, 1972), 708.

Chapter Twenty-One
Interview with Donald McDonald

This interview with Donald McDonald, Dean of the College of Journalism, Marquette University, was published in *Religion* (Santa Barbara, California: Center for the Study of Democratic Institutions, 1963), 31–60.

¹ Dante, *Purgatorio*, bk. 32, 102: "Di quelle Roma onde Cristo è Romano".

² John F. Powers (1828–1902) was the founder (1866) and pastor (1847–1902) of St. Paul Church—later Cathedral—Worcester, Massachusetts. Fr. Powers, who had studied theology in Montreal and later in Paris, where he was ordained in 1858, is a Worcester legend. At the time of his death, Fr. John J. McCoy, a close friend said: ". . . He built the finest church in Worcester, founded the first public hospital the city ever knew, erected a school and orphanage. More, Fr. Powers was a member of the Worcester School Committee and served on the committee which planned the building of the Classical High School. He was a director of the Free Public Library and a charter member of the St. Wulfstan Society, a group of educators, lawyers, physicians, and clergy who presented essays at social gatherings."

³ Thomas F. Coakley was born in Pittsburgh, Pennsylvania, on February 20, 1880 and died in the same city on March 5, 1951. Ordained in Rome, Italy, on May 25, 1907, he served at St. Paul Cathedral (1908–1918), as an Army Chaplain (1918), secretary to Bishop J. F. Regis Canevin (1919), pastor of St. Patrick Church, Pittsburgh (1920–1923), and pastor of Sacred Heart Church, Pittsburgh, from 1923 until his death in 1951.

⁴ *McCall's* (June 1962), p. 158.

⁵ John J. Wright, "Peace, the Work of Justice" *RC* I, 352–62.

Chapter Twenty-Two
Patriotism, Nationalism, and the
World View at the Editor's Desk

[1] Cardinal Laurian Rugambwa was born on July 14, 1912. He was ordained priest in 1943; his episcopal ordination took place nine years later on February 10, 1952. In 1960 Pope Pius XII named him a cardinal.

[2] Cardinal Valerian Gracias was born on October 23, 1900. He was ordained priest in 1926; his episcopal ordination took place on June 29, 1946. In 1953 Pius XII named him a cardinal.

[3] Wright had a lifelong devotion to St. Joan of Arc. See R. Stephen Almagno, O.F.M., "Entrevue avec le Cardinal John J. Wright relative au don de sa collection johannique à la Bibliothèque publique de Boston", *Bulletin de la Société des Amis du Vieux Chinon* (1977), 17–22; R. Stephen Almagno, O.F.M., *Cardinal John Wright the Bibliophile* (Pittsburgh: Pittsburgh Bibliophiles, 1980) and Edward J. Ward, "Joan of Arc Collection Graces BPL's Cheverus Room", *Pilot* (December 7, 1979), 5.

[4] Wright wrote his doctoral dissertation on this topic. See John Wright, *National Patriotism in Papal Teaching* (Westminster, Md.: The Newman Press, 1956).

While in Rome, Wright came under the influence of Fr. J. Edward Coffey, S.J. Coffey (1897–1986) was a true internationalist who appreciated the universality of the Church. He was a social scientist and lectured at the Gregorianum on sociology (14 years), economics (8 years), and ethics (4 years). The study of the family from an ethical and sociological point of view was Fr. Coffey's central interest. See Joseph Fitzpatrick, S.J., "Ed Coffey Dies—Man of International Vision", *National Jesuit News* (October 1986), 15–17. Wright, I repeat, was very influenced by Fr. Coffey, who was both his teacher and confessor. In *National Patriotism in Papal Teaching*, Wright wrote: "The Reverend J. Edward Coffey, S.J., gave most unselfishly of his time and counsel in directing this dissertation. For many more lessons than those which are imperfectly reflected in this book, the author is indebted to the priestliness and scholarship of Father Coffey" (ibid., xiii).

[5] Pericles (c. 500–429 B.C.) delivered the funeral oration at the commemoration of the Athenians who fell in the first year of the Peloponnesian War. See Thucydides, *History of the Peloponnesian War*, trans. C. Foster Smith (New York: Putnam, 1929), 333–35.

Chapter Twenty-Three
The Real Aim of Education

[1] 1 Cor 3:22–23.

[2] Ps 8:6.

[3] Jacques Maritain, *Education at the Crossroads* (New Haven: Yale University Press, 1943), 8–9.

[4] Jacques Maritain, *Education at the Crossroads*, 10–11.

[5] Encyclical *Divini Redemptoris* (March 19, 1937). English translation: *Atheistic Communism* (Washington, D.C.: National Catholic Welfare Conference, 1937), 13.

[6] Pope John XXIII, Encyclical *Pacem in Terris* (April 11, 1963). English translation: *Peace on Earth* (New York: America Press, 1963), 14.

[7] Jacques Maritain, *Education at the Crossroads*, 100.

[8] 1 Cor 3:22–23.

Chapter Twenty-Four
The Education of Women Religious

[1] C. P. Snow, *The Two Cultures: A Second Look* (Cambridge University Press, 1964).

[2] L. J. Suenens, *The Nun in the World; New Dimensions in the Modern Apostolate* (Westminster, Md.: Newman Press, 1962).

[3] In 1962, the then Holy Office—now the Congregation for the Doctrine of the Faith—while in no way impugning Father Teilhard's spiritual integrity, issued a *Monitum* against an uncritical acceptance of his ideas. See *AAS* 54 (1962): 526.

Due to the influence of Frank J. Sheed and the genuine friendship as well as enormous respect that Wright had for the Jesuit scholar-cardinals Henri de Lubac and Jean Daniélou, Wright—while accepting the *Monitum*—changed his ideas about many items in Teilhard's thought. See Frank J. Sheed, *The Church and I* (London: Sheed and Ward, 1974), 152, 223, 276–78, and "La Porpora nella Compagnia di Gesù", *Gesuiti—Annuario della Compagnia di Gesù* (1969–1970), 125–26.

Sometime in 1976, Cardinal Wright told me that when he came to write his autobiography, he definitely wanted to include an item—concerning Teilhard de Chardin and himself—that was completely unknown. The Cardinal mentioned, briefly in that 1976 conversation and at a time when he was already ill, that in 1951 or 1952 Cardinal Spellman had sent him to St. Ignatius Jesuit Residence, Park Avenue, to speak with Father Teilhard. Alas, as with so many other interesting and important vignettes from a life that was so rich, the details of Wright's meeting and conversation with Father Teilhard de Chardin will never be known.

⁴ *Missale Romanum*, "Praefatio de Nativitate Domini".

⁵ St. Bernard, *Sermons for the Seasons and Principal Festivals of the Year* (Westminster, Md.: Carroll Press, 1950), vol. 2, 35–41.

⁶ Thomas Aquinas, *Summa Theologica* I, q. 1, 8 ad 2.

Chapter Twenty-Five
Monsignor Daniel A. Lawless, 1875–1963

This text was published as follows: *Remarks of the Most Reverend John J. Wright, D.D., at the Requiem Mass for Monsignor Daniel A. Lawless at St. Paul's Cathedral, December 23, 1963* (Pittsburgh: Saint Joseph Protectory Printery, 1964), 8 pp.

¹ Heb 8:5.

² Ex 18:13–23.

³ Ex 17:8–15.

⁴ Ex 33:11.

⁵ Lev 19.

⁶ Deut 15:11.

⁷ Deut 34:5–10.

⁸ For thirty-six years as parochial administrator and director of the Diocesan Missionary Confraternity of Christian Doctrine and for sixteen years as pastor, Lawless spent fifty-two years of his priestly life at St. Mary of Mercy Church, Pittsburgh, Pa. He was born in Bridgeport, Pa., on December 7, 1875, ordained on June 14, 1905, and died on December 19, 1963.

Chapter Twenty-Six
Reflections on Conscience and Authority

This address was first published in *The Critic* (April-May 1964): 11–28. Subsequently it was reprinted in *Reflections on Conscience and Authority* (Chicago: Scepter, 1964), 56 pp., and translated into Italian: *Coscienza e Autorità—Tensione e Armonia* (Roma, Città Nuova Editrice, 1970), 89 pp.

Mr. Joel Wells prefaced the address—as it appeared in *The Critic*—with these words: "Before launching into the delivery of the 1964 McGeary Foundation lecture, *Reflections on Conscience and Authority* (which occupies a deservedly large portion of this issue), Bishop John J. Wright took advantage of the presence of the twenty-six hundred people on hand for the twenty-fifth anniversary celebration of the Thomas More Association, February 9, to bite the hand that sponsored him. The fact that it was the hand that writes *Stop Pushing*, and one that very many think needs biting, enlisted great support from the audience." *The Critic* (April-May 1964), 4.

[1] Heb 10:31.

[2] Wright was awarded the Christ the Teacher Medal, designed by Ivan Mestrovic, for the 1964 McGeary Foundation lecture. Five years later, in 1969, when Paul VI made him a cardinal, he was assigned the Church of *Gesù Divin Maestro* (Jesus the Divine Teacher) as his titular church. See chap. 52, note 1.

[3] John G. Deedy was editor of the *Pittsburgh Catholic* from 1959–1967, when he left to become *Commonweal*'s managing editor. He had been with Wright in Worcester, Mass., as editor of *The Catholic Free Press* from 1951 to 1959.

[4] See Chap. 19, note 1.

[5] Pope Pius XII, "Talk to the Roman Rota", October 2, 1945.

[6] Msgr. A. Pailler, "Considerations on the Authority of the Church", in *Problems of Authority*, John M. Todd, ed. (Baltimore, Md.: Helicon Press, 1962), 23–24.

[7] Jacques Leclercq, *La Liberté d'Opinion et les Catholiques* (Paris: Cerf, 1963).

[8] Thomas à Kempis, *The Imitation of Christ*, bk. 1, chap. 1.

[9] E. C. McGuire, *The Religious Opinions and Character of Washington* (New York: Harper, 1836), 45.

[10] *The Century Dictionary and Cyclopedia*, vol. 2 (New York: Century, 1911), 1202.

[11] William Hamilton, *Lectures*, vol. I (Cambridge, Mass., 1870), 154.

[12] Bernard Häring, *The Law of Christ: Moral Theology for Priests and Laity*, trans. Edwin G. Kaiser (Westminster, Md.: Newman Press, 1966).

[13] See my introductory note on pp. 553–54 (Ed.).

[14] Emile J. De Smedt, "Religious Liberty", in *Council Speeches of Vatican II* (Glen Rock, N.J.: Paulist Press, 1964), 237–53.

[15] Ibid., 244.

[16] Ibid., 238–39.

[17] Saint Thomas, *De Veritate*, 17, 5. Much of Eric D'Arcy's *Conscience and Its Right to Freedom* is devoted to Saint Thomas' doctrine on conscience.

[18] John M. Todd, *Problems of Authority*, 3.

[19] Bertrand Russell, *Authority and the Individual* (London: Unwin, 1949), 88.

[20] Romano Guardini, "L'Ateismo e la Possibilità dell'Autorità", in *Humanitas* (January, 1962), 570–81.

[21] John M. Todd, *Problems of Authority*, 4.

[22] Thomas Corbishley, S.J., "Power and Authority", in *The Way* (October 1963), 285–93.

[23] See Phil 2:3–7.

[24] Ps 8.

[25] Yves Congar, O.P., "The Historical Development of Authority in the Church: Points for Christian Reflection", in *Problems of Authority*, John M. Todd, ed., 148.

[26] Charles Journet, *The Church of the Incarnate Word*, vol. I (New York: Sheed and Ward, 1955), 130.

[27] Yves Congar, O.P., in *Problems of Authority*, 127.

[28] Theodore Westow, *The Variety of Catholic Attitudes* (New York: Herder and Herder, 1963).

[29] C. A. Pierce, *Conscience in the New Testament* (London: SCM Press, 1955), 124–25.

[30] Pius XII, "Conscience and Education" (Radio broadcast of March 24, 1952).

[31] Ibid.

[32] Bernard Häring, *The Law of Christ*, 148–49.

[33] C. A. Pierce, *Conscience in the New Testament*, 123–24.

[34] Ibid., 128–29.

[35] Jean Daniélou, S.J., *The Christian Today*, trans. Kathryn Sullivan (New York: Desclée, 1960), 49 and 58.

[36] F. James Kaiser, *The Concept of Conscience according to John Henry Newman* (Washington, D.C.: The Catholic University Press, 1958).

[37] Robert J. Dwyer (1908–1976) was, like Wright, a student and lover of Newman. In Msgr. Ellis' estimation, "Dwyer probably employed his historical knowledge more than any bishop schooled in that discipline." See *Catholic Bishops: A Memoir* (Wilmington, Del.: Michael Glazier, Inc., 1983), 154.

[38] John Henry Newman, *Difficulties of Anglicans*, vol. 2 (London: Longmans, Green and Co., 1901), 249.

[39] Ibid., 250.

[40] F. James Kaiser, *The Concept of Conscience according to John Henry Newman*, 47–49.

[41] Pope John XXIII, Encyclical *Pacem in Terris* (April 11, 1963), English translation: *Peace on Earth* (New York: America Press, 1963).

[42] John Henry Newman, *Apologia* (London: Longmans, Green and Co., 1921), 240–50.

[43] John Henry Newman, *Parochial and Plain Sermons* (San Francisco: Ignatius Press, 1987), 291.

[44] John Henry Newman, *Difficulties of Anglicans*, vol. 2, 253–54.

[45] Ibid., 248.

[46] Wright was, for his own reasons, very circumspect in voicing his opinions concerning President Kennedy. He put his thought on tape, for the John Fitzgerald Kennedy Library, with this proviso:

"General Services Administration
National Archives and Records Service
Gift of Personal Statement
by Most Reverend John J. Wright, D.D.
to the John Fitzgerald Kennedy Library

In accordance with Sec. 507 of the Federal Property and Administrative Services Act of 1949, as amended (44 U.S.C. 397) and regulations issued thereunder (41 CFR 101–10), I, *John J. Wright*, hereafter referred to as the donor, hereby give, donate, and convey to the United States of America for eventual deposit in the proposed John Fitzgerald Kennedy Library, and for administration therein by the authorities thereof, a tape and transcript of a personal statement approved by me and prepared for the purpose of deposit in the John Fitzgerald Kennedy Library. The gift of this material is made subject to the following terms and conditions:

It is the donor's wish to make the material donated to the United States of America by the terms of the instrument available for research in the John Fitzgerald Kennedy Library. At the same time, it is his wish to guard against the possibility of its contents being used to embarrass, damage, injure, or harass anyone. Therefore, in pursuance of this objective, and in accordance with the provisions of Sec. 507(f)(3) of the Federal Property and Administrative Services Act of 1949, as amended (44 U.S.C. 397) *this material or the names contained therein shall not until every person named in the material and the donor himself are dead be made available for examination by anyone*. This stipulation is made formally and without qualification for two specific reasons: it was with this assurance that the material was obtained and prepared, and on principle the donor is deeply opposed to discussion of people that would in anyway embarrass their work or his own.

This restriction shall apply to and include employees and officers of the General Services Administration (including the National Archives and Records Services and the John Fitzgerald Kennedy Library) engaged in performing normal archival work processes.

The donor retains to himself during his lifetime all literary property rights in the material donated to the United States of America by the terms of this instrument. After the death of the donor, the aforesaid literary property rights will pass to the United States of America.

Signed: John J. Wright   Accepted: Robert H. Bahmer
Date: January 20, 1968   Archivist of the United States
              Date: January 23, 1968.

See Theodore C. Sorensen, *Kennedy* (New York: Harper and Row, 1965), 175, 191, and 194.

[47] John Henry Newman, *Apologia*, 249–50.

[48] Dan Herr, "The Man Who Wouldn't Conform", the *Sign* (January 1964), 22.

[49] Thomas à Kempis, *The Imitation of Christ*, bk. 2, chap. 6.

[50] Raymond William Chambers, *Thomas More* (Westminster, Md.: Newman Press, 1949) and Robert Bolt, *A Man for All Seasons* (New York: Random House, 1962).

[51] "Sometimes, I am asked the reason for this strange veneration on the part of a bishop for someone who died at the hands of a bishop—condemned as a witch, a heretic and a sorceress. My reply is now automatic: what saint could be more appropriate as a reminder to a bishop to be very careful when passing judgment, particularly where conscience is involved and where the alleged heretic is appealing over his head to the Pope?" See *Cardinal John Joseph Wright the Bibliophile*, text edited and prepared by R. Stephen Almagno, O.F.M. (Pittsburgh, Pa.: The Pittsburgh Bibliophiles, 1980), 13–14.

[52] Jean Guitton, *The Guitton Journals* (London: Harvill Press, 1963).

[53] Jacques Maritain, "A Propos de la Foi de Jeanne en ses voix", *Bulletin de la Société des Amis du Vieux Chinon* (1962–1963): 319–22.

[54] R. Stephen Almagno, O.F.M., *Cardinal John Wright the Bibliophile* (Pittsburgh: Pittsburgh Bibliophiles, 1980), 13–14.

Chapter Twenty-Seven
A Closed Retreat: Why Me?

[1] This address shows Wright's preoccupation with the question of the human person. Throughout 1963 and 1964 he served on several subcommissions charged with drafting the Council's *Pastoral Constitution on the Church in the Modern World*. He was president of the subcommission on *The Human Person* and a member of the subcommission on *The Signs of the Times* and *The Church of the Poor*. On October 28, 1964, six months after this address, Wright would introduce his specific chapters on the Council floor during the 111th congregation. See Vincent Yzermans, *American Participation in the Second Vatican Council* (New York: Sheed and Ward, 1967), 191.

[2] On August 3, 1962, Wright's sister—Mrs. Harriet Wright Gibbons—gave birth to a daughter, Joan Lorraine.

[3] Wright was never comfortable with most of the new technology. He even had trouble with radio and television dials and buttons. He did, however, love the phone and used it constantly. The following memo illustrates his respect for persons before all else.

TO: Reserved Phone List
FROM: Bishop Wright
DATE: September 15, 1966
RE: New Telephone Numbers

The unpublished telephone number at the Bishop's Residence (MA 1-5470) is being canceled and a new number has been assigned. It is given in confidence to all those to whom it is a convenience in their diocesan work or a service to the Bishop. The new unlisted House number is _____ .

The Sisters of Divine Providence at my house will have a line and a number of their own so that they can receive their Community or personal calls over their own phone. They will give their number to any persons they choose.

The reason for this change is that during 1966 the bishop's house number came into the possession of two disturbed personalities. The result was harassment of the sisters by one of these and a more than usually annoying effort at troublemaking by another.

I do not ordinarily feel disturbed about *nut* calls and usually take them at the office; they are part of the inevitable and sometimes instructive routine of life in our times. However, I do not like to see the sisters who work at my house called upon to cope with disturbed people who really prefer to bother me, not them, and so I ask for maximum discretion in giving out the house number. *It should never be given to anyone whose identity is not completely clear and under no circumstances should be given merely to relay a phone call unevaluated. Thanks!!*

[4] Stephen Vincent Benét, *Selected Works* (New York: Farrar and Rinehart, Inc., 1942), vol. I, 222.

Chapter Twenty-Eight
Facts, Truths, and
The Christian Journalist

This address was published in *Catholic Mind* 62 (October 1964): 5–11.

[1] St. Paulinus of Nola, Carmen XVII (*CSEL* 30, p. 93).

[2] *The Poems of St. Paulinus of Nola*, trans. P. G. Walsh (*ACW* 40, 112).

[3] Carmen XVII.

[4] Ibid.

[5] Ibid.

[6] Jacques Maritain, *Art and Scholasticism* (New York: Scribners, 1962), 36–37.

[7] St. Paulinus of Nola, Carmen XVII.

[8] See Acts 5.

Chapter Thirty
Intervention on Religious Liberty

This address has been published in many books. I will cite only one source: Vincent Yzermans, *American Participation in the Second Vatican Council* (New York: Sheed and Ward, 1967), 653–56.

Commenting on Wright's address, Yzermans wrote: "Bishop Wright of Pittsburgh, an important American member of the doctrinal commission, . . . delivered a brilliant address on 'the question of religious liberty and its exercise' and how it 'ultimately touches the question of the common good'." Yzermans, ibid., 630–31.

Wright's interest in the question of religious liberty went back to his Roman student days and his doctoral thesis, *National Patriotism in Papal Teaching*. And, as Msgr. Stapleton observed: "An interesting comparison might be made of John's thought in his thesis and those developed so effectively by John Courtney Murray, S.J., on Church and State" (Letter of Stapleton to Almagno, February 9, 1982). The fact is that Wright and Murray enjoyed a long friendship and much intellectual exchange.

John Courtney Murray (1904–1967) was one of the principal architects of the Declaration on Religious Freedom approved by the Council in 1965. A Jesuit professor at Woodstock, Maryland, from 1936 to 1967, "he became widely known as an expert on church-state relations as he sought to reconcile the traditions of the Catholic Church with the demands of America's pluralistic society. Among his other concerns were interracial justice, civil rights, the promotion of civil and religious freedom, peace and ecumenism, but the study of church-state relations was his paramount interest. He became the center of controversy in the fifties when his proposal that the Vatican give its blessing to the relationship between church and state that existed in the United States attracted international attention. In 1954 his Jesuit superiors in Rome demanded he stop writing and lecturing on the subject—which he did—and he was required to clear all his writing with Jesuit headquarters in Rome. He came into his own at Vatican Council II when Cardinal Francis Spellman of New York invited him to Rome as his *peritus*." John J. Delaney, *Dictionary of American Catholic Biography* (Garden City, New York: Doubleday, 1984), 413.

The day before the final vote on the Declaration on Religious Freedom, Paul VI concelebrated Mass in St. Peter's Basilica. Among the concelebrants were John Courtney Murray, S.J., and another theologian—now a cardinal—who for years, too, was under a cloud, Hénri de Lubac, S.J. In a text written by Wright for the NCWC News Service, he said: "The American part in the fashioning of the Declaration was in preeminent degree the work of Father John Courtney Murray, for whom the religious liberty document is a kind of trophy paying tribute to the persevering service of truth by a Council *peritus* who is all scholar and all priest. More eyes than his own felt consoling tears of joy at the thought of Father Murray's presence at the papal altar as a concelebrant with the Chief Shepherd of Christendom on the day before the final vote. It was a happy omen and a deserved salute." See also John Deedy, *Seven American Catholics* (Chicago: Thomas More Press, 1978), 125–53.

[1] Acts 17:26–27.

[2] Jacques Maritain, *The Person and the Common Good* (New York: Scribners, 1947), 43.

Chapter Thirty-One
Family Life in a Changing Society

This address was published in *Catholic Mind* (May 1965), 45–51.

Wright's presence in India, during the time of his busy involvement with the Council, affords me the opportunity to make a point so well expressed by Yzermans, namely, that: "Bishop John Wright presented to his colleagues from other nations an image of the American bishop they were not quite prepared to expect. 'I conceived it our duty as American bishops', said Bishop Wright 'to welcome opportunities for the presentation to European audiences of seminarians, priests and laity the Catholic American understanding of the Council and its agenda.'

"Throughout the time of the Council he lectured at 11 seminaries in Rome, addressed 7 meetings of national hierarchies, traveled to 4 countries to speak with 6 groups of university professors and students, attended 4 general congresses and conventions in 3 different countries, granted 15 European press interviews to representatives from 5 different countries and appeared in 4 radio and television interviews over European stations." Vincent Yzermans, *American Participation in the Second Vatican Council* (New York: Sheed and Ward, 1967), 194.

Concerning Wright's visit to India, Dr. Dorothy M. Baker wrote: "In 1964 Bishop Wright came to India with Monsignor Carroll Dozier—now bishop of Memphis—and he stayed in Nirmala, Niketan, our Institute. We gave him the best room in the house and from our terrace we could see the altar of the Eucharistic Congress in the *Oval Maidan*, a park lined with coconut trees, coconut palm trees. . . . Bishop Wright was bothered by the heat and troubled with a rash, but with the help of ice and fans he found a way to adjust. When we had time I took him out to see some parts of Bombay and on the way back after a long tour I happened to mention the Hindu cremation grounds known as *burning ghat*. He was very interested to go but as he was all dressed up in clerical black and red with biretta, I was reluctant to take him because I thought the burying grounds attendants would take offense and not let us in. On the contrary—to my amazement—the Hindu priests, sadhus, etc., welcomed him and took him to a burning body to explain the rites. The son of the person being burned was squatting nearby, crying, and Bishop Wright consoled him and brought a kind of peace and strength to the whole scene" (Letter from Baker to Almagno, November 3, 1983).

1 Mt 10:28.
2 Gen 1:26–31 and 2:18–24.
3 Gen 2:23–24.
4 Jn 6:55–58.
5 Ez 36:26–27.

Chapter Thirty-Two
Conciliar Rome

This article was published in *America* (March 27, 1965), 348–51.

1 James H. Griffiths was born in Brooklyn, New York, on July 16, 1903, and died—auxiliary bishop of New York—on February 24, 1964. Ordained in Rome on March 12, 1927, he served in the Brooklyn Diocese until 1950, when he was ordained bishop and appointed as auxiliary to the Military Vicar. In

1955 he was named as an auxiliary to the archbishop of New York. A learned and active man, Griffiths was a member of the New York City Commission on the United Nations and served as the assistant bishop for United Nations Affairs on the Administrative Board of the NCWC. One of the founders of the Canon Law Society of America, he served as its president from 1941 to 1942. Together with Wright and Dearden, Griffiths was a member of the Council's Theological Commission and was, with Wright, part of the program arranged for United States' journalists assigned to cover Vatican Council II.

[2] Always at ease with the media, Wright was both its critic and at the same time a close friend of many journalists, writers, and radio and television commentators. During the Council he began a lifelong friendship with Father Andrew Greeley. About that relationship, Greeley writes: "I made three good friends in those weeks: Hans Küng, the great Swiss theologian; John Wright, then an auxiliary bishop in Boston; and John Courtney Murray, the American Jesuit expert on Church-state relationships (whom I'd met once before during a retreat at the seminary)—three men who could not possibly be more different, but still three men who had an enormous impact on the council: Küng, with his ideas on ecumenism, and Wright and Murray, on the religious liberty declaration and on the statement on Jews (both of which were of enormous importance to American bishops). In later years when I would visit Rome working on the papal election book, I would always stop by Signor Cardinale's apartment—just up the stairs from Cardinal Baggio's apartment on the Piazza Città Leonina. Wright and I shared a love for Newman and Chesterton, for the Irish heritage and for Catholic literature. On virtually everything else we disagreed. As John put it one night, waving a wine glass at me, 'Andrew, I disagree with everything you stand for. And I shall defend to the death my right to continue to disagree with you.' " Andrew M. Greeley, *Confessions of a Parish Priest: An Autobiography* (New York: Simon and Schuster, 1986), 239.

[3] Lk 17:20.

Chapter Thirty-Three
Seed Ideas—Reflections at
Easter after the Council

As Bishop Bosco has noted in his Introduction to this volume, Wright was "very generous in sharing the experience of the Council with the priests, religious, and laity" of the Pittsburgh Diocese. Upon his return from each session of the Council he conducted a series of public lectures in the form of an adult education course. In each of these lectures Wright stressed that the most lasting fruits of the Council would be what he called the *seed-ideas* of the chapter on collegiality, the chapter on the laity, and the chapter on Our Lady in the Constitution on the Church, as well as the *seed-ideas* of the sections on the person, Christian anthropology, dialogue with atheism, marriage, and peace and war in the Constitution on the Church in the Modern World. Fr. Egbert M. Laufer, O.F.M. Conv., placed Wright's lectures into a synthesis: "Vatican II in 24 Seed Ideas" *Homiletic and Pastoral Review* (October 1966), 23–30.

¹ Paul VI went on pilgrimage to the Holy Land from January 4 to January 6, 1964.

² Paul VI was in India from December 2 to December 5, 1964.

³ Paul VI visited the United Nations on October 4, 1965.

⁴ See *La Visita di Paolo VI alle Nazioni Unite* (Città del Vaticano: Libreria Editrice Vaticana, 1966), 154 pp.

⁵ Angelo Giuseppe Roncalli, later Pope John XXIII, was Apostolic Visitor in Bulgaria from 1925 to 1935, Apostolic Delegate in Istanbul from 1935 to 1945, and Nuncio to France from 1946 to 1953.

⁶ Pope Pius XII, Encyclical *Mediator Dei* (November 20, 1947). English translation: *On the Sacred Liturgy* published in *Catholic Mind*, 46 (June 1948): 321–88.

Chapter Thirty-Four
Franciscan Joy

¹ While still a young priest, Wright joined the Secular Franciscans at Saint Leonard Church, North End, Boston, Massachusetts.

Chapter Thirty-Five
Colonel de Corbiac 1872–1965

¹ In his Introduction to vol. I (The Boston Years: 1939–1950) of *Resonare Christum*, Msgr. Edward G. Murray noted: "With the exception of a summer spent in northern England, all the other summers were spent in Corbiac, a village in the Dordogne. . . . Father Wright stayed at the home of Colonel de Corbiac, and made friendships which lasted until his death. I met the Colonel de Corbiac at London in 1948 with Bishop Wright. He was a man of profound traditional piety, and he spoke of the love that Father Wright had left behind him in France" (*RC* I, 15).

The Colonel's memorial card reads: "Louis Durand de Corbiac / Lieutenant-Colonel de Cavalerie / Officer de la Légion d'Honneur / Croix de Guerre 1914–1918 / Croix de Guerre Belge / D.S.O. / Membre de l'Hospitalité / de N. D. de Lourdes et de N. D. du Salut / Ancien Commissaire aux Scouts de France / Membre de la Légion de Marie / Rappelé a Dieu le 6 Août 1965 / Dans sa 93ᵉ Année."

Chapter Thirty-Six
Discovering One Another
In Facing Great Issues

[1] Richard Wright, *Black Boy: A Record of Childhood and Youth* (New York: Harper and Row, 1969).

Chapter Thirty-Seven
David L. Lawrence 1899–1966

[1] "Lawrence served four terms as mayor beginning in 1945. He resigned in 1959 to become governor, stayed one term, and then served as chairman of the Commission on Equal Rights under Presidents John F. Kennedy and Lyndon B. Johnson. A product of the city's tough Point area and the Hill District, Lawrence was an effective, old-style Democratic politician. As mayor, he joined forces with members of the Richard King Mellon family—former political enemies—to revamp Pittsburgh's national and international image in a Renaissance. He held office longer than any other Pittsburgh mayor and was considered by far the most popular. A heart attack felled him on Nov. 4, 1966, and he died after 17 days in a coma." Jerry Byrd, *The Pittsburgh Press* (December 12, 1982), A-12.

Chapter Thirty-Eight
The Church Is Always Young

[1] Cant 2:11–12.
[2] William H. Prescott, *History of the Conquest of Peru* (New York: Heritage Press, 1957), 266–67.

Chapter Thirty-Nine
The Year of Faith

[1] Mk 9:24.
[2] 1 Cor 1:10–12.

Chapter Forty-One
A Prayer for President Posvar and
The University of Pittsburgh

[1] As Bishop Bosco has noted in his Introduction to this volume, Wright "as a neighbor of the University of Pittsburgh, and loving academia as he did . . . was always interested in the university. He had a close official and personal relationship with Dr. Litchfield, the twelfth chancellor (1956–1965) and came to the university's aid when it was in financial difficulties." See *Statement of Bishop John J. Wright on the Financial Emergency at the University of Pittsburgh* and Robert C. Alberts, *Pitt: The Story of the University of Pittsburgh 1787–1987* (Pittsburgh: The University of Pittsburgh Press, 1986), 341–42.

More, and again quoting Bishop Bosco: "He had a pastoral concern for the spiritual life and growth of the Catholic professors, students, and staff who frequented or worked at the university. So he entrusted this concern to the Fathers of the Oratory, the sons of Saint Philip Neri and Cardinal John Henry Newman, with the hope that they would bring, as indeed they have, a new dimension to the Diocese of Pittsburgh." See John G. Deedy, "A First for Pittsburgh", *Information* 75 (August 1961): 10–14; Raleigh Addington, *The Idea of the Oratory* (London: Burns and Oates, 1966), 95 and 130; "A Sermon for the Combined Celebration of the Lord's Ascension and St. Philip Neri", *Lenten and Easter Sermons of William Clancy* (Pittsburgh: University of Pittsburgh Press, 1984), 31–33, and "Commitment on Campus: Pittsburgh-Carnegie Mellon", in *Time's Covenant: The Essays and Sermons of William Clancy* (Pittsburgh: University of Pittsburgh Press, 1986), 43–77.

When Wesley W. Posvar became the fifteenth chancellor (the title was changed to president in 1984) Wright formed a close friendship with both President and Mrs. Posvar. And, as Bishop Bosco writes: "By his interest in the university and through the friendships he established . . . he remedied what was certainly a defect. Relations between what was known as a *Presbyterian* University and the Roman Catholic Diocese of Pittsburgh were not always what they should have been. John Wright . . . brought about through the Oratory and his own personal contacts the now happy relationship between the University of Pittsburgh and the Roman Catholic Diocese of Pittsburgh." See Robert C. Alberts, *Pitt: The Story of the University of Pittsburgh 1787–1987*, 347–49 and 365.

Chapter Forty-Two
The Use Christ Made of Public Dinners

[1] Lk 7:31–34.
[2] Jn 2:1–11.
[3] Lk 5:29–32.
[4] Lk 7:36–50.
[5] Lk 11:37–42.
[6] Lk 14:1–24.
[7] Jn 6:9.

[8] Jn 6:9.
[9] Jn 6:1–15.
[10] Lk 22:8–20.
[11] Lk 24:18–31.
[12] Jn 21:12–14.
[13] Jn 21:15–17.

Chapter Forty-Three
Martin Luther King Jr., 1929–1968

This tribute was first published in *The Critic* (June-July 1968), 18–19 and 80.

[1] *The Critic* prefaced Wright's text with these words: "Bishop John Wright's *Unspoken Tribute* to Dr. Martin Luther King is literally that. Because of his long-standing friendship with Dr. King, Mrs. King wanted Bishop Wright to attend and address the funeral ceremonies. But, as we all observed on television, the press of thousands and the heat of the day took their toll of time and people. With the ceremonies moving several hours late and dozens fainting, it was decided to forego the eulogy. . . ." *The Critic* (June-July 1968), 1.

Mrs. Coretta Scott King wrote as follows: "As you know, Bishop Wright was a staunch supporter of Martin Luther King, Jr., from the Catholic community. What could better demonstrate Martin's universal message than to ask Bishop Wright to give a tribute at Martin's Memorial Service?

"How unfortunate it is that Bishop Wright's Tribute was never heard. For it was written with the deepest sympathy and sincerity" (Letter of Mrs. Coretta Scott King to Almagno, July 30, 1982).

[2] Acts 17:26–27.
[3] Jn 11:50–52.
[4] Rev 21:1–27.

Chapter Forty-Six
The Catholic Parish

[1] Mt 18:20.

[2] In his liturgical thinking Wright was very much influenced by Fr. Hans Anscar Reinhold (1897–1968). This priest, writer, lecturer, and especially liturgist had because of his anti-Nazi and (then) avant-garde liturgical views not a few difficulties in his life. After Reinhold's troubles with the Archdiocese of Seattle, Washington, Wright—as Reinhold himself wrote—accepted him into the Pittsburgh diocese in 1961 "with his characteristic openheartedness". Fr. Reinhold died in Pittsburgh of Parkinson's disease on January 26, 1968, and was buried from St. Paul Cathedral at a Mass celebrated by Wright with Fr. William Clancy, of the Pittsburgh Oratory, preaching the eulogy. See *H. A. R.: The Autobiography of Father Reinhold* (New York: Herder and Herder, 1968) and "In Memoriam: H. A. R. Preached at the Funeral of Father H. A. Reinhold", in *Time's Covenant: The Essays and Sermons of William Clancy* (Pittsburgh: The University of Pittsburgh Press, 1986), 134–39.

Chapter Forty-Seven
Human Life in Our Day

[1] Wright was the chairman of the drafting committee for the first two postconciliar collective pastoral letters of the American bishops: *The Church in Our Day* (1967) and *Human Life in Our Day* (1968). See *Pastoral Letters of the United States Catholic Bishops*, III, 1962–1974 (Washington, D.C.: National Conference of Catholic Bishops, United States Catholic Conference, 1983), 98–154, 164–94.

When he took his stance in favor of *Humanae Vitae* there began what Wright called—in the outline for his proposed autobiography—"the sudden rise of an unexpected and sometimes painful opposition. Origin: the Pope's encyclical on *Human Life*. Overt channels: Dan Herr, the *National Catholic Reporter*, odds and ends of the hierarchy, Kenneth Woodward and Xavier Rynne" (Manuscript in possession of the Literary Executor). All of this caused in John Wright the "firmer determination than ever to write and fight for human life" (ibid.).

[2] In 1970—and in contrast to what Robert Kaiser has asserted in his book: *The Politics of Sex and Religion*—Wright would use these principles in helping to resolve the conflict between Cardinal Patrick A. O'Boyle and the Washington Nineteen. See Robert B. Kaiser, *The Politics of Sex and Religion* (Kansas City, Mo.: Leaven Press, 1985), 209; Joseph Byron, "The Case of the Washington

Nineteen: A Search for Justice", in *Concilium*, vol. 107 (New York: Seabury Press, 1977), 104–12 and Desmond O'Grady, "Cardinal John Wright: An American with a Roman Connection", *National Catholic Reporter* (August 4, 1972), 15.

[3] As a longtime member of Pax Christi and one who denounced the Vietnam War, Wright was particularly concerned about war and peace issues. See George Weigel, *Tranquillitas Ordinis—The Present Failure and Future Promise of American Catholic Thought on War and Peace* (Oxford and New York: Oxford University Press, 1987), 186, 204, 229, 436, 440, 445; John Deedy, "A Remembrance of Wine and Roses" *The Critic* (Summer 1987): 56–57 and Wright's correspondence with Thomas Merton: *The Hidden Ground of Love: The Letters of Thomas Merton on Religious Experience and Social Concerns*, selected and edited by William H. Shannon (New York: Farrar, Straus, Giroux, 1985), 162, 180, 187, 312, 327, 607–11.

[4] Deut 30:19.

Chapter Forty-Eight
The Formal Call of the Synod

This address was published in *Eighteenth Synod of the Diocese of Pittsburgh* (Pittsburgh: 1971), iii–ix.

[1] *AAS* 54 (1962): 790.

[2] John J. Wright, *A New Year's Letter to the Clergy of the Diocese of Pittsburgh—Setting Forth Some Points for Our Common Priestly Study and Action in Seeking the Renewal Called for by the Second Vatican Council—Epiphany 1966* (Pittsburgh: 1966), 14 pp.

Chapter Forty-Nine
Statement upon Being Named a Cardinal

[1] St. Ignatius of Antioch, *Epistola ad Romanos* (PG 5, 686): ". . . universo coetui charitatis praesidens."

[2] See Chap. 1, note 4.

[3] On March 29, the day after the announcement, the *New York Times* published this editorial: "Since 1875 when John McCloskey became the first American Cardinal, the Archbishop of New York has traditionally received the red hat which symbolizes the Roman Catholic Church's highest honor.

Archbishop Terence Cooke's elevation yesterday by Pope Paul VI reflected that tradition—a fact the new Cardinal acknowledged when he said, 'I am aware that this appointment belongs to the people of New York more than to me personally.'

"But if the honor is traditional, it is no less merited. In the little more than a year in which he has served as head of the New York Archdiocese, Cardinal Cooke has shown himself a man of wide social concerns, sound common sense and impressive tact. In a huge metropolitan community torn with racial and religious conflicts, he is a force for racial justice and ecumenical understanding. All New Yorkers can join his fellow Catholics in welcoming his rise.

"The three other American bishops elevated to the College of Cardinals are also outstanding in different ways. Archbishop John Dearden of Detroit, the president of the National Conference of Catholic Bishops, is a strong progressive leader, while Archbishop John J. Carberry of St. Louis is a distinguished canon lawyer.

"In summoning Bishop John J. Wright of Pittsburgh to a position in the Curia in Rome, Pope Paul has singled out the American hierarchy's most brilliant orator, writer and intellectual. With his incisive intelligence and wide knowledge of men and affairs, Cardinal Wright is likely to be a major force in Rome in shaping the course of the Church in the years ahead. But many will hope that, whatever assignments he has in the Curia, he will not permanently be removed from the American Church, where his influence is much needed."
The *New York Times* (March 29, 1969), 34.

Chapter Fifty
The Resurrection: Fact, or Myth?

This Easter Pastoral was published in pamphlet form: *The Resurrection: Fact or Myth?* (Washington, D.C.: United States Catholic Conference, 1969), 9 pp.

[1] Jn 6:62–69.

[2] Mt 28:13.

[3] 1 Cor 15:5–7.

[4] Rev 1:8.

[5] 1 Cor 15:3–4.

[6] 1 Cor 15:14.

[7] Jn 20:27–28.

[8] Rom 8:11.

[9] *Missale Romanum*, "Praefatio Defunctorum".

[10] Phil 3:20–21.

[11] Jn 12:23–24.

[12] Jn 6:63.

[13] Rev. 2:8.

[14] See Rom 8:16–18.

[15] 2 Cor 4:10.

[16] Job 19:25–26.

[17] Lk 24:13–34.

[18] Jn 20:29.

Chapter Fifty-One
The Church and the Urban Crisis

[1] "Statement on National Race Crisis", in *Pastoral Letters of the United States Catholic Bishops*, vol. III, 1962–1974 (Washington, D.C.: National Conference of Catholic Bishops, United States Catholic Conference, 1983), 156–60.

[2] Ibid., 157.

[3] Ibid.

[4] Ibid.

[5] Ibid.

[6] Mt 11:2–6.

[7] Mt 4:4.

[8] Lk 8:1.

Chapter Fifty-Two
Doing and Teaching

[1] "When Cardinal Wright was first named to the Congregation for the Clergy in Rome, His Holiness Pope Paul VI asked him what he would miss most in giving up his diocese of Pittsburgh. He replied that he would miss more than anything else the many opportunities to teach the Faith.

"Probably more than any other characteristic that dominated his life, Cardinal Wright was a teacher of the Faith. He was not lacking in gifts that made him a natural orator and exponent of the Word of God. Nor did he lack the zeal that permitted him to dedicate these gifts full time to the service of God's Church.

"It was fitting that the titular church assigned to Cardinal Wright by the Pope was the Church of Jesus the Divine Teacher." Donald W. Wuerl,

"Cardinal John Wright—An Appreciation" in *L'Osservatore Romano*, English edition (September 24, 1979), 9.

² Lk 8:1.

³ John Henry Newman, *Parochial and Plain Sermons* (San Francisco: Ignatius Press, 1987), 196; *Sermons on Subjects of the Day* (London: Longmans, Green and Co., 1909), 316; *Discourses to Mixed Congregations* (London: Longmans, Green and Co., 1921), 102; *Sermons on Various Occasions* (London: Longmans, Green and Co., 1921), 22.

⁴ John Henry Newman, *Via Media*, vol. I (London: Longmans, Green and Co., 1918), 354–55.

⁵ Mk 9:23.

⁶ John Henry Newman, *Essays Critical and Historical*, vol. I (London: Longmans, Green and Co., 1919), 244–49.

⁷ Ibid., 219–52.

⁸ *Addresses of Cardinal Newman with His Replies 1879–1881*, ed. W. P. Neville (London: Longmans, Green and Co., 1905), 64.

⁹ Ibid., 68.

¹⁰ Ibid., 67.

¹¹ Ibid., 64.

¹² Ibid.

¹³ Ibid., 69.

Index

567

578